Revealing the Corporation

"Managing and communicating about corporate brands, building corporate identity, and protecting corporate reputation are vital issues in the boardrooms of entities global and local, large and small, corporate and non-profit. *Revealing the Corporation* treats the highly salient realm of corporate branding, identity, image, and reputation. Balmer and Greyser explain the roots of the territory, gather decades of wisdom about it, and interpret its significance and applicability for those who seek to understand and practice effectively in this complicated field.

The book speaks cogently to scholars, teachers, and executives. Scholars will be helped by the substantial commentary on individual articles and the extensive references. Teachers will find the chapter introductions and discussion questions useful. Those in practice – in corporations, communication firms, and brand consultancies – will benefit from the volume's orientation to their perspectives. All readers will welcome the breadth of the anthology, the module essays that analyze the multi-dimensional character of the field, and the future-oriented insights into what the authors call 'corporate-level marketing'."

Professor John A. Quelch
Senior Associate Dean, International Development, Harvard Business School
Former Dean, London Business School

As the concepts of corporate identity, communication, image, and branding have caught the imagination of both scholars and managers, new ways of conceptualizing organizations have arisen. This international and multidisciplinary collection of works captures the quintessence of the corporation and its many inner and outer manifestations. Both editors are pioneers of the field, and in this work they present a new approach to the subject area.

Drawing on their wide experience, Balmer and Greyser have assembled a portfolio of readings from those who practice, study, and research the areas in question, selecting illuminating pieces that stem from the 1950s to the present day to highlight both practitioner and scholarly perspectives. Features include:

- Editors' analysis and commentary
- Original pieces
- Case study
- Discussion questions
- Further reading

The resulting work is an augmented anthology that affords a new way of comprehending organizations, drawing on a range of disciplinary perspectives. This is essential reading for anybody who is serious about understanding the many levels of corporate meaning.

John M. T. Balmer holds the Chair of Corporate Identity at Bradford School of Management, UK, and is on the editorial board of several international journals. He has worked on identity projects for the BBC, Mercedes-Benz, and other organizations. He is a graduate of the Universities of Reading, Durham, and Strathclyde.

Stephen A. Greyser is Richard P. Chapman Professor (Marketing/Communications) Emeritus at Harvard Business School, former *Harvard Business Review* Editorial Board Chairman, and past Executive Director of the Marketing Science Institute. He is a Fellow of the American Academy of Advertising, for career contributions to the field. He is responsible for over 300 published case studies, numerous journal articles, and 15 books and monographs.

For online resources and a lecture guide please visit
www.routledge.com/textbooks/041528421X

Elliot -
nice to meet ose to
PNM. Look forward to
seeing you at MFA!
Best,
SG

Revealing the Corporation

Perspectives on identity, image, reputation, corporate branding, and corporate-level marketing

An anthology selected and interpreted by

John M. T. Balmer and

Stephen A. Greyser

Routledge
Taylor & Francis Group

LONDON AND NEW YORK

First published 2003
by Routledge
11 New Fetter Lane, London EC4P 4EE

Simultaneously published in the USA and Canada
by Routledge
29 West 35th Street, New York, NY 10001

Routledge is an imprint of the Taylor and Francis Group

Typeset in Perpetua and Bell Gothic by RefineCatch Limited, Bungay, Suffolk
Printed and bound in Great Britain by
TJ International Ltd, Padstow, Cornwall

British Library Cataloguing in Publication Data
A catalogue record for this book is available from the British Library

Library of Congress Cataloging in Publication Data
A catalog record for this book has been requested

ISBN 0–415–28420–1 (hbk)
ISBN 0–415–28421–X (pbk)

To Anna-Paolina, Annunziata, John, and Richard; Linda and Naomi

"Remember the rock from which thou wast hewn."

We are like dwarfs on the shoulders of giants
so that we can see more than they,
and things at a greater distance,
not by virtue of any sharpness on our part,
or any physical distinction, but
because we are carried high and
raised up by their giant size.
(Bernard of Chartres, d. *c.* 1130)

Contents

About the Editors

John M. T. Balmer holds the Chair of Corporate Identity at Bradford School of Management, U.K. This is believed to be the first appointment of its kind. Previously he was on the faculty at Strathclyde Business School, Glasgow, where he was the founder/director of the International Centre for Corporate Identity Studies. His research focuses on a range of corporate-level marketing issues including corporate identity, corporate branding, and corporate communications. He is on the editorial board of *European Journal of Marketing, Journal of Marketing Management, Corporate Reputation Review*, and *Corporate Communications*. His work has been published in the above journals as well as in others, including *California Management Review, Long Range Planning, International Studies of Management and Organizations, Journal of General Management*, and the *International Journal of Bank Marketing*. He has worked on major identity/branding projects for organizations such as the BBC, Mercedes Benz, Enterprise IG, and Landor Associates. Since 1994 he has organized a series of International Corporate Identity Symposia and from 1998 the Lord Goold Memorial Lectures. He has given seminars/keynote presentations at a number of leading business schools including those of Harvard, Oxford, Copenhagen, Rotterdam, and Waikato in New Zealand. Before joining academe he was Assistant Administrator of Lord Menuhin's concert agency, 'Live Music Now!' and was subsequently appointed to a senior managerial position within Brighton's Directorate of Arts and Leisure. He is a graduate of the Universities of Reading, Durham (MBA), and Strathclyde (PhD), and has the particular distinction of having taught throughout all echelons of England's educational system.

Stephen A. Greyser is Richard P. Chapman Professor (Marketing/Communications) Emeritus at Harvard Business School, former Editorial Board Chairman of *Harvard Business Review*, and past Executive Director of the Marketing Science Institute. He is a graduate of Harvard College and Harvard Business School (MBA, DBA). He is responsible for 15 books/monographs, numerous journal articles, and over 300 published case studies. His research focuses on corporate reputation and corporate marketing communications, including the edited volume *Improving Advertising Budgeting* (MSI, 1999). He is an elected Fellow of the American Academy of Advertising for lifetime contributions, and the charter member of the MSI Hall of Fame.

He developed the HBS MBA elective on Corporate Communications, involving some forty case studies on efforts to influence constituency opinion. He has also developed courses and written extensively on the business of sports and on arts/cultural administration.

Among his books are *Advertising in America: The Consumer View* and *Managing Cooperative Advertising: A Strategic Approach*. His distinctions include service on the National Advertising Review Board (the U.S. advertising self-regulatory entity), as the first academic board member of both the Advertising Research Foundation and Advertising Educational Foundation, and the first Lord Goold Lecturer (London). He was national vice chair of PBS, the U.S. non-commercial TV system, and a member of over a dozen corporate and nonprofit boards.

Foreword

A reliable reference work on the demanding subject of corporate-level marketing has long been sought by company managers and business academics alike. By producing their book *Revealing the Corporation*, Professors John Balmer and Stephen Greyser have made the wait worthwhile.

At last we have a seminal anthology to depend on and take guidance from as we confront those business fundamentals of identity, image, reputation, and corporate branding. *Revealing the Corporation* is accessible, practical, and thankfully unpretentious. Yet it is also a learned volume. The book has breadth and depth; looks at the new without ignoring the old; and challenges the familiar with the not-so-familiar. Clearly, its scope is global, drawing on the annals of *Harvard Business Review* and other leading journals, including the *California Management Review*.

The list of contributors is impressive. As befits the distinct traditions of Harvard and Bradford business schools, *Revealing the Corporation* celebrates the input of business practitioners as well as scholars.

Essentially, the book's undoubted value stems from the considerable scholarship of Professors Balmer and Greyser, who pilot us with safe hands and clear minds through *Revealing the Corporation*. Their succinct, enthusiastic commentary is both illuminating and entertaining. As they take us further and higher than we have probably been before in the search for the truths of corporate identity, fascinating new perspectives and thought-provoking ideas are revealed.

Stephen Greyser, the eminent Harvard academic and former editorial board chairman of the *Harvard Business Review*, brings to bear his vast experience of course and case study development on corporate identity, communication, and reputation, dating back to the late 1960s. John Balmer draws on a program of academic research and course development started in 1988. It is no coincidence that each of the joint editors is from a top-class seat of business learning: Harvard, the world's foremost business school; and Bradford, England's first university-based business school.

Neither Professor Balmer nor Professor Greyser is a stranger to British Airways. My predecessor as Chairman of the airline, Lord King, gave the keynote address at the first International Corporate Identity Symposium organized by Professor Balmer at Strathclyde Business School in 1994. I followed suit in 2001, by addressing the Eighth Symposium, which took place in London, alongside Lord Browne, Group CEO of BP.

Issues of identity, communication, reputation, and corporate branding have been key areas of strategic focus during my time with British Airways. Our identity as a loss-making, production-led, state-owned corporation in the early 1980s had to change. Thus, the transformation into a customer-driven, profitable enterprise took place and continues to evolve. The day-to-day management discipline of addressing those key, fundamental questions such as "Who are we?," "What are we?," and "What is our brand promise?" is replicated in this book.

Revealing the Corporation is an engaging and enjoyable text. The book demonstrates a new way of thinking about the corporation and a new way of analyzing the tasks and responsibilities of senior management. It is a masterpiece of its kind which I commend to the business community, to academics, and to all who really care about corporate development.

Lord Marshall of Knightsbridge
Chairman, British Airways Plc
Chairman, Royal Institute of International Affairs
Chairman, Board of Trustees, The Conference Board

Acknowledgments

We would like to thank all those who helped to bring this book into fruition. Especial thanks are due to our supportive and enthusiastic editor, Francesca Poynter, who oversaw this initiative from conception to publication. At Routledge we would also like to thank Rachel Crookes together with Marianthi Makra, Natasha Mary, and Jim McGovern. We are also grateful to our copyeditor Peter Harrison for his excellent work. We also wish to thank Lynne Lancaster and Joanne Christie at Bradford School of Management for providing administrative help in the latter stages of this initiative.

Finally, we are indebted to Lord Marshall of Knightsbridge, Chairman of British Airways, who found time in his busy schedule to write the Foreword. Both he and the former Chairman of British Airways, Lord King, have shown us numerous kindnesses over the years and we wish to place our thanks on public record.

The publishers would like to thank the following for permission to reprint their material:

Advertising Association/World Advertising Research Center for permission to reprint David Bernstein, "Corporate Void," *International Journal of Advertising* 1989, 8: 315–320.

Bank One: "The Uncommon Partnership" has been republished with permission of the Design Management Institute, 29 Temple Place, Boston, MA 02111, USA. Phone: (617) 338 6380; web site: www.dmi.org.

Braybrooke Press and Henley Management College for permission to reprint John M. T. Balmer, "The Three Virtues and Seven Deadly Sins of Corporate Brand Management," *Journal of General Management* 2001, 27 (1): 1–17.

California Management Review by kind permission of The Regents of the University of California to reprint John M. T. Balmer and Stephen A. Greyser, "Managing the Multiple Identities of the Corporation," *California Management Review* 2002, 44 (3): 72–86.

Elsevier Science for permission to reprint Stuart Albert and David A. Whetten, "Organizational Identity," in L. L. Cummings and B. M. Straw (eds) *Research in Organizational Behavior* 1985, 7: 263–295; and James E. Grunig, "Image and Substance: From Symbolic to Behavioral Relationships," *Public Relations Review* 1993, 19 (2): 121–139.

Harvard Business School Press by kind permission of the President and Fellows of Harvard College, Walter P. Margulies, "Make the Most of Your Corporate Identity," *Harvard Business Review* 1997 (July–August): 66–77; and Pierre Martineau, "Sharper Focus for the Corporate Image," *Harvard Business Review* 1958 (November–December): 49–58.

Henry Stewart Publications for permission to reprint an extract from Charles J. Fombrun and Cees B. M. Van Riel, "The Reputational Landscape," *Corporate Reputation Review* 1998, 1 (1): 5–13; Kevin Lane Keller and David A. Aaker, "The Impact of Corporate Marketing on a Company's Brand Extensions," *Corporate Reputation Review* 1998, 1 (4): 356–378; and Helen Stuart, 'The Effect of Organizational Structure on Corporate Identity Management," *Corporate Reputation Review* 1999, 2 (2): 151–164.

MCB University Press for permission to reprint John M. T. Balmer and Edmund R. Gray, "Corporate Identity and Corporate Communications: Creating a Competitive Advantage," *Corporate Communications: An International Journal* 1999, 4 (4): 171–176; and Stephen A. Greyser, "Advancing and Enhancing Corporate Reputation," *Corporate Communications: An International Journal* 1999, 4 (4): 177–181.

The Chairman and Council of the Royal Society for The Encouragement of Arts, Manufactures and Commerce for permission to publish Wally Olins, "Corporate Identity: the Myth and the Reality," *Journal of the Royal Society of Arts* December 1978–November 1979, 127: 209–218.

Westburn Publishers Ltd. for permission to reprint the following: Stephen King, "Brand-Building in the 1990s," *Journal of Marketing Management* 1991, 7: 3–13 © Westburn Publishers Ltd. www.westburn.co.uk.

Carcanet Press Ltd. for permission to reprint part of the poem "In Broken Images" by Robert Graves, in *Complete Poems*, edited by B. Graves and D. Ward, Manchester: Carcanet Press, 2000.

Some of the quotations used in this book were taken from Crainer, S., *The Ultimate Book of Business Quotations*, Oxford: Capstone Publishing Ltd., 1997.

We also wish to thank Professor Cees B. M. Van Riel for his essay "Managing Corporate Communication," which was written especially for this anthology.

PROLOGUE
New insights

■ John M. T. Balmer and Stephen A. Greyser

THE CONCEPTS OF CORPORATE IDENTITY, communication, image, reputation, and branding have, at various times since the 1950s, captured the imagination of scholars and managers alike. The result has been new ways of conceptualizing organizations, new management functions and responsibilities, a new family of consultancy, and the emergence of new writing on corporations.

Individually, the concepts cited above have provided new perspectives in comprehending the various facets of corporate meaning. We ascribe this to the skills of invention, to principles derived from practice, as well as to the penetrating insights born out of intellectual prowess and grounded in empirical research. Each of the chapters of this anthology has at least one of the above attributes. Some have several.

Unfortunately, various fault lines have emerged. This fragmentation has, alas, also led to dilution.

Why the confusion? The causes are countless: the divide between practitioners and scholars; the existence of disciplinary silos; the divisions caused by geography, language, and culture.

There is another indictment of those who are concerned with these corporate-level concepts – namely, the magnetism of monomania. As a consequence, one concept is held in particular affection at any one point in time. Currently, the lure of the corporate brand is holding sway. Other recent stars include corporate reputation, corporate communication, organizational identification, and corporate identity. In the 1970s the corporate personality was held in awe, while in the 1950s considerable esteem was accorded to the corporate image. Thus the area has many facets, each with its own intellectual roots and practice-based adherents.

Although individual corporate-level concepts provide a powerful and radical lens through which to comprehend organizations, individual perspectives are necessarily limited. However, when a broad vista is adopted, these corporate-level concepts offer the promise of a critical breakthrough in our conceptualization of organizations, one that serves as a window that throws light on the essence of organizations. In their totality, these rays of light reveal the organization. Such a stance is radical. It affords new ways of comprehending organizations. It represents a tableau that we believe is complex, challenging, and rewarding in equal measure and that is superior to single-perspective approaches.

Marshaling the latent power of *all* the corporate-level concepts is something that we find to be enormously exciting. It forms a leitmotif in *Revealing the Corporation*. It is a theme that is reflected in our opening article "Managing the Multiple Identities of the Corporation," as well as in the Epilogue. Such a perspective, we believe, has the potential to be of significant value to both scholarship and practice.

A daunting visage?

We are frequently asked by our students, by academic colleagues, as well as by managers and consultants for a book of key articles on the area. Some are beginning their exploration of the domain. Others have ventured further but have found themselves confronted by an abyss or, perhaps worse, a cul-de-sac. Invariably, they have become frustrated, if not defeated, by the literature: its size, its impenetrability, and its lack of disciplinary coherence. They are disappointed by our observation that the corpus of work on the area *is* disorganized and that it *is* taxing. Thus the need for this anthology, a need to plug the void and to make a start, however tentative.

In assembling this compilation we have drawn on our wide experiences and discussions relating to research and course development, collaboratively over the past decade but with much earlier origins. Stephen designed and developed numerous practice-based case studies for his MBA elective on the new corporate communications offered at Harvard Business School; his research and writing in the area began over thirty years ago. John, in 1991, introduced an MBA elective on corporate identity and branding that formed part of the syllabus at Strathclyde Graduate Business School. The course is now offered at Bradford School of Management and its affiliate institutions in the Netherlands, Singapore, India, and the United Arab Emirates. The topic has proved to be very popular at executive, postgraduate, and undergraduate levels. Undergraduate registrations for the course have, for the past two years, been in excess of 150.

Both of us, in executive education work, have discovered that many senior managers find the area to be a revelation. We have learned a great deal from examining corporate-level related issues with senior executives and students on our various programs. Scholars of a certain vintage may be familiar with the Latin maxim *docendo discimus* – "we learn by teaching." Certainly this has been, and is, our experience.

Catholic classics

This anthology is eclectic and draws on diverse traditions within the academic and practitioner literatures. It is international in scope and embraces contributions from the U.S.A., the U.K., the Continent, and Australia.

We include a number of practitioner-written classics because, to a considerable degree, many of the areas covered in this anthology have been practitioner led, the earliest example being the 1958 *Harvard Business Review* (*HBR*) article on corporate image by Pierre Martineau. Others are by Walter Margulies, a pioneer in the identity industry, by leading U.K. branding and advertising consultants Stephen King and David Bernstein, and by Wally Olins, the doyen of the identity industry.

Our research has uncovered several "hidden" gems. One of these is a lecture on corporate identity delivered by Wally Olins in 1978 to The Royal Society for the Encouragement of Arts, Manufactures and Commerce in London. The article by Stephen King on corporate branding is another. These early contributions have lost little of their resonance with the passing of years despite their lack of recent visibility.

A representative selection of some of the foremost scholars on the area has also been assembled. This includes the seminal work by Stuart Albert and David Whetten on organizational identification, James Grunig on corporate image, Charles Fombrun and Cees Van Riel on corporate reputation, Kevin Keller and David Aaker on corporate branding, and a specially commissioned exposition on corporate communications by Cees Van Riel.

We have also drawn on our own work. For instance, the anthology opens with a collaborative endeavor between us that details a new framework, drawing on interdisciplinary perspectives, published in the spring 2002 issue of *California Management Review*. The anthology includes a very recent Harvard-style case study written by Peter Phillips and Stephen A. Greyser. This provides a "real-life" context for the numerous issues mentioned in this compilation.

Unanswered questions

The articles included in this collection raise important issues. We conclude that six crucially important questions characterize the area (see Exhibit 1). On reflection it will be seen that these questions relate to the six concepts covered in this compendium.

We begin by outlining the new processes that have led to the growing importance accorded to the area. We continue by discussing the development of the family of corporate-level concepts that are examined within *Revealing the Corporation*. This provides a brief historiography and, as such, a useful introduction to this anthology.

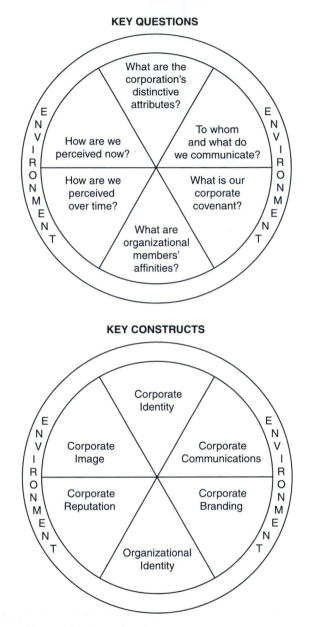

KEY QUESTIONS

What are the corporation's distinctive attributes?

How are we perceived now?

To whom and what do we communicate?

How are we perceived over time?

What is our corporate covenant?

What are organizational members' affinities?

ENVIRONMENT

ENVIRONMENT

KEY CONSTRUCTS

Corporate Identity

Corporate Image

Corporate Communications

Corporate Reputation

Corporate Branding

Organizational Identity

ENVIRONMENT

ENVIRONMENT

Exhibit 1 Key questions and key constructs

Source: Adapted from J. M. T. Balmer, "Corporate Identity," in M. J. Baker (ed.) *The IEBM Encyclopedia of Marketing*, London: International Thomson Business Press, 1999, pp. 732–746

New pressures

A number of authors[1] have noted, regarding identity, image, and reputation, that new environmental pressures on business have led to increasing importance being accorded to these topics and, in overview, also to corporate brands. These pressures include the acceleration of product life cycles; deregulation; privatization programs; increased competition in the public and not-for-profit sectors; increased competition in the service sector; globalization and the establishment of free trade areas; merger, acquisition, and divestment; shortage of high-calibre personnel; public expectations for corporate social responsiveness; and the increased salience to organizations of external stakeholders.

The ten undercurrents listed here, which have been prevalent for the past decade, have accentuated the need for identity, reputation, and corporate branding to be strategically managed. As Balmer and Gray[2] observed:

> Some firms have been affected by many of them whereas others by only a few. It would be difficult, however, to identify any companies that have not been touched significantly by at least one of them. Hence, in the aggregate, they represent the driving force behind the recent upsurge in interest in corporate identity and corporate communication issues.

New concepts

In tracing the evolution of the area covered by the time frame of this anthology, five distinct phases of development can be detailed. Each of them tends to reflect a new or growing interest in a concept, group of concepts, or, in the case of identity, a more profound appreciation of the concept.[3] Exhibit 2 provides a synopsis of the area's historiography.

The anthology's structure

We have divided this anthology into six distinct sections. With the exception of the initial and final sections, each one is concerned with a broad concept *or* with familial concepts as in the case of the third section, which embraces both corporate image and corporate reputation. We open each of these sections with an early, and accessible, example from the *practitioner* literature, to set the stage for more substantial scholarly contributions that follow.

Introductions are provided for each section and each chapter. The former provides a general introduction to the concept(s) under scrutiny in that section. This is followed by a section entitled "Topics for discussion and reflection" followed by another entitled "Further reading," which is self-explanatory. The "Topics for discussion and reflection" should be tackled only when the entire section has been read.

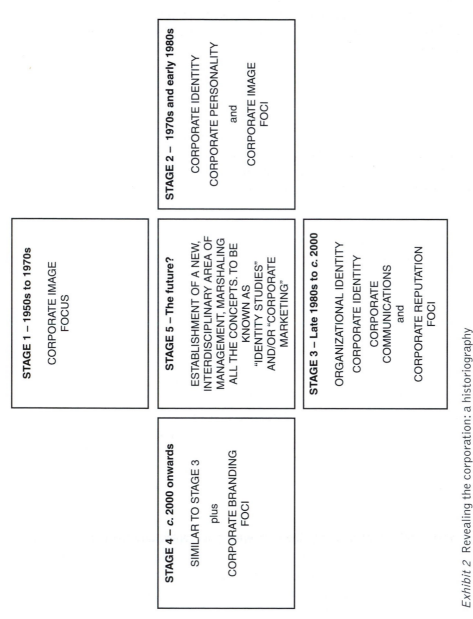

STAGE 1 – 1950s to 1970s

CORPORATE IMAGE
FOCUS

STAGE 2 – 1970s and early 1980s

CORPORATE IDENTITY
CORPORATE PERSONALITY

and

CORPORATE IMAGE
FOCI

STAGE 5 – The future?

ESTABLISHMENT OF A NEW,
INTERDISCIPLINARY AREA OF
MANAGEMENT, MARSHALING
ALL THE CONCEPTS, TO BE
KNOWN AS
"IDENTITY STUDIES"
AND/OR "CORPORATE
MARKETING"

STAGE 3 – Late 1980s to c. 2000

ORGANIZATIONAL IDENTITY
CORPORATE IDENTITY

CORPORATE
COMMUNICATIONS

and

CORPORATE REPUTATION
FOCI

STAGE 4 – c. 2000 onwards

SIMILAR TO STAGE 3

plus

CORPORATE BRANDING
FOCI

Exhibit 2 Revealing the corporation: a historiography

Source: Adapted from J. M. T. Balmer, "Corporate Identity," in M. J. Baker (ed.) *The IEBM Encyclopedia of Marketing*, London: International Thomson Business Press, 1999, pp. 732–746

The editorial commentary that introduces each chapter provides a synopsis highlighting what we believe are the chapter's merits. These interstitial comments provided by the editors aim (a) to assist readers in navigating their way through the myriad issues encompassed by this anthology, and (b) to offer routes for exploring the area in greater detail by contemplating the issues raised in the "Topics for discussion and reflection" section and/or by delving further into the literature using our list of additional readings as a point of departure.

From confusion to fusion

A key premise underpinning this compilation is that the various concepts examined in *Revealing the Corporation* afford perspectives that are both diverse and edifying – that is, viewpoints of assistance in comprehending the multiple dimensions of the corporation. We see the contents not as a disparate collection of insights but rather as parts of a whole – parts of a *new gestalt of the corporation*. As such, this represents a new beginning.

We illustrate how the seemingly disparate elements may be fused together in two principal ways. These two approaches should be viewed as handrails to guide the reader through different levels of understanding rather than handcuffs to be forcibly worn on a predetermined route march envisioned by the editors.

The first of the approaches mentioned above is realized by adopting an identity-based perspective. This is the theme of the opening section, which focuses on the aforementioned article coauthored by the editors in the *California Management Review*. Entitled "Managing the Multiple Identities of the Corporation," it views the concepts examined in this anthology as a variety of identity types that need to be identified, understood, and brought into alignment with corporate strategy and management vision (both of which we characterize as additional types of identity).

The second means of synthesis is examined in the Epilogue. This component of the volume adopts an overtly marketing-focused perspective. We argue that the perspectives explored in this anthology may be considered analogous to a new branch of marketing, that of *corporate-level marketing*. We seek to explain the merits of this marketing-focused umbrella title; the affinity of the image, reputation, communication, and branding concepts to marketing; the salience of mutually beneficial exchange relationships that underpin the marketing philosophy; and the notion that mutual benefit should characterize corporate-level relationships. However, corporate-level marketing will be markedly distinct from traditional marketing in at least two significant ways: it will be multidisciplinary in scope and will have a more strategic/ senior management role. This second avenue of synthesis is explored in the Epilogue.

Readers should note that the sixth section of the volume consists of a case study, that of Bank One. The questions that accompany this case study also facilitate the adoption of an integrated approach, in the manner of the opening article and concluding Epilogue.

The benefits of table d'hôte

There are many articles worthy of inclusion in this anthology. However, space constraints meant that we had to limit the number, and thus exclude some distinguished scholars and practitioners whom we hold in high regard. We hope that none of our colleagues from the worlds of academe or practice will take exception if their work has not been included.

We hope this anthology will be of interest to a wide audience. We are acutely aware that, as with any anthology, what we have offered is table d'hôte rather than à la carte. As we suggested earlier, the complexities of the literature can result in mental indigestion, if not a loss of appetite. Table d'hôte can, we trust, represent good value. We have sought to provide a repast that includes new fare that may even delight the self-professed connoisseur. Whether you are a novice or an aficionado, we hope there will be many aspects of this collection that will interest or delight.

The chapters that follow are articles that we ourselves have close at hand, refer to frequently, and consider worthy of recurrent scrutiny. We hope that if you are new to them you will have a real sense of discovery. If you are not, we hope that the orchestration of the various strands in this anthology will act as a catalyst for rethinking the various dimensions of corporate meaning.

Revisiting the vast and imposing literature of which some is represented here is a humbling experience. Both of us realize the debt *we* have to the many practitioners and scholars who showed us the way.

Both of us stand on the shoulders of these giants.

Notes

1   Ind, N. (1992) *The Corporate Image*, 2nd edition, London: Kogan Page, 1992, pp. 28–44; Gray, E. R. and Balmer, J. M. T., "Managing Corporate Image and Reputation," *Long Range Planning* 1998, 31 (5): 695–702; Balmer, J. M. T. and Gray, E. R., "Corporate Identity and Corporate Communication: Creating a Competitive Advantage," *Corporate Communications: An International Journal* 1999, 4 (4): 171–176.

2   Balmer and Gray, *op. cit.*

3   Balmer, J. M. T., "Corporate Identity and the Advent of Corporate Marketing," *Journal of Marketing Management* 1998, 14 (8): 963–996.

Revealing the corporation: an integrative framework

Acid test n. *a conclusive test of success and value*
Concise Oxford Dictionary

EDITORS' INTRODUCTION AND COMMENTARY

WE BEGIN THIS ANTHOLOGY with an article coauthored by the editors. "Managing the Multiple Identities of the Corporation" appeared in the *California Management Review* in 2002. It details a new, multidisciplinary, and multifaceted framework that can be marshaled to reveal important misalignments that can arise within *any* corporate or organizational entity. The broad vista adopted in this chapter draws on all of the corporate-level concepts covered in this collection.

The idea of a multidisciplinary perspective to the field is not new. Its lineage within the identity literature is well documented. It can be detected in the work of Abratt,[1] Dowling,[2] Van Riel and Balmer,[3] and Balmer.[4] Recently, organizational behaviorists such as Hatch and Schultz[5] have adopted a similar perspective. It is also evident in a contemporary collection of articles dealing with corporate-level concerns edited by a U.S.–Danish triumvirate: Shultz, Hatch, and Larsen.[6]

The antecedents of the AC²ID Test™ framework,[7] particularly the notion of the corporate identity interface (and its companion notion of identity misalignments), are to be found in the pioneering conceptual work on image and identity undertaken by the South African marketing academic Abratt.[8] It was Abratt who, in his conceptual model of the corporate image management process, highlighted the key identity/image interface and observed that a key factor of image management was to ensure that a positive image was underpinned by a positive identity. In other words, perception should mirror reality. The importance of this interface was articulated by the then President of Landor Associates, John Diefenbach,[9] as far back as 1982. Building on the work of Abratt, Balmer[10] argued that *many other* interfaces could have a deleterious effect on an entity.

This framework grew out of a major international identity research project in which both authors were involved. The chapter draws on the most recent developments in relation to the model and draws on the authors' respective research at Bradford and Harvard, including case study explorations. Its genesis can be found in an early articulation of the model by Balmer and Soenen[11] that is accompanied by a detailed examination of the first stage of the research process.

The integrative approach advanced in this chapter is intended to assist the reader in comprehending the following:

- the inherent power of the corporate-level concepts discussed in this anthology;
- the profound insights that may be gleaned about the corporation when these concepts are combined into an integrated framework;
- the utility of marshaling the various disciplinary strands that inform our understanding of the corporate-level concepts examined in this anthology;
- the efficacy of examining the various interfaces and potentially hazardous dichotomies that may exist among current organizational reality (identity), corporate rhetoric and communication (communication), perception (image and reputation), the organization's game plan (strategy), and management vision (leadership).

The model presented here does, we believe, make a significant advance on earlier work. It takes account of the powerful identity categories that are derived from organizational reality, strategy, management vision, perception, and communication. It embraces the fact that each of the five identity categories will possibly inhabit different time frames. It assimilates the perspective that these categories transcend traditional organizational boundaries and have their origin, in some instances, from outside as well as inside the corporation. The article also describes important misalignments or "moments of truth" that have been experienced by a variety of organizations in the U.S.A., the U.K., the Continent, and Asia.

In operationalizing the framework, Balmer[12] recommended recourse to his REDS^2 Acid Test Process™. This involved a five-stage process. It results in the articulation of a strategy to resolve any misaligments among the five identity types. It can be explained as follows:

R = REVEAL   the five identity types
E = EXAMINE   the ten indentity interfaces
D = DIAGNOSE   the problem areas (perhaps place in rank order)
S = SELECT   the interface(s) that should to be brought into alignment (taking into account what is urgent, desirable, and feasible)
S = STRATEGY   identify what type of strategy is required to bring the interfaces into alignment (strategic, visionary, culture, communication, perception, or "reality" change – i.e., what the company does, how it does it, where it does it)

We believe the AC^{2}ID Test™ encapsulates the complexities of the area in a framework that is simple, memorable, rational, and operational. (Note: an expanded version of the framework which is applicable to organizations having a corporate brand is introduced in the editors' introduction to Section Five. The additional (sixth) identity type is called the *covenanted* identity.)

TOPICS FOR DISCUSSION AND REFLECTION

1   What are the strengths and weaknesses of the AC^{2}ID Test™ framework in:
    (a)   comprehending the multidisciplinary roots of identity?
    (b)   addressing identity problems in a real-life context?
2   How might the framework assist senior managers when engaging consultants and in evaluating their work?
3   How might the framework assist consultancies in identity-related work?
4   Using the model and the REDS^2 framework, undertake a desktop analysis of an organization of your choice.
    (a)   If appropriate, prioritize the three identity types requiring alignment and detail recommendations to effect such an alignment.
    (b)   Identify which time frame each of the organization's five identity types occupies.

5   How might the AC²ID Test be deployed in a merger/acquisition situation?
6   Does the AC²ID Test have a utility in other business-related situations? If so,
     how? Explain its use in that situation.

NOTES

1   Abratt, R., "A New Approach to the Corporate Image Management Process,"
     Journal of Marketing Management 1989, 15 (1): 63–76.
2   Dowling, G., "Managing Your Corporate Images," *Long Range Planning* 1993, 26
     (2): 101–109.
3   Van Riel, C. B. M., *Principles of Corporate Communication*, London: Prentice Hall,
     1995.
4   Balmer, J. M. T., "Corporate Branding and Connoisseurship," *Journal of General
     Management* 1995, 21 (1): 24–46.
5   Hatch, M. J. and Schultz, M., "Are the Strategic Stars Aligned for your Corporate
     Brand?," *Harvard Business Review* 2001 (February): 129–134.
6   Schultz, M., Hatch, M. J. and Larsen, M. G., *The Expressive Organization*, Oxford:
     Oxford University Press, 2000.
7   The AC²ID Test™ and The ACID Test™ of Corporate Identity Management have
     respectively been trademarked by J. M. T. Balmer in 1999 and 1998.
8   Abratt, op. cit.
9   Diefenbach, J. M., "Design as a Management Tool: The Strategic Thinking behind
     the Design Process," unpublished paper delivered at the Design Management Insti-
     tute Conference, Boston, December 9–10, 1982.
10   Balmer, J. M. T., "Corporate Identity and the Advent of Corporate Marketing,"
     Journal of Marketing Management 1998, 14 (8): pp. 963–996.
11   Balmer, J. M. T. and Soenen, G. M., "The ACID™ Test of Corporate Identity Man-
     agement," *Journal of Marketing Management* 1999, 15 (1–3): 69–92.
12   Balmer, op. cit.

FURTHER READING

Abratt, R. (1989) "A New Approach to the Corporate Image Management Process,"
     Journal of Marketing Management 15 (1): 63–76.
Balmer, J. M. T. (1998) "Corporate Identity and the Advent of Corporate Marketing,"
     Journal of Marketing Management 4: 963–996.
Balmer, J. M. T. and Soenen, G. M. (1999) "The ACID™ Test of Corporate Identity Man-
     agement," *Journal of Marketing Management* 15 (1–3): 69–92.
Kiriakidou, O. and Millward, L. J. (2000) "Corporate Identity: External Reality or
     Internal Fit?," *Corporate Communications: An International Journal* 5 (1): 49–
     58.
Stuart, H. (1998) "Exploring the Corporate Identity/Corporate Image Interface: An
     Empirical Study of Accountancy Firms," *Journal of Communication Management*
     2 (4): 357–371.

Chapter 1

John M. T. Balmer and Stephen A. Greyser

MANAGING THE MULTIPLE

IDENTITIES OF THE CORPORATION

From *California Management Review* 2002, 44 (3): 72–86. © 2002 by The Regents of the University of California

RECENTLY, COMPANIES HAVE BEEN experiencing a period where the corporate identity landscape has become more active and more crowded. For example:

- Mergers, spin-offs, acquisitions, and alliances have led to many new or meaningfully changed companies, in turn calling for new identities by name and/or business focus.
- The proliferation of dot.com and new technology companies created many new (and differentiated) company identities, albeit often short-lived.
- Some existing companies undertook "re-imaging" as they sought, substantively and/or via communications, to make their identities more technology-oriented.

Consequently, corporate managing of identity and image has become more salient, especially in and for the financial marketplace and for the media. In short,

The authors wish to acknowledge the assistance of Guillaume Soenen, Professor Balmer's research assistant, in the initial stages of the research reported here. Also we are grateful to Enterprise I.G. for providing access to senior staff in London and New York regarding their recent and current practice of identity project management, for financial assistance, and for ongoing encouragement. We also appreciate the cooperation of the various organizations that shared their identity-related experiences. To Opinion Research Corporation, we are grateful for access to selected reputation research data and models. Finally, we appreciate the support of Bradford School of Management, the Strathclyde Business School, and the Harvard Business School.

corporate identity has emerged as a "hot topic" for senior company management and those who advise them as well as for academics studying the territory.

In the wake of this activity has come the rapid growth of consultants in identity, branding, graphic design, communications, and image research – all asserting their competence in serving as advisors to senior management on identity issues. Each offers a useful perspective, but one formed dominantly from only a single discipline. However, our experience points to diagnostic and prescriptive power from marshaling a *variety* of disciplines. While there is a growing consensus as to the salience and strategic importance of corporate identity, identity studies to date have not been characterized by models informed by multidisciplinary perspectives harnessed within a single pragmatic framework. This article describes a model that seeks to fill this void and that meets the needs of senior managers and scholars alike.

The new framework is called the AC^{2}ID Test^{TM}.[1] This is an acronym that encapsulates a mosaic of five identity types – namely, actual identity, communicated identity, conceived identity, ideal identity, and desired identity. The framework is grounded in our field research undertaken in the U.S. and the U.K., much of it conducted within the corporate identity industry; it also incorporates recent trends in identity scholarship. As such, the framework encompasses a variety of disciplinary sources and time frames and also accommodates internal corporate as well as external perspectives.

Prevailing corporate thinking considers identity to be a monolithic phenomenon. At most there is a view that a current corporate identity (or non-identity) needs to be recast into a new, typically vision-inspired, identity. Our research shows that the premise of a monolithic identity is narrow and inadequate. Management needs to have understanding across the five identities within the AC^{2}ID Test. Furthermore, corporate leadership should recognize that multiple identities can co-exist comfortably within a company even if they are slightly different. However, meaningful incongruence between any two (or more) of the five identities can cause problems for a company with its relevant stakeholders.

The framework of the AC^{2}ID Test

"Acid test: a conclusive test of success and value"

Concise Oxford Dictionary (1999)

Figure 1 depicts five identities that are present in any corporate (or organizational) entity. They are:

- *Actual identity* – The actual identity constitutes the current attributes of the corporation. It is shaped by a number of elements, including corporate ownership, the leadership style of management, organizational structure, business activities and markets covered, the range and quality of products and services offered, and overall business performance. Also encompassed is the set of values held by management and employees.
- *Communicated identity* – The communicated identity is most clearly

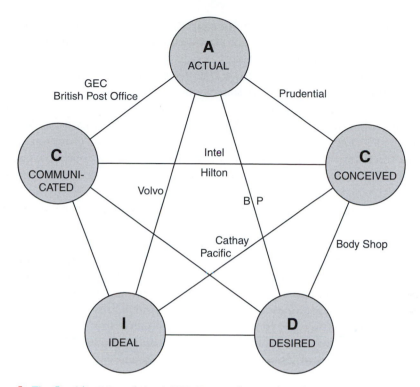

Figure 1 The five identities of the AC²ID Test and examples of misalignment

revealed through "controllable" corporate communication. This typically encompasses advertising, sponsorship, and public relations. In addition, it derives from "non-controllable" communication, e.g., word-of-mouth, media commentary, and the like.

- **Conceived identity** – The conceived identity refers to perceptual concepts – corporate image, corporate reputation, and corporate branding. These are the perceptions of the company – its multi-attribute and overall corporate image and corporate reputation – held by relevant stakeholders. Management must make a judgment as to which groups' perceptions are most important.
- **Ideal identity** – The ideal identity is the optimum positioning of the organization in its market (or markets) in a given time frame. This is normally based on current knowledge from the strategic planners and others about the organization's capabilities and prospects in the context of the general business and competitive environment. The specifics of a given entity's ideal identity are subject to fluctuation based on external factors – e.g., the nuclear power industry after Chernobyl; and industries (such as travel, transport equipment, and security systems) affected negatively and positively by the September 11 World Trade Center catastrophe.
- **Desired identity** – The desired identity lives in the hearts and minds of corporate leaders; it is their vision for the organization. Although this identity type is often misguidedly assumed to be virtually identical to the

ideal identity, they typically come from different sources. Whereas the ideal identity normally emerges after a period of research and analysis, the desired identity may have more to do with a vision informed by a CEO's personality and ego than with a rational assessment of the organization's actual identity in a particular time frame.

Even within one identity type for a particular company may reside several variations of that identity. For example, different stakeholder groups and different market segments may have somewhat different perceptions of a company (Conceived Identity). Managers should be sensitive to these variations, but should be cognizant of the single identity type of which they all are a part. An extensive literature addresses corporate and brand image research, as noted in Table 1, with illustrative references.

The AC²ID Test is grounded in the premise that companies indeed have multiple identities. A corollary premise is that the lack of alignment (or "fit") between any two of the identities causes dissonance that can potentially weaken a company. This dissonance manifests itself as "a moment of truth," such as when corporate rhetoric (Communicated Identity) is meaningfully ahead of or behind reality (Actual Identity); where vision (Desired Identity) is at odds with strategy (Ideal Identity); or when corporate performance and behavior (Actual Identity) falls short of the expectations held by key stakeholder groups (Conceived Identity).

It is a task of the corporate leadership group to manage identities so that they are broadly consonant with each other. At the same time, naturally, management should be tracking trends in the business environment to inform its strategy (Ideal Identity) and eventually affect corporate action and behavior (Actual Identity). The framework of the five identities also takes into account the involvement and influence of various internal and external stakeholder groups. Table 2 shows which stakeholders most affect each type of identity.

Identities emanate from different sources within and outside the company. Different management traditions and disciplines inform our understanding of identity. There are some identities that are formed by a company's communications. Others grow from a corporation's values and cultures, reflecting a company's heritage or its current leadership. Some are influenced by a dominant business unit or the national mores and precepts of a corporation's home country. In considering identities, company top management may want to be assured that the perspectives and disciplines employed are wide-ranging.

Perils of misaligned identities

Organizations must manage their multiple identities to avoid potentially harmful misalignments. Following are descriptions of nine situations where company identities were *not* in alignment and how those firms either successfully acted to make appropriate adjustments (and confront a "moment of truth") or how they continued to struggle with the challenges of reconciling the misalignment.

Table 1 Disciplinary sources of the AC²ID Test

Concept	Management roots/disciplinary origins	Our brief explanation	Links to one or more of the five identity types
Corporate identity	• Marketing • Communications • Graphic design	The mix of attributes which makes any entity distinct.[a]	• Actual • Communicated • Conceived • Ideal • Desired
Corporate branding	• Marketing • Economics • Strategy	Derived from an organization's identity and encapsulated in a branding position statement which delineates the tangible and intangible attributes of the brand. Brand reputation serves as a company's convenant with key stakeholders.[b]	• Actual • Communicated • Conceived • Ideal • Desired
Corporate image and corporate reputation	• Marketing • Economics • Social psychology • Strategy	The perception of the organiza- tion by an individual, group, or groups at one point in time (image), over time (reputation), and the added value accrued from a positive reputation (esteem).[c]	• Conceived
Total corporate communications	• Marketing and communications	The multi-faceted way by which organizations communicate. *Primary* (product performance, organizational and leadership behavior); *Secondary* (advertising, PR, graphic design, sponsorship and other controlled forms); *Tertiary* (word of mouth, third party communications, and "spin").[d]	• Communicated
Corporate personality	• Marketing • Psychology • Organizational behavior	Very similar to the organiza- tional identification concept but also includes the role of the founder's personality in identity formation.[e]	• Actual • Desired
Organizational identity/ identification	• Organizational behavior	Traditionally focuses on an organization's culture(s), with the emphasis on personnel's commitment to the organization.[f]	• Actual
Corporate culture	• Organizational behavior	The mix of values and sub- cultural groups which is a major element of an organiza- tion's actual identity.[g]	• Actual

Table 1 *continued*

Concept	Management roots/disciplinary origins	Our brief explanation	Links to one or more of the five identity types
Organizational leadership	• Organizational behavior	The role of an organization's founders and leaders in shaping an identity.[h]	• Actual • Desired
Organizational history	• Business history • Reputation studies	The salience and ongoing influence of an organization's historical roots.[i]	• Actual • Conceived • Communicated
Corporate strategy	• Strategy	The organization's game plan.[j]	• Ideal
Organizational structure and architecture	• Strategy	The relationship/s between the corporate entity/holding company and its subsidiaries in business units.[k]	• Actual • Ideal
Visual identification	• Graphic design	The system of visual identification used by the organization incorporated on products, staff uniforms, buildings, vehicles, and so on.[l]	• Actual • Communicated • Ideal • Desired

Other related concepts and constructs

Concept	Management roots/disciplinary origins	Our brief explanation	Links to one or more of the five identity types
Corporate identity interface	• Marketing/ multidisciplinary	Usually refers to the identity/ image interface (the degree of congruence between organizational reality and external perception). Other "key" interfaces have been identified.[m]	• Actual • Conceived
Corporate identity mix(es)	• Marketing/ multidisciplinary	The elements which make up an organization's identity.[n]	• Actual
Schools of thought relating to corporate identity	• Marketing/ multidisciplinary	Articulates the various approaches to corporate identity: strategic, behavioral, communications schools and the four graphic design schools.[o]	• Actual • Communicated • Ideal • Desired

a   J. M. T. Balmer, "Corporate Identity and the Advent of Corporate Marketing," *Journal of Marketing Management*, 14 (1998): 963–996; N. Marwick and C. Fill, "Towards a Framework for Managing Corporate Identity," *European Journal of Marketing*, 31/5–6 (1997): 396–409; C. B. M. Van Riel and J. M. T. Balmer, "Corporate Identity: The Concept Its Management and Measurement," *European Journal of Marketing*, 31/5–6 (1997): 340–356.

b   K. L. Keller and D. Aaker, "Corporate Level Marketing: The Impact of Credibility on Corporate Brand Extensions," *Corporate Reputation Review*, 1/4 (1998): 356–378; S. King, "Brand Building in the 1990s," *Journal of Marketing Management*, 7 (1991): 3–13.

Table 1 *continued*

c   K. Boulding, *The Image* (Ann Arbor, MI: University of Michigan Press, 1956); E. R. Gray and J. M. T. Balmer, "Managing Corporate Image and Corporate Reputation," *Long Range Planning*, 31/5 (October 1998): 695–702; S. A. Greyser, "Advancing and Enhancing Corporate Reputation," *Corporate Communications: An International Journal*, 4/4 (1999): 177–181; R. Worcester and J. Downham, eds., *Consumer Market Research Handbook* (London: McGraw-Hill, 1986).

d   J. M. T. Balmer and E. R. Gray, "Corporate Identity and Corporate Communications: Creating a Strategic Advantage," *Corporate Communications: An International Journal*, 4/4 (1999): 171–176; D. Bernstein, *Company Image and Reality* (Eastbourne, UK: Holt, Rinehart and Winston, 1984); C. B. M. Van Riel, *Principles of Corporate Communication* (London: Prentice Hall, 1995).

e   W. Olins, *The Corporate Personality: An Inquiry into the Nature of Corporate Identity* (London: Design Council, 1978).

f   S. Albert and D. A. Whetten, "Organizational Identity" in L. L. Cummings and B. M. Staw, eds., *Research in Organizational Behavior, Vol. 7* (Greenwich, CT: JAI Press, 1985): J. E. Dutton and C. V. Harquail, "Organizational Images and Member Identification," *Administrative Science Quarterly*, 39/2 (June 1994): 239–263; D. A. Whetten and P. C. Godfrey, eds., *Identity in Organizations: Building Theory through Conversations* (Thousand Oaks, CA: Sage, 1998).

g   M. J. Hatch, "The Dynamics of Organizational Culture," *Academy of Management Review*, 18/4 (October 1993): 657–693; M. J. Hatch and M. Schultz, "Relations between Organizational Culture, Identity and Image," *European Journal of Marketing*, 31/5–6 (1997): 356–365.

h   G. R. Dowling, "Developing Your Company Image into a Corporate Asset," *Long Range Planning*, 26/2 (1993): 101–109; W. Olins, *The Corporate Personality: An Inquiry into the Nature of Corporate Identity* (London: Design Council, 1978).

i   J. M. T. Balmer, "Corporate Branding and Connoisseurship," *Journal of General Management*, 21/1 (1995): 24–46; W. Olins, *The Corporate Personality: An Inquiry into the Nature of Corporate Identity* (London: Design Council, 1978); B. Ramanantsoa, (Strategor), *Stratégie, structure, decision, identité: Politique général d'entreprise* (Paris: InterEditions, 1989).

j   K. R. Andrews, *The Concept of Corporate Strategy* (Homewood, IL: Irwin, 1980): B. E. Ashforth and F. Mael, "Organizational Identity and Strategy as a Context for the Individual," in J. A. C. Baur and J. E. Dutton, eds., *Advances in Strategic Management, Vol. 13* (Greenwich, CT: JAI Press, 1996), pp. 19–64.

k   H. Stuart, "The Effect of Organizational Structure on Corporate Identity Management," *Corporate Reputation Review*, 2/2 (1999): 51–164.

l   M. J. Baker and J. M. T. Balmer, "Visual Identity: Trappings or Substance?," *European Journal of Marketing*, 31/5–6 (1997): 63–76; C. Chajet and T. Schachtman, *Image by Design: From Corporate Vision to Business Reality* (Reading, MA: Addison-Wesley, 1991); W. Margulies, "Make the Most of Your Corporate Identity," *Harvard Business Review*, 55/4 (July/August 1977): 66–74.

m   R. Abratt, "A New Approach to the Corporate Image Management Process," *Journal of Marketing Management*, 5/1 (1989): 63–76; J. M. T. Balmer, "Corporate Identity and the Advent of Corporate Marketing," *Journal of Marketing Management*, 14 (1998): 963–996.

n   J. M. T. Balmer, "Corporate Identity, Corporate Branding and Corporate Marketing: Seeing through the Fog," *European Journal of Marketing*, 35/3–4 (2001): 248–291; K. Birkigt and M. M. Stadler, *Corporate Identity: Grundlagen, Funktionen und Fallspielen (Landsberg am Lech: Verlage Moderne Industrie, 1986)*.

o   J. M. T. Balmer, "Corporate Branding and Connoisseurship," *Journal of General Management*, 21/1 (1995): 24–46.

Table 2 Stakeholder groups' impacts on the five types of identity

Type of identity	Key stakeholder groups involved
Actual	Internal (those who "make" the company)
Communicated	Internal (marketing, communications) Marketing partners (e.g., advertising agency, communications firms) Media (interpreting the company)
Conceived	All external publics (e.g., financial community; government/regulatory sector; headquarters/local facility communities; customers/consumers)
Ideal	Internal (e.g., strategic planning) External (e.g., financial analysts, regulatory/legislative entities)
Desired	Internal (CEO/Board)

In illustrating the AC^{2}ID Test's utility, we have adopted an approach that is pragmatic rather than exhaustive. We examine many but not all of the identity misalignments that may occur. Because an organization's current position (Actual Identity) is typically and logically a point of departure for any analysis of potential misalignment, our treatment encompasses all four identity interfaces involving Actual Identity. We have included two Actual–Communicated Identity misalignments because communication is the most frequent – and perhaps most tempting – avenue to try to change an Actual Identity quickly. The allure of deploying a new Communicated Identity in an attempt to rectify deep-seated organizational problems is a common phenomenon. An effective communications platform can assist in modifying an Actual Identity when supported by substantive change in corporate behavior. Otherwise there will be a misalignment – a distorted mirror – between the Communicated and Conceived identities, as shown in the Intel and Hilton examples. The nine companies that illustrate the identity pairs are shown in Figure 1.

Identities misaligned: actual and communicated

GEC was a name that symbolized Britain's manufacturing of electrical systems and electronics for much of the 20th century. Recently, the company divested its defense division. As such, the Actual Identity of the company metamorphosed overnight from one dominantly oriented to electronics to one with its newer focus on information technology hardware. However, the GEC corporate brand name, despite enjoying wide esteem, reflected its past identity and did not communicate the radical change that had occurred. Consequently, the company adopted another historic brand name that was part of its portfolio of brands – Marconi (the company founded by Guglielmo Marconi, the inventor of wireless transmission, whose firm had been acquired by GEC). Thus, having changed its Actual Identity, the company was faced with a pressing need to bring the

Communicated Identity into alignment. The Marconi name not only reflected the new positioning more strikingly, but also drew on the distinct identity strands of the organization's heritage. Alas for Marconi, the strategy has not been successful and a new misalignment has emerged between the new positioning (Actual Identity) and some yet-to-be-disseminated altered strategic direction ("new" Ideal Identity).

Identities misaligned: actual and communicated

The British Post Office encompasses mail delivery (the Royal Mail); retail offices that sell stamps, provide basic banking services, and distribute government benefit payments; and the sending and delivery of packages. In recent years, the British Post Office has been broadening its operations to the Continent. It is also anticipating partial privatization of some services. In these latter contexts, management believed the Post Office name would not adequately differentiate itself from other postal service entities using "post office" in their name. Further, confusion could be caused within the U.K. because "post office" is used for both the retail offices and the corporate umbrella organization. Thus the name Consignia was adopted for the umbrella entity, but three distinct divisions retained the traditional names Royal Mail, Post Office, and Parcelforce. This enables the company to enter prospective new markets under its corporate name. In essence, the new corporate name intends to reflect a potentially wider range of services in a larger geographic footprint and permits potential global delivery systems under an international identity. Also, should Consignia be partially privatized, it can be differentiated in the minds of the global financial community as an international firm. At the same time, the Post Office identifies only the retail outlets within the U.K. and provides clarity for consumers.

Identities misaligned: actual and conceived

Prudential, the large British financial services group (not related to Prudential in the U.S.), confronted a substantial incongruence in the mid-1980s between the reality of its scope (Actual Identity) vs. the widely held perception (Conceived Identity) that it was narrowly focused in life assurance (insurance). Olins describes the situation as one of stark contrast.[2] Prudential was Britain's largest estate agent (real estate firm), beyond its strong insurance base. However, the latter dominated its image among stakeholders; further, its longtime "Man from the Pru" visual imagery reinforced its narrow roots. Olins' firm developed and implemented "a radical solution," in his words, via a design transformation built around the face of Prudence, long a symbol in the company's iconography. The new Prudential visual identity, supported by an extensive marketing communications program (Communicated Identity), succeeded in bridging the identity gap over a period of years.

Identities misaligned: actual and ideal

Volvo, the Swedish automotive and engineering group, faced an identity problem related to the firm's strategic goals. The Volvo group, in addition to its commercial vehicle division, had a car division that enjoyed an enviable quality reputation for its brand name. However, Volvo cars were ranked twenty-third in unit sales volume worldwide. Industry projections pointed towards further consolidation within the automotive sector with predictions of only five to ten global car manufacturers remaining in a few years. However, Volvo's automobile brand values – principally based on safety – were becoming increasingly relevant to consumers. For its part, Volvo did not have the financial clout to support the car brand, especially in the U.S. market. Very simply, in the automobile industry Volvo was a comparatively small company with a large brand. For the company's leadership, the ideal strategic solution was for the Volvo brand to be sold off and the proceeds from the sale to be reinvested in its other competencies of engineering and commercial vehicles. The Volvo group was sold to Ford, and joined their stable of other distinctive high-reputation marques such as Jaguar and Aston Martin. In essence, the present and future of the Volvo car business were misaligned. Having addressed this issue, Volvo now faces another misalignment, that between its Actual and Conceived identities, because the destiny of its same-named cars resides in the hands of another corporation. This illustrates the point that realigning identities can be an ongoing management concern.

Identities misaligned: actual and desired

When BP (formerly British Petroleum) acquired Amoco, it created a corporate entity that embraced both organizations' multiple identities. However, BP's recent (post-merger) corporate positioning strategy emphasized its environmental activities and aspirations (Desired Identity). However, to many this seems to be at variance with organizational reality and the Actual Identity of the organization. BP is quintessentially concerned with oil exploration, refining, and distribution. The environmental activist group Greenpeace, for instance, pointed out that only 1% of BP's activities comes from sustainable sources. What is clear from the above is that the post-merger BP – while it may be less British and more American, and certainly more global in outlook[3] – has not changed its core business. Although BP has a stated corporate aim of being green-oriented, this environmental positioning (Desired Identity) is an aspiration which (to us) bears arguably questionable resemblance to near-term reality; BP's substantive ability to achieve its Desired Identity is constrained, but it may be able to achieve meaningful *relative* "green" advantage over other energy firms.

Identities misaligned: communicated and conceived

Intel launched its advanced Pentium chip in 1994 on the wings of a marketing and communications program built on the widely recognized success of the

company's RandD-driven stream of components. The company had invested heavily in its well-known ongoing "Intel Inside" advertising campaign featuring a core
message of the superiority of Intel-brand components. This communicated identity was supported by the company's track record of successful innovations. The
Pentium chip was the latest entry in this line. However, during the fall of 1994,
murmurs grew louder within the advanced user community that the Pentium
chip was flawed for some complex computations, especially in scientific research.
These user doubts and concerns were spread largely by e-mail. Although aware
of the concerns among part of the user community, Intel did not undertake any
public actions to rectify the underlying product problem. In late November, the
situation burst into the public arena when news of the problem "migrated" into
mainstream media, and very quickly escalated into a major mass-media print and
broadcast news story. The company characterized the concerns as exaggerated
and the problems as likely to occur very infrequently; Intel would replace the
chip only if its own analysis and judgment led it to a conclusion that the problem
was serious. Very soon, as awareness and concern mounted about Intel's Pentium chips, doubts were being cast by key stakeholders – e.g., manufacturers
using Intel chips, distributors, end-users – on the reliability of Intel's positioning
(Conceived Identity). Confronted with a deepening misalignment of its Communicated and Conceived identities, Intel within weeks changed its position
(albeit grudgingly in the eyes of many) to one of greater responsiveness to
customer concerns. Through these actions, the company gradually moved to
restore its traditional reputation for developing and manufacturing high-quality
components.

Identities misaligned: conceived and communicated

Hilton is a world-renowned hotel chain brand. In the mid-1960s, the U.S.-based
company suffered acute financial difficulties which led to much of its non-
American operations being sold off, including the rights to the Hilton brand
name internationally. The non-American operations were eventually acquired by
the British entertainment group Ladbrookes. Both the U.S.-based Hilton and
Ladbrookes used the Hilton brand name. Although consumers generally perceived "Hilton" to be one entity, in reality the brand was owned by two organizations. Over time, the two firms increasingly employed different communications
programs to support the Hilton brand in their markets. This caused brand
identity confusion for those consumers and/or business-to-business customers
who used Hilton in both sets of markets. In identity terms, there was a gap
between the widely held perception of Hilton as a single entity (Conceived
Identity) and the two Communicated identities. By the mid-1990s, the two
management groups realized that this misalignment was weakening the common
meaning and values in the brand. In 1998, the two organizations entered into
a formal marketing and branding alliance, including reservation systems,
technology, marketing programs, and, most noticeably, visual identity.

Identities misaligned: desired and conceived

Body Shop, a cosmetic retailer (and manufacturer), had long positioned itself as a firm with pro-social values, principally through the voice of its founder/CEO Anita Roddick. The company's Desired Identity drove both its philosophy and its strategy. The positioning was reflected especially through the company's environmentally friendly product formulas. The growth and success of the company, and Roddick's style and rhetoric, attracted considerable media attention. (At this time, the Desired and Communicated identities were in alignment.)

The company's vigorous espousal of its values led to some external explorations of the company's actual practices. Some of these suggested that the Body Shop was not living up to its own standards, leading to widely reported accusations and debate about the validity of the company's environmental and ethical credentials. The company undertook an ethical audit; the latter reported a number of inconsistencies between Body Shop's statements of its policies (Communicated Identity) vis-à-vis the underlying reality (Actual Identity). Media coverage of the inconsistencies further fueled the debate, leading to a growing skepticism on the part of the public and a change in perceptions of the company (Conceived Identity). In essence, the misalignments had their roots in the growing distance between the founder's vision (Desired Identity), supported by the company's communications (Communicated Identity) on the one hand, and on the other hand, eventual public perception (Conceived Identity) that the company's Actual Identity was not as distinctive as claimed. (This is an illustration of the classic "promise/performance gap" Greyser has identified as a major corporate communications problem.[4])

The Body Shop experience indicates the multiple interfaces among the five identity types, interfaces that can point to perils for company reputation. Note also that its Actual Identity seemed to migrate over time, further challenging efforts at identity alignment.

Identities misaligned: ideal and conceived

Cathay Pacific, Hong Kong's longtime international airline, confronted a significant strategic identity issue in preparation for the 1997 changeover from British to Chinese control of Hong Kong. The company was generally seen as a quality airline, but one strongly associated with Hong Kong's colonial past. A major challenge for the future was for Cathay Pacific to be perceived as more Asian (rather than British/Asian) in order to strengthen its market abilities in Asia (including attracting a wider Asian customer base), as well as to reflect the changed political realities in Hong Kong. In short, the company needed to align its Conceived Identity with its (new) Ideal Identity. Cathay Pacific chose to undertake this identity realignment through a massive coordinated set of initiatives intended to transform the reality of the company (Actual Identity) to achieve the new perceptions (Conceived Identity) that would reflect the new strategy (Ideal Identity) and permit communications (Communicated Identity) based on the substantive changes. Among the initiatives were: adding aircraft capable of operating in medium-sized airports in Asian markets previously underserved by Cathay Pacific, appointing an increased proportion of Asian nationals (including managers), and changing the on-board food and service to reflect more closely the wider Asian customer base. In addition, Cathay Pacific's visual identity was markedly changed to draw extensively from traditional Chinese imagery including calligraphy and symbolism.

Additional observations

From the above examples and many others we have studied, several additional observations should be noted:

- Multiple identities are pervasive – in public organizations as well as in the private sector, in product firms and service firms, and in global entities and more local ones.
- In merger and acquisition situations, senior managers need to be extra-sensitive to the even larger number of identities present, which in turn may call for harmonization. In our view, the Actual and Desired identities of each firm warrant special attention in terms of the culture and the leader-ship of the combined companies.
- Different identity types tend to inhabit different time frames. Most notice-ably, the Conceived Identity may lag behind the Actual Identity because it often takes time for stakeholder groups to recognize incremental changes in reality. A major task for identity consultants (and a company's com-munications partners) is to signal meaningful change via name changes, visual identification changes, and/or major corporate communications campaigns (usually explaining such things as a company's changed activities or direction).
- Multiple identities can co-exist comfortably within a company even if they are somewhat inconsistent. For example, a CEO may articulate an identity toward which the company is still reaching (Ideal Identity) through a strat-egy of broadening the company's product line portfolio, but the company's current identity (Actual Identity) is still clearly understood.

Conclusion

The AC^{2}ID Test can assist senior company management in researching, analyzing, and managing corporate identities. It can also help in navigating the company through the complexities of identity change and realignment. In-depth examin-ation of corporate identity occurs relatively infrequently, typically at a strategic "fork in the road" such as a major merger, acquisition, or divestment. However, because of changes in the business and competitive environment, regular identity reviews warrant a place on the senior management's agenda. The ultimate guardians and managers of corporate identity reside in the boardroom.

APPENDIX

Methodology of the research

The research reported here brings together several major strands of inquiry. The collaborative TransAtlantic Identity Study focused on the conceptions and analytic approaches on identity projects undertaken by leading industry consultants. Balmer's extensive literature surveys explored the nature of identity, how organizations manage their identities, and "disciplinary schools of thought" (multiple roots) in conceptualizing identity. Greyser drew from his continuing development of Harvard Business School case studies in Corporate Communications, especially on identity and image issues, and also from his field research on corporate reputation.

- *TransAtlantic Identity Study* – With the cooperation and support of a leading global identity and branding consulting firm, we interviewed senior consultants in London and New York regarding their past and current approaches to conducting identity projects. Some 34 interviews were completed, also encompassing previous project experiences with other firms. In addition, the firm's archival material on recent identity and branding projects was made available for study. Further, we examined published material from approximately twenty U.K. identity consultants regarding their principal methodologies.

- *Literature review* – The survey of the identity literature examined publications extending over a 50-year period, from both business and academic researchers in the U.S., U.K., and the Continent. Early examples include the seminal theoretical work of Kenneth Boulding and the pioneering applied studies of Pierre Martineau.[5] Three major comprehensive reviews provided a strong foundation for analysis – by Kennedy, by Abratt, and by Balmer.[6] Other relevant sources include: Barich and Kotler; Gray and Smeltzer; Schultz, Hatch, and Larsen; Van Riel; and Whetten and Godfrey.[7] Analysis of the literature led to: a taxonomy of various identity audit techniques advocated by academics, which in turn permitted a comparison with the techniques employed by consultants; an assessment of the articulated components of corporate identity by different authors, permitting a comparison of the scope of identity audits; and a review of emerging theory regarding corporate identity interface(s), thus illuminating issues of congruence (i.e., alignment) across different types of identity.

- *HBS case studies* – Over several decades, culminating in the development of his Harvard Business School MBA elective on Corporate Communications, Greyser wrote a series of case studies on identity and image issues confronted by corporations and other organizations (e.g., NASA). These clinical studies focused on how these entities were perceived by relevant publics and how they sought to change those perceptions through communications as well as policy initiatives. Additional field research addressed corporate reputation, derived principally from multi-attribute perceptions of companies in large-scale surveys.

A significant insight that emerged from analysis of all the strands was that corporate identity was in truth *multiple* identities. These identities were based on multiple disciplinary roots, via multiple routes, leading to the five types of identity incorporated in the AC²ID Test framework. Table 1 delineates a range of concepts that constitute building blocks of corporate identity, shows the management roots/disciplinary origins for each, provides a brief explanation of the concept, and indicates the links of each to one or more of the five identity types. For each of these concepts there is considerable literature. Representative references have been included in Table 1 for each of them. Of particular pertinence to interested readers is Schultz, Hatch, and Larsen.[8] Its contents reflect the multidisciplinary nature of the fields related to identity.

Notes

1   Trademarked by J. M. T. Balmer, 1999. The framework is also known as DR. BALMER'S AC²ID TEST™, 1999. An earlier version of the framework was reported in J. M. T. Balmer and G. B. Soenen, "The ACID Test of Corporate Identity Management™," *Journal of Marketing Management*, 15/1–3 (1999): 69–92.

2   W. Olins, *Corporate Identity* (Boston, MA: Harvard Business School Press, 1990).

3   CEO Lord Browne recently characterized the company as "global with British roots and headquarters," at the Eighth International Corporate Identity Symposium in London, November 2001.

4   S. A. Greyser and S. L. Diamond, "Business Is Adapting to Consumerism," *Harvard Business Review*, 52/5 (September/October 1974): 38–58; S. A. Greyser, "Advancing and Enhancing Corporate Reputation," *Corporate Communications: An International Journal*, 4/4 (1999): 177–181.

5   Kenneth Boulding, *The Image* (Ann Arbor, MI: University of Michigan Press, 1956). See, also, Pierre Martineau, "The Corporate Personality," in L. Bristol, *Business and Its Public* (Boston, MA: Harvard Business School Press, 1960), pp. 159–170.

6   S. H. Kennedy, "Nurturing Corporate Images: Total Communications or Ego Trip?," *European Journal of Marketing*, 11 (1977): 120–164; R. Abratt, "A New Approach to the Corporate Image Management Process," *Journal of Marketing Management*, 5/1 (1989): 63–76; J. M. T. Balmer, "Corporate Identity and the Advent of Corporate Marketing," *Journal of Marketing Management*, 14 (1998): 963–996.

7   H. Barich and P. Kotler, "A Framework for Marketing Image Management," *Sloan Management Review*, 32/2 (1991): 94–104; E. R. Gray and L. R. Smeltzer, "Corporate Image – An Integral Part of Strategy," *Sloan Management Review*, 26/4 (1985): 73–78; M. Schultz, M. J. Hatch, and M. H. Larsen, eds., *The Expressive Organization* (Oxford: Oxford University Press, 2000); C. B. M. Van Riel, *Principles of Corporate Communication* (London: Prentice Hall, 1995); D. A. Whetten and P. C. Godfrey, eds., *Identity in Organizations: Building Theory through Conversations* (Thousand Oaks, CA: Sage, 1998).

8   Schultz, Hatch, and Larsen, op. cit.

SECTION TWO

Identity: the quintessence of an organization

"... it should come as no surprise to find that the concept of identity, which is so germane to conceiving what it means to be human, also is central to the conceptualization of one of the most complex and fascinating of human creations, the work organization."
(Dennis A. Gioia, 1998)

EDITORS' INTRODUCTION

Untying the Gordian knot

THE IDENTITY CONCEPT IS powerful. Powerful because at its heart resides two profoundly important corporate-level concerns. These are: "*Who are we?*" (a particular concern of organizational behaviorists who focus on *organizational identification*) and "*What are we?*" (a particular concern of marketers and communicators who focus on *corporate identity*). From our perspective we regard the concepts of organizational and corporate identity as alter egos. With these two philosophical questions in mind, it may come as no surprise to the reader to discover that identity studies are characterized by profundity and complexity. Both scholars and practitioners have asserted the importance of identity. However, identity studies reflect different perspectives. The area is akin to the Gordian knot. Any attempt to unravel the various strands of thought can appear a challenging if not a futile task. However, the identity concept as applied to corporations, for all its complexity, is too important to ignore. It has the potential to be of considerable utility to academics and practitioners, albeit problematic in character.

A journey of discovery

For the novice in identity studies this section aims to equip the reader with some basic navigational tools – tools to guide readers along their path through the various perspectives. Hence readers will embark on a journey of discovery.

For some, the journey represents the quest to uncover an all-encompassing definition of identity. From our experience it is the journey itself and not the destination that we have found to be illuminating and rewarding. Once this journey is underway, it is likely to change irrevocably how entities are conceptualized. This helps to explain the allure of identity studies, and why managers and academics have been captivated by the quintessential identity issues of "Who are we?" and "What are we?"

Let us explain a little further why we believe the identity concept is profound and why it has wide utility.

We are of the firm view that the area provides a new way by which corporate and other organizational entities may be conceptualized, comprehended, and managed. As such the concept may have a utility for corporations, holding companies, subsidiaries, and business units, and also for entire industries or industry-wide alliances. Furthermore, many of the same principles may be applied to not-for-profit entities, to churches, and to cities, regions, and supranational bodies. One highly publicized report concluded that some of the methods used by global companies to manage their corporate identities might also be employed by a nation-state to ensure clarity and consistency.[1]

A rich tradition of scholarship

We now turn to the issue of complexity. The Byzantine nature of identity when considered as a whole is a consequence of the rich disciplinary and philosophical traditions that underpin scholarship and practice associated with the area. While some practitioners and scholars have attempted to draw on these multiple perspectives, the area has mainly developed along narrow disciplinary lines. The former approach is not uncommon in Europe and the Commonwealth but the latter is more typical.

We also think that others have avoided the multidimensional and contradictory aspects of identity by finding solace in one of the extant disciplinary perspectives, such as graphic design, corporate communications, or organizational behavior. However, we believe that corporate life *is* complicated and its management is fraught with difficulty. This does not negate the need to try to manage through the complexity; we think the same approach applies to identity studies.

Ignoring issues of identity is not a feasible option, particularly for managers. Indeed, it only tends to exacerbate a problem. Identity issues do not go away, and can surface with a vengeance. All too often managers are bereft of the capacity to address identity issues – a point well illustrated by Bernstein in Section Three.

What *is* clear to us is that seemingly imponderable questions relating to identity come to the fore *in extremis* – for example, when one identity epoch gives way to another, when entities contemplate a corporate fork in the road such as a merger, takeover, or divestiture. To us it becomes apparent that identity change underpins the different stages of the corporate life cycle. To us these represent rites of passage where identity studies can inform scholars and managers alike. To us it becomes clear that identity management should be seen not as a one-off exercise but as an integral part of corporate strategy.

Let us now explain something of the richness that characterizes identity studies and has affected our choice of papers for inclusion in this section.

Identity: an aperture of nine

From our analysis of the literature we have found that the identity concept has been examined in terms of its (a) disciplinary and national roots, (b) schools of thought, (c) philosophical underpinnings, (d) components, (e) characteristics, (f) management, (g) analysis, (h) structure and hierarchy, and (i) relationship with other corporate-level concepts.

These nine streams of inquiry can be briefly explained as follows.

(a) Disciplinary and national roots

In the main it has been marketing/corporate communications,[2] organizational behavior,[3] and graphic design studies[4] that form the three dominant disciplinary strands that underpin identity studies. For that reason, a good deal of the literature conceptualizes identity along one of these narrow disciplinary lines. For instance, the graphic design literature accords particular importance to the role of visual symbolism in identity formation, analysis, change, and management.

From our reading of the literature it also becomes apparent that there are some national differences in relation to the conceptualization of identity. For instance, a small group of marketing academics from the Commonwealth attempt to adopt a multidisciplinary approach. Typically, they emphasize the role of identity in creating favorable external perceptions and accord an important role to corporate communications.[5] Among North American scholars, however, particular importance is accorded to staff identification and to the conceptualization of identity grounded in theories associated with organizational behavior.[6] Also of note is the so-called "French" school of thought[7] with its distinctive methodological approach.

One study of note that specifically compares differences regarding the conceptualization of identity is a Pan-European study undertaken among 200 chairmen and chief executives. It revealed some wide national variations. Whereas in Germany many respondents viewed identity as comprising a multidisciplinary mix of elements including corporate culture, staff behavior, external projection, public image, and visual presentation, in the U.K. and in Scandinavia visual presentation was accorded particular importance. Of note is that the single most important aspect of identity was considered to be corporate culture in every country apart from Belgium, where corporate communication was singled out. There was wide consensus too in identifying the main audience to which an identity is targeted, with existing customers being identified in all countries apart from the U.K., where financial institutions and shareholders were seen as the main target group.[8]

(b) Schools of thought

An early review of the literature by Balmer identified no fewer than seven schools of thought relating to identity.[9] This typified the ways in which scholars and practitioners approached identity studies. They include the strategic, behavioral, communications, and four design schools of thought: design-as-strategy, design-as-behavior, design-as-communication, and design-as-fashion. These are shown in diagrammatic form in Exhibit 1.

That literature review led to the conclusion that the different emphases mirrored not only the different roots of the area, but also the different identity issues that confront organizations at different times, which vary in magnitude. Thus, one identity problem might well be strategic and encapsulate the questions "Who are we?" and "What are we?" Alternatively, the problem might be of a different order altogether and focus simply on updating the logo so that it appears contemporary; this would reflect the design-as-fashion school. Another school of thought discernible in this early review is one that views the various schools of thought as an integral whole, and considers identity studies to be multidisciplinary. In this context, one would draw from different schools of thought to address different organizational concerns. This multidisciplinary approach characterizes the International Corporate Identity

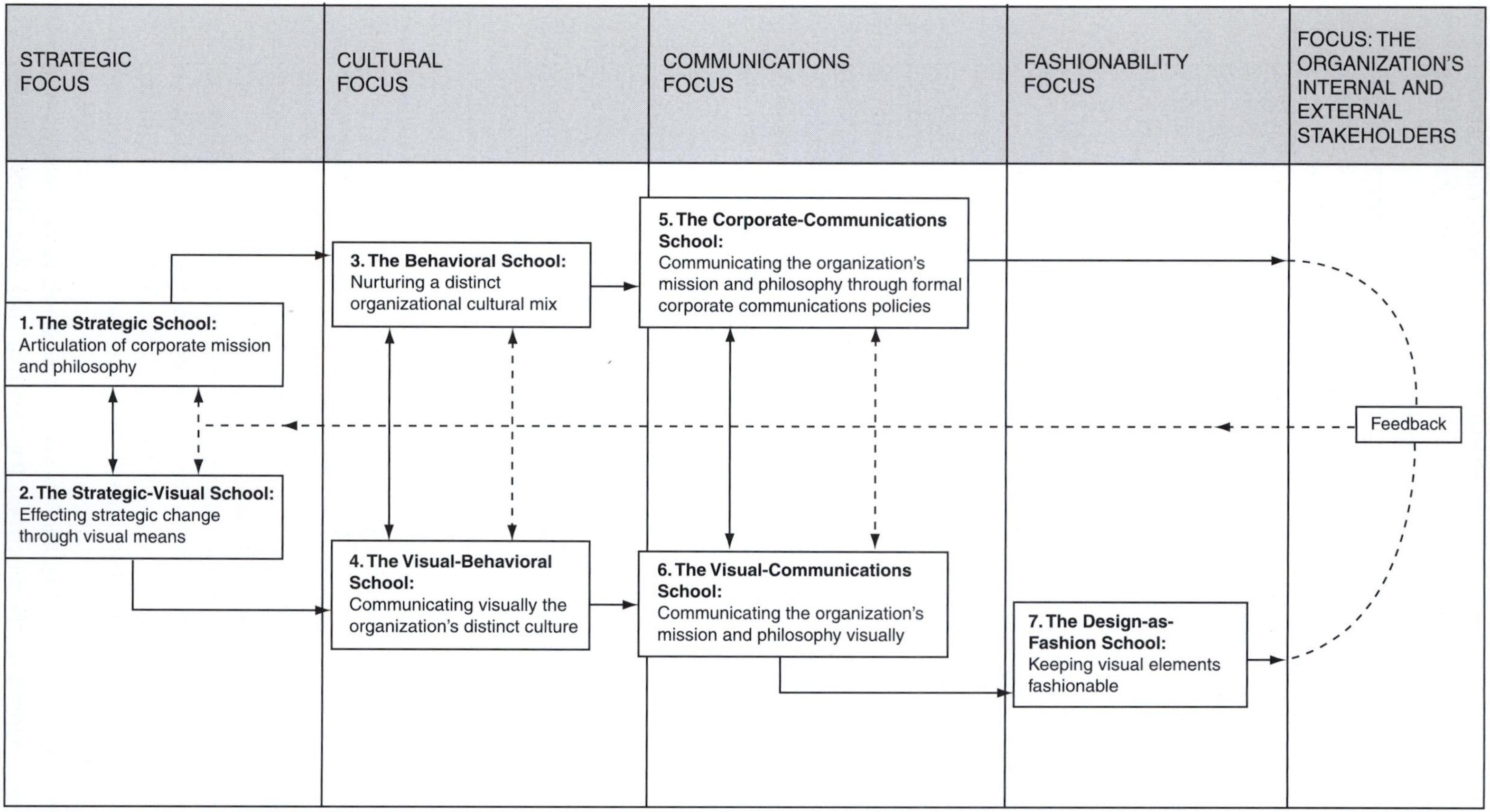
STRATEGIC FOCUS
CULTURAL FOCUS
COMMUNICATIONS FOCUS
FASHIONABILITY FOCUS
FOCUS: THE ORGANIZATION'S INTERNAL AND EXTERNAL STAKEHOLDERS
1. The Strategic School: Articulation of corporate mission and philosophy
2. The Strategic-Visual School: Effecting strategic change through visual means
3. The Behavioral School: Nurturing a distinct organizational cultural mix
4. The Visual-Behavioral School: Communicating visually the organization's distinct culture
5. The Corporate-Communications School: Communicating the organization's mission and philosophy through formal corporate communications policies
6. The Visual-Communications School: Communicating the organization's mission and philosophy visually
7. The Design-as-Fashion School: Keeping visual elements fashionable
Feedback

Exhibit 1 Integrative diagram of the hierachy of schools of thought in strategic corporate identity management

Source: Adapted from J. M. T. Balmer, "Corporate Branding and Connoisseurship," *Journal of General Management* 1995, 21 (1): 22–46. (Based on an analysis of the literature)

Group's initial statement on identity, commonly known as "The Strathclyde State-ment." Shown here is the less frequently referred to *first* version of the statement. For the revised version, see p. 134.

The Strathclyde Statement

Corporate identity management is concerned with the conception, development, and communication of an organization's mission, philosophy, and ethos.
Its orientation is strategic and is based on a company's
values, cultures, and behaviors.

The management of corporate identity draws on many disciplines, including strategic management, marketing, corporate communications,
organizational behavior, public relations, and design.

It is different from traditional brand marketing directed towards household or business-to-business product/service purchases since it is concerned with
all of an organization's stakeholders and
the multifaceted way in which an organization communicates.

It is dynamic, not static, and is greatly affected by
changes in the external environment.

When well managed, an organization's identity results in loyalty from
its diverse stakeholders.

As such it can positively affect organizational performance,
e.g. its ability to attract and retain customers,
achieve strategic alliances, recruit executives and employees,
be well positioned in financial markets, and strengthen
internal staff identification
with the firm.

(John M. T. Balmer and Stephen A. Greyser, 1995)

(c) Philosophical underpinnings

As his exegesis of the identity concept, Gioia[10] explains that there are three para-digmatic perspectives that underpin the study of identity by scholars. The three perspectives are functionalist, interpretative, and postmodern.

The *functionalist* lens regards identity as a social fact. It is thus in sharp con-trast with the other perspectives, which may be viewed as forms of solipsism grounded in the premise that the self is all that can be known to exist. The functional-ist perspective is characterized by the view that identity can be observed, molded, and managed. For the identity scholar the primary foci here are on uncovering, describ-ing, and measuring business identities, with psychometric instruments being one of the principal research tools.

The second paradigm, the *interpretative* perspective, has as its primary focus the understanding of how employees construct meaning of who they are within the work environment. Here identity is seen to be a socially constructed phenomenon; the primary research activity focuses on uncovering the meaning employees attach to their work organization. Much of the research activity is concerned with the study of organizational symbolism.

The third paradigm, the *postmodern* perspective, seeks to disclose power relationships within an organizational context. This perspective views identity as an amalgam of transcendatory perspectives about how employees see themselves. The favored research tools are language and discourse analysis. Typically, scholars adhering to this perspective celebrate the complexity and richness of a given organizational situation.

Gioia gives a ready riposte to those who consider the three paradigms to be incompatible. Any apparent incompatibility, he says, comes about because the existence of these perspectives is indicative of the richness, complexity, and exuberance – and thus importance – of identity studies.

(d) Components

An abiding concern of marketing/communication practitioners and scholars has been to identify the components that fuse together to constitute an entity's identity. In our view this interest probably stems from the field of marketing, where the use of the "mix" metaphor has been so important (the marketing mix, the services marketing mix, and the promotional mix). The existence of various identity mixes illustrates the degree to which marketing and communication scholars have, for some time, embraced the multidisciplinary nature of the field.

The most widely referenced identity mix is that by the German authors Birkigt and Stadler,[11] whose identity mix consists of culture, behavior, and symbolism. Somewhat wider in scope is the mix developed by the Anglo-German consultancy Henrion, Ludlow, and Schmidt,[12] which comprises corporate culture, corporate behavior, market conditions and strategies, products and services, and communication and design. However, a degree of confusion has entered the debate regarding the identity mix. Balmer[13] concluded that many authors failed to make a distinction between the mix of elements that constitute an identity and the mosaic of elements that require orchestration when managing an identity. Accordingly, he advocated that there should be two mixes: the identity mix, which he argues should consist of strategy, structure, communication, and culture; and the identity management mix, which includes the aforementioned but also includes reputations, stakeholders, and the environment. An important caveat here is that identities can never be entirely managed owing to the inseparable link between some subcultural groups in organizations and their affinities to their own multiple identities (e.g., a BBC reporter identifies with both organization and occupation).

(e) Characteristics

A related issue of inquiry to components is the articulation of the characteristics of identity. In this regard the work of Albert and Whetten[14] has, without doubt, been the most influential. Writing from an organizational behavior viewpoint, they said that identity is conceptualized from an employee perspective. The primary focus is on issues relating to employee identification with the organization. They argue that identity comes into being when it is *central* (permeates the entire organization), *distinctive* (is unique to the organization), and *enduring* (has existed for some time.)

Recently there has been considerable academic debate as to whether identities are enduring. The work of the French school of thought on identity also warrants note in this regard,[15] especially the work by Larcon and Reitter.[16] These authors argued that identity occurs when it imbues an organization with *specificity, stability*, and *coherence.*

More recently, Balmer,[17] taking a "big picture" perspective, has argued that identity is characterized by the following three dimensions: its *complexity* (accommodating the multifaceted and multidimensional aspects of the domain, with staff having an affinity to multiple identities and the existence of various identity types as per the AC²ID™ constraints); its *variability* (identities are not sclerotic, they evolve); and, finally, its *heterogeneity* (the need for sensitivity to, and recognition of, the various disciplinary strands that inform our understanding of an organization's identity).

(f) Management

Identity management has been another issue of concern. It has been argued that the management of corporate image,[18] corporate reputation,[19] and corporate communications[20] and corporate brand management[21] needs to take account of and is inextricably linked to the management of identity. Hence there is a concern not only with what should be managed (see components above) but also with who should manage identity. With regard to the latter, many argue that it should be a board-level concern or even that of the Chief Executive Officer (CEO), who (to us) is "the ultimate guardian" of corporate reputation and identity.

(g) Analysis

Among European identity scholars there has been considerable interest in developing techniques and models that seek to analyze and/or measure identity. These include Bernstein's[22] cobweb method. With this approach the researcher solicits the views of senior staff in revealing the key attributes of the organization's identity. Another approach has been used by the French scholar Ramanantsoa.[23] This approach analyzes the organization's history from which the quintessential elements of the organization's identity are manifest. The Dutch scholar Van Rekom[24] focuses on the behavior of employees to reveal the organization's identity using a laddering technique which he has developed.

In the UK, Balmer[25] drew largely on the principles of cultural anthropology to develop a framework for revealing an identity. He went on to argue that an identity can only be adequately understood when the researcher has intimate knowledge of the organization and enjoys wide access. Also of note is the ACID Test of Corporate Identity Management™ developed at Strathclyde Business School by Balmer and Soenen[26] as part of the Transatlantic Identity Study (funded in its initial stages by Enterprise IG). This provides a technique that assesses the degree of misalignment between various identity types. A refined and rearticulated version of the model is discussed in the article "Managing the Multiple Identities of the Corporation," which forms Chapter 1 in Section One of this anthology.

(h) Structure and hierarchy

The relationship between identity and organizational structure and hierarchy has been a line of inquiry for some time. Olins,[27] describing the visual architecture used by organizations, identified three basic types: the *monolithic* (where one visual identity/name is used throughout the organization), the *endorsed* (where a subsidiary or business unit has its own visual identity but where visual reference is also made to the holding company); and the *branded* (where a subsidiary or business unit has its own visual identity but makes no visual reference to the holding company). This approach, grounded primarily on visual identification, offers a useful analysis of the complicated arrangements that increasingly characterize corporate life.

Ind[28] may be seen to have taken the debate further by articulating the strengths and weaknesses of the Olins tripartite characterization. Of particular note is the work of Kammerer,[29] which articulated the various identity structures in terms of the goals of the parent company. The most authoritative work to date is by the Australian scholar Stuart;[30] she provides a thorough examination of the link between structure and identity and concludes that a corporation's structural architecture will be a key determinant of the organization's identity and should determine the system of visual identification used.

(i) Relationship with other corporate-level concepts

Hatch and Schultz,[31] drawing on Saussurian logic, have attempted to clarify the concept of identity by articulating its relationship with the concept of image and culture. This is based on Saussure's view that words are most appropriately defined in terms of how they affect other words. Thus identity, when contemplated through the image lens, may appear to be similar to the concept of culture. Both are tacit and internally focused. When contemplated through the culture lens, identity and image also are difficult to distinguish. Both appear to be superficial and appear to be more concerned with appearances. However, when image and culture are viewed through the identity lens it becomes manifestly clear that identity is distinguishable from both image and culture.

In summary, their approach affords a degree of translucence to an area of scholarship that sometimes may appear to be opaque.

Corporate identity: beyond the visual overstatements?

"Among the heroic types of the latter half of the last century – the corporate whiz kid, the stock trader, the media mogul – should also be counted the corporate identity consultant." This assertion was made in a highly controversial opening article of the *RSA Journal* by Aldersey-Williams.[32] He articulated in a manner that is pithy, if not enlightening, why traditional corporate identity consultancy and the conceptualization of corporate identity simply in terms of *graphic design* has become discredited. (This is not to be confused with the multidisciplinary approaches to corporate identity/identity studies that we have examined in Section One.) He argues that although identity consultants wear the mantle and use the rhetoric of strategy, their focus and work are driven by graphic design considerations. Their overriding concern, he says, is to distill the essence of the corporation in the form of a single logotype.

Aldersey-Williams is by no means the only detractor of the narrow, graphic design perspective accorded to identity. An article by Topalian[33] provides an early critique of the work of graphic designers. Empirical research has also identified shortfalls in the activities of some identity consultancies.[34]

We are of the view that design can play a role in communicating and creating awareness of a corporation's identity. Its contribution has been significant – even at certain times and places, powerful. In many instances its legacy has been enduring. Consider nineteenth-century British railroad companies, which exploited the design functions to considerable effect. Not only was there widespread use of corporate coats of arms, but considerable attention to detail was accorded to architecture, interior design of railroad cars, and uniforms. The recent privatization of the U.K.'s railroad network has resulted in similar types of activities.

In the early twentieth century we acknowledge the pioneering work of Peter Bahrens at AEG, Adriano Olivetti at Olivetti, and Alan Parkin and Edward Johnston at London Underground. These German, Italian, and British organizations achieved a consistency in design that is perhaps without parallel, and that laid the foundations for the field of corporate communications: the notion that corporate communications should be consistent and should be managed.

In the 1950s the work of the British graphic designer F. H. K. Henrion received wide acclaim. His most lasting legacy was his design work for KLM Royal Dutch Airways: key features of his design work have endured. In the 1950s this design activity was called *house style* – a phrase popularized by Henrion (the corporate identity concept was as yet unknown). 'House style' was a concept that was widely understood in the U.K. and the Continent. It was a more accurate appropriate descriptor for the work undertaken by graphic designers than the corporate identity label that came in vogue in the late 1960s. We think the label still has considerable utility.

The narrow sense of the graphic design perspective is not what informs *our* understanding of corporate identity. Many assume that the graphic design lens reflects the dominant viewpoint within marketing. However, an examination of the literature gives the lie to this notion. Indeed, the marketing literature on identity has for some time assumed a multidisciplinary perspective.[35] Such an approach has informed our own understanding of the area and has been a key theme in our individual and collaborative writing and teaching.

However, we *do* recognize the considerable merits of graphic design. It is one of the most powerful and noticeable forms of communication; moreover, it is probably the only aspect of corporate life where management has total control and where change can be effected speedily.

A consideration of an organization's house style/system of visual identification invariably involves designers quizzing senior executives whether they have answers to two key corporate-level questions: "What are we?" and "Who are we?" As such, graphic designers (and their discipline) become the vehicle but not the *only* means by which these deeper issues of the corporation begin to be examined, explored, understood, and revealed. This is not always understood, communicated, or practiced.

The role of graphic design as a vehicle by which deeper issues of the corporation and of corporate life generally are considered can be seen in the establishment of the *Movimento Comunità* by Bahrens and Olivetti. Bahrens and Olivetti's interests metamorphosed from design coordination to the role of corporations in contemporary society. A fundamental tenet of the *Movimento Comunità* was that manufacturers and industrialists should not focus only on maximizing profit and turnover but need to be conscious of their wider corporate responsibility to internal interest groups and to societal concerns as well as to stockholders and end-users. This important facet of their work has been eclipsed by their contributions to the management of design.

Triquadri orbis: corporate, organizational, and visual identities

For the novice of identity studies it may be helpful to regard identity as inhabiting a tripartite world: a *triquadri orbis*.

(i) The first sphere relates to conceptualization of identity along narrow, graphic design terms, detailed above. We call this *visual identification*; an earlier label is *house style*. (In general parlance it is called corporate identity, but some academics and practitioners assign a broader definition to that term: see the third perspective below.)

The principal focus here is to bring communication and reality into alignment via visual means.

(ii) The second landscape focuses on staff identification with the corporation. This has given rise to the *organizational identification* construct. It seeks to address the question "*Who are we?*"

(iii) The third territory adopts a multidisciplinary perspective and relates to the distinct attributes of the organization. This approach is to be found in the marketing literature on the area but can also be found elsewhere. We call this *corporate identity*. (Others call it "identity studies/business identity.") It seeks to address the question "*What are we?*" as well as "*Who are we?*"

Identity: not contingent but necessary

In bringing this short discussion of the identity concept to a close we would like to emphasize two aspects relating to the examination of this concept.

The first is that concepts are either contingent or necessary. Our exploration of the literature shows that the identity concept belongs firmly in the latter category. At the corporate level the discussion of strategy, reputation, image, and communication become difficult, if not futile, unless identity is brought into the equation. As Gioia[36] mused, the concept is fundamental to the conceptualization of the corporation.

The second point is that for us, identities may be compared to organisms. They are constantly shifting and are embryonic. As a result, their comprehension is rarely easy or straightforward.

The following quote relates to both premises voiced above:

> Identity is not something genetic, safe, and secure. It is shaped by history and culture: it is about group feeling; allegiance to the state: it is, too, a common sense of culture, custom and language, to be sure, but in an open society that can be wide and inclusive. It is always in the making and never made.
>
> Michael Wood[37]

Wood's articulation of national identity could easily have been written about a corporation. The wide utility of the identity concept is testimony of its significance.

The articles

We have selected five articles for inclusion in this section. The first two are written by two leading identity consultants of the first generation. The first is an article based on a keynote lecture delivered by the doyen of the identity industry in Europe, Wally Olins. The lecture was delivered to London's Royal Society for the Encouragement of Arts, Manufactures and Commerce. The second article appeared in the *Harvard Business Review* by the celebrated U.S. identity consultant Walter Margulies. He is credited with coining the label "corporate identity."

The first of three academic chapters in this section is the cornerstone paper by Stuart Albert and David Whetten. They may be seen to be the fathers of the distinct organizational behavior school of scholarship, a school that enjoys considerable hegemony in scholarly circles. The fourth chapter is by Helen Stuart, one of the first wave of academics who have acquired doctorates in identity studies and who are happy to take on the mantle and title of identity scholar. The final chapter, by John Balmer and Edmund Gray, is illustrative of the collaboration that is now taking place across management disciplines – in this case between marketing and strategy.

The chapters are international in scope, drawn as they are from the U.S.A., the U.K., and Australia. They cover the last quarter of the twentieth century and represent some of the distinct traditions that we have described: graphic design, marketing, communication, and organizational behavior, as well as the multidiscipli-nary perspective. They range in style from Olins's grandiloquent, irascible, and at times irreverent retrospective to the cerebral and magisterial examination provided by Albert and Whetten.

We believe that all five chapters provide an illuminating introduction to the iden-tity concept. We hope that the reader will concur with us that in their totality these articles demonstrate why identity is one of the most fascinating and important corporate-level concepts of recent times and why it deserves significant attention from scholars and managers alike.

TOPICS FOR DISCUSSION AND REFLECTION

1   Explain why identity issues come to the fore in periods of adversity *or* when an organization is undergoing change.
2   Consider the Strathclyde Statement on corporate identity (the first version, as reproduced on p. 37) in the context of an organization with which you are familiar. What does the statement reveal about (a) corporate identity? (b) the organization?
3   Why and when might corporate identity be seen to be 'strategic'?
4   What are the strengths and weaknesses in viewing identity through the three lenses identified by Gioia (*functionalist, interpretative*, and *postmodern*)?
5   What are the pros and cons in approaching corporate identity from a graphic design perspective? Take the perspective of a graphic design consultant, a corporate strategy manager, and a student of business administration.
6   What role, *if any*, do systems of visual identification have for blind people or those with a severe visual impediment?
7   Consider the degree to which each of the five senses has a utility in articulating the identity of the following:
    (a)   the Catholic Church;
    (b)   universities;
    (c)   the judiciary;
    (d)   radio stations;
    (e)   Singapore Airways;
    (f)   McDonald's;
    (g)   Canada.
8   What entities (countries, regions, towns, religions, clubs, companies, etc.) do you have an affinity with?
    (a)   Is the relationship the same in every instance? Why? Why not?
    (b)   What benefits do you receive from such entities?
    (c)   What benefits does the entity receive from you?
    (d)   How do you/Why do you not demonstrate your membership of the above?
    (e)   Which relationships have been enduring/transitory and why?

9 Referring to organizations of your choice, explain why identity is not contingent but strategic (or vice versa).

10 Explain the nature of identity in an organizational context in no more than one minute *or* in no more than forty words.

NOTES

1 Leonard, M., *Britain™: Renewing our Identity*, London: Demos, 1997.

2 Abratt, R., "A New Approach to the Corporate Image Management Process," *Journal of Marketing Management* 1989, 5 (1): 63–76; Van Riel, C. B. M. and Balmer, J. M. T., "Corporate Identity: The Concept, Its Management and Measurement," Special Edition on Corporate Identity: *European Journal of Marketing* 1997, 31 (5/6): 340–355; Balmer, J. M. T., "Corporate Identity and the Advent of Corporate Marketing," *Journal of Marketing Management* 1998, 14 (8): 963–996.

3 Albert, S. and Whetten, D., "Organizational Identity," in L. L. Cummings and B. M. Staw (eds) *Research in Organizational Behavior* 7: 263–295, Greenwich, CT: JAI Press, 1985 (also this volume, Chapter 4); Ashforth, B. E. and Mael, F., "Organizational Identity and Strategy as a Context for the Individual," in J. A. C. Baur and J. E. Dutton (eds) *Advances in Strategic Management* 13: pp. 19–64; Greenwich, CT: JAI Press, 1996; Hatch, M. J. and Shultz, M., "Relations between Organizational Culture, Identity and Image," Special Edition on Corporate Identity: *European Journal of Marketing* 1997, 31 (5/6): 356–365.

4 Pilditch, J., *Communication by Design: A Study in Corporate Identity*, London: McGraw-Hill, 1970; Topalian, A., "Corporate Identity: Beyond the Visual Overstatements," *International Journal of Advertising* 1984, 3: 55–62; Napoles, V., *Corporate Identity Design*, New York: Van Nostrand Reinhold, 1988.

5 Balmer, J. M. T., "Corporate Identity, Corporate Branding and Corporate Marketing: Seeing through the Fog," Special Edition on Corporate Identity and Corporate Marketing: *European Journal of Marketing* 2001, 35 (314): 248–291; Marwlck, N. and Fill, C., "Towards a Framework for Managing Corporate Identity," Special Edition on Corporate Identity: *European Journal of Marketing* 1977, 31 (5/6): 396–409; Stuart, H., "Exploring the Corporate Identity/Corporate Image Interface: An Empirical Study of Accounting Firms," *Journal of Communication Management* 1998, 2 (4): 357–371.

6 Albert and Whetten, *op. cit.*; Dutton, J. E., Dukerich, J. M., and Harquail, C. V., "Organizational Images and Member Identification," *Administrative Science Quarterly* 1994, 39: 239–263; Whetten, D. A. and Godfrey, P. C. (eds), *Identity in Organizations: Building Theory through Conversations*, Thousand Oaks, CA: Sage, 1998.

7 Larcon, J. P. and Reitter, R., "Corporate Imagery and Corporate Identity," in M. Kets de Vries (ed.) *The Irrational Executive: Psychoanalytic Explorations of Management*, New York: International University Press, 1984, pp. 344–355; Moingeon, B. and Ramanantsoa, B., "Understanding Corporate Identity: The French School of Thought," Special Edition on Corporate Identity: *European Journal of Marketing* 1997, 31 (5/6): 683–395.

8   Henrion, Ludlow, and Schmidt, *Corporate Identity in a Multicultural Marketplace*, Summary of the Third Pan-European Study on Corporate Identity, Henrion, Ludlow, and Schmidt: Consultants in Corporate Identity, London, 1993.

9   Balmer, J. M. T., "Corporate Branding and Connoisseurship," *Journal of General Management* 1995, 21 (1): 22–46.

10   Gioia, D. A., "From Individual to Organizational Identity," in Whetten and Godfrey (eds) *op. cit.*

11   Birkigt, K. and Stadler, M. M., *Corporate Identity: Grundlagen, Funktionen, Fallspielen*, Landsberg am Lech, Germany: Verlage Moderne Industrie, 1986.

12   Schmidt, C., *The Quest for Identity*, London: Cassell, 1995.

13   Balmer, "Corporate Identity, Corporate Branding and Corporate Marketing," pp. 259–263.

14   Albert and Whetten, *op. cit.*

15   Ramanantsoa, B. ("Strategor",) *Stratégie, structure, décision, identité: politique générale d'entreprise*, Paris: InterEditions, 1989.

16   Larcon, J. P. and Reitter, R., *Structures de pouvoir et identité de l'entreprise*, Paris: Nathan, 1979.

17   Balmer, J. M. T., "From the Pentagon: A New Identity Framework," *Corporate Reputation Review* 2001, 4 (1): 11–22.

18   Abratt, *op. cit.*

19   Fombrun, C. J., *Reputation: Realizing Value from the Corporate Image*, Cambridge, MA: Harvard Business School Press, 1996.

20   Van Riel, C. B. M., *Principles of Corporate Communication*, London: Prentice Hall, 1995.

21   Balmer, J. M. T., "The Three Virtues and Seven Deadly Sins of Corporate Brand Management," *Journal of General Management* 2001, 27 (1): 1–17 (also this volume, Chapter 15).

22   Bernstein, D., *Company Image and Reality: A Critique of Corporate Communications*, Eastbourne, U.K.: Holt, Rinehart and Winston, 1984.

23   Ramanantosoa, *op. cit.*

24   Van Rekom, J., "Deriving an Operational Measure of Corporate Identity," Special Edition on Corporate Identity: *European Journal of Marketing* 1997, 31 (5/6): 410–422.

25   Van Riel and Balmer, *op. cit.*

26   Balmer, J. M. T. and Soenen, G. B., "The ACID Test of Corporate Identity Management™," *Journal of Marketing Management* 1999, 15 (1–3): 69–92; Balmer, "From the Pentagon."

27   Olins, W., *The Corporate Personality: An Inquiry into the Nature of Corporate Identity*, London: Design Council, 1978.

28   Ind, N., *The Corporate Image*, London: Kogan Page, 1992.

29   Kammerer, J., *Beitrag der Produktpolitik zur Corporate Identity*, Munich: GBI-Verlag, 1989.

30   Stuart, H., "The Effect of Organizational Structure on Corporate Identity Management," *Corporate Reputation Review* 1999, 151–164 (also appears below as Chapter 5).

31   Hatch, M. J. and Schultz, M., "Scaling the Tower of Babel: Relational Differences between Identity, Image and Culture," in M. Schultz, M. J. Hatch, and M. Larsen (eds) *The Expressive Organization*, Oxford: Oxford University Press, 2000.

32   Aldersey-Williams, H., "Ten Reasons Why Corporate Identity Is Irrelevant," *RSA Journal* 2000, 148 (5495, 4/4): 4–5.

33   Topalian, A., "Corporate Identity: Beyond the Visual Overstatements," *International Journal of Advertising* 1984, 3: 55–62.

34   Balmer and Soenen, *op. cit.*

35   Abratt, *op. cit.*; Van Riel and Balmer, *op. cit.*; Marwick and Fill, *op. cit.*; Henrion, Ludlow, and Schmidt, *op. cit.*; Schmidt, C., *The Quest for Identity*, London: Cassell, 1995.

36   Gioia, *op. cit.*, p. 17.

37   Wood, M., *In Search of England: Journeys into the English Past*, London: Penguin, 2000, p. 305.

FURTHER READING

Corporate identity: articles

Abratt, R. (1989) "A New Approach to the Corporate Image Management Process," *Journal of Marketing Management* 5 (1): 63–76.

Abratt, R. and Mofokeng, T. N. (2001) "Development and Management of Corporate Image in South Africa," Special Edition on Corporate Identity: *European Journal of Marketing* 35 (3/4): 368–386.

Balmer, J. M. T. (1995) "Corporate Branding and Connoisseurship," *Journal of General Management* 21 (1): 24–46.

Balmer, J. M. T. (1998) "Corporate Identity and the Advent of Corporate Marketing," *Journal of Marketing Management* 14 (8): 963–996.

Balmer, J. M. T. (2001) "Corporate Identity, Corporate Branding and Corporate Marketing: Seeing through the Fog", Special Edition on Corporate Identity: *European Journal of Marketing* 35 (3/4): 248–291.

Balmer, J. M. T. and Dinnie, K. (1999) "Merger Madness: the Final Coup de Grace," *Journal of General Management* 24 (4): 53–68.

Balmer, J. M. T. and Dinnie, K. (1999) "Corporate Identity and Corporate Communications: the Antidote to Merger Madness," Special Edition on Corporate Identity: *Corporate Communications: An International Journal* 4 (4): 182–192.

Balmer, J. M. T. and Wilson, A. (1998) "Corporate Identity: There is More to It Than Meets the Eye," *International Studies of Management and Organization* 28 (3): 12–31.

Christensen, L. T. and Askegaard, S. (2001) "Corporate Identity and Corporate Identity Revisited", Special Edition on Corporate Identity and Corporate Marketing, *European Journal of Marketing* 35 (2): 292–315.

Cornelissen, J. and Harris, P. (2001) "The Corporate Identity Metaphor: Perspectives, Problems and Prospects," *Journal of Marketing Management* 17 (1/2): 49–71.

Downey, S. M. (1986/1987) "The Relationship between Corporate Culture and Corporate Identity," *Public Relations Quarterly* 31 (4): 7–12.

Gray, E. R. and Balmer, J. M. T. (1998) "Managing Corporate Image and Corporate Reputation," *Long Range Planning* 31 (5): 695–702.

Harrison, R. (1972) "Understanding Your Organization's Character," *Harvard Business Review* (May–June): 119–128.

Larcon, J. P. and Reitter, R. (1984) "Corporate Imagery and Corporate Identity", in M. Kets de Vries (ed.) *The Irrational Executive: Psychoanalytic Explorations of Management*, New York: International University Press.

Leitch, S. (1999) "From Logo-centrism to Corporate Branding?," *Australian Journal of Communication* 26 (3): 1–8.

Leitch, S. and Motion. J. (1999) "Multiplicity in Corporate Identity Strategy," Special Edition on Corporate Identity: *Corporate Communications: An International Journal* 4 (4): 193–199.

Leuthesser, L. and Kohli, C. (1997) "Corporate Identity: The Role of Mission Statements," *Business Horizons* 40 (3): 59–66.

Levinson, H. (1966) "How to Undermine an Organization," *Public Relations Journal* (October): 82–84.

Ludlow, C. (1997) "The Global Identity Crisis in the Airline Industry," *Journal of Brand Management* 5 (2): 85–91.

Marwick, N. and Fill, C. (1997) "Towards a Framework for Managing Corporate Identity," Special Edition on Corporate Identity: *European Journal of Marketing* 31 (5/6): 396–409.

Marziliano, N. (1998) "Managing the Corporate Image and Identity: A Borderline between Fiction and Reality," *International Studies of Management and Organization* 28 (3): 3–11.

Meijs, M. M. (2002) "The Myth of the Manageability of Corporate Identity," *Corporate Reputation Review* 5 (1): 20–34.

Melewar, T. C. and Harold, J. (1999) "The Role of Corporate Identity in Merger and Acquisitions Activity," *Journal of General Management* 26 (2): 17–31.

Melewar, T. C. and Jenkins, E. (2002) "Defining the Corporate Identity Construct," *Corporate Reputation Review* 5 (1): 76–91.

Moingeon, B. and Ramanantsoa, D. (1995) "An Identity Study of Firm Mergers: The Case of a French Savings Bank,". in H. E. Klein (ed.) *Case Study Method and Application 7*, Needham, MA: WACRA, pp. 253–260.

Moingeon, B. and Ramanantsoa, D. (1997) "Corporate Identity: Understanding the French School of Thought," Special Edition on Corporate Identity: *European Journal of Marketing* 31 (5/6): 383–395.

Morison, I. (1997) "Breaking the Monolithic Mould," Special Edition on Corporate Identity in Financial Services: *International Journal of Bank Marketing* 15 (5): 153–162.

Olins, W. (1991) "Corporate Identity and the Behavioral Dimension," *Design Management Journal* (Winter): 42–45.

Schultz, M. and Hatch, M. J. (1997) "A European View on Corporate Identity: An Interview with Wally Olins," *Journal of Management Inquiry* 6 (4): 330–339.

Siegel, A. (1988) "Common Sense on Corporate Identity," *Across the Board* 25 (6): 27–32.

Spaeth, T. (1991) "Diagnosing Corporate Identities," *Design Management Journal* (Winter): 46–51.

Stuart, H. (1998) "Exploring the Corporate Identity/Corporate Image Interface: An Empirical Study of Accountancy Firms," *Journal of Communication Management* 2 (4): 357–371.

Stuart, H. (1999) "Towards a Definitive Model of the Corporate Identity Management Process," Special Edition on Corporate Identity: *Corporate Communications: An International Journal* 4 (4): 200–207.

Tyrrell, T. (1995) "Managing Corporate Identity," in J. Crainer (ed.) *The Financial Times Handbook of Management*, London: Financial Times/Pitman Publishing, pp. 442–445

Van Rekom, J. (1997) "Deriving an Operational Measure of Corporate Identity," Special Edition on Corporate Identity: *European Journal of Marketing* 31 (5/6): 340–355.

Van Riel, C. B. M. and Balmer, J. M. T. (1997) "Corporate Identity: The Concept, Its Measurement and Management," Special Edition on Corporate Identity: *European Journal of Marketing* 31 (5/6): 340–355.

Westcott Alessandri, S. (2001) "Modeling Corporate Identity: A Concept Explication and Theoretical Explanation," *Corporate Communications: An International Journal* 6 (4): 173–182.

Wilkinson, A. and Balmer, J. M. T. (1996) "Corporate and Generic Identities: Lessons from the Co-operative Bank," *International Journal of Bank Marketing* 14 (4): pp. 22–35.

Organizational identification: articles

Ackerman, L. D. (1988) "Identity Strategies That Make a Difference," *Journal of Business Strategy* 9 (3): 28–32.

Albert, S., Ashforth, B. E., and Dutton, J. E. (2000) "Organizational Identity and Identification: Charting New Waters and Building New Bridges," *Academy of Management Review* 25 (1): 13–17.

Ashforth, B. E. and Mael, F. A. (1989) "Social Identity Theory and the Organization," *Academy of Management Review* 14: 20–39.

Ashforth, B. E. and Mael, F. A. (1996) "Organizational Identity and Strategy as a Context for the Individual," *Advances in Strategic Management* 13: 19–64.

Brickson, S. (2000) "The Impact of Identity Orientation on Individual and Organizational Outcomes in Demographically Diverse Settings," *Academy of Management Review* 25 (1): 82–101.

Brown, A. D. and Starkey, K. (2000) "Organizational Identity and Learning: A Psychodynamic Approach," *Academy of Management Review* 25 (1): 102–120.

Cheney, G. and Christensen, L. T. (1999) "Identity at Issue: Linkages between 'Internal' and 'External' organisational communications," in F. M. Jablin and L. L. Putnam (eds) *New Handbook of Organisational Communication*, Newbury Park, CA: Sage.

Cheney, G. and Tompkins, P. K. (1987) "Coming to Terms with Organisational Identifica-
    tion and Commitment," *Central States Speech Journal* 38: 1–15.
Christensen, L. T. and Cheney, G. (1994) "Articulating Identity in an Organisational
    Age," in S. A. Deetz (ed.) *Communication Yearbook 17*, Thousand Oaks, CA: Sage.
Czarniawska, B. and Wolff, R. (1998) "Constructing New Identities in Established
    Organization Fields," *International Studies of Management and Organization* 28
    (3): 32–56.
Dutton, J. E. and Dukerich, J. M. (1991) "Keeping an Eye on the Mirror: Image and Iden-
    tity in Organizational Adaptation," *Academy of Management Journal* 34: 517–554.
Elsbach, K. D. and Kramer, R. M. (1996) "Members' Responses to Organizational
    Identity Threats: Encountering and Countering the *Business Week* Rankings,"
    Administrative Science Quarterly 41: 442–476.
Fiol, C. M. and Misra, S. K. (1997) "Two Way Mirroring: Identity and Reputation When
    Things Go Wrong," *Corporate Reputation Review* 1 (1/2): 147–151.
Gioia, D. A. and Thomas, J. B. (1996) "Identity, Image and Issue Interpretation: Sense
    Making during Strategic Change in Academia," *Administrative Science Quarterly*
    40: 370–403.
Gioia, D. A., Schultz, M., and Corley, K. G. (2000) "Organizational Identity, Image and
    Adaptive Instability," *Academy of Management Review* 25 (1): 63–81.
Hatch, M. J. and Schultz, M. (1997) "Relations between Organisational Culture, Identity
    and Image," Special Edition on Corporate Identity: *European Journal of Market-
    ing* 31 (5/6): 356–365.
Hogg, M. A. and Terry, D. J. (2000) "Social Identity and Self-Categorization Processes
    in Organizational Contexts," *Academy of Management Review* 25 (1): 121–140.
Pratt, M. G. and Foreman, P. O. (2000) "Classifying Managerial Responses to Multiple
    Organizational Identities," *Academy of Management Review* 25 (1): 18–42.
Scott, S. G. and Lane, V. R. (2000) "A Stakeholder Approach to Organizational
    Identity," *Academy of Management Review* 25 (1): 43–62.

Visual identification: articles

Baker, M. J. and Balmer, J. M. T. (1997) "Visual Identity: Trappings or Substance?,"
    Special Edition on Corporate Identity: *European Journal of Marketing* 5/6 (3):
    366–382.
Foo, C. T., Lowe, A., and Foo, C. T. (2001) "Corporate Identity Strategy: Empirical
    Analyses of Major ASEAN Corporations," *Corporate Communications: An
    International Journal* 6 (3): 137–143.
Green, D. and Lovelock, V. (1994) "Understanding a Corporate Symbol," *Applied
    Cognitive Psychology* 8: 37–47.
Haase, S. J. and Theios, J. (1996) "Understanding Corporate Logos: Lexical and Ana-
    logical Considerations," *Genetic, Social and General Psychology Monographs* 122
    (3): 309–327.
Heaton, E. E. (1967) "Testing a New Corporate Name," *Journal of Marketing Research*
    4: 279–285.

Henderson, P. W. and Cote, J. A. (1998) "Guidelines for Selecting or Modifying Logos," *Journal of Marketing* 62 (2): 14–30.

Lippincott, J. G. and Margulies, W. P. (1957) "The Corporate Look: A Problem in Design," *Public Relations Journal* 13: 4–6.

Melewar, T. C. and Saunders, J. (1998) "Global Visual Identity: Standardization, Control and Benefits," *International Marketing Review* 15 (4): 291–308.

Melewar, T. C. and Saunders, J. (1999) "International Global Visual Identity: Standardisation or Localisation?," *Journal of International Business Studies* 31 (3): 583–598.

Melewar, T. C., Saunders, J., and Balmer, J. M. T. (2001) "Cause, Effect and Benefits of a Standardised Corporate Visual Identity System of UK Companies Operating in Malaysia," Special Edition on Corporate Identity: *European Journal of Marketing* 35 (3/4): 414–327.

Schechter, A. H. (1993) "Measuring the Value of Corporate and Brand Logos," *Design Management Journal* 4 (11): 33–39.

Schmitt, B. H., Simonson, A., and Marcus, J. (1995) "Managing Corporate Image and Identity," *Long Range Planning* 28 (5): 82–92.

Siegel, A. (1993) "Is Corporate Identity Dead?," *Graphics* 49: 11–13.

Smythe, J. (1993) "The Role of Corporate Identity in Managing Change," in P. Bowman and R. Bing (eds) *Handbook of Financial Public Relations*, 2nd edition, Oxford: Butterworth-Heinemann, pp. 123–135.

Stewart, K. (1991) "Corporate Identity: A Strategic Marketing Issue," *International Journal of Bank Marketing* 9 (1): 32–39.

Topalian, A. (1984) "Corporate Identity: Beyond the Visual Overstatements," *International Journal of Advertising* 3: 55–62.

Van Heerden, C. H. and Puth, G. (1995) "Factors that Determine the Corporate Image of South African Banking Institutions: An Explanatory Investigation," *International Journal of Bank Marketing* 31: 340–355.

Van Riel, C. B. M., van den Ban, A., and Heijmans, E. J. (2001) "The Added Value of Corporate Logos: An Empirical Study," Special Edition on Corporate Identity and Corporate Communication: *European Journal of Marketing* 35 (3/4): 428–440.

Books: academic

Cheney, G. (1991) *Rhetoric in an Organizational Society: Managing Multiple Identities*, Columbia: University of South Carolina Press.

Schultz, M., Hatch, M. J., and Larsen, M. (2000) *The Expressive Organization*, Oxford: Oxford University Press.

Van Riel, C. B. M. (1995) *Principles of Corporate Communication*, London: Prentice Hall.

Whetten, D. A. and Godfrey, P. C. (eds) (1998) *Identity in Organizations: Building Theory through Conversations*, Thousand Oaks, CA: Sage.

Books: practitioner

NB: The vast majority of the following are concerned with the conceptualization of corporate identity along graphic design lines. Where a broader approach has been adopted, this is indicated by a double asterisk.

Aldersey-Williams, H. (1994) *Corporate Identity*, London: Lund Humphries.

Blake, J. E. (ed.) (1971) *A Management Guide to Corporate Identity*, London: Council of Industrial Design.

Carter, D. E. (1982) *Designing Corporate Identity Programs for Small Corporations*, New York: Art Direction Book Co.

Chajet, C. and Shachtman, T. (1998) *Image by Design*, 2nd edition, New York: McGraw-Hill.

Garbett, T. F (1988) *How to Build a Corporate Identity and Project Its Image*, Toronto: Lexington Books.**

Henrion, F. and Parkin, A. (1967) *Design Co-ordination and Corporate Image*, London: Studio Vista.

Ind, N. (1992) *The Corporate Image*, London: Kogan Page.**

Jenkins, N. (1991) *The Business of Image*, London: Kogan Page.

Lippincott, A. and Margulies, W. (1987) *America's Global Identity Crisis: A Study of Corporate Communications Executives*, New York: Lippincott and Margulies.

Nagai, K. (1992) *Corporate Image Design*, Tokyo: PIE Books.

Napoles, V. (1988) *Corporate Identity Design*, New York: Van Nostrand Reinhold.

Olins, W. (1978) *The Corporate Personality: An Inquiry into the Nature of Corporate Identity*, London: Design Council.

Olins, W. (1989) *Corporate Identity: Making Business Strategy Visible through Design*, London: Thames and Hudson.

Olins, W. (1995) *The New Guide to Identity*, Aldershot, UK: Design Council.**

Pilditch, J. (1971) *Communication by Design: A Study in Corporate Identity*, Maidenhead, UK: McGraw-Hill.

Pilditch, J. (1976) *Talk about Design*, London: Barrie and Jenkins.

Schmidt, C. (1995) *The Quest for Identity*, London: Cassell.**

Schmittel, W. (1984) *Corporate Design International*, Zurich: ABC Edition.

Selame, E. and Selame, J. (1975) *The Company Image*, New York: John Wiley.

Steidl, P. and Emory, G. (1997) *Corporate Image and Identity Strategies: Designing the Corporate Future*, Warriewood, Australia: Business and Professional Publishing.**

Chapter 2

Wally Olins

CORPORATE IDENTITY: THE MYTH AND THE REALITY

Adapted from *Journal of the Royal Society of Arts,* December 1978–November 1979, 127: 209–218

EDITORS' COMMENTARY

It is fitting that the opening article of this section should be by Wally Olins. Without doubt he is among the premier advocates for corporate identity as an agenda item for senior management. He is a former Chairman of Wolff Olins, an identity and branding consultancy that he cofounded with Michael Wolff in 1964. His work for the graphic design industry was recognized by his award of the honor CBE (Commander of the British Empire).

Of note are his books on identity, which include *Corporate Identity: Making Business Strategy Visible through Design*[1] and *The New Guide to Identity*.[2] However, it was his first substantive work on identity, a work we consider to be his finest exposition of the area, entitled *The Corporate Personality: An Inquiry into the Nature of Corporate Identity*,[3] that propelled him into the limelight within the British business establishment. The title of Olins's treatise appears to owe something to another seminal work, namely Adam Smith's *An Inquiry into the Nature and Causes of the Wealth of Nations*, published in 1776. In its own way Olins's text remains a key source for identity scholars and practitioners, as Smith's does for economists. Having shared a number of conference platforms with Wally Olins, both of us have enjoyed his larger than life character; he is someone who in both his presentations and his writings is erudite, witty, insightful, and challenging.

The chapter "Corporate Identity: The Myth and the Reality" is taken from a lecture that was delivered on December 6, 1978 to the Fellows and members of The Royal Society for the Encouragement of Arts, Manufactures and Trades in London;

this is one of the U.K.'s most respected institutions of its type. It subsequently appeared in the *Journal of the Royal Society of Arts*.

The fact that such an august institution organized a lecture on corporate identity is itself noteworthy. It is testimony to the increasing importance that was being accorded to corporate identity by senior managers in the 1970s in the U.S.A. as well as in the U.K. It can also be seen as the RSA conferring its informal imprimatur on the work of leading identity consultants.

Olins's lecture draws extensively on his book *The Corporate Personality*,[4] which was published in the same year, and reveals him to be a consummate communicator of the strategic importance of identity to corporate entities, whether business or national. In "Corporate Identity: The Myth and the Reality" Olins adopts a broad-brushed, if not eclectic, approach to the area. He presents not one but *several* definitions of identity, reflecting several of the schools of thought pertaining to corporate identity.[5] On the one hand, Olins argues that corporate identity refers to *who* you are and *what* you are as an entity. In this respect, he foreshadows some ideas (noted in the introduction to this section) in recent identity scholarship.

Beyond this, Olins also posits that identity is fundamentally concerned with the way an organization *presents itself* – particularly to external audiences. Here, he reflects the traditional marketing/communications approach to identity as captured in the next chapter, by Margulies, who views identity as something that an organization creates through communication.

Lastly, Olins implies and observes that corporate identity can also be aligned to graphic design, in that systems of visual identification can be variously used as (a) a catalyst for change; (b) an important communications vehicle; and (c) a tool to be deployed for no other reason but fashionability. This perspective reflects his beliefs that identities are developed, made known, and experienced through design.

One aspect of Olins's early work that is articulated in a more pronounced form in *The Corporate Personality*[6] is the role of company founders and leaders in identity formation. This is not typically treated in the literature. Olins argues that when a company is first established it invariably reflects the personality of the founder. However, when the founder leaves or when there is weak leadership, an identity/personality crisis often ensues and thus the identity/personality needs to be managed in order to make up for this deficit.

Indeed, the salience of the leader's personality appears to have informed Olins's decision to accord primary importance to the corporate personality in the title of his seminal text.[7] In his recent writings Olins downplays or disregards this aspect of his work. However, in this chapter he engagingly refers to the roles of Robespierre and Napoleon in shaping French identity as well as drawing on well-known industry figures of his day. Today, Olins would no doubt refer to the role of Bill Gates at Microsoft, Sir Richard Branson at Virgin, and Anita Roddick of the Body Shop, as well as Martha Stewart of her eponymous company.

The complexity of identity, or what identity scholars would call identification, is also outlined. Just as individuals have an affinity to a nation, region, profession, and class, company components are made up of diverse elements, with individuals having multiple affinities. Olins points out that corporations are often a fusion of separate companies as a consequence of mergers and acquisitions.

The chapter is significant in a further regard. This is because Olins identifies the existence of *industry-wide* identities – something that again is often overlooked in the literature. Olins argues that in several instances it is the identity of the industry rather than that of individual companies that is the dominant force – that within a particular industry organizations have more in common with and fewer differences from their competitors, as compared with companies in unrelated industries.

The overriding message from Olins's lecture is that while identity is of critical importance it is often misunderstood and narrowly conceived. We believe that in this eloquently crafted lecture Olins demonstrates why identity is a captivating and engaging area of study. Corporate identity, according to Olins, is a profound and permanent manifestation of the human condition.

NOTES

1   Olins, W., *Corporate Identity: Making Business Strategy Visible through Design*, London: Thames and Hudson, 1989.

2   Olins, W., *The New Guide to Identity*, Aldershot, UK: Gower/Design Council, 1995.

3   Olins, W., *The Corporate Personality: An Inquiry into the Nature of Corporate Identity*, London: Design Council, 1978.

4   *Ibid.*

5   Balmer, J. M. T., "Corporate Branding and Connoisseurship," *Journal of General Management* 1995, 21 (1): 24–46.

6   Olins, *The Corporate Personality*.

7   *Ibid.*

O N THE 14TH JULY 1789 the Bastille was stormed. In September 1792 the French monarchy was abolished. In January 1793 Louis XVI was executed. The Ancien Régime fell.

Within a few days of the storming of the Bastille the Tricolor was seen on the streets of Paris – it soon replaced the traditional Fleur de Lys. In August 1792 the Marseillaise – a new national hymn – was heard. The army's uniforms were also changed. The government announced a series of what we might now describe as local government boundary changes. The historic regions of France were swept away at a stroke: Gascony, Provence, Brittany, Bourgogne, Poitou were replaced by a series of Departments. The Revolutionary government was determined totally to obliterate one way of life and replace it with another. They replaced the traditional weights and measures with new ones – which nearly two hundred years later are making a tentative appearance in this country. They started an entirely new calendar. The Year One began on 19th September 1792; it was followed by Years Two, Three and so on. They also changed the names of the months of the year – these innovations, unlike many, did not last. Indeed in its zeal the Revolution went so far as to replace God. Robespierre celebrated the worship of the Supreme Being in a former church newly redesigned and renamed the Pantheon – a building as unlike a traditional house of worship as it was possible for them to imagine.

They forgot nothing. In order to despatch their opponents in a fashion appropriate to the age they even introduced a new executing machine – the guillotine.

Now that's what I call changing your corporate identity.

Corporate identity – real corporate identity that is – is about behaviour as much as appearance, and certainly about reality, as much as symbolism. Whenever behaviour and appearance are linked, real corporate identity emerges.

The need for a new corporate identity most often manifests itself when a country, or for that matter any organization, is in a volatile state, when its management has changed, when it wants to expand, move in new directions – or alter its structure, when it wants or needs to demonstrate a new sense of direction to the various groups of people among whom it lives.

So going back to late eighteenth-century France, the symbols of change, the elimination of the old regional names, the new weights and measures, the new calendar, the new anthems, titles and uniforms, all emphasized the reality of change and acted as a catalyst to those who were managing the change.

A few years later in another political convulsion in France, things changed once again. To use the business jargon of the twentieth century, after a boardroom struggle a new chief executive emerged with growth plans which make the efforts of the American conglomerates of the 1960s look feeble and half hearted. Even the redoubtable Harold Geneen of ITT has nothing on Napoleon.

Like any really good manager, Napoleon made the most abundant use of corporate identity techniques to emphasize the changes taking place under his direction.

He was a great one for symbolic titles. Initially he became First Consul (the second and third consuls were of no significance), then Emperor. He crowned himself at his own Coronation. He created new Kings and a new aristocracy of Princes and Dukes. Even to-day the Swedish Royal Family is descended from a Napoleonic Marshal. He invented medals and awards – including the Légion d'Honneur. He even devised new countries like the Cisalpine Republic and Grand Duchy of Warsaw. Wherever he went Napoleon took with him his own name, styles, titles, legal codes, uniforms and emblems which symbolized to all who came into contact with them what Napoleonic power and rule really meant.

Corporate identity is about these things. It is about how behaviour and appearance symbolize the reality, reflect the reality and underline the reality all at the same time.

I find it much easier to grasp what corporate identity is really about or at any rate what it should be about by reference to historical, social or political precedents than by plunging into the minutiae of letterhead designs, symbols, logotypes, colour schemes or even, dare I say it, gazing at the corporate identity manuals of companies which have received the Design Management Award of this august Society.

All that type of stuff is, if I may say so, very largely the myth.

There are a number of conceptions and misconceptions, or as I call them in the title of this lecture, myths and realities, about corporate identity with which I should like to cope this evening. To start with, the phrase 'corporate identity' is as imprecise and disagreeable a piece of jargon as is common in any business manual. Personally I can't stand it. Corporate image is even worse though. It is just as imprecise, equally pretentious and on top of all that has sinister overtones all related to allegedly sophisticated techniques of manipulation. 'House style' is superficial and implies drawing up designs for letterheads – which gets me into hot water because I never learned to draw – and all the other phrases which are bandied about suffer from similar handicaps.

Definitions are unfortunately rather important in this business, because most people involved in it, both those who earn their living from creating and selling corporate identity programmes and those who buy and use them, are often vague and imprecise about what they are trying to do.

In real life we all have an identity. We don't consciously create it, although we may consciously for at least part of the time manipulate it and project it, but it's there all the time. Our identity is closely associated with and partly derives from the different groups to which we belong: to our country, to our town, to our district within that town, and of course in Britain, to our social class, to our families, our wives (or husbands), children, mistresses, to the companies in which we work, to particular groups within those companies. All of these different groups have their own language, signs, symbols and personality. What we as people present to the outside world is our own interpretation of the amalgam of those things. So our clothes, our houses, the way we speak, project our identity.

In an advertising agency, for example, it is the expensive informality of the creative director's clothes and style with his open necked shirt, his beard and his leather jacket which are meant to signal his unorthodox and, by inference, creative ways. We can tell from looking at him where he lives, how much he earns, and what at least some of his interests are.

Unhappily until we see it we can only surmise whether his work is as creative as he tries to look.

In most real life situations the outward and visible signs of corporate identity emerge naturally, organically – as part of what is currently called one's life style. We get married, say, we start a family, we live in Islington, we send our kids to the local Comprehensive, we work in journalism, we have a Renault 4, we buy our furniture from Habitat, we vote Labour (even though it isn't in our class interest to do so), the females in our family are draped from head to toe in Laura Ashley. We didn't do any of it on purpose – but it came out that way, so we end up looking a bit like this.

Or, maybe, we get married, we start a family, we live in Gerrards Cross, we send our kids away to school, we work in a merchant bank, we have a BMW, we buy our furniture from Harrods, we vote Tory, the females in our family are draped from head to foot in Jaeger. We didn't do any of it on purpose – it came out that way. And maybe we end up looking like this.

Each conscious individual decision that we take – to pick a particular neigh-bourhood to live in, to buy certain brands of clothes, to furnish our houses in a specific way – adds up collectively to a certain life style which clearly reminds ourselves and signals to the rest of the world what kind of people we are. Although the individual selections which we have made about the different aspects of our life may not consciously have been contrived any more than the French revolutionaries consciously created symbols of their régime, what it all adds up to is a clear corporate identity – a clear projection of self.

We know what we are and so do other people. Our corporate identity symbolizes the reality, emphasizes the reality and is part of the reality all at the same time. When our life style changes, when we divorce, move away, retire from the rat race or whatever, our identity is modified accordingly.

What I have argued so far is that what people call corporate identity, so far from being a fashionable management fad, something to do with logotypes, symbols and colours, charged for by the kilo, by the designer and slapped on with a trowel by the client, is in fact a profound and permanent manifestation of the human condition.

It is certainly the case that corporate identity is also a product sold by

specialized design consultants to companies of all shapes and sizes all over the world. The corporate identity practitioner currently shuffles uneasily from foot to foot in a kind of half light somewhere between the advertising agency, the PR man, the management consultant and the architect. He is normally a graphic designer struggling away with concepts which he, like his client, only partially understands.

Why is this?

What is going on?

How did it happen?

The first really large organizations to emerge in the modern commercial and industrial world were the railways. Intuitively each major railway company developed its own individual identity stemming from its own personality and needs. I have written about the sharply differing identities of the Midland, Great Northern and Great Western Railways clearly manifested in architecture, rolling stock, liveries, uniforms, even down to such things as cutlery. The fact that the Midland was the line for comfort rather than speed while the Great Northern was more concerned with technical advance, is clearly revealed in the neighbouring stations of St. Pancras and King's Cross – the one rich, gaudy and ostentatious, the other modest, austere and simple.

Neither the Midland nor the Great Northern nor for that matter any of the other railway or shipping companies which produced such complex, involved and powerfully idiosyncratic corporate identity programmes in the middle and late nineteenth century needed any outside designers' help to project what they were. It just naturally, organically, emerged. All the architects and engineers, printers, publicists and hundreds of other suppliers they used had an instinct for what the companies really were.

The first time I can trace the use of professional outside assistance in the self-conscious development of corporate identity was in Germany in the early years of this century when the great AEG organization, the major German electrical company, employed the young architect Behrens to design and co-ordinate products, publicity and architecture. His work for them was extremely success-ful. He was able to help them project through the design of his products, and through architecture and exhibitions and publicity material the idea of a very advanced thoughtful company, concerned to use its knowledge of what was then an extremely advanced form of energy – electricity – in a way which would be life-enhancing without being too pi. AEG products were of a piece with the company – modern, well made and thoughtfully designed.

The direction of the Allgemeine Elektricitäts-Gesellschaft was at that time in the hands of Walter Rathenau, a rare combination of industrialist, visionary and as it subsequently transpired, world-class statesman.

Men such as Rathenau were rare, companies as thoughtful, sophisticated and commercially acute as the old AEG maybe even rarer. In Britain a few people like Frank Pick of London Transport also consciously introduced a policy of using a mixture of outsiders and insiders to project through architecture, products and printed material a clear idea about his organization.

The fact of the matter is that when an organization has a clear idea about itself, what its business is, what its priorities are, how it wants to conduct itself, how it wants to be perceived, its identity falls fairly easily into place. Its prod-ucts, buildings, the services it offers, the publicity it conducts, are all of a piece – they are coherent and mutually supportive. The company may need outside help to execute its intentions effectively, but it certainly doesn't need any help in discovering what they are.

If we look at a few contemporary examples, the point becomes clear. Sir Freddie Laker's Laker Airways has a clear identity, so does Terence Conran's Habitat, so does Colin Chapman's Lotus. What these three companies have in common is that their identities directly reflect the preoccupations, the energy, and the attitudes of the people who own and manage them.

But in to-day's world, companies like Laker, Lotus and Habitat are compara-tively small and, more important, comparatively simple. They are fairly easy to understand, to get a grip on.

Another group of companies, usually much bigger and older, which share with these smaller companies a clear idea of what they are about are those like Mercedes-Benz and Marks & Spencer which are obsessed by their own techno-logy. Both Mercedes-Benz and Marks & Spencer have gone beyond the point where the personality of the chief executive is the one thing that holds the culture of the company together. The idea behind the product has taken such

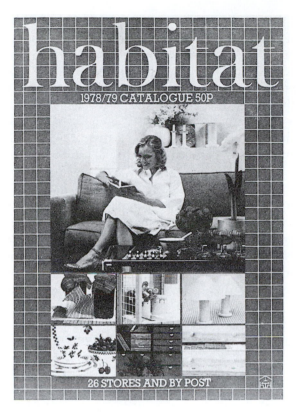

firm root that virtually anyone who works in either of these companies is aware that certain standards in products and product development, in service, in packaging, in technology, in pricing, in human relations, are appropriate to them and what they do and such standards are followed. Life is made much easier for suppliers, customers and everyone else who deals with the company – they have certain expectations, about what the company is prepared to accept and how it will behave, which are comfortably consistent. In these companies those marketing men who sway with the lightest breezes of public opinion are shunned. These companies sturdily and successfully set out to give the consumer what is good for him and not what he wants.

This kind of company, and there are a fair number of them, has a powerful, idiosyncratic and well understood identity. It is usually, contrary to most marketing men's cherished beliefs, highly successful.

Most organizations, however, fall into two quite different groups. There are those whose culture, behaviour pattern, and way of life are so much part of the generic of the industry in which they operate that it is practically impossible for anybody to tell any of them apart.

These are often organizations whose activities are very heavily circumscribed by trade associations, by IATA, say – the International Air Transport Association, which still controls much of the minutiae of airline travel – or, a more homely example, by the Building Societies Association, the trade body controlling the activities of the Building Societies.

In order to prepare for this lecture, I spent some time investigating what Building Societies look, sound and behave like. There is hardly any difference between what one Building Society offers a customer and what another offers. So any differences must stem from their personalities. There is certainly a collective Building Society culture, a collective Building Society way of behaving and doing things, but despite the individual Building Societies' quite considerable efforts to differentiate themselves by advertising, the experience of dealing with them, their offices, their forms, the way in which their employees behave is so similar, that it is virtually impossible to tell one from the other.

Building Societies are extreme versions of the category of organization whose behaviour and appearance and standards are such that it is all but impossible to tell them apart. Two other prominent groups in this category are banks and insurance companies. Theoretically petrol retailing is another activity in which everyone believes the product is much the same, and in which apart from a few minor price variations from time to time there doesn't seem to be a real difference between the major brands. The petrol retailers, unlike the Building Societies, are acutely aware of this problem and have made over many years constant efforts to build in perceptible differences through advertising, through architecture, signs, colours, and even, when they are really desperate, through attempts to improve service.

Organizations like these are amongst those that need help from outsiders to help them understand, define and then execute a corporate identity which will give them some kind of real, distinct and individual personality.

So far we have talked about businesses which have been dominated by the personality of the founder, like Habitat, or by one idea, say the intention to excel, like Rolls-Royce, or even by the rule book and customs of the trade, like Building Societies.

The last, most numerous, and in many ways, most important group of businesses with which I would like to deal this evening has also been dominated at least for a considerable time by one idea – the wish to grow. This idea, which is in many ways valuable and important, is, unless it is very carefully monitored, also potentially self-destructive.

Many, perhaps most, of the world's really major companies have grown cannibalistically, by swallowing first their rivals, then their suppliers, then their customers. They have grown by merger, amalgamation, horizontal and vertical integration into enormous and often shapeless structures. They have formed offensive and defensive alliances, both temporary and permanent, until they have come virtually to dominate the industries in which they traditionally operate and sometimes a few others as well. These companies often have the greatest difficulty in knowing who and what they are and in maintaining clear and consistent standards because they are simply a ragbag of many different traditions, styles and regional and national backgrounds.

In their headlong race for growth, such companies almost always gulp down, sometimes almost without noticing it, a mass of smaller companies, each with its own subsidiaries, with its own traditions, customers, methods of purchasing, distribution systems, community relations activities, methods of accounting, research and development operations, overseas agents, public relations programmes, brands and products and so on.

Each individual unit of which the monster, the colossus company, is made up, has in other words, its own identity, influenced by its own history and the personalities who once dominated it.

Colossus companies are often made up of traditional rivals with mutual and almost hereditary antagonisms. This bringing together of two or more ancient enemies into one corporation is almost always the source of the most vicious in-fighting. In this situation individuals in both companies are not just fighting for dominance in the market place but for the victory of their own way of life – the only way in which they can ensure their own personal survival in the new corporation. There is no war more vicious than a civil war.

Almost always the mergers that directly led to the creation of the colossus have been preceded by a series of previous mergers, sometimes going back forty or fifty years, in each of which there has been played out a smaller but no less violent version of the civil wars which currently wrack the colossus company.

Eventually all this becomes unendurable. The colossus company finds itself with a heaving mass of companies, brands and products, each with different attitudes, different loyalties and different identities, with different reputations in the different market places all over the world in which it operates. It is distracted at every turn – what should its policy be in research and development, in branding, in export, in financial controls, in personnel relations and recruitment? What common elements should the companies in the group possess? What is its own personality?

It may realize that as things stand it has no clear personality itself – that nobody quite knows who it is and what it stands for, and that the absence of such a personality is in itself revealing. It allows the company to be perceived as one dominated by its component parts. Even its business purpose is unclear. Should it be a holding company, only interested in the financial results of its operating units? Should it be a highly decentralized organization, looking after finance, research and development, personnel and one or two other functions while it leaves its operating units to get on with it at the sharp end?

Or should it be the one source which carefully controls and directs all of the activities of its operating units, including recruitment, research and development, marketing policy, pricing and so on?

Should it control or should it be controlled by its operating units?

In the end these questions, all of which concern the relationship of the centre to the whole, cannot be ducked. The decisions the colossus takes have a profound bearing on the way it does its business, what kind of growth it is looking for, what kind of people it wants – and all of these things in turn will affect its identity.

When the centre does not know what its rôle is, it cannot know what it wants from its operating units. It cannot know how it wants them to behave, what it wants them to do. In these circumstances the identity of the individual units continues wildly to rampage – the identity of the colossus continues to wither. The results of all this are in the end dire.

In the end the colossus has to take action – to rediscover its own identity.

Somewhere beneath all those acquisitions there must be a corporate soul, some goals, some intentions, a way of behaving, of doing things, standards of product performance that it feels comfortable with, something which suppliers, customers and people inside all of the companies within the organization can understand and respond to. It is these standards which have to be unearthed and then made visible – so that all companies within the massive organization can respond in a way which everyone else both within the group and outside will recognise.

Or maybe there isn't. Maybe there isn't anything there at all except the will to expand – like the Quatermass monster.

Companies with no real understanding of what they are about are in the end found out. They don't really know where they are going – when the mood of the moment is for expansion, they grow – when it changes and it's fashionable to divest, they get small again. More often than not they get small quicker than they might wish, in a fashion which they may not like.

But all companies, big or small, which want to introduce familial or, if you prefer, corporate behaviour often find it easiest to symbolize it visually – and that's perhaps where the myth of corporate identity comes in.

Many huge companies with massive and complex problems ranging over every aspect of their business, as I have attempted to describe, do not necessarily think of these problems as inter-related. Certainly they do not always or for that matter often think of them as problems of corporate identity or personality. But they are, or at least in part they are, and if they are properly treated they will respond effectively.

In the beginning of this lecture I showed through the example of the French Revolution that corporate identity symbolizes the reality, emphasizes the reality and is part of the reality all at the same time. I also said that corporate identity is about behaviour as well as appearance.

If this is true then the application of a purple stripe and a new way of writing Bloggo in silver is hardly likely to make a profound difference to a corporation in the travail that I have just described. Stripes, new colours, new paint schemes on lorries and a few signs on buildings are in themselves neither here nor there – they are the myth, not the reality.

They only become significant when they act as the symbols and catalysts of change, when they help the management of the colossus to signal both internally and externally that change is taking place – that order is emerging from chaos – that the products the company makes and sells will once again have a consistent and clear reputation, that loyalties will lie not just with one part of the organization, but through one part of it to the totality – that the whole is genuinely greater than the sum of its parts.

That is why corporate identity cannot be confined to graphics. If a company puts fresh bright signs on a squalid and decaying edifice, it indicates not only that it has the wrong priorities, but also that it is not sensitive to the spirit of the age in which we live.

Corporate identity must take into account not just the package but the product that goes inside it and the service that backs it up, not just a sign but the building on which it is placed. Not just uniforms but the way in which people who work for the company think about themselves in relation to it.

That is why corporate identity is an activity which essentially must be directed from within – it is after all the essence of the company. If it is to work it needs the constant commitment of the man at the top. It is best carried out intuitively. Nobody told Robespierre that he was doing a good job with his corporate identity programme. I don't suppose Freddie Laker needs much advice on his corporate identity either.

There is – fortunately for us in the trade – a job for the outside consultant. It is to investigate, to recommend, to monitor, to hold up a mirror and to help implement.

But the process is essentially an internal one. It is the manifestation of the spirit of the organization in a comprehensible form, and nobody can properly be responsible for that but the company itself.

Chapter 3

Walter Margulies

MAKE THE MOST OF YOUR CORPORATE IDENTITY

From *Harvard Business Review*, 1977 (July–August): 66–77

EDITORS' COMMENTARY

It would be unthinkable in an anthology such as this to ignore Walter Margulies, the founder and, at the time the article was written, president of the world-famous identity consultancy Lippincott and Margulies based in New York City. Like the article by Olins, this contribution appeared in the late 1970s when there was heightened interest in the identity concept.

This article's appearance in the *Harvard Business Review* is of particular significance with regard to the genesis of the identity concept, since it brought the concept and the work of identity consultants, aka graphic design consultancies, to the forefront in corporate America. The article was, and remains, influential. It is widely referred to in the literature, and it reflects a distinct, if not dominant, paradigm within identity studies. Its premise is that in order to create a positive image and, over time, a positive reputation, a company must successfully communicate and manage the way it wishes to be viewed by key stakeholder groups. Under this scheme of communication, graphic design is accorded an important and invariably dominant role.

The focus is *external*, the emphasis is on *control*, and the mechanism is *integrated corporate communications*, with a pivotal role being accorded to *graphic design*. This approach is, increasingly, falling out of favor with recent identity scholars.

Margulies's categorization of corporate identity is one-dimensional. His conceptualization is a good deal narrower than that posited by Olins in the preceding article. In the context of Balmer's schools of thought,[1] Margulies would appear to belong to the communication/communication-by-design school of thought.

Margulies accords a good deal of importance to the difficulties that can arise when image does not reflect reality. In time this became known in the literature as the identity/image interface.[2] However, Margulies adopts a narrow perspective in considering this interface. This is because his approach has a narrow, external focus. Thus, the thrust of a good deal of this chapter is that identity management is concerned with bringing a negative image into alignment with a positive identity. The question of what to do if the image is good and the identity (reality) is bad is not addressed.

Margulies presents a number of interesting case vignettes that illustrate the efficacy of effective communication or changing the company name or logo, in order to nudge perception into line with reality. Certainly the problems faced by Humana and United Technologies are likely always to characterize the corporate environment.

One important feature of the chapter is Margulies's injunction to CEOs not only that they should have responsibility for the corporate identity but that it should be managed on an ongoing basis. It is worth noting that Margulies is speaking about visual identity rather than about the deeper characteristics of identity advanced by other authors in this anthology. With the passage of time, Margulies's perspective may appear simplistic. However, this article is of seminal importance within the annals of the corporate identity literature since the communication/communication-by-design schools of thought represent two of the significant practitioner paradigms on identity.

There is another reason to include Margulies in this anthology. Clive Chajet, the successor to Walter Margulies at Lippincott and Margulies, relates how the corporate identity concept was first introduced by Gordon Lippincott and Walter Margulies in 1964. However, a close reading of Martineau's article "Sharper Focus for the Corporate Image" (this volume, Chapter 9) reveals that Margulies was not in fact the originator of the concept! For Martineau as far back as 1958 makes use of the phrase "corporate identity design."

> Johnson's Wax had just bought another company that sold a product entirely different from household waxes – health foods – and it occurred to Gordon and Walter that the wax image might damage the product line of the newly acquired company. Johnson's agreed that a potential problem did exist, and hired Lippincott and Margulies to look into it. Gordon and Walter called the process they undertook to solve the problem "corporate identity." Thus was the term and the discipline invented. It was the first time anyone had defined the relationship between image and identity. Gordon and Walter had come to the conclusion that identity was (in Walter's words) "that component of a corporation's image that can be wholly controlled by the company."[3]

NOTES

1   Balmer, J. M. T., "Corporate Branding and Connoisseurship," *Journal of General Management* 1995, 21 (1): 24–46.
2   Abratt, R., "A New Approach to the Corporate Image Management Process," *Journal of Marketing Management* 1989, 5 (1): 63–76.
3   Chajet, C. and Shachtman, T., *Image by Design*, 2nd edition, New York: McGraw-Hill, 1998, pp. xviii–xix.

CORPORATE IDENTITY PROGRAMS ARE thrust into the limelight every now and then when some large company changes its name or displays its old name or nickname in a strikingly new fashion. Everybody seems to have an opinion about the new look or name, and there is usually much discussion about the good taste, or lack of it, on the part of the executives who made the choice.

This process may seem to involve simply putting one's best foot forward. For a small business such as a single neighborhood store, this could well be so. But for the large corporation with diverse product lines and a national or international scope, putting one's best foot forward in a manner that is compatible with overall capabilities and goals can be a difficult, intricate, time-consuming, and highly rewarding task.

In the somewhat specialized language of the field, *identity* means the sum of all the ways a company chooses to identify itself to all its publics – the community, customers, employees, the press, present and potential stockholders, security analysts, and investment bankers. *Image*, on the other hand, is the perception of the company by these publics.

A corporation influences its image by the way it manages its corporate identity and has a much greater capacity to change the public perception – for better or worse – than many executives realize.

To begin with, let's look at a hypothetical company whose mistakes are typical of several real companies and who succeeded spectacularly in transforming their weak images into *worse* ones by misidentifying their corporate identity needs.

The symptoms, fairly common ones that trouble many companies, were well defined. The diversified manufacturer made high-quality products that were among the best in the industry. Its sales had grown steadily, if not spectacularly, and its earnings performance was about average for the industry with which it was grouped (incorrectly) by security analysts. But its price–earnings ratio was the lowest of the group. Because of the low stock price, the company had difficulty in raising capital for expansion and feared it might become a victim of a takeover bid as well. In addition, it was having difficulty keeping its top salesmen and engineers and recruiting new ones.

The name of the 115-year-old company, the executives reasoned, was too closely identified with the past. It decided therefore that it needed a zippy new name and a sleek new look. The art department came up with a crisp rendition of the company's initials, and the new name was born. The company redesigned its stationery and began replacing the old name with the initials on its packages, a few products at a time, as the supply of old materials ran out.

But things got worse. It turned out that the old name had actually been the strongest element in the corporation's identity. The public – both consumers and the financial community – continued to refer to it by the old name, as did many of its own salesmen.

The only element (the old name) that unified its many products now coexisted, often on the same shelf, with the new initials. Lacking specific instructions as to how to implement the name change locally, many divisions and individual plants never did make the change to the new initials or adopt the new stationery, which further compounded the confusion.

Let's discuss what the company did right and then all the things it either did wrong or failed to do in addressing its identity problem.

First, the company recognized that it had a corporate identity problem. So much for what it did *right*. Now for the failures:

1   The company failed to study its needs in detail.
2   It failed to diagnose its product identity problem – too many products were not identifiable either with each other or with the corporation because of a confusing coexistence of names and designs.
3   It then disposed of its strongest corporate identity asset, the old name, for lack of adequate information.
4   It added to the confusion by failing to coordinate the introduction of the new name on a company-wide basis.
5   It did nothing to clarify to security analysts the industry group to which it correctly belonged or to otherwise improve its standing in the financial community. In fact, its inept handling of the new name had quite the opposite effect.

To sum up, the company had attempted to solve deep problems with cosmetics.

How to get started

A successful corporate identity program certainly requires the involvement and support of the company's chief executive officer. The CEO will, of course, ask many tough questions before endorsing a program. A big one, expressed in the popular catch-phrase, is likely to be "What's the bottom line?"

It is, unfortunately, the wrong question.

If this seems heretical, let me hasten to point out that investors are willing to pay far more for the bottom line of some companies than for others; that is, the price–earnings ratios of even highly similar companies can differ dramatically. A major factor in such discrepancies is the way companies are perceived by present or potential investors and their advisers.

A classic example arose a few years ago, when conglomerates were in disfavor with the financial community. Two giant, nationally known companies were both involved in electronics, EDP, aerospace, aircraft, communications, military supplies, chemicals, marine products, education, transportation, and consumer products. One company, perceived as a conglomerate, had a price–earnings ratio of 6, while the other was not regarded as a conglomerate and had a multiple of 32. In other words, one company's bottom line was worth more than five times as much to the investor, largely as a result of public perception of its performance and prospects. The "conglomerate," incidentally, was LTV; the other company was General Electric.

The argument over conglomerates has since faded, and the price–earnings gap between LTV and GE has narrowed somewhat. But even at present, when sky-high multiples have virtually disappeared, examples of striking discrepancies in the relative market prices of similar stocks are abundant.

The point is that investor perceptions, correct and incorrect, influence a company's ability to perform in the financial marketplace. But, as we have seen, investors are only *one* of the many publics whose perceptions affect corporate success. For many companies, final approval of the sale of their product or service may involve the opinions of a customer's board members about the seller's overall corporate capabilities.

A corporation that is doing a good job of marketing its products effectively could still have difficulty obtaining financing for expansion because the financial community perceives the company as sedentary. It may not be able to recruit the brightest business school graduates; or it may find itself an easy target for a takeover bid because its stockholders have negative sentiments about its management.

It should be remembered that different companies require different financial relations strategies. A company with a small stock float and a company whose shares are widely held by large institutional investors cannot always benefit from the same program. Some case histories of successful corporate identity efforts involving some of the same problems faced by our composite company may serve to demonstrate the techniques that the specialized communications field uses today.

When the name doesn't fit

A decision to change a well-established identity cannot be taken lightly. It would seem foolhardy, as our composite example shows, for a large corporation to substitute an unknown name for one that has become highly esteemed by the public and by the business and financial communities.

Yet U.S. Rubber reached just such a decision and made a highly successful name change to Uniroyal, initially chosen as a cohesive, communicative name and eventually adopted as its new legal name. But the name change, unlike that of our mythical company, was only one result of a corporate identity program that addressed itself to the peculiar difficulties that can arise as a corporation grows and diversifies its operations.

The problem with the old name was twofold: neither "U.S." nor "rubber" correctly described the company's activities. It had become a multinational company with more sales abroad than in the United States, and its product line had come to include chemicals, plastics, fibers, and many other products, in addition to rubber.

The large number of products was a problem in itself. More than 400 brand names were used for the company's thousands of products produced by plants in 23 countries. A company official summarized the problem in these words: "Everywhere, U.S. Rubber seems to be doing business as a small local company. Nobody gets the idea that it is a worldwide corporation."

The search for a new name was begun. It had to be suitable for almost all potential markets; without geographic or cultural restrictions; applicable to all products, divisions, and affiliates; free of embarrassing meanings in major foreign languages; and it should relate, if possible, to major brand franchises. The name also had to be brief, adaptable to visual presentation, unique, and legally available. And, of course, it had to project desirable attributes.

Thousands of possible names were generated by a computer and screened before the name Uniroyal was chosen. This name proved highly suitable to an integrated international enterprise. It expresses the company's international stature, binds together its many parts, and contains nothing to offend nationalistic feelings. It also retains the equity the company had in its largest selling tire, U.S. Royal.

But the corporate identity program did not begin with a new name and certainly could not end at that point. Exploiting the Uniroyal mark required a threefold program of graphics, nomenclature, and application. Research had already shown the graphic versatility of the name. The role of nomenclature was to wed the symbol to the generic names of divisions and affiliates so as to identify every part and function of the company in a uniform way.

Successful performance in these two fields created the opportunity to embrace all potential uses. But application involved an even more extensive effort, which included these steps:

- Preparing a corporate identity manual to ensure uniform application of the symbol's various forms in all possible situations.
- Meeting with company managers and department heads to explain the identity system.
- Indoctrinating all divisional sales executives.
- Discussing the new communications philosophy with union leaders.
- Addressing financial audiences to clearly explain the new name.
- Communicating the change and the rationale behind the name change to the company's shareholders.
- Preparing advertisements for media throughout the world.
- Mailing announcement brochures to 60,000 employees and letters to twice as many major customers.

The public announcement of the new corporate name and logotype, its accompanying internal communications efforts, and the resulting external publicity made the initiation of the new symbol an international event. But the hard work of the week-in, week-out advertising of brand name products, which will eventually have the greatest impact worldwide, is necessarily a continuing activity, as is promoting the name under which the stock is sold.

Humana, Inc. is typical of the many companies that have solved a number of problems with a well-executed identity program. Humana was originally called Extendicare, and in the mid-sixties was a large operator of nursing homes. In the late sixties, it changed its focus to management of health-care institutions and operation of hospitals. The nursing home scandals of other companies rubbed off on Extendicare, and its stock slumped. Research showed that brokers were routing customers away from Extendicare simply because of the industry it was in. After it undertook a corporate indentity program, changing its name to Humana and overhauling all its corporate and financial communications, its market position improved considerably.

Another recent example of the same kind of problem encountered by U.S. Rubber and Extendicare was United Aircraft's case of mistaken identity. While it was and is engaged in designing and building aircraft products, for many years the company had been extending its aerospace-based technological know-how to a wide variety of other fields, including electrical power generation and trans-mission, industrial processes, electronics, communications, marine propulsion, appliance and automotive systems, laser technology, and automotive diagnostics and controls.

Yet the company was less known than many of its subsidiaries, despite the fact that it was among the famous Dow-Jones "30 industrials." It continued to be identified principally with aircraft manufacture, when it was not confused with United Air Lines. Since the security analysts who followed the company were usually those who followed the airframe companies, United tended to share the relatively low price–earnings characteristics of that volatile and cyclical industry dependent on defense contracts. This severely limited its growth potential and its proper recognition.

What all of United's activities had in common was their high technology. A study of the company's communications needs led not only to a new name, United Technologies, but to a clarification and strengthening of the corporation's sense of its own future, as well as a plan for compatible acquisitions.

One immediate result has been that Wall Street interest in United Technolo-gies is no longer confined to analysts who follow the airframe manufacturing group. Its price–earnings ratio has improved. The company now has applied its high-technology capabilities to consumer products and has grown impressively in recent years.

Establishing an identity

Not all corporate identity programs are therapeutic, that is, a response to specific ills. When introduction of a new product or service creates an entirely new business for an established company, an identity program can help the company through the difficult first stages as well as provide a solid base for continuing operation. Such was the case with First Federal Savings & Loan of Lincoln, Nebraska.

Electronic transfer of funds, the computer-based system that enables customers to deposit, withdraw, or transfer money at any location equipped with a special computer terminal, is revolutionary. All the customer needs is a coded plastic card. The implications are immense. The spread of such systems could dramatically change the way people handle their money. But these implications do not translate into an automatic marketing success.

One of the earliest institutions to market the systems was First Federal and its subsidiary, TMS Corporation of America. Computer terminals have been installed in a number of Nebraska supermarkets, and TMS is now licensing the operation in other regions of the country.

TMS quickly recognized the need for a strong identity program. Their efforts began with a series of attitudinal surveys among savings and loan executives nationwide to discover how other institutions felt about electronic funds transfer. The results led to the development of specific marketing strategies, among which was a complete graphics system, including a plastic card designed to accommodate individual signatures of participating institutions.

The card was part of a marketing package called "The Money Service," which included point-of-purchase displays, decals, counter-top posters, booklets, stationery, and business forms. But the identity program did not stop there; it also encompassed a broadcast and newspaper advertising campaign.

Thus the program was a far cry from the mere design of a logotype, and it was rewarded with nationwide success and public recognition of the TMS service.

Going beyond the name

For Hardee's Food Systems anticipation of corporate-identity needs helped to head off potential marketing problems and also served as an immediate stimulus to sales. Hardee's is a highly successful operator and franchiser of more than 1,000 restaurants in 34 states and one of the largest fast-food operations in the country.

Hardee's had to project sales appeal to potential franchisees and investors as well as to its customers, but, in doing so, it had to avoid a hard sell promotional look that many communities were finding objectionable.

A comprehensive communications, marketing, and design audit was conducted. All facets of restaurant operation and appearance were investigated, including signs, menus, roadside visibility, restaurant surfaces, and packaging and paper products. The shape and style of the facilities were also considered. The 12-week audit provided a foundation for Hardee's overall repositioning in the market place as a nationally known fast-food restaurant.

A prototype restaurant featuring an environmentally compatible design served as a model for new units and for remodeling of existing restaurants. It avoided the hard sell appearance that often disturbs zoning boards and was designed to meet requirements for both sales potential and cost control.

The prototype featured a distinctive mansard roof and floor-to-ceiling windows that allowed potential customers a clear view of the restaurant sales area. Specifications for construction materials were flexible, permitting the local businessman to select the roofing and siding that best fitted the site and community standards. Although the size of outside signs was reduced by about half, they were made more visible from a distance. Also, the new signs cost 45% less to make and about half as much to illuminate.

Sales gains averaging 35% have been registered by newly remodeled units, demonstrating that a corporate identity program can be designed to be compatible both with business and with environmental requirements.

In July 1976, shareholders learned that the company had received consent from its long-term lenders to begin a $10.5 million expansion program. The capital probably would not have been available before this effort.

The Hardee situation is an example of a corporation that did not have a name problem but could and did profit from a program to improve its image in light of environmental considerations.

The name may not be the problem

Name changes have been a common phenomenon in recent years. But for a successful change, a company must have a clear idea of why it is necessary and of what results the company expects. When this initial assessment shows that a new name will help the company to communicate with its various publics more effectively, development of the new name can begin.

A name change alone will not modify a corporation's identity. Even the most modest identity programs must include extensive preliminary research and extensive implementation efforts for successful corporate repositioning. In some cases, a corporation's problems are so profound that new nomenclature alone is not likely to be effective. In other cases, an overly rigid imposition of the corporate name on subsidiaries would be counterproductive.

RCA Corporation has chosen to keep separate identities for Random House, which seeks to attract top authors, few of whom can identify with the parent company; for NBC, to avoid the appearance of an overly dominant parent–subsidiary relationship because of potential regulatory problems; and for Hertz, to keep the complaints that are an occupational hazard of its business from rubbing off onto the parent.

For FMC Corporation, on the other hand, the high visibility of many divisions proved undesirable because the parent did not have a well-established identity. This is often the case with industrial companies with relatively small advertising budgets. Such names as Link-Belt, John Bean, American Viscose, and Niagara Chemical obscured the image of the parent, FMC.

The repositioning program for FMC involved a study of its marketing capabilities that resulted in a redefinition of its subcorporate nomenclature and a clarification and regrouping of the company's marketing expertise. Most divisions were renamed generically to express their particular expertise, with the FMC logo added for corporate continuity.

Another example of a nonchange of name was Bendix Corporation. Because extensive consumer advertising had established it as a maker of washing machines, it continued to be identified as such long after it went out of the washing machine business. Bendix industrial products were well respected, but because of the small size of industrial advertising budgets, these operations did not have a strong public identity.

The question that had to be answered was "What is the real Bendix?" Top management became involved in what might be described as a search for the corporate essence, and this was the important first step in successfully repositioning Bendix and cementing its well-established skills to its existing name through a company-wide communications program reaching customers, the financial community, and the general public.

The principal lesson of these examples is that a new name is only a single, though quite visible, part of a corporate identity program. In some cases it is only a cosmetic change, which could obscure rather than enhance corporate identity.

A single negative example may serve to reinforce this point. When Universal Oil Products changed its name to UOP Corporation, it decided to try to register the initials on the public consciousness by running an advertising campaign that asked the question "What is a UOP?" After all the company's expensive efforts, people are still wondering what a UOP is.

The benefits

In summation, a corporate identity program is ideally a systems approach to management of a tangible corporate asset. It should begin with research and in-depth analysis to clarify how the company itself perceives its corporate assets.

When this self-perception is measured against the views that are found among the company's various publics, steps can be taken to refocus the public perception and even, when necessary, the corporation's view of itself. Identity programs that accomplish both are remarkably effective and are also long-lasting.

The program may include stronger financial communications planning, a different marketing thrust, redefinition of product uses, and many other activities. In each case, the action involves intensifying and redirecting an existing strength.

An important benefit is emphasis on the corporation as an integral whole – to employees as well as to other publics. Among Wall Street institutional analysts especially, the whole corporation can indeed be greater than the sum of its parts.

To ensure that the graphics system is used effectively, a management guide to the application of the system is invaluable. A transition to the new identification system under the supervision of a staff officer or a specially appointed identity manager is recommended. Like any corporate program, repositioning of identity must be *managed*.

Classic views of identity

Good name in man and woman, dear my lord,
Is the immediate jewel of their souls;
Who steals my purse steals trash; 'tis something, nothing;
'Twas mine, 'tis his, and has been slave to thousands;
But he that filches from me my good name
Robs me of that which not enriches him,
And makes me poor indeed.

Shakespeare, *Othello*

It is with literature as with law or empire — an established name is an estate in tenure, or a throne in possessions.

Poe, *Poems* [1831]

A good name is like a precious ointment; it filleth all around about, and will not easily away; for the odors of ointments are more durable than those of flowers.

Bacon, *Essays*, "Of Praise"

I would to God thou and I knew where a commodity of good names were to be bought.

Shakespeare, *Hamlet*

Me name is Mud.

Dennis, *The Sentimental Bloke: A Spring Song*

Reputation, reputation, reputation! O! I have lost my reputation, I have lost the immortal part of myself, and what remains is bestial. My reputation, Iago, my reputation!

Shakespeare, *Othello*

What's in a name? That which we call a rose
By any other name would smell as sweet.

Shakespeare, *Romeo and Juliet*

A good name is rather to be chosen than great riches.

Proverbs

Chapter 4

Stuart Albert and David Whetten

ORGANIZATIONAL IDENTITY

From *Research in Organizational Behavior*, 1985, 7: 263–295

EDITORS' COMMENTARY

Without any question, Albert and Whetten's disquisition on the organizational identification concept remains the most influential and most frequently cited academic
work on identity and identification. Their work represents a distinct tradition of
research and scholarship on identity among organizational behaviorists.

This tradition of scholarship has largely developed in isolation from the schools
of thought represented by the articles by Olins and Margulies. It is an approach that
has been highly influential among North American scholars. It is substantially different from the two earlier articles since the focus is mainly *internal*, with primary
importance being accorded to personnel's affinity with the organization rather than
on the acquisition of a favorable image. The authors' expansive overview of organizational identification presented here invariably forms the framework by which the
organizational identification concept is discussed.

The most enduring contribution of this chapter entitled "Organizational
Identity," which appeared in *Research in Organizational Behavior*, is Albert and
Whetten's tripartite characterization of identity. The authors state that in describing
or formulating a statement about an organization's identity, the following three
criteria should be used. It should:

1   capture the essence of the organization (*"the criterion of claimed central
      character"*);
2   distinguish the organization from others (*"the criterion of claimed
      distinctiveness"*);

3   exhibit some degree of sameness or continuity over time ("*the criterion of claimed temporal continuity*").

In its prosaic (and most frequently cited) form, Albert and Whetten's definition of organizational identification is that it encapsulates that which is *central, distinctive, and enduring* about an organization.

For much of the period since the publication of this article, their approach and explanation has gone unchallenged. Recently, however, Gioia, Schultz, and Corley,[1] writing in the *Academy of Management Review*, questioned the last of Albert and Whetten's three criteria, namely "the criterion of claimed temporal continuity" – that is, that identity is "enduring." These authors argued that an organization's identity is relatively fluid if not unstable. It is identity's fluidity and flexibility that is a particular strength and allows organizations to accommodate rapid environmental change. Others have adopted a similar stance. One suggestion is that the third characteristic (enduringness) would be better described as Balmer[2] did, namely as "evolving."

While Albert and Whetten's powerful characterization of identity is without doubt their work's most enduring legacy to identity scholarship, their ideas are notable in at least two other regards. The first is the notion that organizations have *multiple* identities. The second is their proposition that issues of identity come to the fore during different stages of an organization's *life cycle*.

The idea that organizations have multiple identities is discussed in some detail in the chapter. The authors give the example of a modern research university, which may metaphorically be characterized as a church as well as a business. This aspect of the article is important because it challenges the notion that organizations have a monolithic identity, and as such questions some of the firmly held beliefs by identity management, and by consultants. (Our own view of multiple identities is articulated at length in Chapter 1.)

The view that identity is of particular importance throughout different stages of an organization's life cycle is explained by means of the identification of six life cycle stages. Albert and Whetten argue that identity issues come to the fore for the organization: during its formation; upon the loss of the founder; on the accomplishment of an organization's *raison d'être*; during a period of rapid growth; when there is an anticipated change of status brought about through a merger or divestiture; and lastly, during a period of retrenchment.

This somewhat magisterial article is worthy of a good deal of analysis. It is perhaps the most academic of the articles in the anthology, but its importance and continued influence cannot be overstated. Its academic nature should not be dismissed lightly. Isaiah Berlin, Fellow of All Souls College, Oxford, and a consummate exponent of the history of ideas, appears to support our stance even though he was referring to thoughts of *one* professor rather than *two* professors, which is the case here! "Over a hundred years ago, the German poet Heine warned the French not to underestimate the power of ideas: philosophical concepts nurtured in the stillness of a professor's study could destroy a civilisation" (Isaiah Berlin[3]).

NOTES

1   Gioia, D. A., Schultz, M., and Corley, K. G., "Organizational Identity, Image and Adaptive Instability," *Academy of Management Review* 2000, 25 (1): 63–81.

2   Balmer, J. M. T., "Corporate Identity, Corporate Branding and Corporate Marketing: Seeing through the Fog," Special Edition on Corporate Identity and Corporate Marketing: *European Journal of Marketing* 2001, 35 (3/4): 248–292.

3   Berlin, I., in H. Hardy (ed.) *Isaiah Berlin: The Power of Ideas*, London: Chatto and Windus, 2000, p. ix.

THE OBJECTIVE OF THIS chapter is to define and develop the concept of identity[1] within an organizational setting, to consider what the term organizational identity might mean that is clear, distinctive, important, useful and measurable. Historically, identity has been treated as a loosely coupled set of ideas, distinctions, puzzles, and concepts that are best considered as a framework or point of view (Erickson, 1980, 1968; James, 1890; Mead, 1934). The empirical questions and hypotheses derived from this framework are not tightly interrelated and clearly bounded as would be the case in a well developed theory (Blumer, 1969). Our task is to build on this literature, to make the term "organizational identity" scientifically tractable. Specifically, our objective is to define, analyze, and illustrate identity in such a way that multiple empirical questions and hypotheses become visible. So that individual hypotheses and questions can be identified and easily referenced, we use the notation, superscript "Q," to denote statements that are important empirical questions, and "H" to denote statements offered as hypotheses.

Our discussion is organized in two parts. Part I examines a number of issues concerned with conceptualizing and defining organizational identity. Part II illustrates the concept of identity and dual identity in a concrete organization by means of a method that we label *extended metaphor analysis*.

I The three criteria definition of identity

Organizational identity as a concept has two uses. First, it is employed by scientists to define and characterize certain aspects of organizations – the scientific concept of organizational identity; and secondly, it is a concept that organizations use to characterize aspects of themselves (i.e., identity as a self-reflective question). Our goal in the following discussion is to address both uses, to contribute to the development of identity as a scientific concept, and to examine how organizational members use the concept of self-identity.

With respect to an organization's use of the concept, a prototypical sequence leading to questions regarding identity might be the following: an organization may decide which of several new products to market, which of several companies to acquire, which of several divisions to sell. or how to absorb a 20% budget cut internally. In short, organizations face choices of some consequence. Debate surrounding the alternatives is usually carried out, at least ideally, in terms of some model of rationality in which questions of information, probability, and expected utility dominate the discussion. When these considerations are not sufficient to resolve the question, and the importance of the question is inescapable, questions of information will be abandoned and replaced by questions of goals and values. When discussion of goals and values becomes heated, when there is deep and enduring disagreement or confusion, someone may well ask an identity question: "Who are we?" "What kind of business are we in?" or "What do we want to be?"

In this sequence lies a principle of solution; namely, that a problem will be solved in the easiest, most satisfactory way: by obtaining facts if that is easy, by calculation if that is easy, or by discussing values that are easiest to discuss and on which there will most likely be a consensus. Questions of identity will, typically, be raised only when easier, more specific, more quantifiable solutions have failed. When the question of identity is raised, we propose that an organization will form a statement that is minimally sufficient for the purpose at hand. It does so, we speculate, because the issue of identity is a profound and consequential one, and at the same time, so difficult, that it is best avoided. Consequently, under ordinary circumstances, the answer to the identity question is taken for granted.

When the question of identity triggers a search for answers in the organization's culture, philosophy, market position, or membership, we propose, by way of a preliminary definition, that an adequate statement of organizational identity satisfies the following criteria:

1   The answer points to features that are somehow seen as the essence of the organization: *the criterion of claimed central character*.
2   The answer points to features that distinguish the organization from others with which it may be compared: *the criterion of claimed distinctiveness*.
3   The answer points to features that exhibit some degree of sameness or continuity over time: *the criterion of claimed temporal continuity*.

For purposes of defining identity as a scientific concept, we treat the criteria of central character, distinctiveness, and temporal continuity as each necessary, and as a set sufficient. To develop identity as a scientific concept, we bring relevant theory to bear on each of the three criteria of our definition. What we will define as important about an organization will depend on how we characterize the organization as a whole. Consider the notion of organizational culture (Louis, 1981; Pondy, Frost, Morgan, and Dandridge, 1983). Is culture part of organizational identity? The relation of culture or any other aspect of an organization to the concept of identity is both an empirical question (does the organization include it among those things that are central, distinctive and enduring) and a theoretical one (does the theoretical characterization of the organization in question predict that culture will be a central, distinctive, and an enduring aspect of the organization). We will use the three defining criteria of organizational identity as a framework for our discussion. Each criterion, or aspect of a provisional statement of identity, generates a host of empirical questions and poses certain distinctive hypotheses and propositions that together form an emerging research agenda for an identity distinctive framework.

Identity as a statement of central character

What the criterion of central character means is that the concept of organizational identity, whether proposed by a scientist, by another organization, or by the organization itself, must be a statement of identity which distinguishes the organization on the basis of something important and essential. However, no theory at this point is capable of providing a universal list of all aspects of an organization that could be said to be important against those which could be said to be demonstrably unimportant. Often the issues will become important for a purpose. It is therefore not possible to define central character as a definitive set of measurable properties. Instead, for a given organization, a given purpose, and from a given theoretical viewpoint, one must judge what is or is not central.

The central character criterion raises a number of empirical questions about the organization's concept of identity. For example, how do organizations answer the identity question (Q1), and how are their answers affected by the context of the question (Q2)? Just as an individual may supply his fingerprints, name, address or social security number as different forms of identification for different purposes, so an organization may also focus on different essential characteristics depending on the perceived nature and purpose of the inquiry. For example, we expect organizations to provide different answers when they are contemplating acquiring a new subsidiary as opposed to preparing a legal brief supporting a claim for tax exempt status. When making an acquisition, decision makers will likely consider how the alternative business under consideration will affect the culture, product mix, financial status, and strategic goals of the acquiring company. Whereas, in the case of the court battle over a firm's tax classification, the characteristics of its membership, the humanitarian nature of its activities, and the source and use of its revenues will all be scrutinized.

These contrasting statements of identity present an interesting comparison. In the first case, the organization's identity is being discussed between organizational members only and there is no immediate threat to the organization's core identity. In contrast, in the court case the essential characteristics of the organization will be debated openly between adversaries and the outcome will have serious long term ramifications for essential, defining characteristics. A common ingredient in both cases is that the essential characteristics of the respective organizations are the focus of important decision making activities. Organizational leaders are attempting to define the organization's central characteristics as a guide for what they should do and how other institutions should relate to them. Furthermore, the key actors involved are concerned with the impact that future activities will have on the core organizational identity. Thus we see that alternative statements of identity may be compatible, complementary, unrelated, or even contradictory. How organizations elaborate, disambiguate, or defend a given statement of identity in the face of challenge is a fruitful line of research suggested by an identity distinctive framework (Q3).

Identity as a classification that identifies: single, dual and multiple identity

A primary meaning of the term identity in most formulations is that identity is a classification of the self that identifies the individual as recognizably different from others (and similar to members of the same class). This is the sense of identity that Erickson refers to as *individual* identity (Erickson, 1980, p. 109). In this usage, identity is linked with the term identification. Identity serves the function of identification and is in part acquired by identification.

While it is likely that there will be some empirical overlap between the essential and unique criteria of identity (in those cases where an essential element of an organization also makes it unique from others), these criteria are nonetheless logically independent, since all essential characteristics need not be unique and vice versa. For example, in the quest for brand loyalty it is not sufficient for a company to point out to consumers the essential ingredients in a product that justify its purchase. Marketing campaigns go beyond this and emphasize how product x differs from all other competing products, which may share most or even all of the same ingredients.

Organizations define who they are by creating or invoking classification schemes and locating themselves within them. From a scientific point of view (McKelvey, 1983; McKelvey and Aldrich, 1983; Scott, 1981), the classification schemes implied by statements of identity are likely to be highly imperfect. The schemes may not be completely elaborated or defined, their dimensions may be assembled without a consistent plan and without care to their independence. The organization may only be ambiguously or vaguely located within each scheme, and different schemes may be employed on different occasions with self-interest the only principle of selection.

The dimensions selected to define an organization's distinctive identity may be quite eclectic, embracing statements of ideology, management philosophy, culture, ritual, etc. Relevant dimensions may include habitual strategic predispositions: for example, a known willingness to take high risks, as might be the case for a company that is distinctively defined by its entrepreneurial activities. Indeed, in those cases in which a distinctive identity is prized, one might expect organizations to select uncommon dimensions of interorganizational comparison as well as uncommon locations along more widely employed dimensions. In addition, which classification scheme is invoked may well depend on the perceived purpose to which the resulting statement of identity will be put. In this sense there is no one best statement of identity, but rather, multiple equally valid statements relative to different audiences for different purposes.

From our point of view, the formulation of a statement of identity is more a political-strategic act than an intentional construction of a scientific taxonomy. We treat the problem of imprecise, possibly redundant, or even inconsistent multiple classifications at different levels of analysis not as a methodological problem to be solved, nor as a deficiency of the concept of identity, but as a description of the facts of self-classification to be examined and explained. What is of interest is studying the ways in which the organizational self-classification implied and articulated by a statement of identity departs from the requirements of a scientific taxonomy (McKelvey, 1983). It is important to entertain the possibility that precise self-classification may be both impossible and, more importantly, undesirable for a number of reasons (Q4):

1   Ambiguous classification may prevent the organization from being typecast and thereby rendered more predictable than desired;
2   The complexity of the organization may make a simple statement of identity impossible;
3   Since organizations change over time, an overly precise or micro-classification might quickly become outdated;
4   Since identity is usually assumed and only critically examined under certain conditions and then resolved with a minimal answer, we would not expect the formulation of identity to be honed to great precision.

For these, as well as other reasons, our view of organizational identity refers to a process of classification that is typically at variance with the canons of constructing scientific taxonomies (for example, that the same organization must be classified into the same categories by multiple independent observers or judges). Indeed, what we find fascinating about this concept are the dynamics behind cases where agreement is unlikely. This leads us to wonder, "Under what circumstances and on what bases will there be disputes about the issue of identity change, and under what conditions and in what ways will these disputes be resolved?" (Q5).

The identity examination process can be conducted both internally and externally with varying degrees of specificity (Meyer and Rowan, 1977). Externally, the question, "What kind of organization is this?" is asked by scientists to establish boundaries of generalizability, by laymen to facilitate social interaction and commerce, and by public officials to establish responsibility and eligibility. In general, this question can be answered adequately utilizing a fairly gross categorization scheme (e.g., age, business/nonbusiness, approximate number of members, scope of activities, and location). In contrast, the more piercing question, "Who are we?" tends to focus on more specific, sensitive, and central characteristics (e.g., ethical, entrepreneurial, employee-oriented, stagnating, and predatory).

However it is conducted, the search is always for that formulation that will distinguish the organization from others. For the individual, the search for identity has historically sought to distinguish man from machine (what is alive from what is not) and man from other "lower" forms of animals. A traditional answer to what makes man distinctive and therefore provides his identity is that he has a self; whereas, machines and animals do not. The important point is that how distinctiveness is defined depends critically on what other objects of comparison are deemed relevant.

Two issues are closely associated with the notion of identity as a classification that identifies: the issue of distinguishing between public and private identity, and the issue of conveying identity to others.

One of the traditional distinctions within the identity literature is between the presentation of self to outsiders (public identity or personal) and the private perception of self (private identity). This distinction suggests two propositions at the organizational level: First, the greater the discrepancy between the way an organization views itself and the way outsiders view it (keeping "intentional ambiguity" within reason), the more the "health" of the organization will be impaired (i.e., lowered effectiveness [H1]). When organizational members possess a view of the organization's goals, mission, and values, that differs radically from views held by outsiders such as customers, regulatory bodies, financial institutions and competitors, the organization will have difficulty generating the political and resource support necessary to guarantee its survival (Cameron and Whetten, 1983a; Goodman and Pennings, 1977; Pfeffer and Salancik, 1978). Second, publically presented identity will typically be both more positive (H2) and more monolithic (H3) than the internally perceived identity. For example, universities typically present themselves as the realization of different but harmonious purposes, such as teaching, research and service, rather than as organizations torn between conflicting objectives. The university does not make its claim for public resources on the desirability of creatively managing the tension derived from inherently incompatible goals. It prefers to see itself as an umbrella for the synergistic combination of diverse and valued ends.

While information about organizational identity is often disseminated via official documents such as annual reports and press releases, public identity is also often conveyed through signs and symbols. An identity distinctive framework highlights questions surrounding the choice and modification of these symbols, such as logos and sales slogans, product packaging, and the location and appearance of the corporate headquarters. This does not mean that the study of signs and symbols is the exclusive province of an identity framework. However, the study of signs and symbols does naturally arise out of a conception of identity as identification (as in "identification with").

Many credit the miraculous recovery of the Chrysler corporation to the public's (congress, bankers, customers, unions) identification with Lee Iacocca as a dedicated, energetic, innovative leader whose company deserved another chance. He successfully portrayed Chrysler as an underdog who was fighting for survival against great odds. By aligning his company's cause with core societal values, he was able to weld together a diverse coalition of supporters.

Mono and dual identity organizations. In both everyday language and in more formal scientific discourse, we tend to treat most organizations as if they were either one type or another, for example, church or state, profit or nonprofit. This taxonomic tradition assumes that most organizations have a single and sovereign identity. The alternative assumption is that many, if not most, organizations are hybrids composed of multiple types (H4).

By a hybrid we mean an organization whose identity is composed of two or more types that would not normally be expected to go together. Of such an organization we would say that it is part X and part Y, the simplest case of which is a hybrid of two types, a dual identity organization. Thus, it is not simply an organization with multiple components, but it considers itself (and others consider it) alternatively, or even simultaneously, to be two different types of organizations.

We take as indirect evidence for the existence of hybrids the difficulty of applying any taxonomic scheme to any set of existing organizations, which almost always results in a number of cases that are difficult to classify (Scott, 1981, p. 45). Rather than attribute the difficulty of achieving precise classification solely to deficiencies of the taxonomic scheme itself (e.g., imprecise rules of classification, insufficient information about the organization), we prefer to point to the probable existence of genuine hybrids.

We distinguish two forms of duality, one in which each unit within the organization exhibits both identities of the organization and one in which each internal unit exhibits only one identity – the multiple identities of the organization being represented by different units. The former, in which each internal unit exhibits the properties of the organization as a whole, we label the *holographic* form. The latter, in which each internal unit exhibits only one identity, is the *ideographic* or *specialized* form. These two forms of internal structure give rise to very different kinds of organizations.

The ideographic form of dual identity is analogous to Thompson's (1967) concept of buffering an organization's core technology with support systems in that the central mission of the organization is sheltered from external demands by a cadre of specialists who are only marginally involved in the core activities and ideology of the organization. Oftentimes, their primary commitment is to their professional role in the organization, rather than the central institutional values of the organization. An example of this structural arrangement might be a bank that is operated by a religious organization. The central decision makers are also church officials committed to advancing the interests of the church through the bank, as well as ensuring that the bank operates according to the moral code of the church. But the peripheral functions of the banking operation (e.g., accountants and computer operators) are performed by personnel hired primarily on the basis of their technical expertise. Within this structural arrangement the organization's pluralism is evident across units but not within units. Each unit is staffed with pure-types and interaction between units is limited by the normal structural impediments of couple bureaucratic institutions.

In contrast, the holographic form of dualism is more similar to the Theory Z approach to management proposed by Ouchi (1981) in which different, and to some extent conflicting, management styles are blended together and diffused evenly throughout the entire organization. In the case of the bank operated by a religious order, the holographic form would require that all members of the organization be members of the sponsoring church and that their performance would be evaluated using the joint criteria of technical proficiency and religiosity.

It is interesting to speculate about the relative adaptive advantage of the holographic and ideographic organizations. On the one hand the ideographic organization is likely to possess greater variety, since it contains greater specialization and more pure types. (Relaxing the condition that all elements must subscribe to a common value system in a normative organization allows for greater variability.) Hence, following Ashby's law of requisite variety (1962), members of ideographic organizations should be better prepared to monitor diverse environmental conditions and formulate appropriate recommendations for adaptive organizational modifications (H5).

On the other hand, the obvious disadvantage of the ideodentic organization is the relative difficulty it has gaining commitment from its members for a given course of action. While it has become almost axiomatic to state that organizations are composed of political interest groups vying for control over the collective resources (Pfeffer and Salancik, 1978), the conflict in an ideographic organization is more fundamental. It is a struggle, not simply over alternative budget proposals, but over the very soul of the institution. In the case of the religiously owned bank this type of struggle will be signaled by the accountants referring to the controlling administrators as impractical religious fanatics and the accountants being labeled as valueless mercenaries. As the relative power of the various ideological groups builds and diminishes, the identity of the organization as a whole will be altered in complexion, leading outsiders to complain that the organization cannot decide what it wants to be or who it wants to serve. Hence, while the holographic organization has less diversity to draw upon in formulating a "correct" plan of action, once a plan has been proposed leaders will be able to draw upon common characteristics across all units as the basis for establishing consensus (H6).

Identity over time

The temporal aspect of the concept of identity is essential. A central proposition in the identity literature is that loss of identity (in the sense of continuity over time) threatens an individual's health. In fact, it was Erickson's original observations that the disturbances of army personnel after World War II might be derived from their loss of continuity with their previous life that led him to originate the concept of ego identity as a sense of sameness over time which was necessary for psychological health (Erickson, 1968).

Is this the same as saying that change is difficult? In a certain sense, yes, since change may involve loss. But what an identity framework adds that is distinctive is a concern with the characteristic ways human beings deal with loss through mourning, grief, and ritual. Therefore, by applying an identity framework to the study of organizations we are naturally led to ask questions about mourning and grief during changes involving loss, and about the existence, desirability, and feasibility of identity-related rituals [e.g., "organizational funerals" conducted for plants that are closing or subsidiaries that are being sold (Albert, 1984)].

At the individual level, an identity distinctive inquiry is one that examines the interplay between what an individual may potentially become, what is available to him at a given time, and how those sets of roles and identities are themselves changing over time (Lifton, 1970). Specifically, it addresses three issues: (1) the potential of the individual assuming different identities or roles; (2) the kinds of roles or identities currently available; and (3) how the relationship of (1) to (2) is affected by the historical forces operating at the time.

At the organizational level it is interesting to speculate about the analogues of gaining and losing identity-related roles, such as parent and child, friend and enemy, policeman and outlaw, leader and follower, teacher and pupil. Certainly the frequent reference to terms like industry leader, maverick, predator, and entrepreneur in the business literature suggests that organizational roles exist. An identity distinctive framework underscores the need to examine how new roles come into existence, how organizations choose (or back into) one role rather than another, and how that action affects the organization's internal and external identity. The identity interaction model (Cooley, 1922; Goffman, 1959; Mead, 1934) states that individual identity is formed and maintained through interaction with others. At the organizational level this poses the question of whether an organization can be said to undergo socialization into a particular role through interaction with other organizations (Q6). If so, are the general laws that describe the socialization of an organization similar to those that describe the socialization of an individual into an organization?

The identity literature suggests that similar processes indeed occur at both levels. In discussing individual identity formation, Erickson (1968) analyzes the problem of identity formation in terms of a series of comparisons: (1) outsiders compare the target individual with themselves; (2) information regarding this evaluation is conveyed through conversations between the parties ("polite boy," "messy boy") and the individual takes this feedback into account by making personal comparisons with outsiders, which then; (3) affects how they define themselves. It follows from this logic that organizational identity is formed by a process of ordered inter-organizational comparisons and reflections upon them over time (Albert, 1977).

When identity becomes a salient issue: some time-dependent hypotheses. Perhaps the most useful contribution of the individual identity literature to the temporal aspect of identity is in the form of a question: Can we predict when organizational identity will emerge as an issue for an organization as a function of time-dependent processes that affect many if not all organizations (Q7)? While we acknowledge that life cycle development/concepts are controversial, especially at the organizational level (Cameron and Whetten, 1983b), we propose that the concept of identity suggests by analogy a number of intriguing testable hypotheses at the organizational level. Specifically, we suggest that the question of organizational identity will be particularly salient or important during the following life cycle events (H7–12):

1   *The formation of the organization (H7).* When the organization is forming and defining exactly what its niche will be, questions of goals, means, technology (all of which are components of defining who and what the organization is) will be salient.

2   *The loss of an identity sustaining element (H8).* If, for example, the founder of a young organization prematurely leaves, a period of soul-searching about organizational identity will occur in the process of searching for a suitable successor.

3   *The accomplishment of an organization's raison d'etre (H9).* The March of Dimes has become the classic example of an organization that worked itself out of a reason for existing. In that case, the organization maintained its central

mission of raising money for health research and shifted its focus from polio to birth defects. But a wide range of alternatives were examined at the time, including some which would have significantly altered the central focus of the organization.

4   *Extremely rapid growth (H10)*. When the ratio of choices faced by an organization is very high relative to its perceived constraints, a condition that might occur when profits or other resources greatly exceed their habitual use, then we can expect the organization to consider issues of identity. In a sense this is a condition analogous to adolescence when excess capacity is in search of use and direction.

5   *A change in "collective status" (H11)*. Marriage, birth, and divorce have been noted as marker events likely to trigger the reevaluation of a person's self-definition. In organizations, the threat of a hostile takeover, the consummation of a carefully planned merger, the divestiture of a previously central subsidiary, or the acquisition of a firm outside the parent company's industry will likely precipitate sharp debates regarding institutional mission, values, and identity.

6   *Retrenchment (H12)*. Retrenchment necessarily involves the definition of organizational identity because it requires the use of budgeting priorities which in turn require an answer to the question of who and what an organization is and what it wants to be (i.e., its descriptive and prescriptive identity) (Whetten, 1980). We hypothesize that the issue of organizational identity may be most acute during retrenchment following a period of slow rather than rapid growth. When organizations grow slowly, they acquire additional goals, missions, and objectives (and the different definitions of identity which these tend to imply). The incompatibility of the differing definitions remains latent until retrenchment forces their discovery.

We can further develop the issue of identity change over time by means of the following diagram (Figure 1, opposite) utilizing four common life cycle events (Birth, Growth, Maturity, Retrenchment) as markers for the temporal dimension. For purposes of illustration the two poles of the Y axis are labeled U for utilitarian identity, and N for normative identity. These two orientations will be described more extensively in the second half of the paper. For our discussion of Figure 1, it will be sufficient to think of a normative organization as a church, and a utilitarian organization as a business. Five paths are illustrated in Figure 1 representing several hypothetical paths of identity change (or lack of change) that may take place over the organizational life cycle. To simplify the diagram we have shown these paths for only the normative organizations. A complete diagram would also include the mirror image of these five paths for utilitarian organizations. Before we comment on each path we would like to propose a general tendency for the entire set of monotonic curves, specifically the tendency for monoidentity organizations to assume dual identities.

The drift from mono to dual identitities. A common proposition in the life cycle literature is that the identity of organizations frequently shifts from A to B at critical transition points (Kimberly, 1980; Lodahl and Mitchell, 1980). This

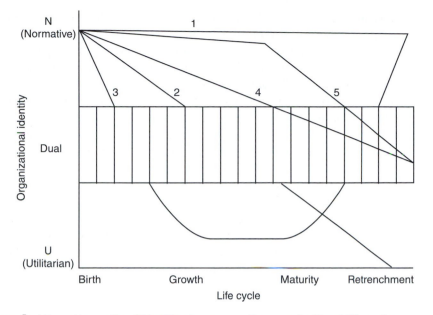

Figure 1 Alternative paths of identity change over the organizational life cycle.

generally occurs very gradually, and hence has been referred to as identity drift. Our proposal is related but different in an important way. We, too, are convinced that a key to understanding the evolution of an organization is tracking shifts in its identity over time, but we are primarily interested in the drift from A, or B, to AB. While the shift in an organization's identity by a process of *substitution* is obviously an important aspect of the life cycle model, it is the shift resulting from the process of *addition* that we feel has been overlooked in the literature thus far. The arrows in Figure 1 illustrate our belief that over time there is a general tendency for monoidentity organizations to acquire a dual identity (H13). With increasing size churches may become more like businesses and businesses may adopt more of the normative structure and values of churches.

There are a number of reasons for postulating a drift towards dualism – reasons which are, in effect, a statement of the advantages and disadvantages of mono vs. dual identity at different points in the life cycle. Without attempting a comprehensive discussion in advance of the empirical documentation of the dualistic shift in a given case, the following reasons for expecting a dualistic shift seem plausible.

1. *Environmental complexity*. If the environment within which the organization is embedded grows more complex over time, presenting a mix of both opportunities and constraints, then a dual identity organization should have adaptive advantages over a monoidentity organization (H14). Again, following Ashby's principle of requisite variety, organizational effectiveness depends in part on the match between organizational complexity and environmental complexity. We propose that over time organizations acquire dual identities both to exploit the opportunities of an increasingly complex and changing environment, and to cope with increases in environmentally imposed constraints and regulations. The rapid increase in administrative ratio in institutions of higher

education during the past two decades in response to a potential expansion in governmental regulation and intervention illustrates this purpose.

2. *Duality by default*. There is a tendency for some organizations, particularly those in the public sector, to acquire multiple identities simply because they become the repository of all things that other organizations will not undertake (H15). For organizations with relatively little control over the scope of their mandate we expect this will be a common path to duality.

3. *The problem of identity divestiture*. It is generally easier to acquire a new identity during growth than to divest an identity during a time of retrenchment (Albert, 1984). Organizations tend to become committed to what they have been and seldom substitute new identifying characteristics for old ones (H16). If this proposition is true, then a drift towards duality would seem to be the necessary result of a process of identity accretion.

4. *Organizational success*. Very often organizations that are eminently successful in pursuing a single identity enter a second domain of activity because of their success in the first (H17). For example, the highly profitable and visible business firms in major metropolitan cities are often invited to assume a major role in supporting the arts. Similarly, a highly successful church may find itself overwhelmed with the administrative and economic detail necessary to meet the needs of its burgeoning congregations. In both cases, the highly successful monoidentity organization tends to acquire a dual identity by virtue of its success.

Path specific hypotheses. Path 1 of Figure 1 illustrates an organization that retains its identity throughout its life cycle. Paths 2 and 3 portray an organization changing its identity over the course of its life cycle, but consistently retaining a single identity (normative followed by utilitarian). In Path 2 this change is permanent, whereas in Path 3 the organization reverses back to its earlier ideological roots after a brief period of trying a new identity. While these shifts may be deliberate, for example, to exploit new opportunities, they are more likely to occur as a result of identity drift, especially for young organizations (H18) (Lodahl and Mitchell, 1980). As noted earlier, the identity of an organization during the growth phase of its life cycle exists often only in a latent form. It is taken for granted and lies submerged under the press of the day-to-day problems of managing growth. Under these conditions organizations often begin to play roles and take on orientations different from those originally envisioned by their founders. But this transformation process often occurs so unobtrusively and at such a slow pace that it is not fully recognized until an organizational crisis forces members to explicitly examine their collective identity. In some cases when the shift is recognized it is welcomed and pursued with great intensity (Path 2), while in others organizational members are shocked by the extent of the drift and take deliberate actions to return to their ideological roots (Path 3).

Fundamentalist churches and medical clinics provide interesting examples of these two paths. Many fundamental Christian denominations have undergone a radical shift in identity with the advent of the "electronic church." Several religious groups sponsor programs on television, including "wholesome family entertainment," Sunday morning services, revivals, talk shows, and fund raising campaigns for Christian colleges. This dramatic change in the form of worship has created considerable debate in the sponsoring church organizations. Advocates point to expanded impact, while detractors lament the loss of intimacy and the apparent intrusion of commercialism into their religious experience. The question, "Are we a church or a broadcasting service?" has led some churches to drop or at least modify their support of religious programming on television.

In a similar fashion when a group of independent physicians join together to form a medical clinic, debates over the identity of the emerging organization are quite predictable. The doctors hire professional managers to handle the business aspects of the clinic, but because they are part owners in the operation they insist on making recommendations for how the clinic could be operated more effectively. However, when the business managers respond to pressures to increase profitability with such measures as cost cutting, the doctors invariably complain about a loss of concern for the welfare of their patients. Discussions between the physicians bearing on the question, "Are we a business or a humanitarian organization?" influence the clinic's movement along Paths 2 and 3.

In general, we hypothesize that with increasing size and over time, a church will begin to look more like a business (H19), than a growing business will look like a church (H20). This occurs for the reasons outlined by Weber (1968) in his discussion of the routinization of charisma. Young, normative organizations are generally founded upon the ideological vision of a charismatic leader. Over time, the success of the movement creates administrative challenges that can be met adequately only by the establishment of formal organizational structures, rules, procedures, etc. Empirical support for this proposition comes from Pettigrew's (1979) study of English public (our private) schools. He found that public schools which were the most successful through their initial growth and maturity phases replaced their entrepreneurial founder with a "steady state manager" capable of routinizing what initially began as an ideologically driven educational program.

However, it is also interesting to examine the case of utilitarian organizations that acquire a normative identity. To some extent this is the path described by Selznick (1957) in his discussion of the process of institutionalization in which the technical activities of an organization become infused with value beyond that associated with their technical function. As part of this process, businesses begin to define their value in terms of their contribution to the broad normative purposes of the society. instead of the more narrow economic marketplace. Selznick argues that institutionalization involves and requires that administrators become statesmen. The assumption of this new role is associated with a new set of incentives to maintain society's values and culture whether through philanthropy, assuming an active role in a private sector sponsored employment and training program (like the National Alliance of Businessmen), or by encouraging executives to take leaves of absence to serve in full time government or ambassadorial positions, teach in universities, and so forth.

A particularly interesting case of the acquisition of dual identity is an economic organization that acquires a normative identity by establishing relations with normative organizations. For example, a business may donate time and money to a charitable organization such as the United Way or the local arts council. If such activities are undertaken over a long enough time period and with enough commitment and emphasis, they may become part of the business' identity as a civic minded organization, a commitment which then becomes part of its fundamental character and which distinguishes it from other businesses. The advantage of a normative identity that is assumed by means of an interorganizational relationship rather than by a transformation of the organization itself is the ease with which such relationships can be modified or terminated when required. On the other hand, it can be argued that establishing an interorganizational link to a normative organization, rather than signaling movement towards the acquisition of a dual identity, is precisely the mechanism for avoiding it. The organization is in the position to claim a normative identity without the internal modification that the acquisition of such identity requires.

If Path 4 illustrates an incremental and long term tendency towards dual identity, Path 5 illustrates the hypothesis that scarcity motivates the acquisition of dual identity (H17). At such times, dual identity can occur for both internal and external reasons. Faced with retrenchment, a church, for example, may hire financial experts who may become so important that the financial criteria they espouse, such as cost effectiveness, may come to directly challenge other principles of decision making and the identity of the organization in the process. In its struggle for economic survival the normative organization may rightly fear the ironic truth of the slogan that it may be necessary to destroy the organization in order to save it. With respect to its external environment the organization may point to the economic benefits of its continued existence. The church in this example may point to its role in providing services to the poor which otherwise would have to be provided by others. Thus, a normative organization under attack can be expected to prepare a utilitarian defense, just as a threatened utilitarian organization will also seek to defend itself on normative grounds (H22). Economic-utilitarian organizations claim not only that they provide jobs and earn a profit for their stockholders, but that they contribute to the community at large. Who, after all, contributed to the museum when it was in need or gave jobs to the poor and absorbed the cost of training them, etc.

Summarizing our discussion of the pressures supporting the adoption of multiple identities, we hypothesize that Path I occurs infrequently (H23) and that Paths 2 and 3 occur less frequently than Paths 4 and 5 (H24).

II   An illustration of dual identity

A strategy for discovering the dimensions of identity

As a scientific concept, identity can be conceived of as a multidimensional construct where the problem is to identify, define, and then measure the dimensions of interest. There is, of course, no mechanical discovery procedure for what dimensions should be considered in a given case, just as, at the level of individuals, there is no agreed upon list of identities or roles that an individual might assume in the world. Our discussion thus far has considered the normative utilitarian dimensions. There are a large number of others that may be of interest but whatever dimensions are selected, the challenging scientific project is always how to define and measure them.

There are two broad, well-established approaches to the problem of definition and measurement (Pondy and Olson, 1977). The approaches differ in the extent that one begins with precisely defined dimensions. One may begin with no dimensions in mind at all. This approach, associated with an anthropological tradition, is purely inductive. A given organization is examined in detail without an explicit preconceived theoretical viewpoint, and those dimensions that define what is core, distinctive, and enduring are arrived at by inductive generalization from the organization's peculiar characteristics. At the other extreme, one may work deductively from a theoretical viewpoint that suggests or supplies relatively well-defined identity-relevant dimensions. For example, the dimension of profit/nonprofit is likely to be considered important in all economic treatments of the organization, and this dimension has achieved some definitional precision based on a body of theory and accepted practice, namely, tax law.

A third alternative that we illustrate here adopts a middle course. If there is no comprehensive theory to predict how many identities an organization has, or how the dimensions of each are to be defined, then another alternative is to *characterize* rather than to define each provisional identity and then carry out what we call *extended metaphor analysis* (EMA) as a way of retrospectively sharpening the definition of each identity and the dimensions that underlie or compose it.

Extended metaphor analysis can be viewed as a method for defining and characterizing one organization in terms of another. With respect to the normative–utilitarian dimension, EMA is a way of asking in what ways a given organization is like a church (representing a normative organization), or a business (representing a utilitarian organization). The ability to sustain two alternative metaphoric descriptions of the organization is the primary test of duality. To establish duality it must be shown that each metaphor can be applied to events of fundamental character that distinguish the organization from others, over time. The hypothesis of duality also assumes power to the extent that the metaphor is capable of being applied to a wide variety of organizational events in short, to the extent that the "fit" between the target organization and its metaphoric analogue is both close and extensive.

The target organization we have selected for demonstrating this method is the modern research university. Our hypothesis is that this organization has a dual identity, that of a church (normative identity) and a business (utilitarian identity). Further, we postulate that the identity of the modern research university has shifted from its normative, largely religious origins towards an increasingly utilitarian posture. This shift from a single to a dual identity illustrates Path 4 in Figure 1.

The discovery that an organization has a dual identity can be an important key in understanding its behavior under any circumstances, but particularly when issues of identity are assumed to be pivotal. One such time, according to our previous analysis, is retrenchment. For this reason we will follow our brief description of the university as a dual identity organization with a description of some of the implications of dual identity for understanding how this type of organization responds to retrenchment. As noted earlier, a dual identity organization facing retrenchment would be expected to encounter a host of difficulties in formulating policy and strategy and coping with internal conflict.

A characterization of the normative–utilitarian dimensions. We will preface our analysis of the comprehensive research university with a more extensive discussion of the normative and utilitarian constructs, drawing on the works of Parsons (1960). Etzioni (1975), and Cummings (1983).

A utilitarian organization is defined as one that is oriented towards economic production (Parsons, 1960). The principal case is the business firm, which will be the subject of our illustration. The business firm is an organization governed by values of economic rationality, the maximization of profit, and the minimization of cost, and for which financial return is both a condition of continuing operation and a central symbol of success. "Products are marketed on a full payment-of-cost basis involving prices governed by marginal utility, not by 'need.' Loyalties and obligations to the organization are defined in terms of 'self-interest.' Remuneration is the major means of control over lower participants and calculative involvement characterizes the orientation of the large majority of participants" (Etzioni, 1975, pp. 31, and 47).

The business firm is expected to "pay its way" on a utility–marginal productivity basis. In the long range it is expected to meet its costs through the monetary proceeds of its operations, with profit the symbol of its success and effective operation. An employee is expected to be paid what his services are worth as determined by a competitive market and will not be blamed for quitting if he can do better.

The business firm is a relatively centralized organization. Its procedures are removed from "democratic" norms. This centralization is legitimized by the expectation that management will be competent and that the interests of management and of the employees will be similar.

The concept of normative identity is typified by Parsons' pattern maintenance organization, the principal examples of which center on organizations with primarily "cultural," "educational," and "expressive" functions (Parsons, 1960, p. 40). Examples of organizations with clear normative patterns are: religious organizations, including churches, orders, and monasteries; a subcategory of political organizations that have a strong ideological program; general hospitals, universities, and voluntary associations. Normative power is the major source of control over most lower participants, whose orientation to the organization is characterized by high commitment. Compliance rests principally on the internalization of organizational directives that are accepted as legitimate. Leadership rituals, manipulation of social and prestige symbols, and resocialization are among the more important techniques of control (Etzioni, 1975).

Utilitarian organizations are largely managed by information, normative organizations by ideology, a distinction between two logical systems of management that was the subject of Cummings' presidential address (Cummings, 1983). As Cummings states:

> Management by information places major emphasis upon the instrumental function of managerial action and of organizational roles in

society. . . . This logic of management is most expressly seen in the technical functions of organizations and in the development of technologies and structures that are appropriate for processing and implementing nonstrategic decisions. Management-by-ideology . . . aims to design . . . organizational systems to serve the expressive functions of organizations in a society. The roles of leaders and followers are quite different in this management system. The purposes of organizations are assumed to be posterior, they are assumed to be basically rationalizations for organizational action. In addition, the cohesiveness of organizations is provided not by information, logic, and rationale, but by the acceptance of shared values, shared beliefs, and intensive socializational experience.

(Cummings, 1981, p. 2)

With these preliminary comments regarding the underlying constructs, we turn now to a description of the university as a dual identity organization.

The university's dual identity as church and as business. The university emerged from the cloistered environment of the monastery as the Age of Enlightenment created a demand for and legitimized the public pursuit of knowledge and understanding (Taylor, 1980). Consequently, it is quite natural to expect that the university of today should contain vestiges of its religious origins (Nisbet, 1979). This can be seen in the fact that both the church and the university have assumed the role of "living in the world, but not of the world." This means that they both assume that they have been given the role of leading the world rather than being led by external secular forces. Members of both organizations view outsiders as heathens to be converted/educated. It is believed that this transformation will make vulgar men virtuous. The value of this metamorphosis is supported in both institutions by an elaborate set of beliefs about the blessings of being righteous/ knowledgable. These include: being released from the bondage of sin/ ignorance; enjoying the benefits of inspiration/wisdom; and earning a sense of personal pride as a result of disciplining base instincts to achieve a higher, more righteous/refined level of development. Personal sacrifices (including financial contributions to the agent of transformation) are justified in terms of enhanced long term rewards (blessings in heaven/enhanced life time earnings).

Neither institution is expected to compete for members (parishioners/ students) in the same way that businesses compete for clients or customers. Indeed, that would be viewed by our society as undignified. (Only recently, as both institutions have suffered significant drops in membership, have they resorted to extensive advertising for support.) In general, society expects both institutions to be slow to change because they both serve as significant repositories of tradition. Universities and churches provide relief from the fast-paced, often meaningless and haphazard, day-to-day activities. Religious and educational traditions, symbols, and rituals provide members with a much needed representation of stability and security in their otherwise chaotic, anomic life. They enable individuals to periodically reaffirm what they feel are society's core values (Kamens, 1977).

For example, churches and universities have constructed elaborate rites-of-passage to commemorate the transitions from youth to adulthood (Bar Mitzvah), single life to married life (marriage), uneducated to learned (graduation). In these ceremonies participants and spectators alike renew their commitment to the underlying value system of their society. Recognizing the importance of these key transitions occurring under the aegis of these ideological institutions, civil marriages and "voc-tech" educational degrees are viewed with contempt by the true believers. They are viewed as instrumental transactions, rather than rites-of-passage. Because they don't recognize that part of the reason for going to college is to become socialized into a culture, and that part of the reason for getting married is to reaffirm support for essential moral values, the legitimacy of these secular imitations of sacred events is discredited by the faithful.

The university is like an ecumenical council. Each department has its own faith (discipline) and the university basically represents a "federation of faiths." The university derives its status from the quality of the federation members (colleges). Its function is to adjudicate disputes between the various denominations (departments) and to facilitate collaboration on issues of common concern. This arrangement accounts for the reluctance of university administrators to allocate resources disproportionately across departments. To say that Department A should have part of its funds withdrawn so that they can be given to Department B is tantamount to saying that the beliefs, values, and claims of one faith are more valid than those of another.

A common problem in all ideological organizations is assessing effectiveness. How can you measure the effectiveness of a teacher in fostering inquisitiveness, or the effectiveness of a minister in increasing faith? Because it is impossible to arrive at a consensus about how to measure ideological goal fulfillment, there is a tendency in churches and universities to substitute measures of efficiency for measures of effectiveness (Whetten, 1981). Since performance measures have a powerful effect on members' allocation of time and effort across activities, the natural consequence is that the organization inevitably becomes means instead of ends oriented.

For example, because we can't determine what percentage of a minister's congregation are admitted into heaven when they die, the quality of a minister's performance is instead judged by the average attendance at his meetings and the size of this congregation's weekly contributions. Similarly, since we can't quantify the long term impact of a teacher on a student we make some assumptions about the maximum number of students a teacher can effectively instruct and then treat faculty/student ratios as indicators of the quality of education.

There are many similarities between the ideology of the professor and the priest. Both universities and churches extol the virtues of poverty. Somehow, being poor is supposed to be enobling. Being rich, on the other hand, is viewed as debilitating because it interferes with one's single minded pursuit of religious/scholarly objectives. This view is of course consistent with the finding that under certain conditions the provision of external incentives for a task can undermine its perceived intrinsic worth (Deci, 1977).

The similarity between the ideology of the professor and the priest is also reflected in the explanation given for either individual forsaking his/her "calling" and joining a secular organization. In both cases, they basically conclude that the personal sacrifices they are required to make as members of the clergy or faculty are not worth the benefits. (These include low salary, restricted choice of places to live, pressures of the job, and in some cases the opportunity to marry and have a family.) In both cases defectors generally do not leave until they are personally convinced that leaving the university or church is not tantamount to ending up in purgatory, i.e., it is still possible to be intelligent, cultured, idealistic, religious, single-mindedly committed to a life of service or learning after leaving the university or church.

Churches and universities have similar socialization practices and reward status hierarchies. Both require a long apprenticeship, or novice period, during which a person is formally scrutinized by senior members of the organization. This period of proving oneself does not simply focus on technical skill proficiency. The commitment of the novice to the ideology of the organization is also critical. Once novices are ordained/given tenure, they have considerable autonomy in the organization. Consequently, the organization is very vulnerable to claims of both malpractice (failure of technical skills) and malfeasance (failure to fulfill normative expectations). Hence the need for very long socialization periods in both organizations (graduate school, post doc, assistant professor/ divinity school, internship, assistant minister).

That a university also has an identity as a utilitarian organization is evident from the claim that its training will be of use to the individual and to society. The concept of utility is at the heart of the notion of service which is part of the trinity of missions (teaching, research, and service) by which the organization justifies its support. The demonstrated utility of applied science and technology during World War II encouraged the view that science and technology were not to be valued for their own sake, but because they were necessary for both an enhanced quality of life and national defense. Federal research support for scientists, for which the university served as a conduit, helped change the identity of the university from a religious institution to a utilitarian one (Moynihan, 1980).

Since that time the university has had considerable difficulty satisfying its normative goal of living in the world but not of the world. As the amount of resources required to support research grew substantially in recent decades, universities found themselves increasingly competing with secular institutions for external support (Coleman, 1973). The requirements for competing successfully in the secular marketplace have resulted in a significant transformation of the academy. Normatively it still clings to its medieval roots as a religious institution, but its reward structure has become increasingly outcome-oriented. For example, faculty are rewarded less for how much wisdom they instill in the next generation, than for the number of publications they produce. The logic underlying this reward structure is that publications are a more fungible commodity than wisdom. The university can take publications and Nobel prizes into the marketplace and use them to barter for resources to buy the newest model of electron microscopes, etc.

The dysfunctional outcome of this trend is that the university is increasingly viewed by its members and external support groups as more instrumental (Jencks and Riesman, 1968; Kerr, 1963). Consequently, the organization is less able to use normative devices for securing commitment to the institution's goals. When faculty members perceive that they are being evaluated on the basis of the volume and quality of the commodities they are producing for the organization to sell in the marketplace, rather than on the basis of their contribution to the organization's missions of spreading the gospel of enlightenment, they respond in kind. One highly visible sign of this shift in commitment is the rapid growth of faculty unions in higher education (Cameron, 1982).

When we state that the university has begun to assume a utilitarian identity as well as a normative one, we mean more than that it has utilitarian goals as part of its mission statement. The internal organizing rules, norms, and attitudes increasingly reflect a utilitarian point of view. Our hypothesis is that the transformation of the university from a normative to a hybrid organization has occurred so slowly that its impact on internal work activities has largely gone unnoticed by participants. The lack of tension between these conflicting personas in the past can also be attributed to the combination of its peculiar organizational structure and relatively abundant resource support. The loosely coupled (Weick, 1976) ideographic structure of the university has acted as a set of boundaries, keeping apart what might be conflicting points of view, philosophies of education, rules of procedure, and priorities. Because it is a loosely coupled system, not only have departments that might be expected to champion normative vs. utilitarian identities been kept separate, but faculty (who as a body represent a normative identity) and administration (who represent a utilitarian orientation) rarely tend to cross the boundary between them. Professors of humanities rarely become accountants and vice versa.

During retrenchment, however, the conflict between normative and utilitarian identities, previously latent during growth and stability, becomes manifest in a series of issues:

Selective vs. across-the-board cuts. Small cuts, perhaps out of a sense of fairness and a desire to avoid the maximum pain caused any one unit will generally be distributed across the board. We hypothesize that a normative organization should be better able to sustain a deep across-the-board cut than a utilitarian one because normative organizations typically require a period of long socialization which generates a feeling of cohesiveness and common faith (H25).

The argument for across-the-board cuts is either that all elements of the organization are equally important to its survival and/or that it is impossible to tell which element is more important than any other. In our previous discussion of the university as an ecumenical council we pointed out that it is difficult to argue that one faith is more important than another on grounds that both faiths can accept. For this reason, university members will prefer that even deep cuts be administered across-the-board (Whetten, 1981).

Normative and utilitarian components within a dual identity organization may be expected to argue that *its* strategic focus is the one that the organization as a whole should adopt. Business and professional schools, and to some extent the sciences, particularly the applied sciences such as engineering, would be expected to propose some version of utilitarianism; namely, the doctrine that things ought to be valued according to their utility as determined in the marketplace. Nonapplied disciplines might well be expected to champion an alternative theory, such as the value of knowledge as an intrinsic good.

What is retained in a normative organization is likely to be different than what is retained in a utilitarian organization if only because the principles on which such decisions are made are quite different (H26). In a normative organization, the principle for determining what ought to be retained is tradition. In a utilitarian organization, the principle is cost-effectiveness (i.e., the instrumental claim that to delete something and retain something else maximizes some overall utility). In the case of the university, we could expect the university's normative components to respond to retrenchment by deleting all forms of knowledge other than those that existed in the medieval university. What is new is suspect. On the other hand, the utilitarian elements of the university should press to retain all that has value in the marketplace regardless of its date of origin. In parallel with this preference, we can expect normative elements of the university to utilize qualitative criteria in making decisions whereas utilitarian elements should prefer quantitative criteria.

Attitudes toward leadership. There is some reason to believe that normative and utilitarian organizations have different patterns of leadership (H27). Stinchcombe states, "Utilitarian organizations tend to have a multi-level, highly differentiated rank structure. . . . Normative organizations tend not only to be comparatively egalitarian, but also to stress the distinction between members and nonmembers, insiders ('believers') vs. outsiders ('heretics'), as the central status criterion, over any internal differentiations" (Etzioni, 1975, p. 278). If this characterization of the difference between normative and utilitarian organizations is true (and we can think of some major exceptions), then members of utilitarian organizations should expect the problem of retrenchment to be solved at the top, while members of normative organizations will demand greater participation and consultation.

Effective leaders of dual identity organizations should personify and support both identities. University presidents who were never professors (ordained members of the priesthood) will always be considered managers, not leaders. This deficiency should impair their effectiveness during retrenchment when they must be perceived as the champion of the normative as well as the utilitarian values of the institution.

Impact of retrenchment on organizational members. In utilitarian organizations, it is expected that members will stay or leave the organization depending primarily on the presence or absence of economic incentives (Hirschman, 1970). A threat to the economic health of the organization will cause members to leave. In normative organizations, however, it is assumed that members will leave only if they suffer a loss of faith. A leader of a normative organization will therefore expect disclosure of an outside threat to bind members more closely to the organization and to mobilize them in its defense. We hypothesize that the reverse will be true for utilitarian organizations (H28). In addition, normative organizations may have a greater tendency to regard themselves as unique than utilitarian organizations. If this is true, then individuals should be especially reluctant to leave since they will feel that they have nowhere else to go.

Organizational learning. Utilitarian organizations can be expected to seek management advice from outsiders more readily than normative organizations, who are probably inclined to believe that only an insider, a true member of the faith, can understand the workings of the organization (H29). For example, when the university has management problems, it is unlikely to hire outside management consultants for fear that they will not understand the culture of the organization or that they will make recommendations alien to it. The university is more likely to form a blue ribbon committee of Nobel prize winners (high priests) to solve internal management problems despite the fact that these individuals have little management expertise.

Planning for scarcity. Normative organizations are often prevented by law, and most certainly by ideology, from storing purely economic wealth against the contingency of future scarcity. Economic wealth not pressed into the service of the normative ideology of the organization would be considered misused. As a consequence, normative organizations will always be economically vulnerable, unless they are able to hide their wealth (from themselves and others) and/or unless they are able to redefine its meaning (H30).

The problems experienced by Boystown, a well-known home for orphans located near Omaha, Nebraska, in the early 1970s reflect this point. A newspaper article in the *Omaha Sun* in 1972, reported that Boystown had an endowment of over $209 million, or $300,000 for every resident – making it one of the richest incorporated villages in the United States. Since fund raising campaigns are based primarily on a perception of extreme need, this revelation was embarrassing to administrators at Boystown and made soliciting extremely difficult for several years. In an effort to justify their wealth, the trustees of Boystown announced an ambitious campaign to fund research on problems of youth.

Merger and divestiture. One common solution to retrenchment is merger since savings can often be achieved by eliminating duplication. Merger, however, is much more difficult if what is being brought together constitutes different faiths (H31). While there are always difficulties associated with merging two units, mergers between utilitarian units can claim justification that both can accept, namely the bottom line. Mergers between normative components or units does not have recourse to this common justification. In extreme cases, the argument is often made that merger is the only means to survival, but the critic is always present who will say that merger entails the loss of the organization, not its survival. Hence, just as it is extremely difficult, if not impossible, to merge faiths, so also is it impossible to divest a faith without a sense of irreparable loss.

Attitudes toward marketing the mission of the organizations. Utilitarian organizations engage in advertising and marketing, while normative/religious organizations engage in missionary work. In both cases, the organization seeks the benefits of increased size and support. Normative organizations, however, sometimes object to advertising on the grounds that selling something of intrinsic worth is demeaning or undignified. The argument seems to be based on the claim that if something of intrinsic worth can be demonstrated to have instrumental value, its intrinsic worth is diminished (i.e., to sell is to diminish the value of what is sold, see Deci, 1977). For this reason, we can expect the normative core of the university to be ambivalent about "selling" the university to outside constituents (H32).

The discovery of priorities. Not only would normative vs. utilitarian organizations be expected to arrive at different priorities in response to scarcity, but perhaps even more importantly, they will differ in the means by which those judgments are formulated (H33). As we have pointed out, normative and utilitarian organizations have different attitudes toward leadership, authority, participation, etc., all of which are involved in formulating priorities. The task of leadership in dual identity organizations undergoing retrenchment is to invent a mechanism for the discovery of organizational priorities that does not a priori value one organizational identity as more important than another; to do otherwise is to prejudge the issue which is at stake.

This example of the university as a church and as a business is intended to demonstrate the face validity of the concept of dual identity and to point to its potential theoretical and practical utility. We have not attempted a full and complete description of a business or a church, nor have we sought to identify all those features within the university to which they might be applied. Both of these tasks form the subject matter for future research along with the consideration of other metaphors and the possibility that a given organization may have more than two identities. The necessary first step however was to demonstrate that at least some aspects of the university could be viewed in terms of those two metaphors. Ultimately, the case for duality should be grounded not merely in the *type and importance* of organizational events that fit within another kind of organization, but by the *extent and distribution* of metaphorically interpretable events throughout the organization. An isolated instance is unlikely to be decisive (although it may be instructive). This was in part the reason that it was important to demonstrate that many aspects of the university could be viewed as churchlike or businesslike. Of course, EMA does not address the question of whether the university in our example *is* a church or *is like* a church (in some ways). If a university's identity as a school (neither church nor business) shrinks, there is a point where one may want to say *it is* a church and/or a business, not that it acts like them. Exactly when this point is reached is not something we can comment on here, but bears further thought.

Further description of extended metaphor analysis

Since the ability to sustain two alternative metaphoric interpretations of those organizational events that are somehow central, endure over time, and differentiate the organization from others is a major test of the hypothesis of dual identity, it is appropriate to comment about EMA in greater detail. EMA is in part a technique of sense making (Weick, 1969). One way in which an individual or organization makes sense of an event is by locating it as an instance of a more general law or framework. This is the hallmark of one form of scientific explanation, that Hempel and Oppenheim call the covering law model (1965). EMA can be conceived of as a method for constructing and elaborating a framework, i.e., an alternative organizational identity, within which events can be located and in terms of which they can be seen as sensible and intelligible. In concrete terms, the method consists of the evocation and testing of comparative and metaphoric statements of the following kind. With respect to some puzzling organizational event, (e), is the organization more like an X organization or a Y organization? Is (e) more likely to occur in X or Y? (frequency criterion)? Is (e) better understood or made sense of if we think of it as occurring in organization X rather than Y (sense making criterion)? Can we predict some new fact if we assume that the organization is like an X rather than a Y (predictive criterion)? If for a given organization we proceed in this manner asking in what ways it is like a large number of different organizations and we consistently come up with only the same two organizations in which a large class of events make sense, then we tentatively entertain the hypothesis of dual identity.

Of course, it is important to point out that metaphors distort and mislead as well as inform and make sense of aspects of organizational life. Hence, as part of the method, it is important also to include the question, in what ways is it misleading or inappropriate to consider a given organization to be like another?

We summarize this discussion of EMA in the following five steps.

1   Assemble a group of puzzles, difficulties, dilemmas, problems, features, characteristics, etc. for a target organization. For example, in our previous illustration take the puzzle that universities tend not to hire management consultants.

2   Characterize and broadly define a set of alternative organizations, institutions, etc. This is a critical step. If the candidates for multiple identity are narrowly chosen: for example, if it is proposed that an organization is both a high tech and a chemical company, it is not clear that this multiple classification will clarify anything of interest. Therefore, it is impossible to determine in the abstract whether an identity candidate will be of practical use.

3   Carry out EMA, as in our example of the university, asking in what ways the target is like each of the metaphor candidates.

4   Determine whether the target organization faces any of the six conditions predicted to be times when the issue of identity is likely to be salient (Figure 1). This suggests the extent to which conflicts over deep seated identity issues are likely to be visible for investigation (and by inference, the extent to which organizational difficulties and conflicts will likely be attributable to conflicts between identities).

5   Using each metaphoric identity predict a new set of difficulties that were not included in the original set obtained in step 1, and/or a new set of difficulties that could arise under another set of conditions, for example, merger rather than or in addition to retrenchment. In this step we treat

organizational identity as a Gestalt of properties. If a candidate identity is that of a church, for example, then we know that rituals will tend to be present along with certain kinds of goal preferences, etc. A description of a church, therefore, provides a domain to be searched for possible analogies. Does the target organization have rituals? In what way are they similar and in what way different to those of the church, etc.? Each metaphoric identity can be searched for areas of similarity and difference to the target organization.

Summary and conclusions

Conceptually, this chapter focused on the meaning, significance, and definition of the term identity as it is applied to organizations. We have presented identity as:

1. A particular kind of question. The question, "What kind of organization is this?" refers to features that are arguably core, distinctive, and enduring. These features reveal the identity of the organization. We have pointed out that identity literature is largely silent on which features an organization will select or claim. What is clear, however, is that organizations are capable of supplying multiple answers for multiple purposes, and that to recognize that fact and study the conditions that provoke different answers and the relationship of those answers to each other is an identity distinctive inquiry.

2. A distinctive framework for investigation. One value of the term identity and its conceptual surround is that it invites us to consider certain issues, ask certain questions, examine certain phenomena in a particular way that, if not exclusive, is at least distinctive. For example, the entire set of propositions examining the life cycle represents an identity distinctive point of view. New questions arise, such as whether organizations are socialized into their societal roles by rules and procedures isomorphic to those that describe and explain how individuals are socialized into organizations.

3. A critique of the monoidentity assumption. A major objective of this chapter has been to introduce and illustrate the concept of dual identity and to explore its implications for the management of organizations.

In general, this chapter should be read as a beginning formulation of the identity of organizational identity in which we have proposed a set of ideas, empirical questions, and hypotheses that together might be considered core, distinctive, and enduring. What the identity literature offers is not a single concept or theory but a diverse set of ideas, modes of analysis, questions and propositions. It is this richness that may be of use to organizational theory.

Note

1   While we will use the terms of organizational identity, organizational culture, and organizational character, we do not intend this usage to imply a principle of reductionism or its opposite. Identity and character usually apply to individuals, culture applies to societies. An organization is neither. Thus, while we use the terms organizational identity and

organizational character, we do not wish to treat the organization as an individual, which is to claim that the whole is like one of its parts; nor, while we retain the term organizational culture, do we wish to treat an organization as identical to the society in which it is embedded, which is to claim that the part is the same as the whole.

References

Albert, S. A design model for successful transitions. In J. Kimberly and R. Quinn (Eds.), *Managing organizational transitions*. Homewood, Ill.: Irwin, 1984.

Albert, S. Temporal comparison theory. *Psychological Review*, 1977, *84*, No. 6, 485–503.

Ashby, W. R. Principles of the self-organizing system. In H. Von Forester and G. W. Zopf (Eds.), *Principles of self-organization*. New York: Pergamon Press, 1962.

Blumer, H. What is wrong with social theory? In H. Blumer (Ed.), *Symbolic interactionism: Perspective and method*. Englewood Cliffs, N.J.: Prentice Hall, 1969.

Calder, B. J. An attributional theory of leadership. In B. M. Staw and G. R. Salancik (Eds.), *New directions in organizational behavior*. Chicago: St. Clair Press, 1977.

Cameron, K. S. The relationship between faculty unionism and organizational effectiveness. *Academy of Management Journal*, 1982, *25*, 6–24.

Cameron, K. S. and Whetten, D. A. *Organizational effectiveness: A comparison of multiple models*. New York: Academic Press, 1983a.

Cameron, K. S. and Whetten, D. A. Models of the organizational life cycle: applications to higher education. *Review of Higher Education*, 1983b, *6*, 269–300.

Coleman, J. S. The university and society's new demands upon it. In C. Kaysen (Ed.), *Content and context: Essays on college education*. New York: McGraw-Hill, 1973.

Cooley, C. H. *Human nature and the social order*. New York: Scribner, 1922.

Cummings, L. L. The logics of management. *Academy of Management Review*, October, 1983, *8*, No. 4, 532–538.

Deci, E. L. Effects of externally mediated rewards on intrinsic motivation. *Journal of Personality and Social Psychology*, 1977, *18*, 105–118.

Erickson, E. H. *Identity and the life cycle*. New York: Norton, 1980.

Erickson, E. H. *Identity, youth, and crises*. New York: Norton, 1968.

Etzioni, A. *A comparative analysis of complex organizations*. New York: Free Press, 1961. Revised edition 1975.

Goffman, E. *The presentation of self in everyday life*. New York: Doubleday, 1959.

Goodman, P. S. and Pennings, J. M. *New perspectives on organizational effectiveness*. San Francisco: Jossey-Bass, 1977.

Hempel, C. G. and Oppenheim, P. Studies in the logic of explanation. In C. G. Hempel (Ed.), *Aspects of scientific explanation*. New York: Free Press, 1965.

Hirschman, A. O. *Exit, voice and loyalty*. Cambridge, Mass.: Harvard University Press, 1970.

James, W. *The principles of psychology*, Vol. 1. New York: Holt, 1890.

Jencks, C. and Riesman, D. *The academic revolution*. Garden City, N.J.: Doubleday, 1968.

Kamens, D. H. Legitimate myths and educational organization: The relationship between organizational ideology and formal structure. *American Sociological Review*, 1977, *42*, 208–219.

Kerr, C. *The uses of the university*. Cambridge, Mass.: Harvard University Press, 1963.

Kimberly, J. Initiation, innovation, and institutionalization in the creation process. In

J. Kimberly and R. Miles (Eds.), *The organizational life cycle*. San Francisco: Jossey-Bass, 1980.

Lifton, R. *Boundaries*. New York: Random House, 1970.

Lodahl, T. M. and Mitchell, S. M. Drift in the development of innovative organizations. In J. Kimberly and R. Miles (Eds.), *The organizational life cycle*. San Francisco: Jossey-Bass, 1980.

Louis, M. R. A cultural perspective on organizations: the need for and consequences of viewing organizations as culture-bearing milieux. *Human Systems Management*, 1981, *2*, 246–258.

McKelvey, B. *Organizational systematics*. Berkeley: University of California Press, 1983.

McKelvey, B. and Aldrich, H. Populations, natural selection, and applied organizational science. *Administrative Science Quarterly*, 1983, *28*, 101–128.

Mead, G. H. *Mind, self and society*. Chicago: University of Chicago Press, 1934.

Meyer, J. W. and Rowan, B. Institutionalized organizations: formal structure as myth and ceremony. *American Journal of Psychology*, 1977, *83*, 340–363.

Moynihan, D. P. State vs. academe. *Harpers*, Dec. 1980, 31–40.

Nisbet, R. The future of the university. In S. M. Lipset (Ed.), *The third century: America as a post industrial society*. Stanford University: Hoover Institute Press, 1979.

Ouchi, W. *Theory Z: How American business can meet the Japanese challenge*. Reading, Mass: Addison-Wesley, 1981.

Parsons, T. *Structure and process in modern societies*. Glencoe, Ill.: Free Press, 1960.

Pettigrew, A. On studying organizational cultures. *Administrative Science Quarterly*, 1979, *24*, 570–581.

Pfeffer, J. and Salancik, G. *The external control of organizations: A resource dependence perspective*. New York: Harper & Row, 1978.

Pondy, L. R. and Olson, M. L. Theory of extreme cases. (Working paper no. 878.) Urbana: University of Illinois College of Commerce and Business Administration, 1977.

Pondy, L. R., Frost, P. J., Morgan, G., and Dandridge, T. C. *Organizational symbolism*. Greenwich, Conn.: JAI Press, Inc., 1983.

Robbins, R. Identity, culture and behavior. In J. Honigmann (Ed.), *Handbook of social and cultural anthropology*. Chicago: Rand McNally, 1973.

Scott, W. R. *Organizations: Rational, natural, and open systems*. Englewood Cliffs, N.J.: Prentice Hall, 1981.

Selznick, P. *Leadership in administration*. New York: Harper and Row, 1957.

Taylor, W. Leadership in higher education. Paper presented at Innovative Approaches to Higher Education Administration, Champaign, Ill., 1980.

Thompson, J. D. *Organization in action*. New York: McGraw-Hill, 1967.

Weber, M. *On charisma and institution building*. Chicago: University of Chicago Press, 1968.

Weick, K. E. Educational organizations as loosely coupled systems. *Administrative Science Quarterly*, 1976, *21*, 1–19.

Weick, K. E. *The social psychology of organizing*. Reading, Mass.: Addison-Wesley, 1969.

Whetten, D. A. Organizational responses to scarcity: exploring the obstacles to innovation in education. *Educational Administrative Quarterly*, 1981, *3*, 80–97.

Whetten, D. A. Sources, responses and effects of organizational decline. In R. Kimberly, R. H. Miles and Associates (Eds.), *The organization life cycle*. San Francisco: Jossey-Bass, 1980.

Chapter 5

Helen Stuart

THE EFFECT OF ORGANIZATIONAL STRUCTURE ON CORPORATE IDENTITY MANAGEMENT

From *Corporate Reputation Review*, 1999, 2 (2): 151–164

EDITORS' COMMENTARY

We first met Helen Stuart at the initial International Corporate Identity symposium held at Strathclyde Business School in 1994. Those were the formative days of identity studies, when academics were first beginning to explore the nature of the identity concept. Her paper was identified as the best academic paper at this event and it comes as no surprise to us that she subsequently won the "best research paper" award from the *Corporate Reputation Review*.

Stuart is one of the first of a new type of university don who specializes in business identity studies. She was one of the first to be awarded a doctorate in corporate identity studies and to offer courses in the area in her native Australia. There is an endearing pioneering spirit with which Helen approaches her subject area. It has an Australian directness − an ability to sort the wheat from the chaff. Her indomitable spirit, vim, and sense of fun is infectious. She is someone to be reckoned with whether on or off the golf course or as a scholar or teacher. Golf, unsurprisingly for a person with Scottish ancestry, is her favorite pastime. This article is very much a whole in one (pun intended)!

This chapter, entitled "The Effect of Organizational Structure on Corporate Identity Management," is particularly significant in that it reflects a distinct tradition of scholarship among a small group of marketing academics within the British Commonwealth.[1] Many of these scholars have been active in developing conceptual models that are broadly concerned with what we would regard as identity management. Unlike organizational behaviorists, who almost exclusively are concerned with the internal concerns and audiences, the approach adopted by marketing scholars from the Commonwealth attaches importance to both external and internal audiences.

Occasionally, this marketing perspective is seen as a counterbalance to the dominant school of thought: that from organizational behavior, with its primary concern in organizational identification. However, a closer examination of many of the conceptual frameworks reveals that a multidisciplinary, boundary-spanning (between the internal and external environment) approach has characterized the area since the 1980s. Whereas the organizational identification literature is gradually being accommodated within the marketing literature, this remains a one-way street.

Stuart's article, which is concerned with showing the inextricable link between corporate identity and structure, reflects the multiple roots of inquiry that now inform a good deal of marketing scholarship in the area. The marketing/Commonwealth approach is far removed from the narrow, graphic design conceptualization of corporate identity as evinced by the earlier article of Walter Margulies.

Stuart observes here that while a good deal of attention has been focused on employee identification, communication, and strategy vis-à-vis identity studies/the corporate identity mix, insufficient attention has been accorded to *corporate structure*. A key presupposition of Stuart's research is that cognizance should be taken of the symbiotic relationship between organizational structure and identity.

To this end Stuart draws on several well-known structural frameworks. These include the famous tripartite revised identity structure devised by Olins[2] (monolithic, endorsed, and branded). She also draws on Kammerer's[3] work; this categorizes the type of management and structural relationships that can exist between a holding company and its subsidiaries and/or business units. Kammerer identifies four types of relationship: financial, organizational, communicational, and single. Lastly, Stuart marshals Mintzberg's[4] framework, which reflects the forces that can influence organizations, these being entrepreneurial, machine, professional, diversified, innovative, and missionary. Stuart concludes that organizational structure should be considered whenever issues of identity are being considered. By this means an important facet of the identity concept can be revealed.

We believe this article demonstrates the maturity and sophistication with which marketing scholars now approach the corporate identity concept.

NOTES

1   Abratt, R., "A New Approach to the Corporate Image Management Process," *Journal of Marketing Management* 1989, 5 (1): 63–76; Abratt, R. and Mofokeng, T. H., "Development and Management of Corporate Image in South Africa," Special Edition on Corporate Identity and Corporate Marketing: *European Journal of Marketing* 2001, 35 (3/4): 368–386; Marwick, N. and Fill, C., "Towards a Framework for Managing Corporate Identity," Special Edition on Corporate Identity: *European Journal of Marketing* 1997, 31 (5/6): 396–409; Morison, I., "Breaking the Monolithic Mould," Special Edition on Corporate Identity in Financial Services: *International Journal of Bank Marketing* 1997, 15 (5): 153–162;

Melewar, T. C., Saunders, J., and Balmer J. M. T., "Cause, Effect and Benefit of a Standardized Corporate Visual Identity System of UK Companies Operating in Malaysia," Special Edition on Corporate Identity and Corporate Marketing: *European Journal of Marketing* 2001, (3/4): 414–427; Dowling, G. R., "Developing Your Company Image into a Corporate Asset," *Long Range Planning* 1993, 26 (2): 101–109; Leitch, S. and Motion, J., "Multiplicity in Corporate Identity Strategy," Special Edition on Corporate Identity: *Corporate Communications: An International Journal* 1999, 4 (4): 193–199; Kirikidou, O. and Millward, L. J., "Corporate Identity: External Reality or Internal Fit?," *Corporate Communications: An International Journal* 2000, 5 (1): 49–58.

2   Olins, W., *The Corporate Personality: An Inquiry into the Nature of Corporate Identity*, London: Design Council, 1978.

3   Kammerer, J., *Beitrag der Produktpolitik zur Corporate Identity*, Munich: SBI-Verlag, 1989.

4   Mintzberg, H., *Minztberg on Management*, New York: The Free Press, 1989.

Introduction

THIS PAPER EXPLORES the significance of organizational structure in relation to the capacity of an organization to develop an effective corporate identity. Although attention has been given to corporate identity structures (Ind, 1992), and the relationship between these structures and internal organizational structures has been explored (Ind, 1997), the effect of organizational structures on the corporate identity management has not been examined in detail. However, van Riel (1995, 47) noted that complex organizational structures have difficulty in effectively communicating the corporate identity and, along with Ind (1997), suggests that a branded identity is the most appropriate corporate identity structure in these cases.

According to Downey (1986/87, 8–9), good corporate identity management means that '. . . the organization can project the kind of focus and commitment that simply wasn't possible before . . . determination of basic identity crystallizes a company's essence and purpose'. Various authors (Kennedy, 1977, Dowling, 1986, Abratt, 1989, Marwick and Fill, 1997, Stuart, 1998) have developed conceptual models of the corporate identity management process. The underlying assumption behind all such models is that, if the corporate identity is well managed, then the resulting corporate image will accurately reflect the values, beliefs and strategic direction of the company. However, although these models have included corporate strategy and culture as variables in the process, attention to other critical variables related to corporate strategy, such as organizational structure, employee identification and corporate identity structure, have not been accounted for.

In fact, most conceptual models of corporate identity management make the assumption that the passage from corporate personality to corporate identity to corporate image is unimpaired if management follows appropriate corporate identity strategies, focusing on *behaviour communication and symbolism* (van Riel, 1995, 32). Organizational identification is assumed to be part of this process. However, a study by Balmer (1994) of BBC Scotland revealed that several sub-cultures existed in this organization, and that factors such as industry ideology, professional ideology and political ideology affected the degree to which employees identified with the overall corporate identity of the BBC. This study revealed that a unified corporate identity is not easily achieved in every organiza-tion, despite organizational commitment to corporate identity management.

Additionally, corporate identity management problems are often perceived as external ones. Balmer's (1995) 'hierarchy of schools of thought in corporate identity' typified the way in which various writers and practitioners depict corporate identity management issues. For example, The Design School was purely concerned with keeping the corporate graphic design fashionable. The Strategic School looked at questions related to corporate strategy and position-ing, whereas the Behavioural Focus School focused on issues pertaining to cor-porate culture. The Communications School was concerned with issues relating to the way in which the company communicates. Balmer perceived these schools of thought as ways in which corporate identity management problems were viewed and this perception affected the way in which practitioners attempted to correct the problems. Although the Behavioural Focus School examines corporate culture, the wider issue of the way in which organizational structure affects the extent of employee identification with a dominant culture is given only passing attention.

Corporate identity structures

Fombrun (1996) wrote that the three factors which account for various types of identities are *products, strategy and corporate identity structure*. The current models of corporate identity management appear to take account of the first two factors. The third, corporate identity structure, is one which Fombrun (1996) addresses in relation to organizational structure indirectly. As in the case of van Riel (1995), the suggestion is made that complex or diversified organizations should adopt branded corporate identity structures. However, a comprehensive investigation of the effect of organizational structure on corporate identity management has not been undertaken.

Ind (1992) noted that there were three basic types of visual structures for corporate identity, namely monolithic, endorsed or branded. The strengths and weaknesses of each structure were described by Ind (1997) and a summary of these is shown in Table 1. As can be seen from this table, each corporate identity structure has its strengths and weaknesses in relation to corporate identity man-agement. However, this perspective does not identify comprehensively the types of structures that are suitable for different types of organizations.

Another way of looking at corporate identity structures was proposed by Kammerer (1988). He identified different structures according to the goals of

Table 1 Corporate identity structures

Identity structure	Rationale	Strengths	Weaknesses
Monolithic	Identity built around a clearly defined idea	High visibility. Economies of communication	Every business under threat in the case of adverse event. May curb innovation due to risk to whole identity
Endorsed	Visible parent company but subsidiary companies are strong brands that keep their own style	Goodwill associated with brands the company has acquired is maintained	Difficult to give sense of purpose to multi-faceted organization. Difficult balancing act
Branded	Wide diversity of businesses within corporate portfolio	Brands are free to develop identities of their own. Suitable for fast moving consumer goods and conglomerates	Difficult to communicate strength to financial audiences. Corporate reputation may suffer due to fragmented identity

Source: Derived from Ind (1997).

the parent company. Four types of identity structures called 'action types' were classified. These are described in Table 2. As can be seen from this table, Kammerer's structures are quite similar to those of Ind. However, Kammerer divided the branded identity into two types: one where there is no involvement of the parent company and the other where the cultures of the subsidiaries are influenced by the parent company. Van Riel (1995) took this approach further by reasoning that the crucial issue is the extent to which the choice of communication policy reveals the parent behind the brand (labeled as 'parent visibility') in combination with the agreement about the common starting points in all company communication (labeled as 'content guiding'). This classification is shown in Figure 1.

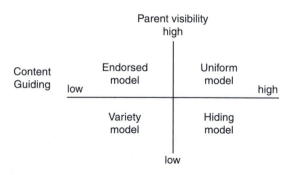

Figure 1 Van Riel's classification of identity structures

Source: Van Reil (1995)

Table 2 Kammerer's identity structures

Action type	Explanation	Advantage
Financial orientation	Subsidiaries are purely financial participants, retaining their own identity and parent company does not interfere	Completely separate identities
Organizational-oriented corporate identity	Sharing of organizational rules by parent company and subsidiaries. Culture of subsidiaries influenced but functioning of corporate identity internal, not visible to outside world	Culture of subsidiaries compatible with parent company
Communication-oriented corporate identity	Fact that subsidiaries belong to parent company is clearly expressed in advertising and symbolism	Conveys size to target groups which increases confidence of subsidiaries
Single company identity	All actions, messages and symbols come across as one consistent whole	Consistency

Source: Derived from Van Riel (1995).

Each schema has its merits in describing the corporate identity structure of an organization. The particular corporate identity structure chosen by an organization may be appropriate in relation to organizational structure at one point in time. However, organization changes such as expansion, diversification, deregulation and so on may mean that, at some point, the type of corporate identity structure chosen does not fit the organizational structure. Therefore, a more comprehensive examination of organizational structure, as developed by Mintzberg (1989), and the effect particular structures have on corporate identity management, is warranted.

Mintzberg's framework for the structure of organizations

Mintzberg (1989) developed a comprehensive framework for the study of organizational structure. This framework is significant in that it focuses on the *forces* that drive an organization. Accordingly, Mintzberg's framework will be used to highlight the effect of organizational structure on corporate identity management and the ways in which organizational structure needs to be considered in designing effective corporate identity management programs.

Mintzberg (1989) developed a model which showed the essence of organizational structure as composed of six parts. These parts included the *operating core, strategic apex, middle line, technostructure* and *support staff*. Mintzberg described the sixth part of an organization as the *ideology or culture* which encompasses the traditions and beliefs which distinguish that organization from any other. He wrote:

> Specifically, an ideology is taken here to mean a rich system of values
> and beliefs about an organization, shared by its members, that dis-
> tinguishes it from other organizations . . . in effect, an integration of
> individual and organizational goals that can produce synergy.
>   (Mintzberg, 1989, 224)

Mintzberg's ideology is closely related to the concepts of 'corporate culture'
(the rich system of values and beliefs) and 'organizational identification' (the
integration of individual and organizational goals) as expounded by Hatch (1993)
and Albert and Whetten (1985). The following extract from Hatch (1993, 682)
exemplifies this:

> In large measure, it is through culture that a person constructs a sense
> of individual and organizational identity and creates images that are
> taken for the self and the organization.

According to Albert and Whetten (1985), an organization has an identity if there
is a shared understanding of the central, distinctive and enduring character or
essence of an organization among its members. As Ashforth and Mael (1989,
p. 27) state:

> The more salient, stable, and internally consistent the character of an
> organization, (or in organizational terms, the stronger the culture),
> the greater this internalization.

There is clearly a relationship between Mintzberg's concept of ideology and the
concepts of organizational identity and culture. This is pertinent as Mintzberg's
framework focuses upon the extent to which each of the six parts, including the
ideology, become the major force driving the organization, depending on its
structure. Mintzberg developed six configurations or types of organizations that
can be explained by the parts that dominate or the major forces or pulls which
the organization experiences. The basic types of organizational structures are
related to these forces which are the major controls in each structure shown in
Table 3.

According to Mintzberg (1989), existing organizations fit into one of the six
configurations although '. . . each configuration is idealized . . . these configurations reflect leading tendencies in organizations'. However, these configurations
are useful in understanding the reasons why the development of a unified corporate identity in some organizations appears problematic and this understanding may be a first step to remedying such problems. This issue was recognized by
Ashforth and Mael (1989) who reasoned that:

> The individual's social identity may be derived not only from the
> organization . . . Albert and Whetten (1985) distinguished between
> holographic organizations in which individuals across subunits share a
> common identity (or identities) and ideographic organizations in
> which individuals display sub-unit specific identities. . . . Given the

Table 3 Mintzberg's organizational structures

Configuration	Prime coordinating mechanism	Key part of organization	Resulting force
Entrepreneurial organization	Direct supervision	Strategic apex	Pull to lead – control over decision-making
Machine organization	Standardization of work processes	Technostructure	Pull to rationalize
Professional organization	Standardization of skills	Operating core	Pull to professionalize
Diversified organization	Standardization of outputs	Middle line	Pull to balkanize
Innovative organization	Mutual adjustment	Support staff	Pull to collaborate
Missionary organization	Standardization of norms	Ideology	Pull together

Source: Adapted from Mintzberg (1989, 110).

comparative rarity of such organizations, however, the notion of a single or blended, organizational identification is problematic in most complex organizations.

In the following section, each type of organizational structure is examined in relation to the most appropriate corporate identity structure and the associated strength of employee identification with the corporate identity. Cases are given to supplement the discussion of organization structures; however, these are not necessarily typical cases. A systematic research study of the topic would be required to explore the issues further.

The basic organizational structures

Entrepreneurial

Entrepreneurial structures are the simplest ones, '. . . run firmly and personally by their leaders. . . . They make for wonderful stories of the building of great empires and of dramatic turnarounds' (Mintzberg, 1989). With a strong force of direction, one would expect such structures to have strong corporate identities, as the environment within entrepreneurial organizations tends to be simple and the sense of mission is strong. The leader will have personal vision for the success of the company. In other words, the corporate personality will be firmly based upon the leader's personality.

However, there are problems inherent in translating the thoughts of the leader into values for the people in such an organization to pursue, as Mintzberg warned.

> The vision must be articulated to drive others and gain their support, and that threatens the personal nature of the vision.
>
> (Mintzberg, 1989, 175)

An example of such an organization is a software development company in Brisbane, where research showed that most clients felt that the company was synonymous with the entrepreneur who developed the company, even though the company was not named after the owner. The main issue for these clients was lack of after-sales service, carried out by staff other than the entrepreneur. The vision was not sufficiently articulated for other staff to follow up when service was required.

Communication mechanisms such as regular face-to-face meetings with staff and an internal newsletter are obviously important so that others within the company share the vision. One Brisbane entrepreneurial firm with a strong leader has regular Friday night WIFLE (What I Feel Like Expressing) sessions where staff discuss issues with the leader to clarify the vision. Even so, the tension between the personal nature of the vision and the way it is projected by others does exist, with clients preferring to deal with the entrepreneur directly.

In relation to corporate identity structure, the choice of a monolithic structure is obvious. The entrepreneurial organization represents the simplest type of organization with the corporate personality of the company derived from the personality of the owner. Employee identification is likely to be strong as the vision of the leader inspires others. However, it is possible that some lack of involvement on the part of employees may occur if the entrepreneur is not able to articulate the vision sufficiently.

Machine

Machine structures work on efficiency as a prime force. Many of these are basically bureaucracies and we are now watching their attempted transformations as they try to become more 'client-centred' and 'marketing-oriented'. Many Queensland government and semi-government agencies are busily engaged in logo design and corporate identity programs.

The weakness in efficiency as a force lies in what Mintzberg (1989, 136) refers to as 'obsession with control'. It is debatable whether such organizations are capable of developing appealing corporate identities since they have such a standardized way of dealing with stakeholders. Although in this situation values can be built into the system, such standardized communication does not produce an endearing character, which means that the usual emotional response from stakeholders, including employees, is primarily negative. Mintzberg wrote that:

> because normalization is anathema to ideology — turning informal beliefs into formal rules imposed down a centralized hierarchy of authority — we would also expect to find strong forces for the destruction of fledgling ideologies in this configuration.
>
> (Mintzberg, 1989, 234)

As an example, Queensland Transport, which is the government department responsible for testing vehicles and drivers, collecting fines and dealing with safety on Queensland roads, has recently attempted a corporate identity program. However, the slogan: 'Better Transport for Queensland' was found to be ineffective. The primary perception of consumers surveyed was that Queensland Transport is a bureaucratic revenue collection agency. The color of the logo was also criticized: the red in the logo was perceived as signifying 'red tape'. (See Napoles, (1988) for color associations.)

Even though Queensland Transport placed emphasis on customer service, this was perceived by external stakeholders to be hypocritical, as the role of the counter staff, who deal most directly with the customer, was to collect revenue such as car and truck registration fees and fines for traffic offences. One solution for this type of organization may be to separate the purely bureaucratic activities from the more human ones using van Riel's endorsed corporate identity structure, or, in Kammerer's schema, a communication-oriented corporate identity. In the case of Queensland Transport, this would mean having one division dealing with collecting revenue from fines, and another division, primarily concerned with safety issues, with a separate but related identity.

An example of a machine organization with greater success at achieving a positive corporate identity is the Brisbane City Council. With a slogan of 'Australia's most livable city', emphasis has been placed on keeping the city green and clean. This provides a good justification for collecting revenue from ratepayers. Also, the current Lord Mayor projects a caring personality (an ex-Catholic priest), and it appears that the organization has developed a 'corporate spirit'.

The Queensland Department of Primary Industries (DPI) has tried the approach of splitting off some areas and calling them Institutes and Research Centres. One such Institute, the Farming Systems Institute (FSI), was investigated because of its apparent lack of recognition among farmers. Research with farmers found that most viewed the Institute as just a fancy name for the DPI, indicating their unwillingness to accept what they perceived to be a change that was merely a name change. Therefore, if such an approach is taken, the benefits need to be carefully explained to the stakeholders, especially if the staff, and hence culture of the division is essentially the same as that of the main organization.

In summary, most machine organizations adopt a monolithic corporate identity structure. However, as indicated above, an endorsed corporate identity structure or a communication-oriented corporate identity structure may be used to create a more human face for the organization, allowing employees in these divisions more scope for organizational identification. This needs to be carefully thought out and promoted to stakeholders, who may be justifiably resistant to a name change which does not appear to embody any significant benefits for them.

Professional

Professional structures emphasize proficiency as a major force, meaning that highly trained specialists operate in a relatively independent way with emphasis on the work they do with their clients, patients and students. They are expected to work in a fairly standard way due to their professionalism and ethical standards. However, as Mintzberg noted:

> . . . no matter how standardized the knowledge and skills, their complexity ensures that considerable discretion remains in their application. No two professionals – no two surgeons or engineers or social workers – ever apply them in exactly the same way. Many judgments are required.
>
> (Mintzberg, 1989, 175)

In addition, professionals may have more loyalty to their profession than [to] the company that employs them, and clients are often more interested in the person dealing with their needs than in the company they work for.

Queensland University of Technology (QUT) has the slogan: 'A university for the real world' and a logo which was designed to resemble a blue chip. The emphasis on the real world approach has been highly successful in attracting students to QUT, but many academics find this enticing slogan disturbing. Academics, like other professionals, have their own unique ways of approaching their work despite the increased emphasis on bureaucratic procedures in universities. Whereas the slightly eccentric professor who was completely absorbed in and passionate about their subject matter was once a prized emissary of a university, standardization of lecture procedures and the use of student evaluation of lectures and lecturers has devalued such professionals. Academics must now 'stick to the party line' and become 'corporate clones'. In other words, possessing knowledge and expertise is progressively less important than managing business relationships with student 'clients'.

Covaleski *et al.* (1998) explored the issue of professional management in the Big Six public accountancy firms in a recent research project. They noted that:

> The issues of managing professionals in formal organizations is not new. . . . Generally it has been concluded that because professionals should have internalized the norms and standards of the profession, the imposition of bureaucratic procedures is not only unnecessary, but it may lead to professional–bureaucratic conflict.
>
> (Covaleski *et al.*, 1998, 293–294)

In professional organizations, developing external communication strategies that emphasize consistency and stability is important. Internally, induction and training procedures can be usefully employed to encourage professionals to behave in standardized ways when dealing with clients. However, these need to be carefully monitored to ensure that a balance between individual creativity and firm goals is struck. The study by Covaleski *et al.* (1998) highlighted the problems with two such induction strategies: MBO (management by objectives) and mentoring. They referred to a policy employed in one accountancy firm where the goal was to remove responsibility from the line partners in an effort '. . . to emphasize that it is the firm that renders client service, not the individual human being'.

Resistance by employees to such control measures was vigorous, since professionals typically enjoy responsibility, are self-motivated and do not view themselves as merely doing a job. However, as the organizational climate shifts more towards client expectations and the firm's business goals, the employees who remain under these conditions become increasingly committed to such practices as MBO, creating a cycle where such practices are mandatory control measures.

Most professional organizations employ a monolithic corporate identity structure and the company is often named after the founder or founders. Employee identification with the corporate identity is a key issue that needs to be addressed sensitively as the study by Covaleski *et al.* (1998) suggests.

Diversified

Diversified structures are based on the strategy of diversification and the synergy achieved by putting together a range of businesses, which then operate autonomously. Units are called divisions and the central administration is the headquarters. There are advantages in this type of structure such as efficient allocation of capital and spreading the risk across different markets. Often what happens in this type of organization is a concentration on performance at the business level rather than the headquarters level. Mintzberg argued:

> This configuration appears to inhibit, not encourage, the taking of strategic initiatives. . . . It is designed to keep the carrot at the right distance in front of the divisional managers encouraging them to strive for better and better financial performance. At the same time, it seems to dampen their inclination to innovate. It is that famous bottom line . . . attention is focused on the carrot just in front instead of the field of vegetables beyond.
>
> (Mintzberg, 1989, 166–167)

Under these conditions the different divisions are only vaguely interested in overall organizational mission. Each division tends to compete with the others in terms of the narrow performance measures instead of overall company values such as integrity and quality. Both Fombrun (1996) and Ind (1997) specifically referred to the difficulties faced by decentralized structures. Employee identification tends to be focused on the division, rather than the overall company.

The diversified structure normally chooses an endorsed or branded identity with all the inherent problems of this type of approach. To achieve 'single-minded and all-encompassing communication strategies' (Ind, 1997) in these situations is difficult, especially when the company is relating to financial audiences. Ind (1997) suggests that such organizations should do everything in their power to compensate by corporate advertising and PR. Internally, employees need to be given rewards based upon their performance in relation to the whole organization.

Kammerer's corporate identity structure schema is useful in the diversified organization, as is van Riel's concept of parent visibility and content guiding. For some diversified organizations, an organizational-oriented structure is appropriate and in others a communication-oriented corporate identity structure is warranted. In some diversified companies, endorsement of the corporate name towards the financial stakeholder (van Riel) is the most appropriate strategy.

An interesting case was provided by a Queensland liquor chain whose corporate image was predominantly 'ockerish'. The liquor chain diversified into outlets that were specifically for wine drinkers. The ambience of these wine stores was completely at odds with the corporate image projected by the liquor chain, yet an endorsed corporate identity structure was chosen, with the liquor chain logo embossed above the wine logo. Contrary to my expectations, research showed that consumers did not perceive that the image of the liquor chain detracted significantly from their image of the wine stores because they felt that the buying power of the liquor chain meant that the prices of the fine wines would be lower. It was suggested that an organizational-oriented corporate identity structure was the most appropriate, so that while the financial backing for the wine stores was still visible, the wine store logo did not include the liquor store logo.

Employee identification was very much related to the division where they worked. Employees at the wine stores tended to be young, attractive and middle-class whereas liquor store employees were typical 'Aussie blokes'.

Innovative

Innovative structures do not rely on any form of standardization or coordination. These types of organizations operate in a dynamic environment which is unpredictable and hence favors an organic structure (Mintzberg, 1989). It is unlike the entrepreneurial structure because it does not rely on a leader and it differs from the professional organization because innovation is the key, not standardization. Mintzberg (1989) believes that this structure is '. . . the structure of our age'.

The fact that there is a lack of standardization in innovative organizations acts as a barrier to effective corporate identity programs. There is, therefore, a lack of philosophies and beliefs and this can inhibit an innovative organization from being able to develop a strong corporate identity. However, this is perhaps how the corporate identity should be projected: with the key positioning statement related to being an innovative company. A study by Keller and Aaker (1993) found that innovative corporate identities had a positive effect on consumers' perceptions of the company.

The usual corporate identity structure for an innovative company would be monolithic, although it is possible for an innovative company to grow out of a large diversified company. As noted in Table 1, innovation may be curbed if there is a risk to the whole identity; therefore organizations with monolithic identity structures may be advised to develop a separate corporate identity for an innovative division. In this case, the degree of parent visibility would depend on a range of factors such as the degree to which the innovation was a common starting point for communication of the corporate identity of the original company.

Missionary

Mintzberg's (1989) final structure, which he did not include in his original work, is the missionary organization. He has some difficulty with defining it as a separate structure. He credits the Japanese for bringing this structure to our attention:

> Sometimes an organization's ideology becomes so strong that its whole structure is built around it. Then a sixth configuration appears, which I labeled the missionary in my power book. But more commonly, it seems to me, organizational ideologies 'overlay' on more conventional structures. . . . Accordingly . . . I shall . . . focus on force as much as form. In other words, the discussion will be concerned with ideology as a force in organization as much as with the missionary as a distinct form of organization.
>
> (Mintzberg, 1989, 222)

In such an organization, the mission may become much more important than the people or cultural and ethical values, leading to an 'end justifies the means' approach which does not tend to produce an appealing corporate identity.

An example of such an organization may be the Brisbane community-based radio station 4ZZZ, which seeks to give a voice to alternative views. It has the slogan 'Agitate, Educate, Organise'. As noted by Mintzberg, this type of organization thrives on the ideology of being different. It has many volunteers who air their particular philosophies on radio, without censorship or modification to fit into a corporate personality. In a sense, the corporate personality is always shifting, depending upon the views of the agitators. However, due to financial problems, the station recently conducted research on corporate identity issues. The main communication problem was how to produce a unifying message, despite the varied convictions of the announcers on a number of current issues. The slogan: 'A Voice for Everyone' was suggested as a way of overcoming the problem.

Amnesty International is another example of a missionary organization where employees and volunteers would be deeply committed to the ideology of the organization. Missionary organizations are predominantly monolithic in identity structure for obvious reasons. Employee identification is strong since few people would work for a missionary organization if they did not feel a strong sense of social identification with the organization.

Summary of issues

A summary of the weaknesses of each structure in relation to corporate identity management, and the preferred corporate identity structure are given in Table 4.

If the organization being studied is not new, it is likely to fit into one of Mintzberg's broad structures or it may be a combination of these idealized

Table 4 Summary of structural weaknesses

Weakness of structure in relation to corporate identity

Structure	CI structure	Main weakness	Effect on employee identification	Possible remedy
Entrepreneurial	Monolithic	Culture not sufficiently defined for people to follow	Strong identification	Staff meetings. Make values part of company systems
Machine	Monolithic/ Endorsed	Focus on standards not beliefs	Weak identification	Develop a corporate soul
	Communication-oriented			Develop divisions that show human face of organization
Diversified	Branded/ Endorsed	Performance of parts emphasized rather than single mission	Weak identification with whole, strong with parts	Performance rewards based on company mission
	Parent visibility to financial stakeholders only			Communicate corporate identity by internal PR and advertising as well as external
Professional	Monolithic	Loyalty to profession not organization	Weak identification with company, strong with profession	Emphasize benefits of corporate culture
Innovative	Monolithic	History and philosophy not important	Moderate identification	Emphasize innovation as a core value
	Organizational-oriented			
Missionary	Monolithic	Ideology overtakes corporate strategy	Strong identification	Find corporate mission within ideology

structures. In every case it is possible to overcome the corporate identity management problems but with some structures, such as the professional, diversified and machine structures, the problems are more complex. However,

an in-depth discussion of the issues concerning power and knowledge in organizations in relation to individual identity (Foucault, 1979, Covaleski *et al.*, 1998)
is beyond the scope of this paper.

Research agenda

A comprehensive program of research needs to be undertaken, examining organizations that fit the various Mintzberg organizational structures, using a case-
study approach. It appears that the basic corporate identity structure schema
(monolithic, endorsed and branded) is rather limited when it is applied to more
complex organizations. The extent to which the approaches of Kammerer and
van Riel can be used effectively by organizations would be an important part of
the research.

   Another area of research would be to examine the extent to which employee
identification is possible and desirable in the different structures. A balance
between organizational goals and individual goals may need to be negotiated so that
employees are still empowered to perform while being subject to some control.

Implications for management and consultants

The message for corporate identity consultants is that organizational structure
must be taken into account when developing corporate identity programs. An
understanding of the forces that drive a particular type of organization is essential in determining an approach to the problem.

   In an interview in the *Harvard Business Review*, the chairman of Levi-Strauss,
Robert Haas, was asked what the changes in his company had meant for
leadership. His reply was:

> There is an enormous diffusion of power. If companies are going to
> react quickly to changes in the marketplace, they have to put more
> and more accountability, authority, and information into the hands of
> the people who are closest to the products and the customers. That
> requires new business strategies and different organisational struc-
> tures. But structure and strategy are not enough. . . . This is where
> values come in. . . . Values provide a common language for aligning a
> company's leadership and its people.
>
> (Howard, 1990, 134)

The type of structure suggested by Haas begins with concentration on the
corporate personality as the major driving force, with the structure being built
around the underlying character of the organization. However, unlike the missionary organization, the corporate personality would not become entirely
dominant but would be an equal partner along with the products and services
and the corporate strategy.

Conclusion

Although a strong corporate identity can act as an umbrella for an organization and be a way to be unique and differentiated, it is advisable to consider carefully the forces acting on its particular structural type. The best time to develop the corporate identity of an existing organization is during an 'identity' crisis, when internal and external forces are such that the form of the structure is breaking down in some way. Then, a strong sense of mission, a new ideological beginning and a reassertion of the fundamental values and history of the organization is appropriate and timely.

In this paper, an examination of the effect of organizational structure on corporate identity management was undertaken for two reasons. The first was to examine the most appropriate corporate identity structure for each organizational type, and the second was to elaborate on the likely extent of employee identification with the overall corporate identity for each organizational type. The cases cited here may not be typical of the problems encountered in corporate identity management. Therefore, a more systematic and comprehensive study needs to be undertaken.

Future models of the corporate identity management process should include organizational structure as an interceding variable. Without an appreciation of the forces that drive an organization, it may be difficult to comprehend the apparent failure of corporate identity programs which appear, from the outside, to be well planned and well executed.

It may be that organizations are beginning to develop structures which champion the corporate personality rather than building organizational structures which are not aligned to the corporate personality. One way of doing this is through the 'empowered' company in which the corporate personality of the organization is the driving force behind everything the company does and is the basis for the mission statement for the organization. The knowledge of the power of corporate identity as a unifying force in an organization may exacerbate the movement away from some organizational structures. As companies move away from the idea of authority as dominance to the expectation of authority as a personal goal of every person, the development of the 'empowered company' may be achieved. However, as most organizations do not act in this way, questions about the extent to which it is desirable for individuals to identify with organizational goals and, ultimately, corporate identity remain.

References

Abratt, R. (1989) 'A New Approach to the Corporate Image Management Process', *Journal of Marketing Management*, 5(1), pp. 63–76.

Albert, S. and Whetten, D. (1985) 'Organizational Identity', in L. L. Cummings and B. M. Staw (eds), 'Research in Organizational Behavior', Vol. 7, pp. 263–295, JAI Press, Greenwich, CT [also this volume, Chapter 4].

Ashforth, B. E. and Mael, F. (1989) 'Social Identity Theory and the Organization', *Academy of Management Review*, 14(1), pp. 20–39.

Balmer, J. (1994) 'The BBC's Corporate Identity: Myth, Paradox and Reality', *Journal of General Management*, 19(3), pp. 33–49.

Balmer, J. (1995) 'Corporate Branding and Connoisseurship', *Journal of General Management*, 21(1), pp. 24–46.

Balmer, J. (1997) 'Corporate Identity: Past, Present and Future', *Working Paper*, Department of Marketing, University of Strathclyde.

Covaleski, M., Dirsmith, M., Heian, J. and Samuel, S. (1998) 'The Calculated and the Avowed: Techniques of Discipline and Struggles over Identity in Big Six Public Accounting Firms', *Administrative Science Quarterly*, 43, pp. 293–327.

Dowling, G. (1986) 'Managing Your Corporate Images', *Industrial Marketing Management*, 15, pp. 109–115.

Downey, S. M. (1986/1987) 'The Relationship between Corporate Culture and Corporate Identity', *Public Relations Quarterly*, Winter, pp. 7–12.

Fombrun, C. (1996) 'Reputation: Realizing Value from the Corporate Image'. Harvard Business School Press, Cambridge, MA.

Foucault, M. (1979) 'Discipline and Punish'. Penguin Books, Harmondsworth.

Hatch, M. J. (1993) 'The Dynamics of Organizational Culture', *Academy of Management Review*, 18(40), pp. 657–693.

Hatch, M. J. and Shultz, M. (1997) 'Relations between Organizational Culture, Identity and Image', *European Journal of Marketing*, 31 (5–6), pp. 356–365.

Hogg, M. A. and Turner, J. C. (1985) 'Interpersonal Attraction, Social Identification and Psychological Group Formation', *European Journal of Social Psychology*, 15, pp. 51–66.

Howard, R. (1990) 'Values Make the Company: An Interview with Robert Haas'. *Harvard Business Review* (Sept/Oct), pp. 133–144.

Ind, N. (1992) 'The Corporate Image', Kogan Page, London.

Ind, N. (1997) 'The Corporate Brand', Macmillan Press Ltd, Basingstoke.

Kammerer, J. (1988) 'Beitrag der Produkt zur Corporate Identity', GBI-Verlag, München.

Keller, K. and Aaker, D. (1993) 'Managing the Corporate Brand: The Effects of Corporate Images and Corporate Brand Extensions', *Research Paper No 1216*, Graduate School of Business, Stanford University.

Kennedy, S. (1977) 'Nurturing Corporate Images', *European Journal of Marketing*, 11(3), pp. 120–164.

Marwick, N. and Fill, C. (1997) 'Towards a Framework for Managing Corporate Identity', *European Journal of Marketing*, 31(5/6), pp. 396–409.

Mintzberg, H. (1989) 'Mintzberg on Management', The Free Press, Glencose, Ill.

Napoies, V. (1988) 'Corporate Identity Design', Van Nostrand Reinhold Company, New York.

Stuart, H. (1998) 'Exploring the Corporate Identity/Corporate Image Interface: An Empirical Study of Accounting Firms', *Journal of Communication Management*, 2(4), pp. 357–371.

Tajfel, H. (1978) 'Differentiation between Social Groups', European Monographs in Social Psychology 14, Academic Press, London.

Van Riel, C. (1995) 'Principles of Corporate Communication', Prentice Hall, Hemel Hempstead.

Van Riel, C. and Balmer, J. (1997) 'Corporate Identity: The Concept, Its Measurement and Management', *European Journal of Marketing*, 31(5/6), pp. 340–355.

Chapter 6

John M. T. Balmer and Edmund R. Gray

CORPORATE IDENTITY AND CORPORATE COMMUNICATIONS: CREATING A COMPETITIVE ADVANTAGE

From *Corporate Communications: An International Journal* 1999, 4 (4): 171–176

EDITORS' COMMENTARY

Urbane, unassuming, unstintingly civil and cheerful, Edmund Gray is the epitome of the gentleman scholar. He is, most certainly, a *gentle*man. Beneath this facade lurks the sharpest of minds. He is no dilettante when it comes to contemplating the concepts of corporate image, reputation, identity, and communications; he is a consummate exponent of their strategic importance in effecting strategic change. His early work on image and reputation is conspicuous not only because he speaks with a clarity to both practitioners and consultants as to the strategic importance of these concepts, but because he was one of the first to do so.[1] This tradition has been maintained in his more recent work.[2]

In that it is concerned with both corporate identity and corporate communication, this chapter provides a bridge with the ensuing section on corporate communication. In it Professor Edmund Gray of Loyola Marymount University, Los Angeles, joined Professor John Balmer (one of the editors of this anthology) to articulate the strategic importance of both corporate identity and corporate communications.

The chapter starts with the authors introducing the principle that as a consequence of recent environmental trends senior managers need to accord greater importance to corporate identity and corporate communication. The authors argue that these trends have blurred the images of many companies both externally and internally. They advance the view that effective corporate identity and corporate communications management can serve as effective antidotes to these situations. Furthermore, they emphasize that corporate identity as well as corporate communications should be viewed as being strategic rather than functional in character.

Apart from the articulation of environmental trends, this chapter is notable in two other regards. The first is the authors' conceptual model of the corporate identity/corporate communications process. It is significant in that the authors view the objective of corporate identity/corporate communications management as investing an organization with a sustainable competitive advantage. This may be compared with earlier conceptual models, such as those by Abratt[3] and Dowling,[4] which saw the acquisition of a favorable corporate image as the objective of effective corporate identity and corporate communications management. Not surprisingly, the model accords particular importance to the role of environmental trends; the importance of these trends has tended to be overlooked in earlier models.

The chapter's second major contribution is in the authors' conceptualization of corporate communications. Reference to the conceptual model reveals that a considerably broader characterization of corporate communications is offered than the tripartite definition offered by Van Riel,[5] which sees corporate communications as a fusion of marketing, management, and organizational communication.

In Balmer and Gray's articulation of what they call "Total Corporate Communication," they argue that this consists of what they call primary, secondary, and tertiary communication. *Primary* communication encapsulates the communication effects of product/service performance, company policies, and employee behavior. *Secondary* communication encompasses the planned, "formal" communications policies of organizations, which typically make use of traditional communications channels such as advertising, public relations, and sponsorship, as well as systems of visual identification. Lastly, *tertiary* communication encompasses the all-important communication effects of third-party communication, which includes, among others, word of mouth, media interpretation, and competitor communication.

The conceptualization of identity in this article is somewhat different from the definitions found in some of the other chapters in this section, such as Stuart's, and Albert and Whetten's. Balmer and Gray define corporate identity as encompassing an organization's distinctive attributes, as shown in the mix of elements forming an identity described in the model. The notion that key elements (but not all elements) of a corporate identity can be viewed as an observable reality, as articulated here, contrasts with other schools of thought that consider identity to be an entirely socially constructed phenomenon.

Several clear messages emerge from this short chapter. First, corporate identity and corporate communications are of strategic importance. Second, when effectively managed they can imbue organizations with a sustainable competitive advantage. Finally, during periods of considerable environmental change, when organizational images are blurred, they afford two means by which organizations can secure distinctiveness in their markets.

NOTES

1   Gray, E. R. and Smeltzer, L. R., "Corporate Image: An Integral Part of Strategy,"
     Sloan Management Review 1985, 26 (4): 73–78.
2   Gray, E. R. and Balmer, J. M. T., "Managing Corporate Image and Corporate Repu-
     tation," *Long Range Planning* 1998, 31 (5): 695–702.
3   Abratt, R., "A New Approach to the Corporate Image Management Process,"
     Journal of Marketing Management 1989, 5 (1): 63–76.
4   Dowling, G., "Developing Your Corporate Images Into a Corporate Asset," *Long
     Range Planning* 1993, 26 (2): 101–109.
5   Van Riel, C. B. M., *Principles of Corporate Communication*, London: Prentice Hall,
     1995.

Introduction

O**VER THE PAST DECADE** corporate identity has become a prominent paradigm and has begun to be linked to the strategic management of organizations (Marwick and Fill, 1997; Morison, 1997). It has been legitimized and promoted through the formation of the International Corporate Identity Group (ICIG) and the subsequent issuance of the Strathclyde Statement (see Appendix). There are a number of literature reviews, and historical surveys, relating to corporate identity particularly within the marketing and communications literatures (e.g. Abratt, 1989; Balmer, 1995, 1998; Van Riel and Balmer, 1997). Such articles would appear, in part, to have fired recent renewed academic and managerial interest in the corporate identity from scholars and practitioners from a broad palette of disciplines including: corporate communications (van Riel, 1995); organisational behaviour (Hatch and Schultz, 1997); marketing (Baker and Balmer, 1997; Wilson, 1997); brand management (Kapferer, 1992; King, 1991); image-research (Barich and Kotler, 1991; Worcester, 1997); and from psychology (Bromley, 1993). This is in addition to those scholars who make an implicit link between corporate strategy and the corporate identity paradigm. In essence, corporate identity is the reality and uniqueness of an organization which is integrally related to its external and internal image and reputation through corporate communication (Gray and Balmer, 1998). Corporate communication is the process through which stakeholders perceive the company's identity and image and reputation are formed. This article will outline the key forces that have created a sense of urgency *vis-à-vis* the effective management of corporate identity and corporate communications within a strategic framework.

The ten environmental forces

The following ten environmental forces prevalent during the past decade have accentuated the need for strategically managing corporate identity. But the trends have influenced companies differently. Some firms have been affected by many of them whereas others by only a few. It would be difficult, however, to identify any companies that have not been touched significantly by at least one of them. Hence, in the aggregate, they represent the driving force behind the recent upsurge of interest in corporate identity and corporate communication issues.

The ten environmental forces contributing to the increased importance of corporate identity and corporate communications are:

(1) Acceleration of product life cycles.
(2) Deregulation.
(3) Privatisation programmes.
(4) Increased competition in the public and non-profit sectors.
(5) Increased competition in the service sector.
(6) Globalisation and the establishment of free trade areas.
(7) Mergers, acquisitions and divestitures.
(8) Shortage of high-calibre personnel.
(9) Public expectations for corporate social responsiveness.
(10) Breakdown of the boundaries between the internal and external aspects of organisations.

Acceleration of product life cycles

The acceleration of product life cycles is one of the critical trends and nowhere is it more evident than in consumer electronics. Consider the audio segment of the market where tapes replaced records and, in turn, were superseded by compact discs, which in the future may be supplanted by digital audio tapes. Companies with high visibility and strong reputations, such as Sony and JVC, have competitive advantage in such fluid markets because their respected names add value to their products by reducing uncertainty in the minds of their customers, retailers and distributors.

Deregulation

The deregulation movement is a second factor affecting corporate identity. As a case in point, deregulation in the financial services industry has allowed firms to compete in new areas but this has left their public images blurred. For instance, in the USA, Glendale Federal Savings Bank and Loan expanded into retail banking and became Glendale Federal Bank. Similarly, in the UK, many building societies such as Abbey National and Alliance and Leicester have become banks. Their principal challenge now is to modify their public persona accurately. The airline industry in both the USA and UK has, as a result of deregulation, under-gone profound change. In the USA this has resulted in the emergence of cut-price airlines such as Southwest Airlines and Alaska Airlines, while within the UK low-cost airlines such as Debonair, Easy-Jet, Go and Ryanair have also emerged.

Privatisation programmes

Privatisation programmes have also left firms vulnerable to identity crises. This has been a particularly salient issue in Britain and continental Europe, especially the former Eastern Bloc nations. Some 90 medium and large companies were privatised in Poland in 1996. The UK has witnessed extensive privatisation in public utilities – gas, electricity, water, telecommunications and rail – giving rise to a plethora of new firms in need of lucid corporate images to differentiate themselves from their competitors as well as their former nationalised positions. Perhaps the greatest privatisation success story is British Airways, which has effectively repositioned itself as a profitable, consumer-friendly, global airline.

Increased competition in the public and non-profit sectors

Heightened competition has touched almost every organisation in the public sector. In Britain, universities are a case in point. The past decade has witnessed the rapid expansion of "new" universities. Although this trend has allowed a greater number of students to read for degrees, it has also resulted in greater competition among universities. Since the principal way universities compete is through their images and reputations, identity management is of great strategic importance. In US universities, identity is also a prominent concern, but for somewhat different reasons. The number of students of college age has declined and consequently many schools which were expanded during the 1970s and 1980s are faced with declining enrolments. Similar problems have also arisen among American hospitals. The social/political movement to reduce medical costs has led to a sharp decline in the demand for hospital beds and consequently an intensified level of competition which, in turn, has sparked interest in devel-oping positive corporate identities. In the UK a number of charities have under-gone various re-positioning exercises in an attempt to achieve differentiation from other charities. A well known example of this was the identity change of the British children's charity, Dr Barnardos.

Increased competition in the service sector

In similar fashion, service industries where competition has clearly intensified in recent years are coming to understand the strategic significance of corporate image and reputation. An example is Hong Kong-based Cathay Pacific which recently repositioned itself as an Asian rather than a British airline. This identity strategy was not simply a reaction to the ending of British Colonial rule in the Crown Colony but, more importantly, a response to increased airline competition and the desire to cater to its customer base, which is primarily Asian.

Globalisation and the establishment of free trade areas

A pervasive image and favourable reputation can be a powerful competitive weapon for a firm expanding internationally. Coca-Cola, McDonald's, and Baskin-Robbins are salient examples of companies that have been able to expand throughout the world more easily than lesser known firms because of their high-profile, positive identities. On a more limited scale, the advent of a single European Market has provided the potential for companies to grow and gain market share by positioning themselves as European throughout the trade zone. The Dutch banking group ING and the Belgian bank Fortis are examples of this trend. The mooted merger between the UK and German aircraft manufacturers British Aerospace and Dasa is an attempt by these institutions to operate on a global scale. Taking advantage of the above opportunities does, however, require a significant investment in developing and communicating a new regional and/or global identity.

Mergers, acquisitions and divestitures

Still another trend is the continuing high level of mergers, acquisitions and divestitures which has radically altered the business profile of many companies. A recent example in the oil industry is the creation of a behemoth with the merger of BP and Amoco. Commonly, a significant outcome of these moves is a deleterious gap between a company's public image and its true identity. Such incongruence can confound financial markets as well as customers, resulting in diminished support for the company from one or both sources. A classic example is US Steel Corporation which, in the mid-1980s, was deriving about two-thirds of its revenue from oil and gas sales but continued to be evaluated by financial analysts as a member of the depressed American steel industry. Only after the company changed its name to USX did its status within the financial community change. Another example is the divestiture of the quality car marque of Rolls-Royce and Bentley by Vickers and the resultant Byzantine agreement whereby Volkswagen will own the Rolls-Royce and Bentley marques for several years and will finally surrender the use of the Rolls-Royce marque to BMW. Both BMW and VW will need to devote a good deal of effort in establishing identities for their respective companies.

Shortage of high calibre personnel

For today's knowledge organisations, the key to staying competitive is the ability to attract and retain skilled and motivated employees. A favourable reputation can play a major role in achieving this, because the organisation's reputation provides a certain psychic income to the individual. To a large extent, this explains why highly reputed organisations such as the BBC, Merek, McKinsey and Company and Harvard University have little trouble attracting and retaining top-notch employees. Furthermore, high calibre personnel can play a prominent role both formally and informally in communicating the firm's identity to the outside world.

Public expectations for corporate social responsiveness

Another trend is society's growing demand for high levels of corporate social responsiveness. There is clear evidence that an increasing number of consumers are concerned about the social performance of business firms. Surveys in both North America and western Europe indicate many consumers are not only concerned about the impact that commercial producers have on the environment, but are also willing to pay extra for environmentally benign products. Entrepreneurs have been quick to respond to this trend. Consider such well-known adolescent companies as Ben and Jerry's, Patagonia, the Body Shop, and Tom's of Maine. Each has built its core strategy around projecting a socially and environmentally responsible image. Moreover, many older and larger firms, such as Britain's Co-operative Bank, awakening to public expectations, are zealously trying to protect socially responsible identities through programmes ranging from ethical investment policies, and using environmentally benign packaging, to providing inner city schools with computers, and creating and maintaining bird sanctuaries.

Blurring of boundaries between organisations and between stakeholders

Finally, the once rigid demarcation between internal and external aspects of organisations is beginning to crumble. Many organisations view relationships with suppliers, consultants, and franchise partners as well as joint-venture partners as important dimensions of their *raison d'être*. The creation of alliances in the airline industry, such as "Star Alliance" and "The One World Alliance", is indicative of this. It is, quite clearly, a two-way process since such an alliance itself may be seen as a new form of identity *vis-à-vis* its competition. Another case is the common rebranding and corporate communications exercise for Hilton, where two independent companies use a common corporate brand name, the Hilton brand being owned by Hilton Hotels in the USA and by Ladbrokes Ltd in the UK and the rest of the world.

Discussion

What is implicit in the above trends is that senior executives are being compelled to think strategically about their company's identity and how it is being communicated to key stakeholders. The ten forces outlined above have modified and blurred the image of many companies throughout the world. They obviously represent a threat to the strategic position of the company. But in another sense they present an opportunity for companies to present a clear image that reflects a positive identity, one that leads to an enviable reputation. We argue that corporate communication plays a vital role in bringing the above to fruition, but for this to be achieved corporate communications needs to be radically re-appraised. Drucker (in Crainer, 1997) remarked, "The most important thing in communications is to hear what is not being said." We also postulate that it should be viewed not so much as a functional aspect of management but one that is inherently strategic. Consequently, a much expanded view of corporate communications is advocated by the authors, who categorise corporate communications as a three-part focus – primary, secondary and tertiary. The authors' broader framework builds on the approaches advocated by Schultz *et al.* (1994), which focuses on integrated marketing communication (IMC). The integration of management, organisational and marketing communications as "corporate communications" advocated by Van Riel (1995) and Aberg's (1990) emphasis on "Total communications" as well as Balmer's (1995, 1998) "Total corporate communications" approach whereby everything an organisation says, makes and does is seen to communicate. Recently, Scholes and Clutterbuck (1998) have emphasised the strategic importance of stakeholder communications and present a cogent argument for a holistic view of corporate communications to be adopted by an organisation's senior management.

Figure 1 is a new model which articulates the corporate identity and corporate communications process. It marshals the authors' understanding of the communications process(es) in a conceptual, operational model. It is pragmatic in nature and has the aim of showing not only the inseparability of corporate identity, corporate communication, corporate image and reputation in securing a corporate advantage, but also depicts the pivotal rôle of the three components of the corporate communications system. It will be seen that corporate communications forms a tri-partite bridge between an organisation's identity and the resultant image and reputation. Figure 1 also provides brief descriptions of each component of the model.

Conclusion

The corporate identity/corporate communication paradigm represents a relatively new but crucially powerful lens through which management scholars, practitioners and advisers can regard and respond to important strategic concerns encountered by organisations of every hue.

This article has detailed the ten forces which have highlighted the need for senior managers to manage effectively their organisation's corporate identity and corporate communications process communications. In addition, the authors have postulated that corporate communications is of particular import in that it does, *de facto*, form the nexus between an organisation's corporate identity and the coveted strategic objective of acquiring a favourable corporate reputation.

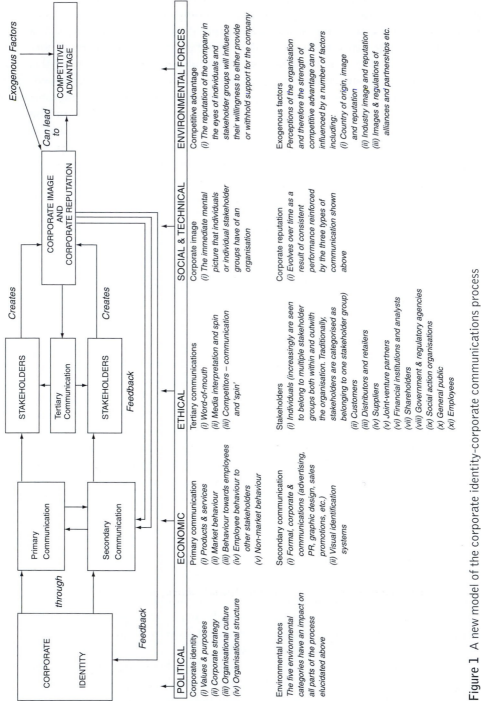

Figure 1 A new model of the corporate identity-corporate communications process

However, just as there has, in recent years, been a growing *consensus gentium* among management scholars that corporate identity has been narrowly conceived with undue emphasis being accorded to graphic design, the authors conclude that some of the same traits may be seen in the related nascent paradigm of corporate communications. Thus, the authors posit that a much broadened view be adopted *vis-à-vis* corporate communications with the paradigm being categorised as encompassing a trio of elements which the authors describe as primary, secondary and tertiary forms of corporate communications. It is concluded that the marriage of corporate identity and the broadened view of corporate communication advocated here be reviewed as strategic fields. As such, the authors conclude that in today's volatile business environment corporate identity and corporate communications, when viewed and managed from a strategic perspective, can imbue many organisations with a distinct competitive advantage.

References

Åberg, L. (1990), "Theoretical model and praxis of total communications", *International Public Relations Review*, Vol. 13 No. 2, pp. 13–16.

Abratt, R. (1989), "A new approach to the corporate image management process", *Journal of Marketing Management*, Vol. 5 No. 1, pp. 63–76.

Baker, M. J. and Balmer, J. M. T. (1997), "Visual identity: trappings or substance?", *European Journal of Marketing*, Special Edition on Corporate Identity, Vol. 31 No. 5/6, pp. 366–82.

Balmer, J. M. T. (1995), "Corporate branding and connoisseurship", *Journal of General Management*, Vol. 21 No. 1, Autumn, pp. 24–42.

Balmer, J. M. T. (1998), "Corporate identity and the advent of corporate marketing", *Journal of Marketing Management*, Vol. 14, pp. 963–96.

Barich, H. and Kotler, P. (1991), "A framework for marketing image management", *Sloan Management Review*, Vol. 32 No. 2, pp. 94–104.

Bromley, D. D. (1993), *Reputation, Image and Impression Management*, John Wiley & Sons, Chichester.

Crainer, S. (1997), *The Ultimate Book of Business Quotations*, Capstone, Oxford.

Gray, E. R. and Balmer, J. M. T. (1998), "Managing corporate image and corporate reputation", *Long Range Planning*, Vol. 31 No. 5, pp. 695–702.

Hatch, M. J. and Schultz, M. (1997), "Relations between organisational culture, identity and image", *European Journal of Marketing Special Edition on Corporate Identity*, Vol. 31 No. 5/6, pp. 356–65.

Kapferer, J. N. (1992), *Strategic Brand Management*, Kogan Page, London.

King, S. (1991), "Brand-building in the 1990s", *Journal of Marketing Management*, Vol. 7, pp. 3–13.

Marwick, N. and Fill, C. (1997), "Towards a framework for managing corporate identity", *European Journal of Marketing*, Special Edition on Corporate Identity, Vol. 31 No. 5/6, pp. 396–409.

Morison, I. (1997), "Breaking the monolithic mould", *The International Journal of Bank Marketing*, Special Edition on Corporate Identity in Financial Services, Vol. 15 No. 5, pp. 153–62.

Scholes, E. and Clutterbuck, D. (1998), "Communicating with stakeholders: an integrated approach", *Long Range Planning Special Edition on the Stakeholder Corporation*, Vol. 31, April, pp. 227–338.

Schultz, D. E., Tannenbaum, S. I. and Lauterborn, R. F. (1994), *Integrated Marketing Communication: Pulling It Together and Making It Work*, NTC Business Books, Chicago, IL.

Van Riel, C. B. M. (1995), *Principles of Corporate Communication*, Prentice-Hall, London.

Van Riel, C. B. M. and Balmer, J. M. T. (1997), "Corporate identity: the concept, its management and measurement", *European Journal of Marketing*, Special Edition on Corporate Identity, Vol. 31 No. 5/6, pp. 340–55.

Wilson, A. (1997), "The culture of the branch team and its impact on service delivery and corporate identity", *The International Journal of Bank Marketing*, Special Edition on Corporate Identity in Financial Services, Vol. 15 No. 5, pp. 163–8.

Worcester, R. M. (1997), "Managing the image of your bank: the glue that binds", *The International Journal of Bank Marketing*, Special Edition on Corporate Identity in Financial Services, Vol. 15 No. 5, pp. 146–52.

Further reading

Balmer, J. M. T. and Soenen, G. (1999), "The acid test of corporate identity management", *Journal of Marketing Management*, Special Edition on Brand Reality, 15 (1–3): 69–92.

Balmer, J. M. T. and Wilson, A. (1998), "Corporate identity: there is more to it than meets the eye", *International Studies of Management and Organisations*, Vol. 28 No. 3, Fall, pp. 12–31.

Ind, N. (1997), *The Corporate Brand*, Macmillan, Basingstoke.

Appendix: the International Corporate Identity Group's (ICIG) statement on corporate identity. "The Strathclyde Statement"

Every organisation has an identity. It articulates the corporate ethos, aims and values and presents a sense of individuality that can help to differentiate the organisation within its competitive environment.

When well managed, corporate identity can be a powerful means of integrating the many disciplines and activities essential to an organisation's success. It can also provide the visual cohesion necessary to ensure that all corporate communications are coherent with each other and result in an image consistent with the organisation's defining ethos and character.

By effectively managing its corporate identity an organisation can build understanding and commitment among its diverse stakeholders. This can be manifested in an ability to attract and retain customers and employees, achieve strategic alliances, gain the support of financial markets and generate a sense of direction and purpose. Corporate identity is a strategic issue.

Corporate identity differs from traditional brand marketing since it is concerned with all of an organisation's stakeholders and the multi-faceted way in which an organisation communicates.

Dr John M. T. Balmer (University of Strathclyde, Director, International Centre for Corporate Identity Studies).

David Bernstein (Vice President of ICIG).

Adrian Day (Managing Director, Landor Associates, London).

Stephen Greyser (Professor of Business Administration, Harvard Business School).

Nicholas Ind (Identity Consultant).

Stephen Lewis (Director, MORI).

Chris Ludlow (Managing Partner, Henrion, Ludlow & Schmidt).

Nigel Markwick (Consultant, Wolff Olins).

Cees van Riel (Director, Centre for Corporate Communications, Rotterdam).

Stephen Thomas (Director, CGI Identity Consultants)

This is a revised version of the original statement which was drafted at Strachur, Loch Fyne, Argyll, Scotland, UK, on 17 and 18 February 1995.

Corporate communications: a dimension of corporate meaning

"Seek first to understand, then to be understood."
(Stephen Covey)

EDITORS' INTRODUCTION

A tumult of two?

THE COMMUNICATIONS REVOLUTION, via the utilization of new technology, is unremitting. It has given rise to inventive, often pervasive forms of communication that have become staples of modern life for businesses and consumers alike. It has transformed the business and societal landscape. It has resulted in new industries and new organizational functions. The ringing in of the new has been accompanied by the din of the death-knell for older technologies, modes of employment, and types of social and commercial discourse. Its unalleviated growth has altered how, where, and with whom we work and converse. We seem to be speaking more but saying and interacting less. It has altered prerequisites for employment. While we *appear* to inhabit a smaller, more transparent planet, the fate of many is to inhabit the shadows.

However, the above is only context for the importance of the communications revolution to the reader. The revolution has also brought with it a realization that corporate communications activities are an integral and important concern for organizations. Management is comprehending that organizations need to be engaged in an ongoing dialogue with a wide spectrum of constituents both within and outside the corporation. All too often this has been accompanied by the painful realization by senior managers when confronted by a cataclysm that there is fragmentation of responsibility, function, and message vis-à-vis their organization's communications.

Embarkation: the New Corporate Communications Wheel

Bernstein's[1] corporate communications wheel provides, in our experience, a useful introduction to corporate communications. It affords one means by which the depth, breadth, and complexity of corporate-level communications can begin to be appreciated. We have made some slight modifications to the wheel to accommodate a few salient characteristics of the business environment that were not so prevalent in the 1980s. Exhibit 1 shows *our* version of the wheel, which we have termed "The New Corporate Communications Wheel."

The wheel shown here will *not* be apposite for all organizations. Substantive changes will be required depending upon whether the company is a holding corporation, a subsidiary, or operating in the not-for-profit sector. The framework presented here has more in common with a large corporation operating within the private sector.

The model aims to assist managers and scholars to:

● prioritize stakeholder and interest groups in communications campaigns;
● select the most efficacious channels of communication to reach such groups;
● appreciate the effect of dissonance on these communication efforts caused by factors such as country of origin, industry, and business partners factors; and
● appreciate the huge task of designing corporate communications campaigns.

Here is the process that Bernstein suggests should be followed. (Each organization should produce its own version of the wheel.) The initial step is to prepare two specific lists, then narrow them to the most important elements, and take into account other factors. More specifically:

1   The main stakeholder groups should be identified. (This should form the outer circle of the wheel.)
2   The variety of communication channels available to an organization should be listed. (This forms the inner of the two outer circles.)
3   Stakeholder groups should be prioritized according to their importance.
4   The most appropriate communication channels for each group should be identified. (Bernstein suggests that the inner circle should literally be turned so that each communication channel is considered in line with each stakeholder group.)
5   The effect of country of origin and industry image should be taken into account at this stage.
6   In our model we incorporate other factors requiring consideration: the corporate branding covenant (see Section Five), partnerships, and the effect of environmental factors.

The vast scope of the task is illustrated by the sheer variety of elements that conceivably might be considered. In our version of the model the 11 stakeholder and interest groups and the 11 communication channels result in 121 considerations alone! For a holding company with seven subsidiaries the magnitude of the problem becomes readily apparent. Further, several of our communication channels encompass, in effect, a variety of channels – New Media being a case in point. This crucially important recent dimension of the communications revolution noted in our opening paragraph was not included in Bernstein's framework, which dates back to 1984.

Further complexity is caused by the fact that individuals invariably belong to multiple stakeholder groups. (This will be examined below.)

Realistically, each organization will engage in a meaningful reduction of the elements contained in the wheel in the course of prioritization, and will find its own ways of using the wheel.

The communications odyssey

Bernstein's early overview[2] of the importance of corporate communications is of particular significance. Written with a communications expert's experience, it still provides a useful and accessible introduction to the broad field of study.

In relation to academic developments within the field of corporate communications, the work of Van Riel[3] and, more recently, Cornelissen, Lock, and Gardner[4] details what may be seen as the corporate communications odyssey. This has reached the point where corporate communications has now emerged as a distinct area of

Exhibit 1 The New Corporate Communications Wheel: Balmer and Greyser
Source: Adapted from D. Bernstein, *Company Image and Reality: A Critique of Corporate Communications*, Eastbourne, U.K.: Holt, Rinehart and Winston, 1984

management and scholarship: academic chairs in corporate communications are becoming more commonplace.

This odyssey has been characterized by various debates concerning the issue of integration: integration of the marketing communications functions, integration of the marketing communications and public relations functions, and, finally, integration of all communications functions. The latter gives rise to corporate communications.

An early proponent of integrated marketing communications was the German author Meffert.[5] This idea soon became a notable theme within the literature, with the work of Knecht[6] and Schultz, Tannenbaum, and Lauterborn[7] being of particular note.

Much debate has taken place regarding the integration of marketing communications and public relations. Some of the literature focuses on their differences;[8] other authors emphasize their similarities[9] while some see advantages in integration.[10]

A growing acceptance of the need for company-wide integration of communication has led to a debate as to how integration should be effected. Some authorities propose that it should be achieved by *process* rather than by function.[11] Recently, researchers have concluded that there might not be one optimum way of integrating corporate communications because environmental, structural, and organizational considerations will necessitate different responses to coordination.[12]

Pluribus in unum: targeting whom?

A particular problem for corporate-level communicators is the question of targeting. Large organizations still tend to have communications departments that have a specific responsibility for seemingly discrete stakeholder groups: customers, stockholders, employees and trade unions, government, and the media, for example. Such an approach takes little account of the fact that individuals invariably belong to multiple stakeholder groups. In an extreme case scenario it is possible for a single individual to be a customer, a stockholder, an employee, a trade union official, a member of the local council, and an occasional columnist in a local newspaper. This raises another important point: individuals may transcend the traditional internal/external corporate boundaries. The same is true for some independently owned organizations in the supply or distribution chains that are seen to be integral to and thus, in essence, a part of the company. The same can be the case for alliance members and for some types of consultants; all can be seen by consumers or customers as "wearing the company uniform."

Corporate communication: a broader vista

The above debates may be regarded as a prelude to an organizational-wide integration of effort and the gradual recognition of the importance of corporate communications. At this juncture mention can be made of Åberg and Siegel, who adopted a broad-brushed approach to corporate-level communications.

Åberg,[13] a Finnish writer, argued that there needed to be integration of all communications activities within the organization. He offered four reasons why such integration was efficacious: it was crucial to the processes of control, persuasion, integration, and informing. It was an important means by which an organization's mission and strategy could be achieved. He devised a detailed communications mix in illustrating the eclectic nature of his approach.

In the U.S.A. Alan Siegel focused on the issue of corporate integration of message. He coined the phrase *corporate voice* to characterize his area of concern in two articles that appeared in the *Design Management Journal*.[14] He argued that in order to communicate the corporation's distinctive personality, vision, and positioning there needed to be a fusion of content, language, and design. A similar line of thought has been developed by van Riel, who developed the notion of common starting points,[15] and by those academics who have advocated an approach based on the sustainable corporate story.

Common starting points and the sustainable corporate story

Van Riel,[16] the Dutch communications authority, proposed that consistency in organizational-wide communications could be achieved through utilizing his *common starting points* (CSPs) process. The CSPs approach is *de facto* an early example of an integrative, interdisciplinary approach, one that takes account of (a) *strategy*, (b) *identity*, and (b) *image*. The CSPs process entails representatives from the corporation's various communications departments articulating points (a), (b), and (c) above. From this, enduring commonalities are established, and these commonalities are used in formal company communications, thereby ensuring a degree of consistency. (It is not clear whether the descriptions of the three dimensions forming the CSPs are as construed by the participants, or are indeed based on fact.)

More recently the *sustainable corporate story* has been advocated as a means by which congruence can be achieved across the controllable communication elements within organizations.[17]

What is it? The sustainable corporate story aims to provide a comprehensive narrative about the whole organization, including its origins, vision, and mission.[18] As such, it is a realistic and relevant description of key aspects of the organization.[19] Such stories are not only believable but also memorable.[20]

How is the corporate story distinct? Corporate stories develop out of the organization and this makes them distinct.[21]

Perceived benefits? Not only does it provide a means of achieving consistency across the organization,[22] but it promotes understanding and helps to differentiate the organization, including its products and services.[23]

Van Riel[24] offers four criteria that need to underpin corporate stories: they should be *realistic* (based on the organization's identity – that is, its distinctive and enduring characteristics), *relevant* (offer added value elements for stakeholders), *responsive* (allow for dynamic two-way symmetrical communication), and *sustainable* (need to meet the sundry demands of key stakeholder groups as well as the organization's objectives). He also offers a six-stage process as a basis for establishing a corporate story:[25]

1   establish the most efficacious positioning for the company;
2   establish the organization's actual and ideal identity as *construed* by managers;
3   establish the corporation's reputation;
4   create the corporate story (the key promise), taking care to articulate the key promise, to provide evidence that the promise is being delivered, and establish an appropriate tone of voice;
5   implement the story by individual units by drawing on the CSP principles (see above);
6   conduct ongoing evaluation.

The corporate communication mix

The structural elements that constitute corporate communications have been another subject of academic literature, with the work of Van Riel being the most influential to date. He proposed that corporate communication entails the orchestration of three forms of communication comprising management communication, marketing communication, and organizational communication.[26]

Management communication has organizational members as its primary focus. Under this category communication is used for command, control, awareness, and motivational purposes. Managers aim to secure a shared vision and trust, and thus effect change.[27]

Marketing communication has end-users (and those involved in purchase decisions) as its primary focus. The principal objectives are to create awareness of and interest in an organization's products and/or services. It involves the orchestration of several controllable communications instruments including advertising, sales promotion, product PR, direct mail, and packaging. These activities fall within the traditional jurisdiction of the marketing department.

Organizational communication is characterized by having multiple constituencies as its foci. Typically, there is an interdependent relationship between the organization with individual constituencies: often there is a network of dependent relationships. These constituencies include stockholders, employees, governments, suppliers, and the media. In addition, organizational communications encompasses a plethora of corporate-level communications functions such as investor relations, corporate public relations, public affairs, employee and recruitment communications, internal communication, media relations, corporate advertising, and environmental communication.

The total corporate communications mix

An alternative approach to the corporate communications mix has been offered by Balmer and Gray.[28] The key point of difference between their mix and that of Van Riel is that the former (a) encompasses the communication effects of products, services, management actions, and corporate behavior, and (b) acknowledges the importance of third-party communication such as the discourse between different constituencies about the company in the media (media commentary on an organization being a specific case in point). This helps to explain why their mix is entitled "the total corporate communications mix."

They also make the important point that organizations should aim to achieve congruence in *vertical* as well as in *horizontal* corporate communications. Vertical consistency is achieved through multiple channels of communication while horizontal consistency is achieved over time.

Balmer and Gray's tripartite mix encompasses:

- primary communications: the communications effects of products, services, management, staff, and corporate behavior;

- secondary communications: the communications effects of controlled forms of communications; in effect this embraces Van Riel's marketing communication mix;
- Tertiary communications: the communication activity relating to the corporation that exists among third parties; it includes such things as competitor and media commentary, and interest group communication, e.g., Greenpeace vis-à-vis the Shell/Brent Spar incident.

Marketing communications and corporate communications: the principal differences

A number of key differences are to be found regarding the conceptualization of marketing communications in relation to corporate communications. Corporate communications focuses on multiple stakeholder and interest groups; it has an important internal dimension in that it encompasses employee communication; it has a role regarding communications between the parent company and its subsidiaries; it embraces numerous communication functions; and it encompasses a variety of communications channels.

In contrast, marketing communications uses a smaller palette of communications vehicles that are focused on a finite number of stakeholder groups, with primary emphasis being given to business-to-business customers and household consumers.

Retrospective

By way of summary, it seems clear to us that whereas consumer/customer-directed marketing communications and corporate public relations have held secure places within many organizations, the same cannot be said for corporate communications, which until comparatively recently has experienced a somewhat uneven acceptance within the business community and as a subject studied at business schools. In part, corporate communications appears to have shared some of the same problems encountered by other corporate-level concepts such as corporate identity. All too often it has been seen to be of minor importance and has been accorded a cavalier or simplistic approach. However, major debacles in the field of corporate communications, such as the *Exxon Valdez* and Brent Spar controversies have brought with them the painful realization that effective corporate communications is not so much a luxury as a requisite.

In our estimation two authors, one a practitioner and one an academic, are worthy of special note, since through their published work they have advanced the general understanding of the importance of corporate communications. Not surprisingly, both these authors have been selected for inclusion in this section. Both have had the same dream, a *rêve à deux*, namely, that corporate communications should be part of an organization's strategic deliberations.

Rêve à deux: Bernstein and Van Riel

The first author is David Bernstein, a UK-based advertising agency creative and guru and consultant who has made corporate communications his core speciality. His book *Company Image and Reality*[29] provides an accessible introduction to the area. Although it was written with the senior manager in mind, it is significant that this text regularly surfaces within academic articles. The second author is an academic, Professor Cees Van Riel of Erasmus University in the Netherlands, whose text *Principles of Corporate Communication*[30] remains in wide currency as one of the first major academic texts on the area to emerge.

In his text Bernstein argues that many business failures are attributable to a failure to communicate effectively. He argues that the time and cerebral prowess that are invested in a corporation's strategic plan should to some considerable degree be mirrored in the formulation of an entity's corporate communication plan. Yet all too often corporate communications is regarded as a Cinderella among management disciplines. Moreover, organizations are often bereft of an overarching corporate communications strategy; they suffer from internal fragmentation among advertising, PR, and internal communications departments. He argues that companies have a *duty* to communicate – to communicate not only to their stakeholders but also to their industry and to society in general. Managers all too often abrogate their responsibility to communicate, he states. And the effect is often disastrous.

Van Riel's book provides an authoritative overview of corporate communications.[31] He also argues that the lack of coordination of corporate communications within organizations results in a communications approach that may be diffuse, confusing, contradictory, and sometimes prolix. Van Riel advocates that organizations coordinate the entire spectrum of company-specific communications.

Van Riel's text is notable in that it marshaled a good many hitherto unknown sources extant within mainland Europe. Because of language barriers, these had been known to relatively small practitioner and scholarly communities.

The articles

This section opens with a clear and instructive piece written for the practitioner section of the *International Journal of Advertising* in 1989 by David Bernstein. Bernstein is a raconteur *par excellence*. In this article he rails against those organizations that adopt a quiescent approach to corporate communication. Bernstein argues that such a tactic invariably backfires. This is because the absence of communication is *de facto* a form of negative communication. Attempting to build rapport with stakeholder groups only in times of crisis almost certainly will be seen by them as cynical, and will most likely falter. This is a point made in the most telling fashion in his chapter, which appropriately is entitled "Corporate Void." The chapter relates the story of a fictitious company than has manifestly failed to take corporate communications seriously. Bernstein's work has influenced a number of scholars, including Van Riel.

Van Riel, in a specially written article for this anthology (Chapter 8), provides a svelte and somewhat whistle-stop tour of the corporate communications domain. The two pieces together make for an appealing *pas de deux*.

Today, corporate communications remains firmly on the agenda of a good many senior managers and scholars alike. The launch of specialist journals on the area, such as the European-based *Corporate Communications: An International Journal*, is testimony that corporate communications has come of age.

Let us bring this introduction to a close by saying we are of the firm view that not only what organizations say, but also to whom and how they say it, provides another level of corporate meaning. Let us add our further belief that what companies communicate must also be supported by the reality of company behavior.

TOPICS FOR DISCUSSION AND REFLECTION

1   Explain the differences between corporate communications and marketing communications in terms of:
    (a)   target groups;
    (b)   communications channels;
    (c)   purposes.
    What dangers, if any, are there in relying on traditional marketing communications mix elements (advertising, marketing support, public relations, sales promotion, direct marketing, etc.) and on the marketing department generally for corporate communications?

2   How might the New Corporate Communications Wheel be altered so as to reflect:
    (a)   a holding company?
    (b)   a subsidiary?
    (c)   a police force?
    (d)   a city wishing to host the Olympic Games?
    (e)   a company that is subject to a hostile takeover bid?

3   What are the relative strengths and weaknesses of relying upon (a) common starting points, and (b) the sustainable corporate story as means of achieving consistency in corporate communications?

4   Examine Van Riel's Corporate Communication Mix and Balmer and Gray's Total Corporate Communications Mix in terms of:
    (a)   mirroring the corporate communications domain;
    (b)   their practical applicability.

5   Explain how environmental factors such as country of origin, industry sector, and association with business partners (e.g. franchises) may (or may not) affect corporate communications.

6   "It is not necessary for any one department to know what the other department is doing. It is the business of those who plan the entire work to see that all of the departments are working . . . towards the same end" (Henry Ford, 1863–1947). Discuss.

7   Imagine that you are the Director of Corporate Communications of the

company that has made a hostile takeover bid for the corporation depicted in Bernstein's "Corporate Void" (Chapter 7; see pp. 153–160). What communications strategy would you have in place for this bid with regard to:

(a) the stakeholder groups of your company?

(b) the company subjected to the bid?

8   What insights can be gleaned from "Corporate Void" in terms of

(a) the nature of corporate communications;

(b) their importance;

(c) their responsibilities;

(d) their link with identity?

9   Assess the efficacy of Robert Worcester's suggestion that corporate communications should address the following issues in the following order: *This is who we are. This is what we make. This is what we believe in.*

10   "In communications, familiarity breeds apathy" (William Bernbach, advertising executive). "Never express yourself more clearly than you are able to think" (Niels Bohr, 1885–1962, Danish physicist). Weigh the relative merits of the two statements.

NOTES

1   Bernstein, D., *Company Image and Reality: A Critique of Corporate Communications*, Eastbourne, U.K.: Holt, Rinehart and Winston, 1984.

2   *Ibid*.

3   Van Riel, C. B. M., *Principles of Corporate Communication*, London: Prentice Hall, 1995.

4   Cornelissen, J. P., Lock. A. R., and Gardner, H., "The Organisation of External Communication Disciplines: An Integrative Framework of Dimensions and Determinants," *International Journal of Advertising* 2001, 20: pp. 67–88.

5   Meffert, H., *Praxis des Kommunikationsmix*, Munster: BDW, 1979.

6   Knecht, J., *Geintegreerde Communicatie*, Amsterdam: BvA en VEA, 1989.

7   Schultz, D. E., Tannenbaum, S. I., and Lauterborn, R. F., *The New Marketing Paradigm: Integrated Marketing Communications*, Lincolnwood, IL: NTC, 1993.

8   Kotler, P. and Mindak, W., "Marketing and Public Relations, Should They Be Partners or Rivals?," *Journal of Marketing* 1978, 42 (16): 13–20; Cutlip, S. M., Center, A. H., and Broom, G. H., *Effective Public Relations*, 5th edition, London: Prentice Hall, 1985; Ehling, W. P., White, J., and Grunig, J. E., "Public Relations and Marketing Practices," in J. E. Grunig (ed.) *Excellence in Public Relations and Communication Management*, Hillsdale, NJ: Lawrence Erlbaum, 1992, pp. 357–383.

9   Broom, G. M., Lauzen, M. M., and Tucker, K., "Public Relations and Marketing: Dividing the Conceptual Domain and Operational Turf," *Public Relations Review* 1991, 17 (3): 219–225; Grunig, J. E. and Grunig, L. A., "The Relationship between Public Relations and Marketing in Excellent Companies: Evidence from the IABC Study," *Journal of Marketing Communications* 1998, 4 (3): 141–162; Kitchen, P.

and Moss, D. A., "Marketing and Public Relations: The Relationship Revisited," *Journal of Marketing Communications* 1995, 1 (2): 105–119.

10   Schultz *et al., op. cit.*; Nowak, G. J. and Phelps, J., "Conceptualizing the Integrated Marketing Communications Phenomenon: An Examination of Its Impact on Advertising Practices and Its Implications for Marketing Research," *Journal of Current Issues and Research in Advertising* 1994, 16 (1): 49–66.

11   Gronstedt, A., "Integrated Communications at America's Leading Total Quality Management Corporations," *Public Relations Review* 1996, 22 (1): 25–42; Varey, R., "Locating Marketing within the Corporate Communication Management System," *Journal of Marketing Communications* 1998, 4 (5): 177–190.

12   Cornelissen *et al., op. cit.*

13   Åberg, L., "Theoretical Model and Praxis of Total Communications," *International Public Relations Review* 1990, 13 (2): 13–16.

14   Siegel, A., "Clarifying the Corporate Voice: The Imperative of the '90s," *Design Management Journal*, Winter 1994: 40–46; Siegel, A., "Beyond Design: Developing a Positive Corporate Voice," *Design Management Journal*, Fall 1989, 1 (1): 64.

15   Van Riel, *op. cit.*

16   *Ibid.*

17   Boje, D. M., "The Storytelling Organization: A Study of Story Performance in an Office-Supply Firm," *Administration Science Quarterly* 1991, 36 (1): 106–126; Van Riel, C. B. M., "Sustaining the Corporate Story," in M. Schultz, M. J. Hatch and M. H. Larsen (eds) *The Expressive Organization*, Oxford: Oxford University Press, 2001, pp. 157–181; Shaw, G. G., "Planning and Communicating Using Stories," in Schultz *et al.* (eds) *The Expressive Organization*, pp. 182–195; Larsen, M. L., "Managing the Corporate Story," in Schultz *et al.* (eds) *The Expressive Organization*, pp. 196–207.

18   *Ibid.*, p. 197.

19   Van Riel, "Sustaining the Corporate Story," p. 157.

20   Shaw, *op. cit.*, pp. 183, 190.

21   Van Riel, "Sustaining the Corporate Story."

22   Roth, G. and Kleiner, A., "Developing Organizational Memory through Learning Histories," *Organizational Dynamics* (Autumn): 43–60.

23   Larsen, *op. cit.*, p. 197.

24   Van Riel, "Sustaining the Corporate Story," pp. 157–158.

25   *Ibid.*

26   Van Riel, *Principles of Corporate Communication.*

27   *Ibid.*, p. 9.

28   Balmer, J. M. T. and Gray, E. R., "Corporate Identity and Corporate Communications: Creating a Competitive Advantage," *Corporate Communications: An International Journal* 1999, 4 (4): 171–176.

29   Bernstein, *op. cit.*

30   Van Riel, *Principles of Corporate Communication.*

31   *Ibid.*

FURTHER READING

Åberg, L. (1990) "Theoretical Model and Praxis of Total Communications," *International Public Relations Review*, 13: 2.

Argenti, P. A. (1988) *Corporate Communication*, Irwin/McGraw-Hill, Burr Ridge, IL.

Arnold, J. E. (1998) "Communications and Strategy: The CEO Gets the Message," *Public Relations Quarterly*, Summer: 5–11.

Balmer, J. M. T. and Gray, E. R. (1999) "Corporate Identity and Corporate Communications: Creating a Competitive Advantage," *Corporate Communications: An International Journal* 4 (4): 171–176. Reprinted as Chapter 6 of this volume.

Bernstein, D. (1984) *Company Image and Reality: A Critique of Corporate Communications*, Eastbourne, U.K.: Holt, Rinehart and Winston.

Blakstad, M. and Cooper, A. (1995) *The Communicating Organization*, London: Institute of Personnel and Development.

Boje, D. M. (1991) "The Storytelling Organization: A Study of Story Performance in an Office-Supply Firm," *Administration Science Quarterly* 36 (1): 106–126.

Broom, G. M., Lauzen, M. M., and Tucker, K. (1991) "Public Relations and Marketing: Dividing the Conceptual Domain and Operational Turf," *Public Relations Review* 17 (3): 219–225.

Cornelissen, J. P., Lock, A. R., and Gardner, H. (2001) "The Organisation of External Communication Disciplines: An Integrative Framework of Dimensions and Determinants," *International Journal of Advertising* 20: 67–88.

Dentsu Public Relations Inc. (1998) *Koporeto Komyunikeshon* (Corporate Communication), Tokyo: Dentsu.

Ehling, W. P., White, J., and Grunig, J. E. (1992) "Public Relations and Marketing Practices," in J. E. Grunig (ed.) *Excellence in Public Relations and Communication Management*, Hillsdale, NJ: Lawrence Erlbaum Associates, pp. 357–383.

Foo, C. T. and Lowe, A. (1999) "Modelling for Corporate Identity Studies: Case of Identity as Communication Strategy," *Corporate Communications: An International Journal* 2: 89–92.

Foster, T. R. V. and Jolly, A. (1997) *Corporate Communications Handbook*, London: Kogan Page.

Gayeski, D. (1993) *Corporate Communications Management: The Renaissance Communicator in Information-Age Organizations*, Boston: Focal Press.

Goldhaber, G. (1986) *Organizational Communication*, Dubuque, IA: W. C. Brown.

Goodman, M. B. (1994) *Corporate Communication: Theory and Practice*, Albany, NY: State University of New York Press.

Goodman, M. B. (1997) *Corporate Communication for Executives*, Albany, NY: State University of New York Press.

Goodman, M. B. (2000) "Corporate Communication: The American Picture," *Corporate Communications: An International Journal* 6 (2): 69–74.

Goodman, M. B. (2001) "Current Trends in Corporate Communication," *Corporate Communications: An International Journal* 6 (3): 117–123.

Gronstedt, A. (1996) "Integrated Communications at America's Leading Total Quality Management Corporations," *Public Relations Review* 22 (1): 25–42.

Heath, R. L. (1994) *Management of Corporate Communication*, Hillsdale, NJ: Lawrence Erlbaum.

Horton, J. L. (1995) *Integrating Corporate Communications*, Westport, CT: Quorum Books.

Knecht, J. (1989) *Geintegreerde Communicatie*, Amsterdam: BvA en VEA.

Kotler, P. and Mindak, W. (1978) "Marketing and Public Relations, Should They be Partners or Rivals?," *Journal of Marketing* 42 (10): 13–20.

Kreps, G. L. (1990) *Organizational Communication*, New York: Longman.

Larsen, M. L. (2001) "Managing the Corporate Story," in M. Schultz, M. J. Hatch and M. H. Larsen (eds) *The Expressive Organization*, Oxford: Oxford University Press, pp. 196–207.

Marion, G. (1998) "Corporate Communications Managers in Large Firms: New Challenges," *European Journal of Management* 16 (6): 660–671.

Meffert, H. (1979) *Praxis des Kommunikationsmix*, Munster: BDW.

Noda, M. (1994) *Zaibie nikkei kopo reto Komyunikeshon katsudo jittai choas hokokusho 1988–1993* (Survey Report on the State of Corporate Communication Activities of Japanese Companies in the United States, 1988–1993), Tokyo: Institute of International Business Communication.

Nowak, G. J. and Phelps, J. (1994) "Conceptualizing the Integrated Marketing Communications Phenomenon: An Examination of Its Impact on Advertising Practices and Its Implications for Marketing Research," *Journal of Current Issues and Research in Advertising* 16 (1): 49–66.

Oliver, S. (1997) *Corporate Communication: Principles, Techniques and Strategies*, London: Kogan Page.

Oliver, S. (2000) "Symmetrical Communication: Does Reality Support Rhetoric?," *Corporate Communications: An International Journal* 6 (1): 26–33.

Scholes, E. and Clutterbuck, D. (1998) "Communicating with Stakeholders: An Integrated Approach," *Long Range Planning* 31: 227–338.

Schultz, D. E., Tannenbaum, S. I., and Lauterborn, R. F. (1993) *The New Marketing Paradigm: Integrated Marketing Communications*, Lincolnwood, IL: NTC.

Shaw, G. (2001) "Planning and Communicating Using Stories," In M. Schultz, M. J. Hatch, and M. H. Larsen (eds) *The Expressive Organization*, Oxford: Oxford University Press, pp. 182–195.

Siegel, A. (1989) "Beyond Design: Developing a Positive Corporate Voice," *Design Management Journal* 1 (1): 64.

Siegel, A. (1994) "Clarifying the Corporate Voice: The Imperative of the '90s," *Design Management Journal*, Winter: 40–46.

Steiner, C. J. (2001) "How Important is Professionalism to Corporate Communication?," *Corporate Communications: An International Journal* 6 (3): 150–156.

Swan, W., Langford, N., Watson, I., and Varey, R. J. (2000) "Viewing the Corporate Communication as a Knowledge Network," *Corporate Communications: An International Journal* 6 (2): 97–106.

Van Riel, C. B. M. (1992) "Corporate Communications in European Financial Institutions," *Public Relations Review* 18: 161–175.

Van Riel, C. B. M. (1995) *Principles of Corporate Communication*, London: Prentice Hall.

Van Riel, C. B. M. (2001) "Sustaining the Corporate Story," in M. Schultz, M. J. Hatch, and M. H. Larsen (eds) *The Expressive Organization*, Oxford: Oxford University Press, pp. 157–181.

Varey, R. and White, J. (2000) "The Corporate Communication System of Managing," *Corporate Communications: An International Journal* 5 (1): 5–11.

Varey, R. (1998) "Locating Marketing within the Corporate Communication Management System," *Journal of Marketing Communications* 4 (3): 177–190.

Yamauchi, K. (2001) "Corporate Communications: A Powerful Tool for Stating Corporate Missions," *Corporate Communications: An International Journal* 6 (3): 131–136.

Chapter 7

David Bernstein

CORPORATE VOID

From *International Journal of Advertising* 1989, 8: 315–320

EDITORS' COMMENTARY

Author, dramatist, raconteur, occasional speech-writer to HRH The Prince of Wales, columnist for *Design Week*, founder and chairman of The Creative Business, David Bernstein approaches the various aspects of his work with a missionary zeal and fervor. His natural habitat? Corporate headquarters, industrial bodies, major international conferences, business schools, and airport business lounges. His business? The business of communication. His calling? To promulgate the nature and salience of corporate communications to successive generations of industrialists, faculty, and students.

He has great presence, personally as well as on the global stage.

Bernstein's considerable commercial expertise, keen sense of satire and theater, and general *joie de vivre* make him a keynote[1] and after-dinner speaker without compare. The epitome of sartorial elegance, he cuts a distinctive and debonair figure in his natural milieu. His signature bow tie habitually parades a bacchanalian riot of colors. The ties are always in exquisite taste, sometimes bespoke and *always* hand-tied.

David's delight of the irreverent is tempered by considerable perspicacity and intellect. This mix of sagacity and profanity has proved to be a winning formula both in his presentations and in his written work. The latter includes books, papers for organizations such as the Confederation of British Industry (CBI),[2] and at least one television drama. He is the only individual we know who has had the distinction of having one of his television plays interrupted by one of his commercials.

Put It Together – Put It Across: The Craft of Business Presentation[3] and

Creative Advertising: For This You Went to Oxford?[4] are two of his better-known books. However, it is his book *Company Image and Reality: A Critique of Corporate Communications*[5] that has won him the greatest plaudits. It is regularly referred to within the literature. Like all his written work, it is erudite and skillfully crafted.

The article reproduced here, "Corporate Void," appeared in the *International Journal of Advertising*. It is part parable and part commentary. It adds up to a powerful whole. Like any good parable, it has lost nothing of its veracity with the passing of time. We view "Corporate Void" as something akin to a Damascene conversation, albeit a corporate one. However, this conversation takes place at the eleventh hour, with the chief executive finally appreciating the importance of both corporate communications and corporate identity.

From our experience, the scenario described in "Corporate Void" is far from fanciful. In this fictitious case history Bernstein relates the saga of an organization which, although it accords considerable importance to its product-line brands, its share price, and company profits, has abrogated its responsibility to engage in effective and ongoing corporate communication. In this woeful tale of neglect we learn that the organization is bereft of a department, let alone an individual, with day-to-day responsibility for communicating with the organization's key stakeholder groups. We learn that the company does not have a good or a bad image but rather that it has no image at all. Awareness of the company is depressingly low.

Having made this important point, the parable might have drawn to a close, but as with any good drama there is an unexpected twist and the *Sturm und Drang* intensifies. Bernstein relates that just as the CEO realizes the efficacy of corporate communications he learns that his company is the focus of a predatory takeover bid. At this juncture it becomes apparent that corporate communications is both a strategic issue for organizations and an issue that requires ongoing investment in terms of time, money, and management. As the company is dragged down by the currents caused by years of neglect of corporate communication we see the CEO struggling to keep afloat. He realizes that such is the corporation's predicament that garnering a new visual identification system and press relations campaign is woefully inadequate to address the ensuing catastrophe.

Bernstein not only rails against using any of the above as a surrogate for ongoing corporate communications management but argues that corporate communications activities generally should be rooted in the company's culture. In essence Bernstein advocates that identity, communication, and image need to be coordinated. Moreover, he advocates that corporate communications management should be undertaken not only because it makes good business sense but because companies have a moral duty to communicate: it is a question of integrity.

Bernstein leaves the story at the height of the storm. It seems improbable that the company will be able to fend off the takeover or that the company's senior management will emerge unscathed from the debacle.

The moral of the parable? A profitable company that has rich product-brand assets but swims in the dark and in the deep is not easily heard or seen when under predatory attack.

The prognosis is invariably bleak.

NOTES

1   Bernstein, D., "Corporate Branding: Back to Basics," the Third Lord Goold Memorial Lecture delivered at Bradford School of Management, November 2000 at the Seventh International Corporate Identity Symposium. To be published in a special edition on Corporate and Services Branding: *European Journal of Marketing*, 2003. Forthcoming.

2   Bernstein, D., *Working for Customers*, London: Confederation of British Industry, 1983.

3   Bernstein, D., *Put It Together – Put It Across: The Craft of Business Presentation*, London: Cassell. 1988.

4   Bernstein, D., *Creative Advertising: For This You Went to Oxford?*, London: Longman.

5   Bernstein, D., *Company Image and Reality: A Critique of Corporate Communications*, Eastbourne, U.K.: Holt, Rinehart and Winston, 1984.

LET US IMAGINE you are the chief executive of a major British manu-facturing company. Your brands are well known, many of them successfully marketed throughout Europe. Your shares have held up. Your end-of-year profits figure is ahead of the analysts' expectations. You enter the new financial year in good heart. You deserve this break in Barbados. You'll get some rest. And catch up on that file of not-so-urgent reading.

Three days of sun and you open the file. You read a report. You discover you are running not a company, but an enigma.

Your *brands* are well known. But, among those audiences whom you respect and need, the company itself has a very blurred image. Mind you, you had hints of this before. An acquaintance at your club, when you mentioned your company name, got you confused with another manufacturer in a totally different line of business. A marketing journalist associated you with one of your brands but had no idea you owned another four times the size.

A sample of two – you remind yourself – is not research. But then, out of the blue, arrives this research report. It comes from a quality national newspaper. It has employed a respectable market research company. Opinion leaders have been asked their opinions about leading companies.

How can opinion leaders be so ignorant! The researchers presented the respondents with a list of attributes, e.g.:

Their products are leaders in their field.
Honest in the conduct of their business.
Good company to work for.
Their prices are too high.
Make too big a profit.
You can believe in their advertising.
A well-managed company.

The scores worry you. Respondents were not specifically antagonistic. Frankly they could not mark you because they *did not know much about you*.

In the accompanying literature you learn that the key finding of corporate communication research in the USA and the UK is this: familiarity leads to favourability. Respondents are more likely to think favourably of those companies they know about.

You examine the figures. The companies with the highest scores are those you would expect. Their images are clear in *your* mind. They have invested heavily over the years – and *consistently* – in a coherent communications programme.

In three years' time the European Single Market will be here. The stakes will be bigger, the opportunities greater – and the competition tougher.

So you make a New Year resolution. You will seriously address this issue. You will make your company known by those publics whose current ignorance is a liability – e.g., the financial community, government, the media and, with an eye to the future, universities.

But what exactly will you do? You know what the problem is – you are not well known. But the solution? Where does it lie? Advertising? A new logo (or corporate identity scheme)? A public relations campaign? Sponsorship even? All of these will make you better known. The question is: known *for what*? And this brings you back from media to content. What do you want to say about yourself?

Tomorrow morning you are taking a boat trip. That will give you time to think . . . .

You begin with the fundamentals. This is who we are. This is what we make. This is what we believe in. (Robert Worcester of the opinion research company MORI insists that these subjects have to be addressed in that order. It is no good telling people what you believe in if they have no idea who you are.)

Now this should not be difficult. After all, we know who we are and what we make. What we believe in may be a *bit* harder. But is anybody out there going to be *interested*? After all, it is not simply a matter of what we want to say, but of how we say it. How do we make it interesting and, above all, distinctive?

How do we do that? Distinctive means different from everyone else. It also means being true to oneself. So that everything emanating from the company is *in character*.

Everything? Well those companies with the highest scores, they *do* act single-mindedly: ICI looks like ICI wherever you encounter it. The advertisements may differ from country to country but the message is common: 'World Class'. And the logo is identical. As Anne Ferguson, ICI's corporate marketing and publicity manager, says, 'The image is now the same whether you go to an ICI plant in Korea or India, Frankfurt or Phoenix, Arizona'.

Look at Lufthansa, Olivetti, Sony. . . .

Or Coca-Cola for that matter, you muse, as you sip your pre-lunch rum and coke and the boat turns for home. Maybe you need some help.

You decide to ring the office the moment you get back to shore. Who do you ring? Is there someone there specifically in charge of corporate affairs or corporate communications? Well no, not exactly. It falls between the marketing director and the company secretary. So you decide to speak to the chairman.

You ring. He sounds relieved to hear you. 'I think we need some help with our image.' He thinks so too. 'Some outside company.'

'What sort of company?' he asks.

You think.

'Hullo', he says. The pause has added three pounds to your hotel bill, but you are no nearer your solution. Where *do* you go?

'Surely corporate communications is big business in the UK?' you say.

'Yes', he says, 'they are all into it. Design companies. Public relations companies. Advertising agencies. Creative consultants. Management consultants.'

'Do we need all of them?'

'Oh no. I suppose we could start with a design consultant.'

'You think we need a new logo?'

'Bit late for that.'

'Late?'

'It could be a PR programme. Or an advertising campaign.'

'What you're saying is it depends who we go to?'

'Frankly', he replies, 'they are more interested in selling solutions than answering problems. But in the circumstances I think we need a corporate advertising campaign. And quick.'

'Why?'

'The bid.'

'Bid. What bid?'

'You mean you didn't get the fax or the telex?'

'I've been at sea.'

'I think we all have', says the chairman.

By the time the average company thinks it needs to do something about its image it is probably too late. In the USA last year 1864 companies changed their names because of mergers and acquisitions. (Report of Anspach, Grossman and Portugal quoted in *Campaign*, 27.1.89.) In the unlikely circumstance that a company has *no* image it may be able to project its identity as it were onto a blank screen. Most probably, however, an image of sorts already exists. Blurred. Muddy. A mosaic of half-formed impressions. And almost certainly out of date.

The new corporate advertising campaign is meant to erase all that. (The whitewash analogy is appropriate.) Instead it adds contrasting pieces to the mosaic. Coherent it ain't.

To believe that corporate advertising or any other item of corporate communication (e.g., a press relations campaign, inspired sponsorship, a new corporate identity) can correct a company's image is to believe that painting the lavatory door will cure the plumbing. A quick image fix may satisfy a few people in the short term, particularly the opportunistic and unprofessional design company, but it means, as Daniel Boorstin put it in his book *The Image*, that the company has decided on a change of face rather than a change of heart. In the words of Rodney Fitch, 'a new letterhead and logo is no substitute for a new board of directors'.

Corporate advertising *is* about the heart of the company. And a company – particularly a public company – has to wear its heart on its sleeve. Why? Because it is evidence of what it is about. Because it differentiates one company from another. Because it is, above all, a *brand*.

If a company is a brand, then the chief executive is a brand manager.

Try the exercise from the parable above. Think of a successful company. Then think of its visual manifestations and your experiences, direct and indirect with the company. I will bet they are all of a piece.

It matters to that company that they should be. Just as it matters that each packet of whatever FMCG it makes and brands delivers the identical consumer benefit or that every widget it manufactures is identical in size to a micro-tolerance.

But whereas a company may see the need for careful brand monitoring and guardianship, it often pays far less attention to its most important brand, the company itself. Indeed, when asked who is *in charge* of that it may point in several directions or none. Responsibility may fall between the desks of the managing director and the press relations officer. Or it may be the part-time responsibility of an overworked assistant to the chief executive. In one of the UK's major companies the role of the executive in charge of media relations was fundamentally to prevent information about the company appearing in the media. That company was recently the object of a hostile bid. It subsequently embarked upon a campaign of external corporate communications.

Responsibility for the company brand must reside at or near the desk of the chief executive. He 'can no more delegate the responsibility for communication than he can for earnings per share' (Chairman of the Eaton Corporation, USA).

And if he is responsible for the brand's communication he must equally be responsible for knowing what the brand *stands for*. What *is* at its heart? Has that been defined? And articulated? Is it known in the company? If so at what level? Has it been codified in some form of mission statement? Or does management dismiss such practice as an unnecessary, alien (i.e., US or Japanese) practice?

'Corporate philosophies all sound the same' it is argued. That is largely true. After all the number of corporate values is finite. But if a company believes in something should it not say so and swear to live by it? Should it omit to say it merely because it does not differentiate the company from other companies? Surely what differentiates one company from another is not its philosophy, but how that philosophy is carried out. *Style* is the discriminator. The personality of the company. Personality is the sum total of characteristics which makes a person *that* person, a company *that* company. And that needs articulating as much as the company's philosophy.

Corporate advertising must reflect both – the philosophy and the personality. It must proclaim the company's core beliefs not in tablets of stone, but by example. And its manner of telling that story must be consistent with its personality. The advertising must be true to the company culture, that mixture of beliefs and behaviour which is generally felt rather than expressed, but which is recognized by all who work there and deal with it. And every communication from that company, every encounter an individual customer or potential customer experiences must be coherent.

Why? Because it says *integrity*, that's why. And that's no accidental semantic felicity. Integrity is the key to branding. When a product moved from commodity to brand the owner stamped it with his name or mark. 'We have given our word.' A brand is a reminder of past performance and a guarantee of future satisfaction. And everything that bears that mark is part of that promise. And anything which, bearing that mark, fails to match it diminishes the brand.

Michael Wolf makes an interesting comparison between Mercedes and Rover. 'From the spare parts manual, and the enthusiasm of a service mechanic, to the canteen in the factory every detail represents the Mercedes-Benz attitude. . . . On the other hand, what is now called the Rover Group is a container of details which can be flung together to make contradictory experiences and confusing emotions – and usually are. Many of the details come from past containers such as Leyland' (Michael Wolf, The Identified Corporation, in *Management 89: The Challenge of Competition*, IMC 1989).

For a company's communications to be coherent, so that every item is felt to emanate from the identical source, the company needs first to have something to be coherent *to*. When a company elects to mount a corporate advertising campaign – to handle a 'local difficulty' or a tactical exercise – it should not need to ask itself about fundamentals, i.e., philosophy or tone of voice. Yet how many times has the opinion-leading public been faced with worthy statements of belief and intention which are unidentified with that company because either they sit uneasily with past reputation or they are indistinguishable from similar corporate utterances.

Philosophies may be the same but, as we saw, that is no reason why the *expression* of belief has to be identical. Yet corporate advertising, with some notable recent exceptions, still has a homogenizing effect. It still seems to iron out differences between companies, even between those in totally different areas.

In product advertising those very same companies would be careful to keep identities constant. They would differentiate. This would make products *brands*. The fundamental physical differences between products may be minimal. But the totality of the package which constitutes the brand (the ingredients, pack, performance, advertising, etc.) will be significantly different. The way the product is seen, the imagery which is applied, the consumer identification it elicits, the strength of the advocacy – all succeed in enlarging the minuscule gap between the product and its competition and make that product a 'brand'.

Conversely, corporate advertising which takes as its raw material a company of diverse human beings and diverse activities in diverse locations and even diverse products and markets, more often than not succeeds in summing it up in a phrase of numbing ordinariness and proclaiming a virtue to which all businesses lay claim.

All of which led me to propose Bernstein's Law. It states:

Product Advertising takes minor differences and maximizes them

whereas

Corporate Advertising takes major differences and minimizes them.

However, if a company believes it can differentiate itself only through its corporate advertising it might as well save itself the expenditure. Creativity is not a substitute for the truth. It uses facts and transmutes them. It is not a substitute for a philosophy. It is the philosophy made manifest. It is not a substitute for a corporate personality. It is a means of illuminating it.

To repeat – what are the corporate communications being coherent *to*?

There is a *bon mot* much beloved of conference speakers on corporate matters. Corporate advertising is like growing asparagus. I should have started three years ago.

To which I add a rider. What should have started three years ago was not necessarily corporate advertising, but the analysis of corporate purpose and behaviour and its clear and cogent articulation.

Chapter 8

Cees B. M. Van Riel

THE MANAGEMENT OF CORPORATE COMMUNICATION

EDITORS' COMMENTARY

The Dutch corporate communications scholar Professor Cees Van Riel is a person who is always on the move. He is a person in a hurry, an individual whose feet are rarely on the ground (no pun intended even for a subject of a kingdom whose citizens have become adept in taming the North Sea). In a very real sense he is the quintessential *Flying* Dutchman. Van Riel is not only an accomplished academic but also a sportsman of considerable prowess. He is equally at home on the football pitch or, in the winter, on Holland's frozen canals where he is, by all accounts, a most adroit ice skater. For relaxation his thoughts turn to Cuba, since among his close colleagues and friends he is known to be an inveterate cigar smoker. Smoking appears to be one of the rare occasions where his lips are the only things on the move apart from his eyebrows, which touch the heavens and thereby divulge Cees's utter rapture.

Professor Van Riel is the Director of the Corporate Communication Center at Erasmus University, Rotterdam, and Managing Director of the Reputation Institute. He is one of the first European scholars to specialize in corporate communication. Along with Charles Fombrun he is coeditor of the *Corporate Reputation Review*, a journal primarily devoted to corporate reputation research but which also covers other corporate-level subjects such as corporate communication and corporate identity.

His book *Principles of Corporate Communication*[1] is one of the first academic texts to have an explicit corporate communications focus. This seminal work did much to establish the field of corporate communications as an area in its own right within Europe.

For Van Riel, corporate communication represents *the key* construct within the broad area of corporate-level marketing. It is an umbrella title under which he subsumes corporate identity, reputation, and branding.

In this chapter, which has been specially written for this anthology, Van Riel places corporate communication in a historical context by explaining that communications have traditionally been seen to fall within the responsibilities of marketing and/or public relations. Van Riel points out that at the corporate level a somewhat jaundiced view of communication used to prevail, with these two functions together being assigned the responsibility for corporate communication. However, corporate communications has experienced exponential growth over recent years, as manifest by the emergence of departments concerned with investor, environmental, and recruitment communications, to name but a few.

The rise of all forms of corporate communications being emitted from the organization via multiple channels has often led to fragmented if not contradictory messages being received by individuals both within and outside the organization. Accordingly, there has been, and remains, a pressing need for corporations to coordinate their communications. This management concern has been picked up by Van Riel and remains an important theme of his writings and one of his key scholarly interests.

In this chapter Van Riel explains that organizations have attempted to overcome some dichotomies associated by corporate communications by introducing rules and structures, sequencing, organizational routines, and group problem-solving.

Certainly, Van Riel has been very active in scholarship relating to the coordination of corporate-level communication. We have mentioned above his *common starting points* (CSPs) concept, based on the notion that corporate communication can be coordinated by delineating the key cultural characteristics of an entity; these are then used as a basis for ensuring consistency in corporate communications. However, this approach has a downside, namely that CSPs are capable of replication by other entities.

A good deal of this chapter is concerned with the current interest in the sustainable corporate story. This aspect of coordination has largely eclipsed the notion of the common starting points. This is because a corporate story cannot be easily replicated.

As we have noted in the section introduction, Van Riel advocates that corporate stories have a utility when four criteria are met. They should be *realistic* (based on fact), *relevant* (with regard to the organization's stakeholder groups), *responsive* (should allow for dialogue between the organization and its stakeholders), and *sustainable* (should meet the wants and needs of the variety of stakeholder groups as well as having a utility for the organization concerned).

This composition provides an encyclopedic introduction to the field of corporate communication. We again thank Cees for his time in preparing this essay. With its publication Cees's thoughts may once again turn toward Cuba. We rather hope so.

NOTE

1   Van Riel, C. B. M., *Principles of Corporate Communication*, London: Prentice Hall, 1995.

Introduction

CORPORATE COMMUNICATION HAS in recent times evolved into a full field of study, both in practice and in scientific theory. During the past two decades, the theoretical basis has particularly grown through the significant increase in insight in the core issues provided by researchers from different disciplines (including marketing, organisational studies, strategic management and communication) and stemming from both Europe and the United States. Of at least equal importance is the emergence of a group of researchers (corporate communication, reputation management) who take an integral approach in tackling research problems in the field of corporate communication.

In this chapter I will try to reach two goals. In the first place, I will try to make it clear to the reader what the field of corporate communication entails (definition, type of (research) questions, who is active in this field, etc.). Second, I will present an overview of what in my opinion are the most important views expressed in the literature pertaining to a core concept of corporate communication: management of communication. In particular, I will explain my views about a so-called Sustainable Corporate Story, as a source of inspiration to be drawn on for all internal and external communication. At the end of the chapter I will draw some conclusions regarding the future of corporate communication research.

The field of corporate communication

At the beginning of the twenty-first century, most universities pay attention to corporate communication. The names used vary greatly; among them strategic communication, company communication, organisational communication and of course corporate communication. The type of research one specialises in is of course coloured by the nature of the field of study of the faculty within which the research takes place. Corporate communication has been located within business administration and economics since the 1970s. Initially it was part of economics, particularly concerning marketing communication, and later it was to be found within business administration, but latterly a more integrated approach to identity and reputation issues has evolved.

Corporate communication can in my opinion be described as the orchestration of all the instruments in the field of organisation identity (communication, symbols and the behaviour of the organisation's members) in such an attractive and realistic manner as to create or maintain a positive reputation for groups with which the organisation has a dependent relationship. This results in a competitive advantage for the organisation. Theoretically speaking, corporate communication can be divided into three main forms of communication: management communication, marketing communication and organisational communication.

Management communication is the communication of managers (on different levels) with internal and external target groups. In particular, researchers concentrating on internal communication have frequently shown how essential the role of managers is in bringing about a positive communication climate (Smidts *et al.*, 2001). In the literature on strategic management, researchers have discussed the role of the CEO in the realisation of a positive reputation (Deephouse, 2000). This research has also shown that managers play a crucial role (or at least they should) in the communication field. However, not all managers are aware of the role they play in communication.

That does not necessarily mean that they are not doing a good job. They are simply not always aware of the fact that they are involved in communication. In their eyes, communication is the task of the people in the organisation specially hired for that purpose. Depending on a company's history, these departments have names such as internal and external communication, corporate communication, company communication, marketing communication, sponsoring, investor relations, job market communication, issues management, etc. This kaleidoscope of communication specialities can roughly be divided into two main groups. On the one hand, different forms of sales-supporting communication can be grouped under the term 'marketing communication'. On the other hand, reputation-enhancing (indirectly sales-promoting) activities can be designated 'organisational communication'. In companies, the accent – especially in budgetary terms – lies on marketing communication: advertising, direct mail, personal sales, sponsoring, etc. Besides this a whole range of organisational communication modalities can be distinguished: public relations, public affairs, investor relations, environment communication, corporate advertising, internal communication, and such like. Until recently, communication was the exclusive domain of the public relations and marketing communication department. However, this era has passed for good with the rise of new communication specialities within functional management units such as 'financial management' (investor relations), 'production management' (environment communication), 'human resources' (job market communication), that mostly communicate with internal and external target groups 'outside' the jurisdiction of the traditional communication departments.

In practice, the diversity of internal 'senders' leads to fragmented and sometimes even contradictory communication statements concerning the organisation as a whole. Organisations are aware of the dangers of fragmented communication. Not only are they wary of painful incidents, but they especially want to keep communication activities in their totality as effective and efficient as possible. This explains the clear trend now to strive towards an increase in the mutual cohesion of all forms of communication. This effort is based on the assumption that a coherent communication policy makes a positive contribution to the creation of a favourable reputation for the collective, which is responsible for the overall organisational behaviour. Apart from that, a favourable reputation is no goal in itself, but a necessary condition (therefore a means) to attain a good (commercial) starting position, which will serve to increase success (in the broadest definition of the word). Recent research has provided empirical proof of this assertion (Fombrun and Shanley, 1990; Maathuis, 1999; Rao, 1997).

Most researchers – whom I would personally like to call corporate communication specialists – concentrate their scientific investigations primarily on issues related to organisational communication and management communication. Nevertheless, it is impossible, either for researchers or for professionals in practice to erect a Chinese wall between the different forms of communication. Moreover, the building of an appealing identity and reputation for an organisation can only be investigated in an adequate manner (and realised in practice) when not only the extent of the consistency between all forms of communication is looked at, but also the coherent application of symbols and – last but not least – the behaviour of members of the organisation are investigated.

The field of measurement of reputation measurement and conceptualisation of identity has, at the beginning of the twenty-first century, been researched most thoroughly. Relatively underdeveloped, however, are the measurement of identity, corporate branding and especially the mutually consistent coordination of different forms of communication. In the following section I will summarise the currently available knowledge in this field. First I would like to reflect on what in my opinion should be the central questions in the field of corporate communication. They can be divided roughly into three clusters:

1   *Identity cluster.* How can the identity of an organisation be determined? What is the influence of certain aspects of the identity on the performance of the organisation? Is identity a single (unambiguous) or plural (hybrid) concept?

2   *Reputation cluster.* How can the reputation of an organisation be determined? What is the influence of reputation (positive and negative) on the performance of an organisation? What factors exert the largest influence on a positive or on a negative reputation?

3   *Management of communication.* Why is it important to try to tune the different forms of communication used by an organisation to each other? What factors simplify consistency in the overall communication policy? How can organisations orchestrate 'communication', 'symbols' and 'behaviour of the organisation's members' in a consistent manner? How can a Sustainable Corporate Story increase the degree of consistency in corporate communication?

The interrelationship between these questions is illustrated in Figure 1. *In this chapter I will concentrate solely on 'management of corporate communication' or orchestration of the corporate identity mix.*

Management of communication

Coordination of tasks within an organisation

Organisations are increasingly aware of the fact that the joint communication efforts by all specialists in this field in an organisation are not always effective. Communication is sometimes fragmented or even contradictory. The magic phrase by which solutions to this problem are often looked for seems to be 'integration of communication'. This can be achieved in several ways. The

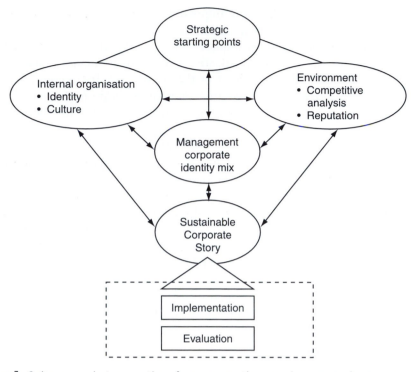

Figure 1 Coherence between the four core themes in research on corporate communication

longest tradition in this field is that of corporate design ('house style'). Other examples are working with common starting points, using the same operational systems and cooperating in the making of decisions pertaining to (marketing) communication.

Orchestration of communication is in essence no more and no less than the solving of a coordination issue. In the literature on 'organisational behaviour' (Grant, 1996; Lawrence and Lorsch, 1967; March and Simon, 1958; Ouchi, 1979), a wealth of relevant information can be found about this, which is also applicable to the field of communication management. It goes without saying that interesting information on this topic can also be found in areas concerned more with communication than in coordination, such as in public relations (Grunig, 1992) and marketing (Nowak and Phelps, 1995; Schultz *et al.*, 1994) and strategy (Cornelissen *et al.*, 2001).

Grant (1996) has in my opinion tackled the most important issues in the area of coordination, because his approach can relatively easily be 'translated' to the coordination of all forms of communication. He argues that there are four mechanisms within an organisation that integrate specialist knowledge (such as communication knowledge). These are:

- 'rules and instructions': procedures, rules, standardised information and communication systems;
- 'sequencing': the organisation of the primary process in a sequential

manner, such that the input of every specialist seems independent because it is allocated its own 'time slot';

- 'organisational routine': application of professional action in a relatively automatic manner, with the use of implicit protocols;
- 'group problem-solving': to be implemented when the complexity increases, a more personal and communication-intensive form of integration.

Applied to communication coordination, this classification results in the matrix shown in Table 1, by which the 'orchestration mechanism' is categorised inside one of the four categories shown in the table.

Coordination is a means by which to find a solution for efficiency and effectiveness problems in businesses. Its logical counterpart is differentiation, the stimulation of entrepreneurship of individuals and/or their business units, thereby allowing them to be responsible for their own decisions in commercial or non-commercial areas.

Despite the popularity of decentralised decisions in organisations, it is still necessary – especially in the field of corporate communication – to establish clear mutual agreements. There should at least be agreement on the question of who is responsible for what, and preferably also on what the common denominators in the communication are.

Table 1 Classification communication management

Rules	Sequencing	Routinisation	Group problem-solving
House style (parent visibility)	Organisation of communication function: tasks, responsibilities, budget	Training an education of protocol for press contact, campaign presentation, implementation, investor relations, etc.	Steering committee
Common starting points (content coordination)	Connecting communication to commercial life cycle		Annual/quarterly evaluations
Guidelines for working with external offices, internal budget responsibilities			Ad hoc meetings

Source: C. B. M. Van Riel, *Principles of Corporate Communication*, London: Prentice Hall, 1995.

Common starting points in communication

Common starting points (Van Riel, 1995) can be seen as central values that may be used as a basis for the steering of the content of all forms of communication used by an organisation. The determination of common starting points is especially useful for the creation of clear priorities, for example, the support of the control and evaluation of the total communication policy. However, common starting points do have their limitations. They are usually 'but' words that can be easily imitated by competitors, and – an even graver problem – they can be explained in too many different ways. A better alternative in this context is to link the words that form the common starting points in sentences and then to arrange these sentences in the form of a story.

Sustainable Corporate Story (SCS)

Communication provides businesses with the means to establish a dialogue in order to create consciousness, understanding and appreciation of the strategic goals of a company. In the ideal scenario, this results in an increase in the competitive advantage of the company. In my opinion, stakeholders will more readily accept a corporate story when they perceive its contents as being coherent and attractive. It should contribute to their personal advantages and, even more imporant, should not arouse any irritation. In my opinion, communication is more effective when a so-called Sustainable Corporate Story can be relied on as a source of inspiration for all internal and external communication activities. After all, stories are difficult to imitate and they simplify the consistency in all the messages propagated by the organisation.

A corporate story will be most effective when four criteria are met. First, the story should be realistic. This is the case when the stakeholders see the content of the story as typical for the organisation and as truly distinguishing it with regard to competitors. It should also be typical for the organisation as a whole and not only for the finest jewels in that organisation's crown. Second, the story should be relevant. The stakeholders should perceive the story as adding value to their daily lives. Third, the communication style used by the organisation to communicate the story should be 'responsive'.

A corporate story is a dynamic entity, developed and redeveloped by the permanent, ongoing interaction between internal and external stakeholders. A continuous dialogue in the testing of the relevance and the reality of the Sustainable Corporate Story, and readiness to apply changes resulting from the dialogue, will have a positive effect on the attractiveness of the story. Recent developments in technology (web sites) make it easier for businesses to show a responsive attitude. However, it is not the technology that should be the determining factor; rather, it is the mentality actually to be willing to react to opinions from society that makes the essential difference. For example, reference to an Internet site is hardly useful if the organisation does not want to react to messages arriving through the site.

The fourth characteristic with which the effectiveness of the corporate story can be improved is the extent to which the story can be characterised as 'sustainable'. A corporate story will be 'sustainable' only when it succeeds in finding and maintaining the right balance between the competing demands of all relevant stakeholders and the wishes of the members of the organisation itself. An extensive discussion of my views regarding the corporate story can be found in *The Expressive Organization* (Van Riel, 2000).

Conclusions

Research in corporate communication has grown substantially in the past decade. This has, for example, resulted in elaborated knowledge in orchestration of communication at a holistic company level. Consistency in communication is one of the crucial factors in increasing success with corporate communication. This implies the necessity of ensuring clarity about who is responsible *for* what and especially *about* what. I introduced the concept 'Sustainable Corporate Story' in this chapter as a tool for increasing internal coherence in communication. Such a story should be used, in my opinion, as the common source of inspiration for all specialised areas of communication within an organisation.

Such stories are of great importance in three ways. First, they increase the distinguishing power of an organisation. After all, a story can more easily be remembered and is more difficult to imitate. Second, they simplify the orchestration of communication. As soon as agreement on the company story has been reached, the chance that – implicitly and explicitly – the same accents are applied to all communication increases. Third – and this might be the most important reason – the building of a story through the common efforts of the top management, the human resources department and the communications department is at least as important as the use of the story for external (and internal) goals. The building of a story creates such a bond between these people that they – legitimately – start to see it as their own creation. It goes without saying that this increases their enthusiasm to actually live the Sustainable Corporate Story.

References

Cornelissen, J., Lock, A. and Gardner, H. (2001) 'The organization of external communication disciplines: an integrative framework of dimensions and determinants', *International Journal of Advertising* 20: 67–88.

Deephouse, D. L. (2000) 'Media reputation as a strategic resource: an integration of mass communication and resource-based theories', *Journal of Management* 26 (6): 1091–1112.

Fombrun, C. J. and Shanley, M. (1990) 'What's in a name? Reputation building and corporate strategy', *Academy of Management Journal* 33: 233–258.

Grant, R. M. (1996) 'Toward a knowledge-based theory of the firm', *Strategic Management Journal* 17: 109–122.

Grunig, J. E. (ed.) (1992) *Excellence in Public Relations and Communication Management*, Hillsdale, NJ: Lawrence Erlbaum.

Lawrence, P. and Lorsch, J. (1967) *Strategic Media Planning*, Lincolnwood, IL: MTC Business Books.

Maathuis, O. (1999) 'Corporate branding: two empirical studies on the value of the corporate brand', doctoral thesis, Rotterdam School of Mangement, Erasmus University, Rotterdam.

March, J. and Simon, H. (1958) *Organisations*, New York: John Wiley.

Nowak, G. J. and Phelps, J. (1995) 'Geïntegreerde marketingcommunicatie', *Tijdschrift voor Strategische Bedrijfscommunicatie*.

Ouchi, W. (1979) 'A conceptual framework for the design of organisational control mechanisms', *Management Science* 25: 833–848.

Rao, H. (1997) 'The rise of investor relations departments in the Fortune 500 industrials', *Corporate Reputation Review* 1 (1/2): 172–177.

Schultz, D. E., Tannenbaum, S. I. and Lauterborn, R. F. (1994) *Integrated Marketing Communications*, Chicago: NTC Business Books.

Smidts, A., Pruyn, A. and Van Riel, C. B. M. (2001) 'The impact of employee communication and external prestige on organizational identification', *Academy of Management Journal* 49 (5): 1051–1062.

Van Riel, C. B. M. (1995) *Principles of Corporate Communication*, London: Prentice Hall.

Van Riel, C. B. M. (2000) 'Corporate communication orchestrated by a sustainable corporate story', in M. Schultz, M. Hatch and M. Holten Larsen (eds) *The Expressive Organization*, Oxford: Oxford University Press, pp. 157–182.

Corporate image and reputation: the other realities

In Broken Images

He is quick, thinking in clear images;
I am slow, thinking in broken images.
He becomes dull, trusting to his clear images;
I become sharp, mistrusting my broken images.
Trusting his images, he assumes their relevance;
Mistrusting my images, I question their relevance.
Assuming their relevance, he assumes the fact;
Questioning the relevance, I question the fact.
When the fact fails him, he questions his senses;
When the fact fails me, I approve my senses.
He continues quick and dull in his clear images;
I continue slow and sharp in my broken images.
He in a new confusion of his understanding;
I in a new understanding of my confusion.
(Robert Graves)

EDITORS' INTRODUCTION

Corporate image: an exceptional inheritance

After 2000 years of human progress it seems that the real nature of things remains as inaccessible as it was to Aristotle.

THIS OBSERVATION, MADE BY Lord Saatchi[1] in The Times Lecture at Worcester College, Oxford University, reflects an enduring perspective held by the sagacious. It is that *images* are *the* basic element of thought. This conviction has underpinned the work of Plato and Aristotle in earlier times and John Locke, David Hume, and John Stuart Mill in more recent ones.

With the advent of business studies in the twentieth century an organization's image was soon identified as a key issue. While it is unclear who can be credited with introducing the concept of corporate image, two writers stand out: Kenneth Boulding and Pierre Martineau. Both exerted a pivotal role in generating interest in perception in business and organizational contexts during the 1950s.

Boulding: paterfamilias of corporate image studies

Boulding, an eminent English economist working at the University of Michigan, wrote a profoundly influential book entitled *The Image*[2] during a sabbatical year spent at Stanford University. Its diminutive size belies the significance of two insights that were seized upon with relish by the business community. Boulding noted that humans have to rely on images; he also concluded that there was an a priori link between an individual's *image* of an organization and that person's *behavior* towards the organization. From the perspective of the twenty-first century these observations may seem unremarkable, but in the 1950s their impact was considerable. The sobriquet of paterfamilias of corporate image studies is one that in our opinion Boulding richly deserves.

Martineau: opening the floodgates

Two years later corporate image studies received a further lift with the publication by Martineau in the *Harvard Business Review* (*HBR*) of an article entitled "The Personality of the Retail Store."[3] Martineau's studies revealed that a favorable image provided an organization with a distinctive competitive advantage. Martineau followed this article by another, more broadly oriented *HBR* article, "Sharper Focus for the Corporate Image."[4] It is this article we selected to open this section on corporate image and corporate reputation. This article opened the floodgates to a stream of articles and books on corporate image.[5]

The writing on image was reflected in the increasing use by business of image and image research. Among the organizations with a long tradition of conducting such research are Opinion Research Corporation (ORC) based in the U.S.A., and Marketing and Opinion Research International (MORI) in the U.K.

In the context of this anthology, the corporate image construct enjoyed hegemony among corporate-level concepts from the 1950s until the 1980s. In one sense it *still* remains one of the highest-profile concepts on the area. (An examination of the practitioner books on visual identity at the end of the introduction to Section Two reveals how many graphic designers refer to their work in terms of corporate image.)

Corporate image: problems

Notwithstanding its utility, there are a number of difficulties associated with the image concept. This in part explains its eclipse by other concepts such as corporate reputation.

Five problems have been identified with the corporate image:[6] (a) its multiple meanings; (b) its negative associations; (c) its difficulty or impossibility to control; (d) its multiplicity; and (e) the different image effects on different stakeholder groups.

Brown,[7] in his comprehensive literature review, concluded that the general understanding of the *antecedents* and *consequences* of corporate image is skeletal.

Corporate image: schools of thought

The fascination with image and also with perception has resulted in the emergence of several distinct schools of thought.[8]

In general, images are categorized according to one of four perspectives. The first focuses on the corporation as the *transmitter of images*. The second considers image from the *receiver end* of the equation. The third category relates to the *focus of images*. This includes the image of the industry or of the country of origin. The fourth perspective is concerned with *construed images* – in other words, *beliefs about beliefs*, such as employees' perception of the image of the corporation held by external stakeholders. The various image categories of the four perspectives are detailed below.

Transmitted images (image management categories)

Projected image: The creation and projection of a *single* image to multifarious stakeholder groups. (This may not be grounded in reality.)[9]

Visual image: Similar to the above, but based on the notion that this is achieved via visual identities and logotypes.[10] This school is often married with the desired future image, explained next.

Desired future image: The articulation by the corporation of a sought-after image to be held at some future date by all stakeholders. (This may also be viewed as a variant of the projected image based on the vision of senior managers.[11])

Receiver-end image categories

Transient image: The immediate, but *fleeting*, mental picture that is construed by a receiver through the direct observation and interpretation of symbols, formal communication, etc. emitted by the organization.[12] (Some hold this to be the clearest application of the corporate image concept.)

Corporate reputation: Judgments made of the organization over time based on the organization's behaviors, performance, and the collective experiences of the organization. Corporate reputations tend to be stable,[13] although in our view subject to change in the wake of significant external or internal events such as an industry disaster (e.g., Chernobyl's effect on nuclear power firms) or an ethical lapse by a company.

The brand user image: The image of the corporation or product that most closely corresponds to the self-image of the stakeholder/stakeholder group.[14]

Stereotype image: The holding of *shared beliefs* across *all* stakeholder groups. In principle this applies to a variety of image-types. This does not imply that perceptions are identical – rather that *some dimensions* are the same – for example, that Rolls-Royce cars are luxurious. Unlike the construed external image the focus here is on the *recipient* rather than on the *transmitter* of images. This image-type would appear to be less prone to fluctuation.[15]

Focus-of-image categories

The brand image: The perception of a brand in relation to others in the same industry or product class.[16]

The industry (product-class) image: The image of an entire industry or industry sector.[17]

Exhibit 1 illustrates the cluster of image categories.

Construed-image categories

A number of categories fall into this zone. In a simplified form it relates to what one group believes another group believes.

Construed corporate image: relates to how *employees* envision that external audiences perceive their corporation.[18]

Construed strategic corporate image: relates to how *senior management* envision that external audiences perceive the corporation.

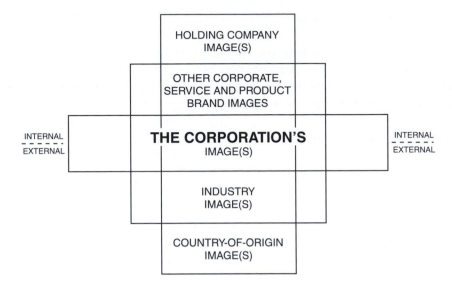

Exhibit 1 The family of business-related images

Construed brand user image: relates to how the *corporation* envisions that different stakeholder groups see the corporation in the context of their self- (stakeholder) image.

Construed stereotype image: relates to how the *corporation* envisions commonly held shared beliefs about the corporation held by all stakeholder groups.

Construed brand image: relates to how the *corporation* envisions how stakeholders view the organization in the context of other corporations operating in the same industry.

Construed industry (product-class) image: relates to how the *industry in its entirety* envisions how other stakeholder groups see that industry.

It will be seen that while some schools focus on the corporation as the *emitter of images*, others consider image from the *receiver end* of the equation. This distinction is not always highlighted or understood. Grunig explores this aspect of image in his article, the second chapter in this section. The third category detailed above, the construed image, relates to *beliefs about beliefs*. The Chinese saying, "One bed, two dreams," captures something of the difficulty in dealing with the image concept: not only is it multifaceted but the existence of construed images adds to its complexity. Thus when talking about image it is essential to ascertain what image type is being referred to.

Corporate image: a common theme

The importance accorded to the image construct by various writers is a common theme. Abratt's[19] model of the corporate image management process is a case in point. However, the use of controlled communication such as advertising to create positive images has been called into question.

The seminal work of Kennedy[29] is important in this regard. She questioned the very notion of image management and the role of marketing communications in changing perceptions. Her study found that organizational members were the most important conduit by which perceptions of the organization were transmitted. Her work has continued to exert a profound influence on marketing scholars in the field of identity studies within Europe and the Commonwealth.

Corporate reputation

Since the 1990s increasing attention has been focused on corporate reputation rather than on corporate image. Within the literature, many writers conclude that a corporate reputation has two distinctive characteristics, namely that they are:

- formed over time;[21]
- based on what the organization has done and how it has behaved.[22]

These two characteristics distinguish the corporate reputation construct from that of corporate image. (Some writers use the concepts interchangeably, however.)

The ascendancy of corporate reputation has been elevated in the world of academe from books such as Bromley's *Reputation, Image and Impression Management.*[23] However, the widespread business interest in the concept may be attributed to the publication of corporate reputation ratings in management periodicals as well as in the quality press. These include the *Financial Times, Asian Business,* and the *Far Eastern Economic Review*. The best-known example of the genre is published by the U.S.-based *Fortune* magazine.

The interest in the concept, and the disquiet shown toward the methodologies deployed by magazines in ranking reputations (especially *Fortune*), have given rise to new methodologies such as the Reputation Quotient.[24] More recently (2001) Rating Research LLC initiated reputation ratings of leading companies on key intangible characteristics, extending to ethics. Also of note is the launch of a new academic journal, *Corporate Reputation Review*, which accords primary importance to the corporate reputation construct.

Why all this interest in corporate reputation?

A favorable reputation brings a distinctiveness and a strategic advantage to a corporation that are not easily duplicated. Moreover, a (positive) reputation can materially contribute to profits and act as a bulwark when an organization is confronted with adverse stakeholder reaction.[25] The ability of a positive reputation to counter adverse external reaction will be explored by Greyser in Chapter 12, the last of this section.

Balmer has argued that corporate reputations (both good and bad) may act as quasi-control mechanisms for corporations. This is because the organizational reputation (the understanding of employees of their corporation's reputation) may provide the standard that governs certain behaviors. It is based on internal rationalizations to planned actions by organizational members which take the form of the following question: "*Would my actions be in line with the organization's reputation?*" Reputations clearly are used in other situations such as recruitment. Here recruiting executives are likely to consider the following question: "*Would this person maintain our enviable reputation?*"

Balmer has called the above "The DEAR principle": *D* decisions, *E* evaluated, *A* against, the *R* reputation.[26] The important point to remember with regard to the above is that reputations can serve as a control mechanism in that they can be impeccable, dire, unwanted, unearned, and/or obsolete.

The reputation concept is not limited to corporations as a whole. It may be applied to other manifestations of the organization such as the corporate brand.

Both corporate image and corporate reputation should be placed in the context that individuals as well as stakeholder groups will have differing anxieties, interests, and aspirations that result in multiple evaluations of their perception of the organization.[27]

One word of caution. Although a good reputation will in many instances be a valuable strategic resource, it is on its own no guarantee of business survival or success. Olivetti had an enviable reputation as a leading producer of typewriters but took insufficient account of technological developments that led to the widespread adoption of computers. Concorde has earned a sterling reputation for its technological prowess but in commercial terms has not been successful, with only two carriers (British Airways and Air France) adopting the plane. Production of it has long ceased.

One more time: corporate image and corporate reputation – what of their importance?

The broad area of perception provides alternative avenues by which to comprehend and reveal the corporation. Such perspectives may be favorable or dark. Perceptions held of the corporation can also be current, impending, outdated, erroneous, inequitable, or just whimsical. Without question, corporate image and corporate reputation in their various guises represent other expressions of reality. Why? Because all of us respond to *perception* in the same way as we do to *reality*. *Quod erat demonstrandum.*

The articles

Four articles have been selected for this section on corporate image and corporate reputation.

The chapters by Martineau and Grunig are concerned with corporate image. Martineau's seminal article on corporate image, an early classic, appeared in *HBR* in 1958. Grunig's chapter presents a thorough examination of the corporate image construct and marshals the extensive literatures on the area.

The chapter by Fombrun and Van Riel and that by Greyser explore the related concept of corporate reputation. Fombrun and Van Riel provide a concise overview of the disciplinary perspectives that inform our understanding of corporate reputation, while Greyser, drawing on an international study on reputation undertaken by Opinion Research Corporation, outlines the numerous benefits that can be accrued from having a positive reputation.

We believe all four chapters to be revelatory.

TOPICS FOR DISCUSSION AND REFLECTION

1   Scrutinize Boulding's (1956) contention that image affects behavior. Selecting two contrasting organizations, contemplate how their image might/might not affect the behavior of the following stakeholder groups:
    (a)   consumers;
    (b)   a graduate seeking post-commencement/post-graduate employment;
    (c)   legislators;
    (d)   investors.

2   "You can't build a reputation on what you are going to do" (Henry Ford, 1863–1947); "Facts are the images of history just as images are the facts of fiction" (E. L. Doctorow, b. 1931). Explore the significance of these observations.
    In addition, consider the usefulness of images and reputations as viewed through the time frames of the past, present and future.

3   "A good reputation is more valuable than money" (Publius Syrus, c. 42 BC). What evidence is there to support (or not support) the above proposition in a business context? What implications (if any) does this have for the role of reputation:
    (a)   in strategic planning?
    (b)   as an influence on decision-making?
    (c)   contemplating a merger with another organization?

4   Kennedy's (1977) research revealed that personnel had a key role in influencing external perceptions. What are the implications of her findings for:
    (a)   organizations generally?
    (b)   collaborative endeavors between the corporate communications and human resources departments?
    (c)   organizations with poor staff morale/with a record of contentious industrial relations?
    (d)   recruitment policies in services industries?
    (e)   "image-building" campaigns?

5   What insights, if any, can be gleaned from Robert Graves's poem "In Broken Images" (p. 171), when placed in a business context?

6   Consider the salience of the following image-types:
    (a)   transient;
    (b)   stereotype;
    (c)   construed.

7   Study the following quotation from David Bernstein (1984):

> Image is a reality.
>
> It is the result of our actions.
>
> If the image is false and our performance is good, it's our fault for being bad communicators.
>
> If the image is true and reflects our bad performance, it's our fault for being bad managers.
>
> Unless we know our image we can neither communicate nor manage.

What evidence is there to support the above from:

(a)   the literature?

(b)   practice?

Explain how corporate reputation is similar to/different from corporate image. Write two versions of Bernstein's statement: one for corporate image and the other for corporate reputation. (Make alterations and provide additions where necessary. Each statement should *not* exceed sixty words in length.)

   Give explanations of why you have/have not adapted Bernstein's original in penning your two statements.

8   "My reputation is a media creation" (John Lydon, aka Johnny Rotten, singer, b. 1956); "Journalists say a thing that they know isn't true, in the hope that if they keep on saying it long enough it will be true" (Arnold Bennett, 1867–1931). To what extent do these observations shed light on the significance of construed corporate images and/or reputations?

   What roles (if any) do the media play in the building, maintenance, and destruction of corporate reputations? Provide examples.

   What lessons are there (if any) for managers regarding the above?

9   Give illustrations (real or hypothetical) of corporate reputations that fall into the following categories:

(a)   good;

(b)   bad;

(c)   good but underserved;

(d)   bad but underserved;

(e)   out of date.

10   "The blaze of reputation cannot be blown out, but it often dies in the socket; a very few names may be considered as perpetual lamps that shine unconsumed" (Dr Samuel Johnson, 1709–1784); "A great reputation is a great noise, the more there is of it, the further does it swell. Lands, monuments, nations, all fall, but the noise remains, and will reach to other generations" (Napoleon Bonaparte, 1769–1821). What implications flow from the above statements?

   Has the reputation of Napoleon Bonaparte stood the test of time? What is (or what do you think is) his reputation in:

(a)   France?

(b)   the U. K.?

(c)   your country/another country of your choice?

What, if anything, does this tell us about reputations?

NOTES

1   Saatchi, Lord, "Perception is Reality," The Times Lecture delivered at Worcester College, Oxford University, in *The Times*, Business Features, May 1, 1998, p. 23.

2   Boulding, K., *The Image*, Ann Arbor: University of Michigan Press, 1956.

3   Martineau, P., "The Personality of the Retail Store," *Harvard Business Review* 1958 (January–February): 47–55.

4   Martineau, P., "Sharper Focus for the Corporate Image," *Harvard Business Review* 1958 (November–December): 49–58 (also this volume, Chapter 9).

5   Bolger, J. F., "How to Evaluate Your Company Image," *Journal of Marketing* 1959, 24 (October); Bristol, L. M. (ed.), *Developing the Corporate Image: A Management Guide to Public Relations*, New York: Scribner, 1960; Budd, J., "A Mirror on the Corporate Image," *SAM Advanced Management Journal* 1969, Part 34 (January): 45–50; Crespi, L. P., "Some Observations on the Concept of Image," *Public Relations Quarterly* 1961, 25 (Spring): 115–119; Swanson, C. E., "Branded and Company Images Changed by Advertising," *ADMAP* 1957: 302–318; Tyler, W. P., "The Image, the Brand and the Consumer," *Journal of Marketing* 1957, 22 (October): 162–165.

6   Balmer, J. M. T., "Corporate Identity and the Advent of Corporate Marketing," *Journal of Marketing Management* 1998, 14 (8): 963–996.

7   Brown, T. J., "Corporate Associations in Marketing: Antecedents and Consequences," *Corporate Reputation Review* 1997, 1 (3): 215–233.

8   Balmer, *op. cit.*; Gioia, D. A., Schultz, M., and Corley, K. G., "Organizational Identity, Image and Adaptive Instability," *Academy of Management Review* 2000, 25 (1): 63–81; Worcester, R. M., "Corporate Image," in R. M. Worcester and J. Downham (eds) *Consumer Market Research Handbook*, London: McGraw-Hill, 1986, pp. 601–666.

9   Alvesson, M., "Organization from Substance to Image?," *Organizational Studies* 1990, 11 (3): 373–394; Bernstein, D., *Company Image and Reality*, Eastbourne, U.K.: Holt, Rinehart and Winston, 1984.

10   Margulies, W., "Make the Most of Your Corporate Identity," *Harvard Business Review* 1977 (July–August): 66–72.

11   Gioia, D. and Chittipeddi, K., "Sensemaking and Sensegiving in Strategic Change," *Strategic Management Journal* 1991, 12: 443–448; Gioia, D. and Thomas, J. B., "Image, Identity and Issue Interpretation: Sensemaking during Strategic Change in Academia," *Administrative Science Quarterly* 1996, 41: 370–403; Balmer, J. M. T., "From the Pentagon: A New Identity Framework," *Corporate Reputation Review* 2001, 4 (1): 356–381.

12   Berg, P. O., "Organizational Change as a Symbolic Transformation Process," in P. Frost, L. Moore, M. R. Louis, C. Lundberg, and J. Martin (eds) *Reframing Organizational Culture*, Beverly Hills, CA: Sage, 1985, pp. 281–300; Gray, E. R. and Balmer, J. M. T., "Managing Corporate Image and Corporate Reputation," *Long Range Planning* 1998, 31 (5): 695–702.

13   Fombrun, C. J., *Reputation: Realizing Value from the Corporate Image*, Cambridge, MA: Harvard Business School Press, 1996.

14   Worcester, *op. cit.*

15   Martineau, "Sharper Focus."

16   Worcester, *op. cit.*

17   *Ibid.*

18   Dutton, J. E. and Dukerich, J. M., "Keeping an Eye on the Mirror: Image and Identity in Organizational Adaptation," *Academy of Management Journal* 1991, 34 (3): 517–554; Dutton, J. E., Dukerich, J. M., and Harquail, C. V., "Organizational Images and Member Identification," *Administrative Science Quarterly* 1994, 39: 239–263.

19   Abratt, R., "A New Approach to the Corporate Image Management Process," *Journal of Marketing Management* 1989, 5 (1): 63–76.

20   Kennedy, S. H., "Nurturing Corporate Images: Total Communications or Ego Trip?," *European Journal of Marketing* 1977, 11 (1): 120–164.

21   Fombrun, C. J. and Shanley, M., "What's in a Name? Reputation Building and Corporate Strategy," *Academy of Management Journal* 1990, 33 (2): 233–258; Gray and Balmer, *op. cit.*; Herbig, P. and Milewicz, J., "To Be or Not to Be . . . Credible That Is: A Model of Credibility among Competing Firms," *Marketing Intelligence and Planning* 1995, 13 (6): 24–33; Smythe, J., Dorward, C., and Reback, J., *Corporate Reputation: Managing the New Strategic Asset*, London: Century Business Books., 1992.

22   Balmer, "Corporate Identity"; Fombrun, C. J. and Rindova, V. P., "Reputation Management in Global 100 Firms: A Benchmarking Study," *Corporate Reputation Review* 1998, 1 (3): 205–214; Levitt, T., *Industrial Purchasing Behavior: A Study of Communications Effects*, Cambridge, MA: Harvard Business School Press, 1965.

23   Bromley, D. B., *Reputation, Image and Impression Management*, Chichester, U.K.: John Wiley, 1993.

24   Fombrun, C. J., Gardberg, N., and Sever, J., "The Reputation Quotient: A Multistakeholder Measure of Corporate Reputation," *Journal of Brand Management* 2000, 7 (4): 241–255.

25   Fombrun, C. and Rindova, V. P., "The Road to Transparency: Reputation Management at Royal Dutch/Shell," in M. Schultz, M. J. Hatch, and M. H. Larsen, *The Expressive Organization*, Oxford: Oxford University Press, 2000.

26   Balmer, "Corporate Identity," p. 973.

27   Bromley, *op. cit.*; Carter, S. and Deephouse, D., "Tough Talk and Soothing Speech: Managing Multiple Reputations," *Corporate Reputation Review* 1999, 2 (4): 308–332.

FURTHER READING

Books

Bernstein, D. (1984) *Company Image and Reality*, Eastbourne, U.K.: Holt, Rinehart and Winston.

Boorstein, D. (1961) *The Image*, Gretna, LA: Pelican.

Boulding, K. (1956) *The Image*, Ann Arbor: University of Michigan Press.

Bristol, L. H. (1960) *Developing the Corporate Image: A Management Approach to Public Relations*, New York: Scribner.

Bromley, D. B. (1993) *Reputation, Image and Impression Management*, Chichester, U.K.: John Wiley.

Fombrun, C. (1996) *Reputation: Realizing Value from the Corporate Image*, Cambridge, MA: Harvard Business School Press.

Jolly, A. (2001) *Managing Corporate Reputations*, London: Kogan Page.

Smythe, J., Dorward, C., and Reback, J. (1992) *Corporate Reputation: Managing the New Strategic Asset*, London: Century Business.

Articles on image and reputation

Abratt, R. (1989) "A New Approach to the Corporate Image Management Process," *Journal of Marketing Management* 5 (1): 63–76.

Alvesson, M. (1990) "Organization from Substance to Image?" *Organizational Studies* 11 (3): 373–394.

Anand, V. (2002) "Building Blocks of Corporate Reputation: Social Responsibility Initiatives," *Corporate Reputation Review* 5 (1): 71–75.

Balmer, J. M. T. (1998) "Corporate Identity and the Advent of Corporate Marketing," *Journal of Marketing Management* 14 (8): 963–996.

Bennett, R. and Kottasz, R. (2000) "Practitioner Perceptions of Corporate Reputation: An Empirical Investigation," *Corporate Communications: An International Journal* 5 (3): 224–234.

Berg, P. O. (1985) "Organizational Change as a Symbolic Transformation Process," in P. Frost, L. Moore, M. R. Louis, C. Lundberg, and J. Martin (eds) *Reframing Organizational Culture*, Beverly Hills, CA: Sage, pp. 282–300.

Bromley, D. (2002) "Comparing Corporate Reputations: League Tables, Quotients, Benchmarks or Case Studies?," *Corporate Reputation Review* 5 (1): 35–50.

Brown, T. J. (1997) "Corporate Associations in Marketing: Antecedents and Consequences," *Corporate Reputation Review* 1 (3): 215–233.

Budd, J. (1969) "A Mirror on the Corporate Image," *SAM Advanced Management Journal* 34 (January): 445–450.

Carter, S. and Deephouse, D. (1999) "Tough Talk and Soothing Speech: Managing Multiple Reputations," *Corporate Reputation Review* 2 (4): 308–332.

Corley, K. and Gioia, D. (2000) "The Rankings Game: Managing Business School Reputation,", *Corporate Reputation Review* 3 (4): 319–333.

Craven, P. (1986) "Managing Your Corporate Images," *Industrial Marketing Management* 15 (2).

Davies, G. and Miles, L. (1998) "Reputation Management: Theory versus Practice," *Corporate Reputation Review* 2 (1): 16–27.

Davies, G., Chun, R., de Silva, R. V., and Roper, R. (2001) "The Personification Metaphor as Measurement Approach for Corporate Reputation," *Corporate Reputation Review* 4 (2): 113–128.

Deephouse, D. (2002) "The Term 'Reputational Management': Users, Uses and the Trademark Trade-off," *Corporate Reputation Review* 5 (1): 9–19.

Dowling, G. R. (1993) "Developing Your Corporate Image into a Corporate Asset," *Long Range Planning* 26 (2): 101–109.

Duimering, P. R. and Safayeni, F. (1998) "The Role of Language and Formal Structure in the Construction and Maintenance of Organizational Images," *International Studies of Management and Organization* 28 (3): 57–85.

Dutton, J. E. and Dukerich, J. M. (1991) "Keeping an Eye on the Mirror: Image and Identity in Organizational Adaptation," *Academy of Management Journal* 34 (3): 517–554.

Dutton, J. E., Dukerich, J. M., and Harquail, C. V. (1994) "Organizational Images and Member Identification," *Administrative Science Quarterly* 39: 239–263.

Flatt, S. and Kowalczyk, S. J. (2000) "Do Corporate Reputations Reflect External Perceptions of Corporate Culture?" *Corporate Reputation Review* 3 (4): 351–359.

Fombrun, C. J. and Rindova, V. P. (1998) "Reputation Management in Global 100 Firms: A Benchmarking Study," *Corporate Reputation Review* 1 (3): 205–214.

Fombrun, C. J. and Rindova, V. P. (2000) The Road to Transparency: Reputation Management at Royal Dutch/Shell," in M. Schultz, M. J. Hatch, and M. H. Larsen, *The Expressive Organization*, Oxford: Oxford University Press.

Fombrun, C. J. and Shanley, M. (1990) "What's in a Name? Reputation Building and Corporate Strategy," *Academy of Management Journal* 33 (2): 233–258.

Fombrun, C. J., Gardberg, N., and Sever, J. (2000) "The Reputation Quotient: A Multi Stakeholder Measure of Corporate Reputation," *Journal of Brand Management* 7 (4): 241–255.

Gardner, B. B. and Levy, S. J. (1955) "The Product and the Brand," *Harvard Business Review* (March–April).

Gardner, B. B. and Rainwater, L. (1955) "The Mass Image of Bug Business," *Harvard Business Review* (November–December).

Gioia, D. and Chittipeddi, K. (1991) "Sensemaking and Sensegiving in Strategic Change," *Strategic Management Journal* 12: 443–448.

Gioia, D. and Thomas, J. B. (1996) "Image, Identity and Issue Interpretation: Sensemaking during Strategic Change in Academia," *Administrative Science Quarterly* 41: 370–403.

Gray, E. R. and Balmer, J. M. T. (1998) "Managing Corporate Image and Corporate Reputation," *Long Range Planning* 31 (5): 695–702.

Gray, E. R. and Smeltzer, L. R. (1985) "Corporate Image: An Integral Part of Strategy," *Sloan Management Review* 26 (4): 73–78.

Gray, J. (1986) *Managing the Corporate Image*, London: Quorum Books.

Herbig, P. and Milewicz, J. (1995) "To Be or Not to Be . . . Credible That Is: A Model of Credibility among Competing Firms," *Marketing Intelligence and Planning* 13 (6): 24–33.

Kennedy, S. H. (1977) "Nurturing Corporate Images: Total Communications or Ego Trip?" *European Journal of Marketing* 11: 120–164.

Kosnik, T. J. (1991) "Designing and Building a Corporate Reputation," *Design Management Journal* 2 (1): 9–16.

Lindquist, J. (1974–1975) "Meaning of Image," *Journal of Retailing* 50 (4): 29–38.

Martineau, P. (1958) "The Personality of the Retail Store," *Harvard Business Review* (January–February): 47–55.

Martineau, P. (1958) "Sharper Focus for the Corporate Image," *Harvard Business Review* (November–December): 49–58 (also this volume, Chapter 9).

Sobol, M. G. and Farrell, Y. (1988) "Corporate Reputation: A Function of Relative Size of Financial Performance?," *Review of Business and Economic Research* 24 (1): 45–59.

Spector, A. J. (1961) "Basic Dimensions of the Corporate Image," *Journal of Marketing* 25: 47–51.

Vendelo, M. T. (1998) "Narrating Corporate Reputation," *International Studies of Management and Organization* 28 (3): 120–137.

Worcester, R. (1997) "Managing the Image of Your Bank: The Glue That Binds," Special Edition on Corporate Identity in Financial Services: *International Journal of Bank Marketing* 15 (5): 146–152.

Chapter 9

Pierre Martineau

SHARPER FOCUS FOR THE CORPORATE IMAGE

From *Harvard Business Review* November–December 1958: 49–58

EDITORS' COMMENTARY

Pierre Martineau, corporate researcher and writer, was one of the earliest pro-
ponents of the importance of corporate image and its management. This chapter is
one of two articles written by him that appeared in the *Harvard Business Review*
(*HBR*) in 1958. In addition to his numerous research studies for the *Chicago Tribune*, it is upon these works that his reputation largely rests. The significance of
two *HBR* articles on corporate image penned by the same author being published
in the same year is testimony to the importance attached by the *HBR* and its
legendary editor Edward C. Bursk to Martineau's scrutiny of the corporate image
concept.

His first article, entitled "The Personality of the Retail Store,"[1] concluded that
image was a powerful driver in consumer buying behavior. The findings revealed that
customers were able to differentiate among retail stores: customers felt most at ease
in those retail outlets that mirrored their own perceived social standing. In addition,
Martineau concluded that nonprice factors were important in imbuing a store with
distinctive attributes. (This finding may be seen to be a precursor to one school of
thought relating to corporate identity, namely that, in part, it focused on the distinct
attributes of an organization.)

This chapter is the second of his articles to appear in *HBR*. Entitled
"Sharper Focus for the Corporate Image," it is an undisputed classic. It provides
a useful vehicle by which present-day scholars and practitioners can explore the
utility of the corporate image concept through the lens of the late 1950s. The
essay captures the ardor of the period toward two areas of interest: corporate

image and consumer motivation. Martineau's observations on the importance, complexity, and management of corporate image still have a contemporary resonance.

The chapter opens in a Socratic mode. Martineau posits six questions that he concludes are germane to his examination of the corporate image concept. We recapitulate these six questions as follows: *Is the (corporate image) concept important? Does a favorable company image make a difference? Is there a framework for projecting a corporate image? Can a single image please all people all of the time? What is the role of advertising in corporate image formation? Is undue focus given to public relations in corporate image formation?* These questions provide the basic framework for Martineau's exposition of the corporate image concept.

Martineau concludes that corporate image *should* be managed, but argues that a reliance on PR alone would *not* be sufficient in projecting a suitable image. Rather, organizations should devote more attention to advertising in projecting an image. (From our twenty-first-century perspective, the latter conclusion may well be viewed as somewhat rudimentary, particularly since public relations has developed into an important element in shaping corporate images.)

In addressing the issue as to whether corporate image is important, Martineau's answer is affirmative. He cites Boulding,[2] who remarks that people relate to companies on the basis of belief rather than on the basis of facts and figures. In other words, people are concerned not so much with what is true as what they believe to be true.

The complexity of the corporate image concept and the difficulties associated with managing image are also addressed by Martineau. The complexity of the concept can be seen in relation to the fact that organizations are engaged in discourses with multiple publics, with the likelihood of different publics holding different images of the company. Martineau acknowledges that this may appear to be an insurmountable difficulty. (That would be particularly true at the time, since mass media – especially TV – reached large and broad audiences, rendering virtually impossible a multiple-message strategy.)

However, Martineau's research identifies a crucially important mitigating trait: the notion of the *stereotype image*. Martineau defines the stereotypical image in a somewhat terse fashion, namely "*what everybody knows about the company.*" This provides his rejoinder to those who harbor misgivings about the usefulness of the image concept. Thus, while perceptions of the organization may be different among different individuals and groups, there will be important stereotype elements that will be similar across stakeholders.

Having revisited this, one of our favorite early articles of the genre, we are struck by the salience of Martineau's observations on image even today. While we may not concur with every part of his commentary (some of it seems a little naive), we broadly share his view of the importance of the construct. This is particularly the case today where in the globe of ideas the image construct has earned particular prominence – no more so than in business studies, where brand, product, services, corporate, and employee images, to mention a few, exercise the minds of a veritable phalanx of scholars. As such, Martineau's deliberations on the stereotype image may possibly offer something that is original, distinctive, and, potentially, valuable.

NOTES

1   Martineau, P., "The Personality of the Retail Store," *Harvard Business Review* 1958 (January–February): 47–55.
2   Boulding, K., *The Image*, Ann Arbor: University of Michigan Press, 1956.

- THERE HAS BEEN A lot of talk about something called the "corporate image." Is this just another loose notion – or is the idea an important one?
- Many hardheaded businessmen seem to have an uneasy feeling that promoting the corporate image is little more than a vague gesture of public good will. Does it *really* make any difference if a company's image is favorable or not?
- Does the corporate image have to be focused by hit-or-miss methods and trial and error, or are there right and wrong ways to project it effectively? Can one corporate image please all of the people all of the time?
- To what use can advertising be put in creating a clear image? Have we overlooked one of our most powerful channels of communication while concentrating on public relations?

The promptness with which management and public relations consultants have adopted the notion of the corporate image would indicate that the concept fills a very real vacuum. Apparently some such concept is needed for the sake of completeness in our thinking. If it is important to be concerned with the psychological overtones and impact on buyer attitudes of the company's individual brands, it also seems important to be concerned with these factors as they affect the company itself.

In one sense, the idea of a corporate image is certainly not new. Companies have done institutional advertising for many years, and sophisticated public relations people have long stressed the significance of many kinds of intelligent effort in building up a general reservoir of good will for a firm. But the concept of a corporate image has given much greater meaning to these efforts. Against the background of thinking about brand images and product-area images, it offers something new, distinct, and valuable.

Author's note: I am indebted to the following consultants for their provocative ideas on the subject of the corporate image: David Cox of Cox and Cox, Leo Shapiro of Leo Shapiro and Associates, Burleigh Gardner of Social Research, Inc., and Ray Winship of *Fortune*.

Mirage or reality?

Because the transition from brand image to corporate image has proceeded so fast, many of the component parts of the corporate image concept are still muddy and need to be overhauled in the light of other knowledge and experience. Businessmen are doing and saying things that do not make sense. For instance:

- One current estimate of how much United States business spends each year to make itself better liked is $1 billion. But when the average president is asked what impression he is trying to create in the public mind, he emphasizes "selling good products at reasonable prices."[1] Is this all? Is this the way the public assesses corporations? Or is this a primitive kind of thinking on the subject of corporate images?
- For many years leading corporations such as American Telephone and Telegraph and Standard Oil Co. (New Jersey) have conducted public opinion surveys hoping to learn the climate of public feeling toward them. Are such studies measuring anything of significance? Are they measuring what they assert to be measuring? What does it mean when the index of negative reactions drops – a more favorable (less critical) image or a weaker (more apathetic) image?
- The literature on the subject implies that the task of molding a corporate image is essentially a public relations function. Is it? Is this the most important way for a company to convey meaning about its image?
- One study purporting to show the corporate image of the steel manufacturers asked the respondent which company he would recommend as a place for a young executive to start working and which company he would invest $5,000 in if he had $5,000 to invest. In defense of the study, it was asserted that the image of the company as a place to work would be indicative of its future growth possibilities. Is this plausible? Is there any such logical relation between the different aspects of the corporate image?

Company personality

In order to put the corporate image in perspective as a workable concept, we need to understand where companies are trying to go with it. And what started this line of thinking in the first place?

In a remarkably few years the goals of advertising and marketing in the consumer field have been broadened past the functional stages. Today sophisticated strategy embraces a conscious effort to create a distinctive and, of course, positive brand image. The successful brand invariably has psychological meanings and dimensions which are just as real to the purchaser as its physical properties, and in many instances the purely subjective attributes play a far more important

---

1 Kenneth Henry, "Creating and Selling Your Corporate Image," *Dun's Review and Modern Industry*, July 1958, p. 32.

role in the brand's fortunes than do the functional elements. But in every case the aura of the symbolic dimensions contributes to the value and the public estimate of the brand.

Often the scope of the problem becomes widened to include a whole product area. Furriers want to know why women buy fewer fur coats. Retailers in the men's clothing field are concerned about their decreasing share of the consumer dollar. Trade associations in the beer industry are asking themselves why per capita beer consumption is declining, whereas wine consumption is increasing. Obviously what is involved is essentially not price, not distribution, not the physical products, but the sets of attitudes which are bearing on and directing consumer behavior in a whole area.

To go a step further in the complexity of images, perceptive retailers everywhere are sensing the vital importance of the many nonprice components of their operations which contribute to their store character. Speakers at leading 1958 conventions in both the supermarket and the department store fields have urged the development of store personality as a primary objective of retailing today.[2] Theorists readily acknowledge that the decision maker in the department store relies more and more on nonprice factors as a major competitive weapon for building sales volume.[3] In other areas of retailing, management is learning how to "sell the store" as a commodity, just as it learned how to sell products. For example:

- The Kroger grocery chain is launched on a major operating and advertising program specifically designed to project a favorable company image.
- Jewel Food Stores, though operating in only one market, has become one of the largest grocery chains by marching under the banner of a pleasing store personality. What started out years ago merely as a promotional idea – "Shop at your friendly Jewel Store" – has long since become a religion for management.

The merchant is realizing that unless the prospective customer can consciously or unconsciously see a "fit" between her own self-image and the image of the store, she will not patronize it, no matter what price offerings are made. It is perfectly logical, therefore, for the manufacturer to inquire whether a similar attraction or repulsion may be taking place between the consuming public and his company's personality which would have tangible bearing on the sale of his products.

Distinction or extinction

To be sure, the corporate image is complex and diverse. Yet there is considerable logic now for attempting to mold it into a clear, distinctive form. Westinghouse,

---

2 Pierre Martineau, "The Personality of the Retail Store," *HBR*, January–February 1958, p. 47.
3 Perry Bliss, "Non-Price Competition at the Department Store Level," from *Marketing in Transition*, edited by Alfred L. Seelye (New York, Harper and Brothers, 1958), pp. 161–170.

for instance, has embarked upon an extensive corporate advertising program designed to build a public image of an inventive and friendly company, because it believes that this will influence sales by raising company stature.[4] The very considerable institutional advertising beamed at the public by such companies as General Electric, General Motors, Goodyear, Firestone, U.S. Steel, Kaiser, and countless others undoubtedly is inspired by a similar wish to control the company image.

Business magazines in the industrial field – particularly those addressed to top management – carry much corporate advertising that contains no attempt to extol products. Container Corporation of America, the largest manufacturer in the fiber-box container field, uses a very imaginative advertising program which does much to mold an image of the company without ever discussing its products. Indeed, the number of hitherto staid corporations in the industrial field that feature abstract art and symbols in their corporate messages has assumed the proportions of a major shift in advertising style.

Obviously, the aim of such advertising is to impart distinctions and meanings in an area where it is difficult to create distinctions and meanings on a functional basis. There are precious few products that can be sold today on the basis of a demonstrable product superiority, and this is particularly true in the industrial field. We have developed an economy based on mass production, and mass production depends on standardization. Both buyers and sellers have managed to level off any real differences in the products they deal with. There are countless people in the laboratories and at the drawing boards who are trying to build in or design in actual superiorities, yet our competitive system will seldom permit one product to remain superior for long.

Too much to focus?

Much of the confusion over the corporate image stems from somewhat conflicting sources. On the one hand, some people are likely to be uneasy over the fact that so little can say so much. On the other hand, a great deal of skepticism exists that such a conglomeration of activities as the modern corporation *can* lend itself to compact expression.

In the strictest sense, every company can be said to have a corporate image. Every bank, every railroad, every manufacturer has a personality or reputation consisting of many facets. The corporate image of American Airlines embraces infinitely more meaning than some airplanes flying in the sky; it symbolically projects associations of waiting rooms, stewardesses, type of equipment, excellence of meals, interior décor of the planes, how fast the baggage is unloaded, the extra fare flights, attitudes toward serving liquor, the company's color scheme and trademark, and so on. The vague generalized image behind the specific is called into mind by some specific facet. Yet it is the vague part, the set of many associations and meanings, which the image really refers to.

But, as if the subtlety of the problem were not enough to bother people,

4 "How Westinghouse Builds an Image," *Printers' Ink*, July 4, 1958, p. 40.

there is also its complexity. For example, I know of one consultant who questions that these complex images even exist. Why? He argues that the manufacturer, if a large one, operates in so many different areas that no one image is possible. The company is a workshop, a research laboratory, a training school for executives, a source of employment for hundreds of workers, a civic institution, a buyer, and, among these many other things, a maker of profit. The point is, he argues, that it has no one single image because it cannot have. It is far too complex.

Or, to use a more concrete illustration, what is the corporate image of the Chicago Tribune Company? It publishes newspapers. But also it operates radio and television stations; it is an office-building landlord in both Chicago and New York; it syndicates comic strips and feature articles to newspapers throughout the country; it operates a fleet of ocean-going boats; it is one of the largest paper manufacturers and one of the largest owners of timberlands; it has built and maintains an entire Canadian city; it has important hydroelectric developments; and it is part owner of a major aluminum-manufacturing project.

The business scene today is characterized by an infinitude of corporations with just such sprawling structures and diverse holdings in many totally unrelated areas. Look, for example, at these two companies:

- W. R. Grace, among other things, is a major factor in steamships, airlines, insurance, banking, and outdoor advertising; it is one of the largest manufacturers in South America with an immensity of products; and in a relatively few years it has become one of the largest chemical manufacturers in this country.

- International Harvester has long since become far more than a manufacturer of farm equipment and harvester machinery. Besides its steel mills, it is one of the very largest makers of such diverse products as motor trucks, ball bearings, sisal, and construction equipment, and only recently it withdrew from the fields of home refrigeration and household appliances. Presumably, few of the buyers in these fields would be impressed with the corporate image of a farm equipment manufacturer. The motor trucks carry the insignia "International Trucks," not "International Harvester Trucks."

"Let the product speak"

In each particular product area, the buyer would generally be concerned only with the activities of the company as a manufacturer in that field, and give very little thought to the baffling complexities of the corporate image. This is why the particular consultant I have mentioned contends that management thinking should be solely about the product at the point of sale. What is important in organization thinking is what happens at this critical spot, he argues. Naturally he turns a jaundiced eye on institutional advertising. Not only is it ineffective, in his viewpoint, but it might give rise to misunderstandings about the company's motives. "Let the product speak for you," is his advice. If there is such a thing as a corporate personality, he does not feel that it is viable – that it will pass coin from one public to another.

There is still another problem. The multiline company not only has to address a number of buying publics but also many other significant groups that have to be influenced in extremely diverse ways. For example, the labor unions who bargain with International Harvester are surely not impressed with its attractive "I H" design or the excellence of its machinery. And the investing public is probably only concerned with the dividend and earnings record, and the general character of management: whether it is progressive, competitive, and stockholder-oriented. May it not be, then, that there is not only too much for the modern corporation to say but also too many different people to say it to?

Direction and indirection

In trying to unravel some of the misunderstandings about the corporate image, I must grant at the outset that much or even most institutional effort is ineffective and not communicating what the company hopes it will. It does not follow, however, that these meanings cannot be imparted with a different kind of communication.

I think that if advertising is viewed as a communication process, it will be seen that there are many other ways to convey and mold the corporate image besides the customary platitudinous messages to the effect that the company is visionary, honest, friendly, considerate, dependable, trustworthy, brave, with unbelievable resources, and so on and on. Certainly management should evolve advertising strategy which not only has such rigid meanings but particularly will cause us to like the corporate personality just as we like a person. But it must do so by indirection. To illustrate:

- In the Westinghouse study previously mentioned, readers of strictly corporate advertising stated that Westinghouse is a very stable company, its stock is a good thing to own, it is a leader in research, the company's appliances are good and the new lines are greatly improved, and that Westinghouse is a good place to work. *Yet the advertising said none of these things.* All of these comments were provoked voluntarily by corporate advertising showing six applications of atomic reactors.

While I have deliberately pointed out the difficulties of abstracting one simple symbol for a complex corporate image, nevertheless that is the way the human mind tends to think. To pragmatic persons who say, "Why all of this bother about images? Let's just run our companies," I should like to refer to what is undoubtedly the best book on the subject: *The Image* by Kenneth E. Boulding.[5] The author points out that it is not mere knowledge and information which direct human behavior, but rather it is the images we have – not what is true but what we

5 Ann Arbor, University of Michigan Press, 1956.

believe to be true. In any situation these patterns of subjective knowledge and value act to mediate between ourselves and the world.

The human mind can only handle so many complexities. It has to over-simplify and abstract a few salient meanings. We bundle up whole nations in simple cartoon figures like Uncle Sam or John Bull. The simple symbolic images act as a rough summation or index of a vast complexity of meanings. We personalize them and like them or dislike them because this is the only way we can interact with things — to endow them with the attributes of people.

Built-in filters

The business executive cannot afford to scoff at this subject of images because people are acting toward his company on the basis of them — not on the basis of facts and figures. Once these stereotyped notions are formed in people's minds, they are extremely difficult to change. They serve as emotional filters which are used by everyone in listening and seeing. Facts or no facts, these images cause us to reject what we do not agree with. On the other hand, we allow agreeable material to pour in unchallenged. The good image has a halo effect, so that it gets credit for all sorts of good things which might be quite contrary to truth. To illustrate:

- In a study by the *Chicago Tribune*, United Airlines was the only major airline not mentioned in connection with fatal accidents, though actually it had recently been involved in three spectacular plane crashes.
- By contrast, when a certain newspaper with the image of being sensational and for lower-status people scored a news scoop of considerable significance to the business community, it sold no extra papers whatever on the newsstands in the financial district. Because the image was negative to the people of this class, they simply refused to believe their senses. The image prevented them from "seeing" the headlines of this paper.

Power of stereotypes

I have pointed out that the image is a kind of stereotype. It is an oversimplification. In a sense, therefore, it negates the complexity of the modern diversified corporation. But this does not make it less workable as an operational tool. Far from it. In fact, it is the reality that creates the need for the illusion.

The hidden perceivers

To begin, I think it would be most fruitful to look a little closer at the notion that the corporation is addressing itself to many different publics, each of which is looking at the corporate image from behind a different set of lenses. Many public relations people who acknowledge this in theory behave in practice as if there were only one public to be addressed.

While it is certainly true that the various publics overlap and are not discrete, they all see the image differently because their perceptions, their expectations, and their wishes differ. Compare the viewpoints of the following groups:

1   *Stockholders — sophisticated people who determine the company's access to capital.*
2   *Consumers — relatively unsophisticated people who buy the company's products for any number of reasons.*
3   *Potential customers — people who could buy the company's products but do not.*

Whereas companies generally address consumers and nonconsumers alike, in our experience at the *Chicago Tribune*, they may be poles apart in their attitudes. Consumers like the products, they are familiar with them, they read the advertising to support their favorable opinions. But nonconsumers very often have negative stereotypes of the company which prevent them from learning anything about the products. Their negative attitudes in some way have to be altered; otherwise they will always act as a barrier to getting information through.

4   *Employees — top management, middle management, and the rank and file of production workers.*

Here it is worth noting that each group will have very different perceptions of the company as a place to work. The perennial sin of employee publications and employee benefits is that they are conceived and remain embedded in the mental set of top management.

5   *Vendors in the distribution system — retailers, wholesalers, manufacturer's agents.*

A very large part of so-called consumer advertising is really designed to influence the vendors. In the Antitrust Division's action to prevent the Procter & Gamble Company's merger with Clorox Chemical Company, considerable stress was placed on Procter & Gamble's ability to secure overnight retail distribution for its new products, such as Crest Toothpaste and Comet Cleanser. The retailer's image of the saleability of Procter and Gamble's products constitutes a very tangible factor in its greater resources.

6   *Suppliers — those who furnish credit, services, materials, and prices.*

The attitudes they form about a company can be very important. For example, if the bank believes the company will ultimately be successful, it allows much greater credit leeway. Thus, fabricators are (as they should be) deeply concerned with the attitudes of textile mills and steel mills that are their suppliers.

7   *Neighbors — the community where the company has plants or general offices.*

If a company operates stockyards or quarries or stream-polluting mills, or anything like that, obviously local opinion becomes very important. Local officials assess taxes and pass zoning ordinances. So of course such companies have to make themselves welcome to the communities where otherwise they would be regarded as a nuisance.

In a broader perspective, nearly all companies recognize the importance of a favorable public climate at the local community and plant city levels. Presidents speak at civic occasions, executives are active in local charities, educational scholarships are created, and many corollary activities are undertaken with the purpose of creating an image of a good neighbor and a responsible citizen. I think this aspect of the corporate image is extremely important in dealing with government functionaries. And also in lawsuits. Remember that railroads and public utilities constantly face the problem of excessive and unreasonable verdicts in personal injury cases because the judgment of the typical juror is swayed by his unfavorable images of these companies.

Between each of these publics and the company are surrogate groups that in reality act for them. For instance, the union is not really a public, but acts for the employees. Investment counselors, bond houses, and stockbrokers are the surrogates for the shareholders, and in most instances it is more important for them to perceive a favorable corporate image than for the shareholders; they are, after all, the "influentials." The retail dealer has wholesalers, distributors, and manufacturer's agents between him and the company. And the retail dealer finally is the ultimate link in the chain of surrogates between the consumer and the company.

"What everybody knows"

While it may be true that the ordinary housewife does not care about the complex operations of business as such, she clearly pays some heed to the particular units that make or sell the individual products she buys. For example, in our studies of retail advertising, the reader invariably asks herself some question about the goals of the store owner, either consciously or unconsciously, before she will allow herself to consider patronizing the store: "Are they dependable? How will they treat me in case I need service? What is their attitude about exchanges? Are they just trying to sell me?" I am convinced that the same kinds of questions are asked about the refrigerator manufacturer or the mail-order house.

The consumer may come into contact with only a small part of the manufacturing operations of an organization like Pillsbury, General Electric, Eastman Kodak, Scott Paper, Ford, Revlon, or Borden. What does it matter if the typical motorist is in total ignorance of the industrial activities of the Standard Oil Co. (Indiana)? It is entirely sufficient that for him it is just a company selling gasoline, tires, and car accessories. In this buying context he definitely has a corporate image of the company that deeply influences his purchases of motor products. It makes a decisive difference at the point of retail sale whether the product partakes of the Westinghouse aura or is a totally unknown brand.

Here is where I disagree with those who disdain the corporate image. I know, on the basis of research, that at the critical point in time when the product, the buyer, and the manufacturer come together, the buyer generally gives some heed to the character of the maker. The buyer shares the public stereotype – "what everybody knows" about the company. It is always surprising to me how widespread these public stereotypes are – and most have *some* basis in fact. While it is perfectly true that the buyer may not have a sharp and detailed mental picture, he does have access to the broad, general, diffused stereotypes which permit him to make first decisions whether to purchase or not. It is these broad stereotypes which cause him to patronize Montgomery Ward or Marshall Field, to fly Eastern or Delta, to buy Philco or Kelvinator products.

Another reason for respecting the corporate image is that among the subjective elements that constitute a brand image, there generally are some aspects of the corporate image playing an important role. For instance:

- In a study of the sales position and consumer desirability of various packaged meat products in the Chicago and Los Angeles areas, the critical difference was the corporate image of the various packers. Meat is meat. Animals are animals. The consumer *knows* all this. Moreover, Armour and Swift were shown in this research to have communicated all the dutiful and dull virtues of quality, value, and dependability. But the consumers surveyed overwhelmingly preferred the products of a regional packer who had acquired an image of youthfulness, fun, imagination, inventiveness, and sincerity. In umbrella fashion these qualities of the packer's image were held over his meat at the self-service displays in the stores to make it distinctively different and far more desirable. Demonstrably, the corporate image, and only that (because meat is meat), must have been the decisive factor in the economic mix.

Industrial marketing

I would argue that the same is true of industrial marketing when and if the manufacturer creates a distinctive corporate image with some applicability to his products. I cite the case of one purchasing agent for a manufacturer of heavy industrial equipment. This individual frankly justifies his purchases and his preference for the products of a principal supplier because of the president's reputation for constantly and enthusiastically discussing his company stock with security analysts. In the words of this purchasing agent, he can always justify his buying from this company because he has a feeling of confidence stemming from a corporate image of dependability and progressiveness built by the seemingly unrelated activities of the chief executive.

The buyer very definitely recognizes that people run companies, and it does make a critical difference what kind of people they are. Because they are human, they must have a value system, and it is important to sense how well-intentioned they are toward the buyer. Who dominates the company? Container Corporation, for example, is obviously a style-and-design company because of its executives; it is not just another production company manufacturing containers at a price.

Molding the image

Let us turn now to the practical question of how to create a clear, persuasive corporate image. Let us consider such aspects of the question as what products the company should identify itself with, how one company can be distinguished from another, and the relative roles of public relations and advertising.

Idealized identifications

The consumer is always asking: "What do they want me to do? Do they want me to clean my desk? Do I scrub floors, or do I enjoy myself?" As the woman looks at dishwashing compounds, she senses that the company not only wants to sell her something but asks her to do something unpleasant. A vacuum cleaner company is persuading her to perform a nasty, thankless chore. A scouring powder forces a woman to do hard, dirty work, and the subjective conclusion may be that any maker with such goals does not like women. By contrast, the maker of an electric toaster or a new gas range wants her to be happy and appreciated.

In advertising, therefore, the company has to be careful about which products it appears to "love" and which it just handles. Procter and Gamble just "handles" detergents and scouring powders. But it identifies with Zest and Camay soaps, which have significant emotional connotations as toiletries of beauty and scent, and with Ivory soap, which is identified with child-loving.

Too often companies identify with products they like instead of products that the consumer finds pleasant. It is, of course, important to discern which products the consumer likes and to identify the company with those. It *does* make considerable difference whether the company identifies with products like meat or cosmetics as compared to items that force one to do disagreeable tasks. "Cooking is a chore, but my family will love me, will compliment me, will realize I am indispensable and very capable. Hand lotions, lipsticks, hair sprays will make me attractive. The company wants me to be beautiful. How nice! What a nice company."

The products and services that the consumer identifies a company with have a far more important bearing on the image than all the knowledge of economists and antitrust lawyers who know the "big picture." To illustrate:

- I think a primary reason why the government failed to whip up any public feeling toward Atlantic and Pacific Stores in its antitrust suit was because people did not see Atlantic and Pacific as some powerfully big corporation – the largest retailer. Rather, people knew individual A and P stores that trimmed lettuce, sold aromatic-smelling coffee, and accommodatingly carried out heavy bundles.

- How can the public dislike General Motors? In the public eye, it is not seen as a huge corporation dominating the automobile field. At the point of public contact, the GM image has filtered down to become one of pleasant people making and selling cars at retail, figuring out trades so the prospect can have a car with a radio, white sidewall tires, and blue windshield glass. "GM bargains with me; it wants me to be happy with a new car."

- Jersey Standard is not "the biggest oil company"; rather, it handles Flit and radiator cleaner, just like any small company handling small things. So people can like Jersey. "How can you hate a company that makes Flit?"

● United States Steel brought itself within public awareness by promoting a "White Christmas"; people like the notion of appliances for Christmas, and therefore U.S. Steel is simple and nice.

At the point where the consumer, the public, and the company all meet, the corporate image has to be uncomplicated so that it can be expressed quickly in feeling or logic. The public must accept the various deeds of the manufacturer so that it can fit them together logically or emotionally; if it cannot find a simple motive for some corporate activity, then it is liable to impute a wrong motive. Accordingly, Lever Bros. should not put out vitamins and Schenley should not manufacture penicillin, for these are illogical steps. They do not fit the pattern of the corporate image. But if a company should make a success of some such maverick enterprise, then the public reconstructs its logic to accept the company in this new field.

Common pitfalls

Molding and shaping the corporate image is a highly positive, constructive job, which needs to be approached with vigor and enthusiasm. There are, however, several problems that management should frankly face up to – and some that it may have to live with.

First there is the problem of "living modern" in times of continuous change. It is quite true that, today as always, there is no substitute for the excellence of a company's products. But we have an economy which has emerged from the production and refinery stage. Unless all products in the market place are good in a functional sense, they die an immediate and unlamented death. Now we are in the era of promotion and merchandising, where the fortunes of a company depend far more on its abilities to advertise and merchandise and promote its products, because it is taken for granted that all products will perform their functions. But in my experience there are far too many mental "DP's" at the management level who cannot shift their perspective from the long-gone days when there were distinctive product differences to dramatize.

Take the case of an advertiser selling electric motors. One $\frac{1}{2}$-horsepower motor performs exactly like another. Yet the maker typically has such a dearth of imagination and of communicative skills that his only recourse is to spell out ten or twelve points of superiority. The buyer knows that $\frac{1}{2}$-horsepower motors are identical. Furthermore, he will recognize that all of the points the manufacturer alludes to are of such miniscule importance as to be valueless. I have heard my wife spontaneously object to dull TV commercials: "What are they telling me such nonsense for? Who cares?"

Generally when it dawns on the executive group that there is such a thing as a corporate image, it fails to distinguish between two general sets of meanings: (1) the functional meanings, which have to do with quality, reliability, service, price, and the like; and (2) the emotive meanings, which have to do with the subjective viewpoints or "feeling tone" of the various publics. In large measure we believe what we wish to believe. Modern communication theory recognizes that our feelings steer our senses.

If a company or a brand is saddled with a negative image, even the most realistic and functional qualities of its products will be colored and altered. We find reasons to reject what we do not like. And at the other extreme, when the feeling tone is favorable to the corporate image, we persistently look for the good side of every experience with this company and its products. This is why any consideration of corporate images has to be concerned with feeling tone and emotive components as well as with the functional and intellectual meanings.

The extreme difficulty of changing a negative image stems from the fact that the individual's attitudes are embedded in a subrational matrix of feeling. He remains immune to logic. In our *Chicago Tribune* studies of nonconsumers in the newspaper field, these groups remained stubbornly oblivious to any changes or improvements in the newspapers they did not like. They will go on for years parroting the same attitudes which long since have ceased to have any basis in fact at all. For example, a newspaper, which had changed its name 13 years ago and had been sold in the meantime, was still associated with the same name and the same ownership as far as these nonconsumers were concerned. Their feelings simply would not let them accept reality.

In the task of molding a favorable corporate image, the public relations people can and should play an important role; there is an infinity of meanings and situations that cannot be approached with direct advertising. Public relations is a tool, however, that is little understood by management. For the most part, its use is still mired in the primitive notions of grinding out news releases or arranging for the president to speak. Public relations itself suffers from a poor image. Too many executives still characterize it as glib press-agentry. They associate it with some company frantically trying to get off the hot seat after particularly bad publicity. Rarely is it thought of as a dynamic on-going program, like the company's advertising, which in its own way can mold public attitudes.

Imaginative imagery

The most direct, overt way for the company to project its character to the public is by advertising. I do not mean traditional institutional advertising. Much of it, in my opinion, is too stilted, too impersonal, too management-oriented, and too much the same to be effective in achieving its goal of creating a favorable climate of public feeling. Certainly, sameness of approach will not build a sense of psychological uniqueness and richness for the corporate image in the public mind – and I think that is necessary. Fortunately, however, neither dullness nor conventionality is necessary. Advertising is a field for originality and imagination.

Let us begin by looking at the meaningful intangibles which advertising can develop. Taking a cue from the increased attention given to abstract symbols in corporate advertising, and from the greatly increased importance of product design and package design, it is worth exploring the nonverbal elements of advertising as significant carriers of meaning. We seem to have the habit of overlooking them.

A European social scientist singles out as an idiosyncrasy of the American mind *our tendency to evaluate all things and actions in objective and quantifiable terms.*[6] This stems from our pioneer heritage, from the settler's need for a simple way to evaluate strangers. As Americans, we have to quantify everything to prove its validity. And with this national tendency, we lose sight of the fact that humans and things can be assessed in many dimensions of meaning which are nonquantifiable, nonobjective, and nonrational. Certainly our relationships with our friends and our relatives are not formed on the basis of quantifiable meanings. Thus, individuality and richness of meaning can be created for the corporate image by approaches other than the quantifiable and rationalistic approaches of traditional institutional advertising.

This is where abstract and aesthetic symbols come into the picture. Look at what some companies are doing:

- Alcoa pulled together many aspects of corporate meanings when it began using abstract symbols as a sort of trademark.
- United States Steel has just changed its corporate identity symbol for the fifth time since 1930; the letters are exactly the same, USS, but the change in design is expected to modernize and strengthen the mark.
- The Ralston Purina Company no longer believes it necessary to stress the company name on its products; the red checkerboard design has more meaning and identity than does the company name. Many diverse products such as breakfast cereals, crackers, poultry feeds, and insecticides are given family identity by means of the checkerboard square.
- The typical corporate advertising of the aircraft manufacturers and engineering consultants should make it irrefutably clear that it is possible to create highly significant character without resorting to the sententious clichés and rudimentary functional claims customarily associated with institutional advertising.
- All the rational qualities of the small car have so much social currency today that it is unnecessary for Volkswagen to spell them out: the company symbol and style of advertising are sufficient to evoke all of these associations while still preserving the distinctiveness of Volkswagen.

Tone and style

The style of advertising — literally how it is done — contributes enormously to brand and corporate images. Olivetti, for example, has used a unique style of abstract advertising to create a very distinctive quality image in the field of office machines. Any competitive manufacturer could duplicate whatever words Olivetti might choose to say about itself, but no one could retrace the corporate image created by this particular style.

The big department store has generally sensed this much better than the manufacturer. The astute store manager knows that all of his activities are acting as

6 Jurgen Ruesch, "American Perspectives," *Communication — The Social Matrix of Psychiatry*, edited by Jurgen Ruesch and Gregory Bateson (New York, W. W. Norton & Co., 1951).

symbols to project to his public the store's inherent character, and therefore they should be expressive, distinctive, and congruent. In the manufacturer's terms, this means that his advertising style, his trademarks, his packaging, his stationery, his reception rooms, his general offices, his reports to stockholders, and his color schemes should be expressive – all saying the same things about the company.

The annual financial reports have become a meaningful and distinct channel of communication – and they say more than the words alone convey. For example, after looking at a Bell and Howell report, it is easy to understand the enthusiasm of investment counselors for the company. The format of the report eloquently conveys that this is a youthful, dynamic, years-ahead organization. All of this is totally apart from the content of the report. By contrast, the report of Pacific Gas and Electric unmistakably relays an image of a staid, old-fashioned management.

The retailer rarely uses straight institutional advertising. Rather, he sees every merchandise offering as institutional advertising. At the same time that he features timely merchandise, the tone and style of the advertising are proclaiming volumes of meaning about the personality of the store itself. This is why the manufacturer should see his regular product advertising as contributory to the corporate image. Regardless of how little or how much it is conveying about the company as a maker of the product, it is saying *something*.

Conclusion

There is no one corporate personality. There cannot be because every firm has different publics, and the four primary ones – stockholders, employees, vendors, and buyers – will see different aspects of the corporate image.

Creating and selling a corporate image is far more than a task for the public relations staff. Every activity of the company adds some meaning to the public's picture of the management that is running the organization. Regardless of the complexity of the corporate structure, at the point where product and buyer come together the consumer also weighs in the balance some associations about the maker of that particular product. Many corollary meanings emerging from the corporate image can play a role in the actual purchase decision at the moment of sale.

Because any functional and price attributes of the product will be filtered through an emotional lens in the buyer's mind, it is important for the corporate image to be liked. This is why it is so necessary to consider what I call the "feeling tone" and the emotive meanings as well as the functional and rational dimensions of the corporate image.

Many channels of communication by which we humans customarily and believably convey meaning to each other are mostly overlooked by management. These avenues of meaning are particularly important in molding positive brand and corporate images. Creating a spectrum of meaningful intangibles is a dual responsibility. In advertising, for instance, the agency as the creative force has to propose symbols which will communicate successfully to the company's publics. And management has to allow such creative effort instead of holding to narrow rationalistic approaches.

Chapter 10

James Grunig

IMAGE AND SUBSTANCE: FROM SYMBOLIC TO BEHAVIORAL RELATIONSHIPS

From *Public Relations Review* 1993, 19 (2): 121–139

EDITORS' COMMENTARY

James Grunig is a Professor in the College of Journalism at the University of Maryland, U.S.A. He is among the most celebrated public relations scholars of his generation. His tomes on public relations (PR) provide some of the most esteemed commentaries on the theory and practice of PR in its many forms.[1]

His article "Image and Substance: From Symbolic to Behavioral Relationships" appeared in the *Public Relations Review* in 1993. The article provides an authoritative exposition of the corporate image construct and draws on the extensive literatures pertaining to corporate image. Although written with a PR constituency clearly in mind, Grunig's exploration of the corporate image construct deserves a much wider audience.

Grunig's approach to the corporate image concept may at first appear to be something of a paradox. He notes that there is a genuine fascination with the concept among PR practitioners and scholars and management theorists. He comments upon the ubiquity of the concept in common parlance. He testifies to the veracity that underpins the construct. Clearly the concept warrants investigation.

Contrast this with Grunig's loathing for the term. He generally disregards it in his writing, and (we are told) has proscribed any reference to the concept by his students.

One explanation for Grunig's abhorrence of the term "corporate image" is its multiple meanings. Grunig points out that it can be used as a synonym for other concepts including message, reputation, perception, cognition, attitude, credibility, belief, communication, and relationship. The omnipresence of the concept has led

Grunig to the view that it has become degraded; it has, in his estimation, become little more than a proxy for corporate-level communication.

Grunig's article has been profoundly influenced by the work of Olasky.[2] The latter argued that there is a correlation between the size of an organization and its role as the focus of symbolic relationships with its stakeholders. Olasky's hypothesis is based on the premise that small companies are characterized by the closeness of their relationships with their key publics. However, maturity brings growth and expansion; consequently the closeness of association with these publics tends to vaporize.

In response, and in an attempt to fill the void, organizations resort to formal communication. This serves, in their estimation, as a surrogate for behavioral relationships. Grunig, like Olasky, inveighs against such an approach.

This provides the setting for the principal inference from Grunig's article, namely that there is a paradigm struggle between (a) those who regard image-building in terms of the *symbolic relationships* between organizations and stakeholders, and (b) those who are convinced that image-building can be achieved only when based on *substantive personal (behavioral) relationships*.

(At this juncture let us call attention to the empirical work of Kennedy[3] published some sixteen years earlier, which confirmed the crucial role of behavioral relationships, particularly by personnel, in image formation. She also derided the reliance on formal communications in image-building.)

However, Grunig is of the view that behavioral and symbolic relationships should not be antithetical but rather synthetical. He concludes that symbolic and behavioral relationships should be intertwined like the strands of a rope, something that is strong, robust, and enduring. The same can be said for his article, which makes for compelling and insightful reading.

NOTES

1   Grunig, J. E. and Hunt, T., *Managing Public Relations*, New York: Holt, Rinehart and Winston, 1984; Grunig, J. E. (ed.), *Excellence in Public Relations and Communications Management*, Hillsdale, NJ: Lawrence Erlbaum, 1992.
2   Olasky, M. N., *Corporate Public Relations: A New Historical Perspective*, Hillsdale, NJ: Lawrence Erlbaum, 1987.
3   Kennedy, S., "Nurturing Corporate Images: Total Communications or Ego Trip?," *European Journal of Marketing* 1977, 31 (1): 120–164.

Abstract

The preoccupation of many public relations practitioners with the concept of image suggests that public relations is concerned only with symbolism – with what the organization says about itself. A paradigm struggle is occurring in

public relations, therefore, between practitioners who use only superficial symbolic activities — the quest for positive images — and those who build substantive
behavioral relationships between organizations and publics.

Communication of symbols alone does not make an organization more
effective. Nevertheless, symbolic and behavioral relationships are "intertwined
like the strands of a rope."

This article deconstructs the meaning of image as it is used in several fields of
communication and psychology. It suggests that "image" disguises the more
precise concepts of perception, cognition, attitude, and schema — concepts that
identify symbolic objectives for public relations. Over the long term, however,
organizations must evaluate the contribution of these objectives to the behavioral
relationships with publics if they are to help organizations achieve their goals and
missions.

James E. Grunig is a professor in the College of Journalism at the University
of Maryland.

THIRTY YEARS AGO, the Foundation for Research on Human Behavior
held a conference on corporate image in Ardsley-on-Hudson, New York.
The foundation invited a number of social and behavioral scientists and business
executives to discuss what Riley (1963) called the behavioral science issues that
were being ignored in the then "superficial interest in corporate image" (p. viii).

At the conference, Gerhard Wiebe, then dean of the School of Public Communication at Boston University, pointed out that research on public relations
should go beyond images to deeper relationships among organizations and their
publics:

> Thinking, discussing, and planning about the so-called corporate
> image too frequently stop with considerations of appearance and too
> seldom reach into the substance behind the appearance. The percep-
> tion of the corporate image too often remains in the area of publicity
> and only infrequently extends, where it more properly belongs, into
> the social dynamics that relate corporations to the society at
> large. . . . The rapport between corporations and their publics is
> neither as firm nor as well understood as it ought to be. Perhaps the
> time has come when progress in public relations research for leading
> corporations lies less in further refinements of image measurement
> than in re-examining the nature of the company-public *relationships*
> [emphasis mine] that lie — or might lie — behind the corporate image.
> (Wiebe, 1963, p. 12)

At an earlier time, according to Wiebe, organizations were small and generally located in single communities. Executives then had personal relationships
with people in the community. They and their organizations also had a personal
stake in the well-being of the community because they lived there themselves. As

organizations grew larger, however, those personal relationships broke down and executives began to feel little involvement in the communities where their organizations operated. As a result, organizations turned to the media to build symbolic rather than personal – behavioral – relationships with publics.

Symbolic relationships meant little to most people, Wiebe added, because they neither thought about nor cared about the organizations trying to communicate with them. The result was a lot of pointless publicity and a lot of frustration by organizations because publics did not respond to their appeals for support. The solution, according to Wiebe (1963), was for organizations to "nurture the larger society from which they receive their sustenance" and to "participate in the solution of what members of these publics perceive to be their own problems" (p. 23).

In a similar vein, Olasky (1987) wrote a critical history of public relations in which he maintained that public relations specialists were directly responsible for leading organizations from substance to image in their relationship with publics. Olasky maintained that in the 19th century corporations practiced what he called private relations. Like Wiebe, Olasky pointed out that corporate executives at this time communicated directly with the media and others outside the corporation without the need for the intervention of the public relations practitioner. Often they kept their business to themselves.

At the beginning of the 20th century, however, public relations innovators, including Ivy Lee and Edward Bernays, entered the picture, helping corporations to manipulate their communication and beginning what Olasky (1987) called the story of convoluted philosophy and tawdry practice. Olasky recommended two solutions to the ethical problems of public relations: responsibility that begins at home and private relations. Responsibility at home means dealing directly with people affected by corporate actions, not papering over the activities with "an extra gift to a local charity or by Thanksgiving turkeys to the faithful" (p. 151). Private relations means saying "none of your business" when that is appropriate.

Most historians and contemporary observers of public relations do not share Olasky's extreme negative assessment of public relations. Nevertheless, the distinction between superficial symbolic activities – the quest for "positive images" – and substantive behavioral relationships between organizations and publics constitutes perhaps the most important paradigm struggle in the field today – just as it did 30 years ago.

Patrick Jackson, a principal in the public relations firm of Jackson, Jackson and Wagner and editor of *pr reporter*, has argued in the pages of *pr reporter* (e.g., July 30, 1990) that public relations must move beyond cognitive effects – image – to effects on behavior. He has developed a model of cognitive and behavioral processes in which awareness leads to latent readiness to respond. When there is a latent readiness to respond, the model continues, a triggering event can produce behavior. These first two stages describe symbolic relationships. The succeeding stages of triggering events and behaviors describe at least some aspects of behavioral relationships.

Jackson can be interpreted as saying that public relations must be concerned both with behavioral and symbolic relationships and not with symbolic relationships alone. Likewise, Wiebe (1963) can be interpreted as saying that organizations too often devote all of their attention to symbolic relationships – to image – and do not pay enough attention to behavioral relationships – the actual interaction between an organization and its publics.

This article, therefore, explores the nature of symbolic and behavioral relationships in public relations. Although I consider long-term behavioral relationships to be the essence of public relations, I do not dismiss symbolic relationships. Symbolic and behavioral relationships are intertwined like strands of a rope. What publics think of an organization is a product of communication as well as of their experience and the experience of others with the organization. Communication – a symbolic relationship – can improve a behavioral relationship, but a poor behavioral relationship can destroy attempts to use communication to build a symbolic relationship or to improve a behavioral relationship.

Although it may be difficult for large organizations to communicate personally with all members of their publics, they have means other than the media to communicate with publics. Publics today do not sit still when an organization refuses to address problems as they see them or to nurture the larger society – to use Wiebe's words. They form into activist groups that pressure or boycott the organization or seek regulation, legislation, or litigation that can severely constrain the ability of an organization to accomplish its mission. Public relations practitioners, therefore, can build personal relationships with publics by establishing personal contact and communication with the leaders of activist groups who represent large publics.

Over the short term, then, public relations practitioners can set objectives for communication programs to improve symbolic relationships with publics. Over the long term, however, public relations should examine behavioral relationships with publics – relationships that directly affect the behavior of the organization – its ability to accomplish organizational goals.

This article begins, therefore, by examining the concept of "image." Practitioners and some scholars use the term loosely to describe symbolic relationships. Because the term "image" is used so frequently, this article articulates several concepts often disguised by the term to help understand the nature of symbolic relationships. It then examines the nature of behavioral relationship and the interaction between symbols and behavior.

Image as a public relations concept

> I loathe the word image and Kotler is an image devotee – he tells his readers and audiences that "image is the set of beliefs, ideas, and impressions that a person holds of an object." My Webster's tells me an "Image is a reproduction or imitation of a person or thing." If Kotler knew Latin, he would know image is derived from *imitari* – imitation. We in PR must be concerned with that good old-fashioned word, *reputation* – not image.
>
> Scott M. Cutlip (1991)

"Image" is a term that arouses great passions and great conflict among public relations practitioners and scholars in the United States. Like Cutlip, I always have loathed the term. I never used it in my textbook, *Managing Public Relations* (Grunig and Hunt, 1984), unless I put it in quotation marks to suggest that I did not know what the term really means. For years, I have asked students not to use the term in my public relations classes.

I have disliked the term image in large part for technical reasons. Image has almost as many meanings as the number of people who use it. It has been used as a synonym for such concepts as message, reputation, perception, cognition, attitude, credibility, belief, communication, or relationship. If a term has many *denotative* meanings, a theorist cannot define, measure, or observe it.

On a more emotional level, however, image has many negative *connotative* meanings. The average person sees image as the opposite of reality – as an imitation of something, as Cutlip put it. In everyday language, images are pro-jected, manipulated, polished, tarnished, dented, bolstered, and boosted. Ber-nays (1977) pointed out that "image" suggests that public relations deals with shadows and illusions rather than reality. Image-making suggests that organiza-tions can create and project an image out of nothing and that their behavior and their relationships with publics count for little. Journalists, especially, equate public relations with the image-making activities of press agents – for whom image-making essentially means getting good publicity in the media.

In spite of the confusion about the nature of public relations inherent in the concept of image, one cannot help but recognize the pervasiveness of the term in public relations practice. Although few practitioners define the term when they use it, it appears regularly in professional publications and in proposals for public relations work. Outside the United States, the term might be even more popular. In studies of public relations in Greece (Lyra, 1991) and India (Sriramesh, 1991), for example, nearly all public relations practitioners interviewed defined public relations in terms of image-making of one sort or another. Image also appears frequently in books about international public relations (e.g., Wouters, 1991).

The ubiquitous use of the term image in public relations suggests that some-thing important underlies the concept. As the authors of one public relations textbook said:

> Of course, image is not a bad word, and practitioners should not have their mouths washed out with soap every time they use it. In the communication process, the goal of the sender-communicator is to convey a message to the receiver-audience in a form as identical as possible to what is in the mind of that sender. What the receiver gets after the message is encoded, sent, and decoded, however, is really an image or reproduction of the thoughts or feelings of the sender, not the thoughts or feelings themselves.
>
> (Haberman and Dolphin, 1988, p. 15)

Haberman and Dolphin's comments suggest that the concepts of cognition and attitude – two psychological concepts affected by communication – are embedded within the concept. In fact, image conceals several psychological concepts that are the products of public relations. The solution to the image problem in public relations, therefore, is to deconstruct the meaning as it is used by scholars and public relations practitioners. Deconstruction of the concept suggests that image refers to a number of symbolic relationships that are important complements to the building of behavioral relationships between an organization and its publics.

Concepts of images

Determining where the concept of image originated and when and how it entered the vocabulary of public relations is difficult. Cutlip (1991) said the term originated with the Latin term for imitation. Horowitz (1978) said the root meaning of image is replica (p. 4). Those meanings seem related to the use of the term image in art and literature, where an image is a replica of something else. The fact that artistic images can be constructed or projected would seem to suggest the origin of the projection vocabulary in public relations.

The artistic concept of image, therefore, sees image as something that a communicator creates – constructs and projects or gives to other people – who often are called receivers. In psychology, in contrast, receivers construct meaning – images – from their personal observations of reality or from the symbols given to them by other people. Most psychologists have a precise concept of image in mind, however. They see images as mental images or ideas that are visual, sensory, or spatial analogues of reality (Anderson, 1980, p. 64; Denis, 1991, p. 103). That is, people literally "see" an image, although what they see is not an exact picture of reality.

The concept of mental images has had a long history in psychology. Horowitz (1978) traced the concept to Aristotle who considered images to be the basic elements of thought. Horowitz added that philosophers such as John Locke, David Hume, and John Stuart Mill followed Aristotle in conceptualizing images as the major components of thought. As should be apparent, however, these early philosophers and contemporary cognitive psychologists conceptualized images more narrowly than the concept used today by public relations practitioners. To psychologists, images are a type of cognition. To public relations people, however, images seem to be everything that takes place in the mind.

Public relations and marketing practitioners and theorists typically use the terms sum total or composite when they define image from the standpoint of the receiver of messages (e.g., Baskin and Aronoff, 1988, p. 62; Clavier and Wright, 1987, p. 27; Kotler and Andreason, 1987, p. 624; Markin, 1990, p. 21). This sum total usually consists of several concepts such as attitudes, cognitions, perceptions, or beliefs – concepts that, if measured, are so different that they cannot be added into a composite index.

At the same time, many public relations and marketing writers do not distinguish carefully between concepts of image as a message produced by the organization and image as some sort of composite in the minds of publics – the difference between the artistic concept of image as symbols and the psychological concept of image as something constructed by receivers of those messages (see, e.g., Kotler, 1991, p. 300 for the artistic concept and p. 570 for the

receiver concept). All of this confusion about image production and consumption and about the different ways in which people consume messages (perception, cognition, and attitude) suggests that image is an umbrella term covering all
of the communication activities and their effects that occur between an organization and its publics – at least as the concept of image is used in public relations. In
another sense, image defines the symbolic relationships among organizations and
publics – relationships that occur strictly through communicative interaction.

To clarify the confusion that surrounds the concept of image, then, we turn
first to production concepts of symbolic relationships – i.e., the projection of
images.

Production of images

Image consulting of varying types has become a multimillion-dollar-a-year business. One type of image consultant – which Robert Dilenschneider (1990), the
former CEO of Hill and Knowlton, called image quacks – tells individuals how
to dress, comb their hair, and shake people's hands. Dilenschneider (1990) said
he had little respect for these image makers: "I have long believed that your
'power center in business' is indeed your head, except it is what's in your head,
not what's on or around it that matters" (p. 26).

Not too far removed from these individual image consultants – but apparently more professional – are the corporate image consultants. Corporate image
consultants essentially are experts in the design – in visual symbols. For a price,
these consultants will design a new logo, trademark, or name for your
organization.

Olins (1978) called this image design work the creation of corporate identity. Clive Chajet, the chairman of Lippincott and Margulies, Inc., one of the
oldest and largest image design firms, made clear the distinction between identity and image in a more recent book (Chajet and Shachtman, 1991) – in essence
the difference between the consumption and production of images. Image is
what audiences perceive of an organization. Identity is what an organization
chooses to use to shape those perceptions (p. 4).

A good identity consultant will point out, however, that a new identity alone
cannot cover up faults in the organization. Chajet and Shachtman (1991) pointed
out that:

> . . . many chairmen still believe that a new identity can cover sys-
> tematic faults. Nothing could be further from the truth. Conjuring a
> new identity to respond to mismanagement is never, never, never a
> solution. . . . Good image-making marries the reality with the image,
> and bad image-making deliberately distorts the image in order to
> mask, protect, or otherwise prevent the accurate understanding of
> the underlying reality.
>
> (p. 8)

Both Olins (1978) and Chajet and Shachtman (1991) pointed out that symbols of identity can help an organization communicate its culture, its mission, the aspirations of its employees, and its mission to publics. Once an organization understands its own identity, it can use symbols to communicate that identity to external publics.

It is only a small step, then, from visual symbols to oral and written symbols that organizations can use to communicate with their publics. This concept of image is used frequently in the fields of rhetorical and literary criticism (Moffitt, 1991, p. 3). Scholars in those fields typically examine the messages sent by writers, film editors, or political candidates and critique the image that they believe consumers of the messages construct (see, e.g., Heath and Toth, 1992). From the perspective of the social sciences, one of the best developed theoretical approaches to the production of images is that of impression management – where an image can be seen as the impression that a person or organization makes on someone else. Impression management originated from Goffman's (e.g. 1959, 1974) dramaturgical approach to the sociological theory of symbolic interaction. Goffman saw society as a stage in which people use interpersonal communication and organizations use organizational communication as actors trying to create an impression on other people or groups. Infante, Rancer, and Womack (1990), for example, defined image as a "total impression" (p. 242).

Most of the research on impression management deals with how individuals can manage the impressions they make by monitoring their own behavior, varying their dress, what they say and do in a placement interview, taking part in team projects, or the timing of their arrival at or departure from work (see, e.g., Giacalone and Rosenfeld, 1989). As Snyder and Copeland (1989) added, however, organizations also try to create impressions "through advertisements and other media of communication, including recruiting programs at colleges and universities" (p. 7).

Much of the rhetoric of impression management, of course, sounds a great deal like the rhetoric of image-making in public relations. Like image-making in public relations, impression management can be deceptive and manipulative. *pr reporter's* (1991) *purview* supplement recently reviewed Giacalone and Rosenfeld's (1991) second book on impression management and warned, "tactics used in career enhancement and other applications are deceptive, but some of the chapter's authors see them as a normal aspect of impression management" (p. 2). Moberg (1989) added, "Many contemporary treatments of impression management also have a cynical tone" (p. 172).

Moberg (1989) weighed several possible rules for evaluating the ethics of impression management. One rule seems most reasonable, "employees should not manage impressions deceitfully" (p. 174). Moberg said this rule has been most popular among those who "advocate openness and trust in organizational communications" (p. 175). He added, however, that some psychologists have countered that bargaining works best when the bargaining parties "select a middle course between the extremes of complete openness toward, and deception of the other. Each must be able to convince the other of his [sic] integrity while not at the same time endangering his [sic] bargaining position" (pp. 175–176).

This discussion of the ethics of impression management resembles the discussion of asymmetrical and symmetrical world views in public relations

(J. Grunig and White, 1992). Symmetrical public relations sees an organization's relationships with publics as balanced – relationships in which both adjust their behavior to each other. Asymmetrical public relations strives for an imbalanced relationship with publics – using communication to get members of a public to do what the organization wants them to do.

Some theorists (e.g., Murphy, 1991) have pointed out that a combination of symmetrical and asymmetrical public relations – a mixed motive model – might be the most realistic way to practice public relations. Most public relations practitioners see themselves as advocates for their organization even though they are concerned with the welfare of the publics it affects. Thus, organizations usually are not willing to be completely open in public relations or to reveal all of their motives and plans in a dialogue with a public.

The dilemma is similar with impression management. Both individuals working in organizations and the organizations themselves want to look good – to have a good image. But they also are advised not to try to create images that do not reflect reality. Thus, the deceit criterion seems to be reasonable. Organizations do not have to tell everything about themselves as they manage the impressions others have of them. Yet they should not deliberately deceive people into believing they are something they are not.

The production of images – or more accurately, the choice and use of symbols to communicate impressions of an organization – is, in summary, an obviously important part of public relations. Public relations theorists and researchers should be able to provide practitioners with research to identify the most ethical and effective methods of symbolic communication. Such research is being done by scholars applying rhetorical and critical methods to public relations (see, e.g., Heath and Toth, 1992).

For semantic clarity, I prefer to call this production component of public relations the communication of symbols or the giving of messages rather than image-making. Thus, image is not a good term to describe the production of messages. Other terms – symbols, messages, communication – are more precise. Next, we will see that there is a different problem when image is applied to the consumption of symbols by publics. Image disguises at least four concepts, which should be conceptualized and measured separately.

Consumption of symbols (images)

Definitions of image that group a number of psychological concepts into a sum total, or composite, define image loosely as everything that goes on inside the mind. We can make sense of these vague conceptions of image by examining the major concepts of cognitive and social psychology – concepts that most definitions of image include but do not define.

General theories of cognitive psychology conceptualize three levels at which people process messages and sensory inputs – sensory processes, perception, and cognition. Social psychologists use the concept of attitude to add a fourth level, evaluation. All of these theories also address the impact of mental processes on behavior – although that effect is not always addressed by each specific theory.

Theories of cognitive psychology begin with the *sensory processes* of sight, sound, taste, touch, and hearing (Gleitman, 1987, Chap. 5). People do not recognize or "see" all of this sensory input, however. Thus, cognitive theories require a second stage of message consumption known as *perception*. To see or pay attention to objects in or messages from their environment, people must perceive them – that is, recognize objects or see patterns in sensory stimuli (Anderson, 1985, Chap. 2).

Before people can remember or think about the objects or symbolic messages they receive, however, they most construct mental representations – which also are known as concepts (Gleitman, 1987, p. 214) or cognitive units (Anderson, 1983, p. 76). This second stage of message consumption is *cognition* – the process through which people develop beliefs about what is real or come to understand – from their perspective, of course – what they perceive.

Public relations practitioners frequently use the expression "perception is reality" to point out that people do not act on what an organization considers to be fact or reality but on their own understanding of that reality. The perception is reality cliché, however, does not represent an accurate use of the term perception. It would be more accurate to say that cognition is reality. For our purposes in public relations, cognitions are the most important components of image because sensory processes and perceptions represent mostly the input and attention phases of mental processes.

There has been much argument over the years about the nature of thought. The linguistic relativity hypothesis of Edward Sapir and Benjamin Whorf (see, e.g., Carroll, 1956) maintained that thought takes place in the categories of languages. Cognitive psychologists now generally agree that thought takes place in abstract cognitive units rather than in language (see, e.g., Anderson, 1983). Communication theories pick up at this point by adding that people construct thoughts from words or other symbols as well as from direct sensory inputs from the environment and that they choose words and other symbols to try to communicate their abstract thoughts to others (J. Grunig, Ramsey, and Schneider [aka L. Grunig], 1985).

Cognitive psychologists have identified several types of cognitive units. Some cognitive units link *objects and attributes* (e.g., Scott, Osgood, and Peterson, 1979; Carter, 1979). For example, an object–attribute concept might link the attributes of intelligent, attractive, or tall with a person (object). Likewise, another cognitive unit could link two objects such as the Chrysler Corporation and Lee Iacocca. Another could link two or more attributes, such as conservative, rigid, and old-fashioned. Or people could link an organization such as Exxon (an object) with the attributes of irresponsible, dangerous, and polluting as the result of its Valdez accident in Alaska.

Marketing writers usually have an objective–attribute cognition in mind when they describe brand image (e.g., Kotler and Armstrong, 1991, p. 151), product image (p. 292), or organizational image (p. 612). For example, Kotler and Armstrong (1991) described a brand image and brand beliefs when they said, "The consumer's beliefs may vary from true attributes because of his or her experience and the effect of selective perceptions, selective distortion, and selective retention" (p. 151).

A second type of cognitive unit is called a *proposition* (e.g., Anderson, 1983). Propositions link subjects and predicates in the same way that a subject–verb–object sentence does. For example, people may remember Union Carbide as the company that killed thousands of Indians in an industrial accident. Propositions seem to take the form of active sentences not because thought is shaped by language but because most languages reflect the inherent propositional nature of thought.

A third type of cognitive unit is a *mental image*, as that concept was described earlier in this article. Cognitive images are mental analogues of reality. According to Denis (1991), "the notion of 'mental analogues' reflects the idea that the mental representations constructed through imagery attain a high degree of structural isomorphism with the objects they stand for" (p. 103). John Locke originally envisioned images as mental pictures or the equivalent of photographs (Horowitz, 1978). Now, psychologists believe images capture spatial relationships, although not in exact detail (J. Grunig, Ramsey, and Schneider [aka L. Grunig], 1985, p. 104).

If we move to social psychology, we can add the concept of attitude to perceptions and cognitions. In essence, attitudes are evaluations of the objects and attributes in cognitions or of the possible behaviors that are implied by cognitions. For example, Petty and Cacioppo (1986) defined attitudes as "general evaluations people hold in regard to themselves, other people, objects, and issues" (p. 4). And, as Gleitman (1987) added, an attitude is "emotionally tinged" and "predisposes people to behave" (p. 297). In addition to being evaluations, then, attitudes also can be seen as a behavioral intent (Fishbein and Ajzen, 1975).

Social psychologists have researched and debated for many years whether attitudes predict behavior (for a review of this debate, see J. Grunig and Hunt, 1984, pp. 122–127). However, research shows that attitudes defined as situational evaluations predict behavior better than attitudes defined as cross-situational or general evaluations. Attitudes are situational when people re-evaluate people, objects, issues, or behaviors as situations change. Attitudes are cross-situational when these evaluations remain stable across situations. For example, a negative evaluation of George Bush's position on taxation would predict a person's voting behavior better than would a negative evaluation of all conservatives.

In summary, then, perception, cognition, and evaluation (formation of attitudes) are the major processes that take place in the mind. Gleitman (1987) concluded the section on cognition in his basic textbook on psychology by saying there are no clear boundaries between perception, memory, and thinking, "these areas are not sharply separated intellectual domains, with neat lines of demarcation between them. They are simply designations for somewhat different aspects of the general process of cognition" (p. 237). Likewise, research on attitudes now is dominated by cognitive-response theories (Petty and Cacioppo, 1981; Markus and Zajonc, 1985) that recognize the importance of the link between cognition and attitude in predicting changes in attitudes and behavior. The cognitive theories of attitudes show that people who construct new cognitive units – think about – persuasive messages are most likely to change their attitudes, especially when they are highly involved in a situation to which the attitude applies. Finally, research based on cognitive response theories of attitudes shows that people who develop attitudes based on elaborated rather than simple cognitions are most likely to change their behavior over the long term as a result of attitude change (Petty and Cacioppo, 1986, p. 21).

Even though there are linkages and overlaps among these mental processes, concepts of imagery that ignore the complexities of cognitive, affective, and behavioral processes mislead public relations practitioners into believing that messages alone can produce desired images in the members of publics with which they are trying to communicate. There are many effects of communication – perceptual, cognitive, attitudinal, and behavioral – some of which are easier to attain than others. Generally, the further a person progresses in the process from perception to behavior, the less likely it is that a given message will have an effect. That difference is extremely important for a public relations practitioner who wishes to choose measurable objectives for public relations programs and then to measure them and do evaluative research to determine whether those effects have been achieved.

In *Managing Public Relations*, J. Grunig and Hunt (1984) developed a taxonomy of these effects based on McLeod and Chaffee's (1973) coorientation model. The taxonomy separates perceptual, cognitive, attitudinal, and behavioral effects and provides a set of objectives for both planning and evaluating public relations.

For the short-term planning of public relations programs, therefore, it is important to separate the mental processes that are confounded when image is defined as a composite. However, an additional concept in cognitive and social psychology, that of a *schema* (see, e.g., Anderson, 1980, 1985), comes close to the definition typically given to image. The concept of schema, however, is much better conceptualized and researched than is the concept of image.

Over the long term, people – members of publics – organize their cognitions and attitudes into complex units of knowledge called schemas or schemata. Schemas are broader units of knowledge than are single cognitive units such as objects and attributes, propositions, or mental images. They are sets of cognitive units. People retain symbols or direct sensory inputs by encoding them from short- to long-term memory as cognitive units. In long-term memory, however, they organize those cognitive units into more comprehensive schemas.

Social psychologists, as well as cognitive psychologists, have researched schemas. Some social psychologists have argued that schemas are strictly cognitive and do not include attitudes (Fiske and Linville, 1980). Others have countered that schemas are "little more than a complex of interrelated attitudes" (Smith, 1982, p. 39). I would choose the middle ground between these extremes by accepting the fact that schemas can include the evaluations and behavioral intentions – attitudes – associated with cognitions as well as the cognitions themselves.

Schemas, therefore, begin to sound a lot like images when they are defined as composites or sum totals. In fact, if we look at Boulding's (1956) influential book, *The Image*, we find that his description of an image sounds almost identical to contemporary descriptions of schemas:

What I have been talking about is knowledge. Knowledge, perhaps, is not a good word for this. Perhaps one would rather say my *Image* of the world. Knowledge has an implication of validity, of truth. What I am talking about is what I believe to be true: my subjective knowledge. It is this image that largely governs my behavior

(pp. 5–6)

Schema theories add substantially to the loose definition of image as a composite. Psychologists have learned that schemas are organized but that they can be organized in different ways. Some schemas are organized in a hierarchical structure, but most often the mind groups cognitions and attitudes because they have a "family resemblance" (Anderson, 1980, pp. 133–137). A family resemblance explains why people often retain bits and pieces of information about an organization that may seem illogical to a public relations practitioner who has organized his or her knowledge about that organization logically and hierarchically. People remember and associate cognitive units that seem relevant and similar to them – i.e., cognitive units that resemble each other in the same inexact way that family members do. That family resemblance pattern is the subjective knowledge to which Boulding referred.

Although single messages seldom change schemas, schemas are dynamic and subject to change. Schemas help people to assimilate new information; they make sense of information by fitting it into an existing schema. Schemas also can distort information because people sometimes make sense of information by fitting it into a pre-existing but inappropriate schema. At the same time, schemas are dynamic; they grow and change to accommodate new information, much as scientific theories change to accommodate new research.

Boulding (1956) said, similarly, that messages can have one of three effects on images. First, they can have no effect, "if we think of the image as a rather loose structure, something like a molecule, we may imagine that the message is going straight through without hitting it" (p. 7). Second, Boulding said a message "may change the image in some rather regular and well-defined way that might be described as simple addition" (p. 7). But third, according to Boulding, messages might change images in a way that "might be described as revolutionary change" (p. 8).

Theories of schemas, therefore, seem to add substance to the ideas about images that Boulding introduced 25 years ago. Yet, as Markus and Zajonc (1985) pointed out, schemas also have taken on diverse meanings in cognitive and social psychology. In particular, theorists gradually came to postulate that a rather rigid schema exists in the mind for each set of related behaviors that a person engages in. Rather quickly, it would seem, the mind would become cluttered with thousands, if not millions, of schemas. If schema is equated with the public relations definition of image, for example, we would come to believe that each person has a schema – an image – for every organization. Public relations practitioners do indeed harbor such beliefs about their organizations – that every person has an image for their organization that can be managed and controlled.

Schema theorists have overcome the problem of schema clutter by conceptualizing schemas more as processes than structures. That is, having a schema means simply that people associate relevant cognitive units dynamically in long-term memory at a time when they have reason to think about an organization, object, or set of ideas. Then they assemble the cognitive units that are relevant to the situation and that have a family resemblance pattern. If I have a reason to think about Exxon, for example, I may bring together memories of the Valdez as well as of my friendly service station up the street. For Union Carbide, which has no consumer products, Bhopal may be the only cognitive unit on my mind unless I work for or know someone who works for the company.

To explain the dynamic nature of schemas, cognitive psychologists have used Craik and Lockhart's (1972) concept of depth of processing. To Craik and Lockhart, depth of processing meant that people apply extensive semantic or cognitive analysis to incoming messages. Cognitive psychologists concluded later that Craik and Lockhart's original concept of depth of processing should, more accurately, be described as breadth of processing, where breadth meant "number of elaborations" (Anderson and Reder, 1979, p. 391).

Both Anderson and Reder (1979, p. 390) and Craik (1979, p. 449) distinguished breadth from depth of cognition. Breadth represents the quantity of cognitive units associated in a schema, whereas depth is the quality of those elaborations. According to Craik (1979), depth means that a cognition has "abstract symbolic properties" (p. 457). Markus and Zajonc called depth subjective "theories about how the social world operates" (p. 145). In short, schemas have breadth when people simply add cognitive units to their overall understanding of an organization or issue.

Pavlik (1983) developed a public relations theory of cognitive breadth and depth that he used to evaluate the effects of health communication campaigns. He found that campaigns more often increase breadth than depth. J. Grunig and Childers [aka Hon] (1988) studied the differing effects on breadth and depth that messages have when directed to active and passive publics as identified by J. Grunig's situational theory of publics (see, e.g., J. Grunig and Hunt, 1984, Chap. 7). In general, they found that public relations programs more often add to cognitive breadth than depth. They also found that such programs are more likely to add to depth when the receiving public is active rather than passive and has a high level of education. In short, though, public relations research shows that communication programs seldom have the large-scale revolutionary changes in schemas mentioned by Boulding (1956). More often, they simply add an additional cognitive unit to the breadth of cognitive associations people make.

Theories of and research on schemas, therefore, show that the grand designs that many public relations practitioners have for shaping, changing, projecting, and polishing images generally have only incremental effects on the breadth of cognitive processes. Seldom do these programs affect cognitive depth. That conclusion suggests the paramount importance of continuing good behavior by organizations — of good relationships with publics — as people learn about an organization and develop informal theories about its motivations — the reasons for its behaviors. Once people accumulate cognitions and attitudes, they continue to store them in long-term memory and associate them when they have reason to think about an organization. A "reputation" — if that term is equated with schema – has a long life. It is best to earn a good reputation early, because it is difficult to replace an existing reputation with a new one.

From symbolic to behavioral relationships

This article began by describing the difference between image (symbolic relationships) and substance (behavioral relationships) in public relations as one of the major paradigm struggles in the field. Yet, I quickly added that the two kinds of relationships are complementary rather than competing. The struggle, therefore, is more between symbolic relationships addressed in isolation from behavioral relationships and the two kinds of relationships viewed as intertwined strands of a rope. We have examined carefully the concepts involved in symbolic relationships. Our last step, then, is to look at their interaction with behavioral relationships.

Ferguson (1984) argued that relationships between organizations and their publics should be the central unit of study for public relations researchers. Ferguson identified several attributes of relationships that scholars and practitioners of public relations can use to define and measure the quality of an organization's behavioral relationships with strategic publics: (1) dynamic vs. static, (2) open vs. closed, (3) the degree to which both organization and public are satisfied with the relationship, (4) distribution of power in the relationship, and (5) the mutuality of understanding, agreement, and consensus.

To this list, I would add two concepts that are stalwarts of theories of interpersonal communication, trust and credibility, and the concept of reciprocity, which Gouldner (1960) has said is a norm in most societies. Finally, Pfeffer (1978) defined another relevant attribute of relationships – organizational legitimacy or the "congruence between social values and organizational actions" (p. 159). A relationship of legitimacy, therefore, would be one in which both parties recognize the importance of the other.

Researchers and practitioners could use any of these concepts to measure the quality of the behavioral relationships of organizations, but the following seem to be most important: reciprocity, trust, credibility, mutual legitimacy, openness, mutual satisfaction, and mutual understanding.

If we then combine these behavioral relationships with the symbolic relationships disguised by the term image, we can see the nature of the paradigm struggle clearly. When symbolic relationships are divorced from behavioral relationships, public relations practitioners reduce public relations to the simplistic notion of image-building. Public relations practitioners then offer little of value to the organizations they advise because they suggest that problems in relationships with publics can be solved by using the proper message – disseminated through publicity or media relations – to change an image of an organization.

For public relations to be valued by the organizations it serves, practitioners must be able to demonstrate that their efforts contribute to the goals of these organizations by building long-term behavioral relationships with strategic publics – those that affect the ability of the organization to accomplish its mission. To do so, public relations practitioners must demonstrate effectiveness at two levels

– the micro level of individual programs to communicate with different publics and the macro level of overall organizational effectiveness.

At the micro level of public relations programs practitioners should use the concepts of perception, cognition, attitude, schema, and behavior to derive objectives for communication programs and to develop measures to evaluate their effectiveness. Micro-level communication programs build symbolic relationships with publics, but symbolic relationships alone cannot solve public relations problems. At a more macro level, organizations need public relations because their behaviors affect publics and the behavior of publics affects them. Over the long term, therefore, organizations must evaluate the quality of their macro-level, behavioral relationships with publics if they are to determine the contribution that public relations makes to achieving organizational goals and missions.

Symbolic relationships and behavioral relationships are intertwined like the strands of a rope. As a result, public relations practitioners must strive to build linkages between the two sets of relationships if their work is to make organizations more effective.

References

Anderson, J. R. (1980). *Cognitive Psychology and its Implications*. San Francisco: W. H. Freeman.

Anderson, J. R. (1983). *The Architecture of Cognition*. Cambridge, MA: Harvard University Press.

Anderson, J. R. (1985). *Cognitive Psychology and its Implications, (2nd ed.)* San Francisco: W. H. Freeman.

Anderson, J. R., and Reder, L. M. (1979). "An Elaborative Processing Explanation of Depth of Processing." Pp. 385–403 in L. S. Cermak and F. I. M. Craik (Eds.), *Levels of Processing in Human Memory*. Hillsdale, NJ: Lawrence Erlbaum.

Baskin, O. W., and Aronoff, C. E. (1988). *Public Relations: The Profession and the Practice (2nd ed.)*. Dubuque, IA: Wm. C. Brown.

Bernays, E. L. (1977). "Down with Image, Up with Reality." *Public Relations Quarterly*, 22(1): 12–14.

Boulding, K. E. (1956). *The Image*. Ann Arbor: The University of Michigan Press.

Carroll, J. B. (Ed.) (1956). *Language, Thought, and Reality: Selected Writings of Benjamin Lee Whorf*. Cambridge, MA: MIT Press.

Carter, R. F. (1979). "A Journalistic Cybernetic." Pp. 475–487 in K. Krippendorff (Ed.), *Communication and Control in Society*. New York: Gordon and Breach Science Publishers.

Chajet, C., and Shachtman, T. (1991). *Image by Design: From Corporate Vision to Business Reality*. Reading, MA: Addison-Wesley.

Clavier, D. E., and Wright, D. K. (1987). "Research." Pp. 15–30 in C. Degan (Ed.), *Communicators Guide to Marketing: International Association of Business Communicators*. New York: Longman.

Craik, F. I. M. (1979). "Levels of Processing: Overview and Closing Comments." Pp. 447–461 in L. S. Cermak and F. I. M. Craik (Eds.), *Levels of Processing in Human Memory*. Hillsdale, NJ: Lawrence Erlbaum.

Craik, F. I. M., and Lockhart, R. S. (1972). "Levels of Processing: A Framework for Memory Research." *Journal of Verbal Learning and Verbal Behavior*, 11: 671–684.

Cutlip, S. M. (1991). "Cutlip Tells of Heroes and Goats Encountered in 55-year PR Career." *O'Dwyer's PR Services Report*, 5(5): 12, 51–56.

Denis, M. (1991). "Imagery and Thinking." Pp. 103–132 in C. Cornoldi and M. A. McDaniel (Eds.), *Imagery and Cognition*. New York: Springer-Verlag.

Dilenschneider, R. I. (1990). *Power and Influence*. New York: Prentice-Hall Press.

Ferguson, M. A. (1984). *Building theory in public relations: Interorganizational relationships*. Paper presented to the Association for Education in Journalism and Mass Communication, Gainesville, FL.

Fishbein, M., and Ajzen, I. (1975). *Belief, Attitude, Intention, and Behavior*. Reading, MA: Addison-Wesley.

Fiske, S. T., and Linville, P. W. (1980). "What Does the Schema Concept Buy Us?", *Personality and Social Psychology Bulletin*, 6: 543–557.

Giacalone, R. A., and Rosenfeld, P. (1989). "Impression Management in Organizations: An Overview." Pp. 1–4 in R. A. Giacalone and P. Rosenfeld (Eds.), *Impression Management in the Organization*. Hillsdale, NJ: Lawrence Erlbaum.

Giacalone, R. A., and Rosenfeld, P. (Eds.) (1991). *Applied Impression Management: How Image-Making Affects Managerial Decisions*. Newbury Park, CA: Sage.

Gleitman, H. (1987). *Basic Psychology (2nd ed.)*. New York: W. W. Norton.

Goffman, E. (1959). *The Presentation of Self in Everyday Life*. Garden City, NY: Doubleday.

Goffman, E. (1974). *Frame Analysis: An Essay on the Organization of Experience*. Cambridge, MA: Harvard University Press.

Gouldner, A. W. (1960). "The Norm of Reciprocity: A Preliminary Statement." *American Sociological Review*, 25: 161–178.

Grunig, J. E., and Childers (aka Hon), L. (1988). *Reconstruction of a situational theory of communication: Internal and External Concepts as identifiers of publics for AIDS*. Paper presented to the Association for Education in Journalism and Mass Communication, Portland, Oregon.

Grunig, J. E., and Hunt, T. (1984). *Managing Public Relations*. New York: Holt, Rinehart and Winston.

Grunig, J. E., and White, J. (1992). "The Effect of Worldviews on Public Relations Theory and Practice." Pp. 31–64 in J. E. Grunig (Ed.), *Excellence in Relations and Communication Management*. Hillsdale, NJ: Lawrence Erlbaum.

Grunig, J. E., Ramsey, S., and Schneider (aka Grunig), L. A. (1985). "An Axiomatic Theory of Cognition and Writing." *Journal of Technical Writing and Communication*, 15: 95–130.

Haberman, D. Z., and Dolphin, H. A. (1988). *Public Relations: The Necessary Art*. Ames, IA: Iowa State University Press.

Heath, R. L., and Toth, E. L. (Eds.) (1992). *Rhetorical and Critical Approaches to Public Relations*. Hillsdale, NJ: Lawrence Erlbaum.

Horowitz, M. J. (1978). *Image Formation and Cognition*. New York: Appleton-Century-Croft.

Infante, D. A., Rancer, A. S., and Womack, D. E. (1990). *Building Communication Theory*. Prospect Heights, IL: Waveland Press.

Kotler, P. (1991). *Marketing Management (7th ed.)*. Englewood Cliffs, NJ: Prentice-Hall.

Kotler, P., and Andreason, A. R. (1987). *Strategic Marketing for Nonprofit Organizations (3rd ed.)*. Englewood Cliffs, NJ: Prentice-Hall.

Kotler, P., and Armstrong, G. (1991). *Principles of Marketing (5th ed.)*. Englewood Cliffs, NJ: Prentice-Hall.

Lyra, A. (1991). *Public relations in Greece: Models, roles, and gender*. Unpublished M.A. thesis, University of Maryland, College Park, MD.

Markin, G. A. (1990). "Corporate Image – We All Have One, but Few Work to Protect and Project It." *Public Relations Quarterly*, 35(1): 21–23.

Markus, M., and Zajonc, R. B. (1985). "The Cognitive Perspective in Social Psychology." Pp. 137–230 in G. Lindsey and E. Anderson (Eds.), *Handbook of Social Psychology (Vol. I)*. New York: Random House.

McLeod, J. M., and Chaffee, S. H. (1973). "Interpersonal Approaches to Communication Research." *American Behavioral Scientist*, 16: 469–500.

Moberg, D. J. (1989). "The Ethics of Impression Management." Pp. 171–188 in R. A. Giacalone and P. Rosenfeld (Eds.), *Impression Management in the Organization*. Hillsdale, NJ: Lawrence Erlbaum.

Moffitt, M. A. (1991). *A cultural studies, ethnographic approach toward understanding the articulation of corporate image: A case study of State Farm Insurance*. Paper presented to the Speech Communication Association, Atlanta.

Murphy, P. (1991). "The Limits of Symmetry: A Game Theory Approach to Symmetric and Asymmetric Public Relations." *Public Relations Research Annual*, 3: 115–132.

Olasky, M. N. (1987). *Corporate Public Relations: A New Historical Perspective*. Hillsdale, NJ: Lawrence Erlbaum.

Olins, W. (1978). *The Corporate Personality: An Inquiry into the Nature of Corporate Identity*. New York: Mayflower Books.

Pavlik, J. V. (1983). *The effects of two health information campaigns on the complexity of cognitive structure: An information processing approach*. Unpublished Ph.D. dissertation, University of Minnesota, Minneapolis.

Petty, R. E., and Cacioppo, J. T. (1981). *Attitudes and Persuasion: Classic and Contemporary Approaches*. Dubuque, IA: Wm. C. Brown.

Petty, R. E., and Cacioppo, J. T. (1986). *Communication and Persuasion: Central and Peripheral Routes to Attitude Change*. New York: Springer-Verlag.

Pfeffer, J. (1978). *Organization Design*. Arlington Heights, IL: AHM.

pr reporter (1990). "Behavioral Model Replacing Communication Model as Basic Theoretical Underpinning of PR Practice: Key is Stimulation Latent Readiness and Creating Triggering Events." (July 30).

pr reporter purview (1991). "Book Examines Application of 'Impression Management' Techniques." (Dec. 23).

Riley, J. W., Jr. (Ed.) (1963). *The Corporation and Its Publics: Essays on the Corporate Image*. New York: John Wiley & Sons.

Scott, W. A., Osgood, D. W., and Peterson, C. (1979). *Cognitive Structure: Theory and Measurement of Individual Difference*. New York: John Wiley & Sons.

Smith, M. J. (1982). *Persuasion and Human Action*. Belmont, CA: Wadsworth.

Snyder, M., and Copeland, J. (1989). "Self-Monitoring Processes in Organizational Settings." Pp. 7–19 in R. A. Giacalone and P. Rosenfeld (Eds.), *Impression Management in the Organization*. Hillsdale, NJ: Lawrence Erlbaum.

Sriramesh, K. (1991). *The impact of societal culture on public relations: An ethnographic study of south Indian organizations*. Unpublished Ph.D. dissertation, University of Maryland, College Park, MD.

Wiebe, G. D. (1963). "The Social Dynamics of Corporation–Public Relationships: A Model and a Parable." Pp. 12–23 in J. W. Riley, Jr. (Ed.), *The Corporation and Its Publics: Essays on the Corporate Image*. New York: John Wiley & Sons.

Wouters, J. (1991). *International Public Relations: How to Establish Your Company's Product, Service, and Image in Foreign Markets*. New York: AMACON.

Chapter 11

Charles J. Fombrun and
Cees B. M. Van Riel

THE REPUTATIONAL LANDSCAPE

Adapted from *Corporate Reputation Review* 1998, 1 (1): 5–13

EDITORS' COMMENTARY

Charles Fombrun, Professor of Business Administration at Stern Business School, New York University, is a leading academic authority in corporate reputation. His book *Reputation: Realizing Value from the Corporate Image*[1] did much to confirm his international standing. He is the author of numerous scholarly papers on corporate reputation.[2]

The extract reproduced here is from the opening article of the inaugural edition of the *Corporate Reputation Review*, a journal whose principal goal is to advance the general understanding of corporate reputations. Entitled "The Reputational Landscape," the article is coauthored by the journal's two editors, Charles Fombrun and Cees Van Riel. (We have discussed Van Riel earlier, Chapter 8.)

"The Reputational Landscape" provides an excellent introduction to the corporate reputation construct. It provides an accessible and concise overview of the various literatures that inform the general understanding of corporate reputation. Thus the corporate reputation construct is examined from different disciplinary perspectives: economics, strategy, marketing, organizational behavior, sociology, and accountancy.

Readers will note that there are a number of similarities shared by the identity, image, and reputation constructs. Each has its attendant schools of thought. Each is widely used in business parlance. Each comes to the fore in times of crisis. Each concept affords a complex, albeit critically important, perspective on organizations. Each concept tends to be narrowly conceived. Each concept, along with corporate communication, is contiguous. Each concept has the aim of ensuring business success and survival. Each concept at various times and places has been treated as a chimera.

The extract ends with a definition of corporate reputation penned by Fombrun and Rindova.[3] They identify corporate reputation along five dimensions, concluding that reputations are: (a) historically rooted; (b) of concern to internal and to external stakeholders; (c) based on past actions and achievement; (d) assessed on the benefits accrued by individual stakeholder groups; and (e) used to position the company in terms of both its competitors and its business environment.

In "The Reputational Landscape" Fombrun and Van Riel appear to share Grunig's perspective (see Chapter 10) that behavior is a key determinant of a corporate image/corporate reputation.

At this juncture, as we move from a consideration of the corporate image construct to that of corporate reputation, it is worth reiterating the perspective adopted in this anthology. Revealing the corporation is akin to examining a mosaic. In this regard corporate reputations provide perspectives that are insighful but ones that necessarily form part of a whole. Fombrun, in an astute piece of analysis taken from his book, reflects the importance of considering *multiple* perspectives. We reproduce it here:

> To focus on a company's reputation is to determine how it deals with all of its constituents: it is to focus on a company's character or identity. Identity constrains what actions a company takes, how it makes decisions, how it treats it employees, how it reacts to crises. Managers and employees tend to act in ways consistent with the company's identity. Identity is therefore the backbone of reputation. Identity develops from within and limits a company's long term actions and its performance as benchmarked against rivals. Identity explains the kind of relationship companies establish with their most critical constituencies, employees, consumers, investors and local communities.[4]

NOTES

1   Fombrun, C. J., *Reputation: Realizing Value from the Corporate Image*, Cambridge, MA: Harvard Business School Press, 1996.

2   Fombrun, C. J., Gardberg, N., and Sever, J., "The Reputation Quotient: A Multi Stakeholder Measure of Corporate Reputation," *Journal of Brand Management* 2000, 7 (4): 241–255; Fombrun, C. and Rindova, V. P., "The Road to Transparency: Reputation Management at Royal Dutch/Shell," in M. Schultz, M. J. Hatch and M. H. Larsen (eds) *The Expressive Organization*, Oxford: Oxford University Press, 2000; Fombrun, C. J. and Rindova, V. P., "Reputation Management in Global 100 Firms: A Benchmarking Study," *Corporate Reputation Review* 1998, 1 (3): 205–214; Fombrun, C. J. and Rindova, V., "Who's Tops and Who Decides? The Social Construction of Corporate Reputations," *New York University: School of Business Working Paper* 1996; Fombrun, C. J. and Shanley, M., "What's in a

Name? Reputation Building and Strategy," *Academy of Management Journal* 1990, 33 (2): 233–258.

3   Fombrun and Rindova, "Who's Tops."

4   *Ibid.*, p. 111.

Corporate reputation: a crossroads of converging disciplines

ALTHOUGH CORPORATE REPUTATIONS ARE ubiquitous, they remain relatively understudied (Fombrun, 1996). In part, it is surely because reputations are seldom noticed until they are threatened. In part, however, it is also a problem of definition. According to the 'American Heritage Dictionary' (1970: 600) 'reputation' is 'the general estimation in which one is held by the public'. Yet how does such a definition apply to companies? Who constitutes 'the public' of a company, and what is being 'estimated' by that public? Given the diversity of audiences companies address themselves to, whose perceptions and judgments count the most? Those of investors, employees, financial analysts, communities, regulators, CEOs?

The lack of systematic attention to corporate reputations can be traced to the diversity of relevant academic and practitioner literatures that explore different facets of the construct (Fombrun and Rindova, 1996). We point here to six distinct literatures that are currently converging in their emphasis on corporate reputations as key but relatively neglected features of companies and their environments.

The economic view

Economists view reputations as either traits or signals. Game theorists describe reputations as character traits that distinguish among 'types' of firms and can explain their strategic behavior. Signaling theorists call our attention to the informational content of reputations. Both acknowledge that reputations are actually perceptions of firms held by external observers.

Weigelt and Camerer (1988: 443) point out that '. . . in game theory the reputation of a player is the perception others have of the player's values . . . which determine his/her choice of strategies'. Information asymmetry forces external observers to rely on proxies to describe the preferences of rivals and their likely courses of action. Consumers rely on firms' reputations because they have less information than managers do about firms' commitment to delivering desirable product features like quality or reliability (Grossman and Stiglitz, 1980; Stiglitz, 1989). Similarly, since outside investors in firms' securities are less informed than managers about firms' future actions, corporate reputations increase investor confidence that managers will act in ways that are reputation-consistent. For game theorists, then, reputations are functional: they generate perceptions among employees, customers, investors, competitors, and the general public about what a company is, what it does, what it stands for. These perceptions stabilize interactions between a firm and its publics.

Signaling theorists concur: reputations derive from the prior resource allocations managers make to first-order activities likely to create a perception of reliability and predictability to outside observers (Myers and Majluf, 1984; Ross, 1977; Stigler, 1962). Since many features of a company and its products are hidden from view, reputations are information signals that increase an observer's confidence in the firm's products and services.

Naturally, then, managers can make *strategic* use of a company's reputation to signal its attractiveness. When the quality of a company's products and services is not directly observable, high-quality producers are said to invest in reputation-building in order to signal their quality (Shapiro, 1983). Their prior investments in reputation-building allow them to charge premium prices, and may also earn them rents from the repeat purchases that their quality products will generate. In contrast, low-quality producers avoid investing in reputation-building because they do not foresee repeat purchases (Allen, 1984; Bagwell, 1992; Milgrom and Roberts, 1986).

In fact, similar dynamics may operate in the capital and labor markets. For instance, managers routinely try to signal investors about their economic performance. Since investors are more favorably disposed to companies that demonstrate high and stable earnings, managers often try to smooth quarterly earnings and keep dividend pay-out ratios high and fixed, despite earnings fluctuations (Brealy and Myers, 1988). Sometimes companies pay a premium price to hire high-reputation auditors and outside counsel. They rent the reputations of their agents in order to signal investors, regulators, and other publics about their firm's probity and credibility (Wilson, 1985).

The strategic view

To strategists, reputations are both assets and mobility barriers (Caves and Porter, 1977). Established reputations impede mobility and produce returns to firms because they are difficult to imitate. By circumscribing firms' actions and rivals' reactions, reputations are therefore a distinct element of industry-level structure (Fombrun and Zajac, 1987).

Reputations are difficult to duplicate because they derive from unique internal features of firms. By accumulating the history of firms' interactions with stakeholders they suggest to observers what companies stand for (Dutton and Dukerich, 1991; Freeman, 1984). Reputations are also *externally* perceived, and so are largely outside the direct control of firms' managers (Fombrun and Shanley, 1990). It takes time for a reputation to coalesce in observers' minds. Empirical studies show that even when confronted with negative information, observers resist changing their reputational assessments (Wartick, 1992). Therefore, reputations are valuable intangible assets because they are inertial (Cramer and Ruefli, 1994).

Like economists, then, strategists call attention to the competitive benefits of acquiring favorable reputations (Rindova and Fombrun, 1997). They implicitly support a focus on the resource allocations that firms must make over time to erect reputational barriers to the mobility of rivals (Barney, 1986). Since primary resource allocations also stand to improve organizational performance directly, however, it proves difficult to isolate their unique impact on performance and reputation. This explains why empirical studies have had difficulty untangling a causal ordering: both are produced by the same underlying initiatives (Chakravarthy, 1986; McGuire, Sundgren, and Schneeweis, 1988).

The marketing view

In marketing research 'reputation' (often labeled 'brand image') focuses on the nature of information processing, resulting in 'pictures in the heads' (Lippmann, 1922) of external subjects, attributing cognitive and affective meaning to cues received about an object they were directly or indirectly confronted with. 'Objects' in marketing research are predominantly 'products' (beer, detergents, computers), while consumers seem to be the principal 'subject' of analyses.

According to the notions of the Elaboration Likelihood Model of Petty and Cacioppo (1986), information processing results in three layers of elaboration: high, medium and low. A high degree of elaboration of information about an object results in a complex network of meanings chunked in memory, enabling a subject to give a sophisticated description of an object. A low degree of elaboration results in simple descriptions like 'good/bad' or 'attractive/unattractive'. A medium degree of elaboration creates a set of attributes enabling a subject to describe an object in terms of salient beliefs and evaluations (Fishbein and Ajzen, 1975; Poeisz, 1988). The degree of elaboration is a consequence of the existing knowledge of an individual, the level of involvement of the subject with the object, and the intensity and integrated nature of the marketing communications (Schultz, Tannenbaum and Lauterborn, 1994) through which a company tries to create an attractive, desirable brand.

Building brand equity requires the creation of a *familiar* brand that has *favorable, strong and unique* associations (Keller, 1993). This can be done both through the initial choice of the brand identity (the brand name, the logo) and through the integration of brand identities into the supporting marketing program so that consumers purchase the product or service.

Companies apply three types of branding strategies (Kotler, 1991; Olins, 1978): individual names for all products without any explicit mention of the company; all products refer to the company, identifying the company name on all products; or combining the company name with the product brand names. Preference for one of the three branding strategies has to be based on the similarity between the endorser and the inferred product/service. Most marketing literature deals with an endorsement of one brand by another brand in the same product category (image transfer by line extensions, Aaker and Keller, 1990; Park, Milberg and Lawson, 1991), products complementing each other (co-branding, Rao and Ruekert, 1994) or linking organizational associations (e.g. social responsibility and financial performance) to product associations (Belch and Belch, 1987). An endorsement will be more successful if consumers perceive similarity between the core brand and its extension (Boush and Loken, 1991).

Umbrella branding (Dawar and Parker, 1993; Kapferer, 1992) or more specific 'corporate branding' (all processes that are inclined to enhance the value of the corporate brand, Maathuis and Van Riel, 1996) will be more successful if the information asymmetry between buyer and seller creates an incentive for service providers to capitalize on a firm's reputation and introduce new services for existing customers (Nayyar, 1990); when consumers perceive a high degree of risk acquiring the product/service; and finally, when the endorser's attributes are highly relevant in the context of the intended processes of image transfer (Brown and Dacin, 1997; Keller, 1993).

The organizational view

To organizational scholars, corporate reputations are rooted in the sense-making experiences of employees. A company's culture and identity shape a firm's business practices, as well as the kinds of relationships that managers establish with key stakeholders. Corporate culture influences managers' perceptions and motivations (Barney, 1986; Dutton and Penner, 1992). Corporate identity affects how managers both interpret and react to environmental circumstances (Dutton and Dukerich, 1991; Meyer, 1982). Shared cultural values and a strong sense of identity therefore guide managers, not only in defining what their firms stand for, but in justifying their strategies for interacting with key stakeholders (Miles with Cameron, 1982; Porac and Thomas, 1990).

Thick cultures homogenize perceptions inside a firm and so increase the likelihood that managers will make more consistent self-presentations to external observers. By creating focal principles, that is, general understanding of the right way of doing things in a firm, thick cultures contribute to the consistency of firms' images with stakeholders (Camerer and Vepsalainen, 1988).

Identity and culture are related. Identity describes core, enduring, and distinctive features of a firm that produce shared interpretations among managers about how they should accommodate to external circumstances (Albert and Whetten, 1985). For instance, a comparative study of Bay Area hospitals showed how each institution responded differently to a strike because of their distinct self-images (Meyer, 1982). A case study of how the Port Authority coped with the problem of homelessness in New York demonstrated how an organization's self-image as a high-quality, first-class institution played a central role in constraining managers' action to cope with the problem (Dutton and Dukerich, 1991). These reports suggest that firms with strong, coherent cultures and identities are more likely to engage in systematic efforts to influence the perceptions of stakeholders. Managers in such firms will probably attend carefully to how their firms' key audiences feel about them (Albert and Whetten, 1985).

The sociological view

Most economic and strategic models ignore the socio-cognitive process that actually generates reputational rankings (Granovetter, 1985; White, 1981). In contrast, organizational sociologists point out that rankings are social constructions that come into being through the relationships that a focal firm has with its stakeholders in a shared institutional environment. Firms have multiple evaluators, each of whom apply different criteria in assessing firms. However, these evaluators interact within a common organizational field and exchange information, including information about firms' actions relative to norms and expectations. Thus, corporate reputations come to represent aggregated assessments of firms' institutional prestige and describe the stratification of the social system surrounding firms and industries (DiMaggio and Powell, 1983; Shapiro, 1987).

Faced with incomplete information about firms' actions, observers not only interpret the signals that firms routinely broadcast, but also rely on the evaluative signals refracted by key intermediaries such as market analysts, professional investors, and reporters. Intermediaries are actors in an organizational field. They transmit and refract information among firms and their stakeholders (Abrahamson and Fombrun, 1992a, b). An empirical study of firms involved in nuclear-waste disposal and photovoltaic cell development demonstrated how in both these industries reputational status depended, not only on structural factors like company size and economic performance, but also on a firm's position in the interaction networks linking firms in each institutional field (Shrum and Wuthnow. 1988).

To sociologists, then, reputations are indicators of legitimacy: they are aggregate assessments of firms' performance relative to expectations and norms in an institutional field. Sociologists point to the multiplicity of actors involved in the process of constructing reputations and their interconnectedness.

The accounting view

A vocal group of academic accountants has recently acknowledged the insufficiency of financial reporting standards in documenting the value of intangibles. They highlight the widening gap between factual earnings reported in annual statements and the market valuations of companies. They also criticize accepted practice that requires managers to expense research and development (R and D) activities, advertising, and training expenses – activities which strategists recognize as critical enhancements of firms' actual and perceptual resource positions (Lev and Sougiannis, 1996; Scheutze, 1993). As Deng and Lev (1997: 2) suggest, current accounting practice induces a mismatch in the allocation of costs to revenues, and so misleads observers about the earning capabilities of firms and the true value of their assets. In regards to the valuation of R and D, they conclude that '. . . hundreds of corporate executives, along with their auditors appear to be able to value R and D and technology in the development stage. This apparent inconsistency between the current regulatory environment which sanctions immediate expending of R and D and a fast developing business practice, obviously deserves a careful examination . . .'

Instead, many accounting researchers are now calling for a broad-based effort to develop better measures of how investments in branding, training, and research build important stocks of *intangible* assets not presently recorded in financial statements – assets that, not coincidentally, are said by strategists to build higher reputational assessments among observers (Barney, 1986; Rindova and Fombrun, 1997). Appropriate capitalization of these expenditures would better describe the value of a company's investments in what are fundamentally reputation-building activities.

Towards an integrative view

Jointly, these five academic literatures suggest that reputations constitute subjective, collective assessments of the trustworthiness and reliability of firms, with the following characteristics (Fombrun and Rindova, 1996).

–   Reputations are *derivative, second-order* characteristics of an industrial system that crystallize the emergent status of firms in an organization field.
–   Reputations are the external reflection of a company's *internal identity* – itself the outcome of sense-making by employees about the company's role in society.
–   Reputations develop from firms' prior resource allocations and histories and constitute *mobility barriers* that constrain both firms' own actions and rivals' reactions.
–   Reputations summarize *assessments of past performance* by diverse evaluators who assess firms' ability and potential to satisfy diverse criteria.
–   Reputations derive from multiple but related images of firms among all of a firm's stakeholders, and inform about their *overall attractiveness* to employees, consumers, investors, and local communities. Simplifying the complex construct of performance helps observers deal with the complexity of the marketplace.
–   Reputations embody two fundamental dimensions of firms' effectiveness: an appraisal of firms' *economic performance*, and an appraisal of firms' success in fulfilling *social responsibilities* (Etzioni, 1988; Lydenberg et al., 1986).

Consistent with these characteristics, we therefore propose the following definition (Fombrun and Rindova, 1996): *A corporate reputation is a collective representation of a firm's past actions and results that describes the firm's ability to deliver valued outcomes to multiple stakeholders. It gauges a firm's relative standing both internally with employees and externally with its stakeholders, in both its competitive and institutional environments.*

References

Aaker, D. and Keller, K. L. (1990) 'Consumer evaluations of brand extensions', *Journal of Marketing*, January, 54: 27–41.

Abrahamson, E. and Fombrun, C. (1992a) 'Forging the iron cage: Interorganizational networks and the production of macro-culture', *Journal of Management Studies*, 29: 175–194.

Abrahamson, E. and Fombrun, C. (1992b) 'Macrocultures: Determinants and consequences', *Academy of Management Review*.

Albert, S. and Whetten, D. (1985) 'Organizational identity', in Cummings, L. L. and Staw, B. M. (Eds.), 'Research in Organizational Behavior', pp. 263–295, Greenwich, CT: JAI Press. [Also this volume, Chapter 4.]

Allen, F. (1984) 'Reputation and product quality', *Rand Journal of Economics*, 15: 311–327.

Bagwell, K. (1992) 'Pricing to signal product line quality', *Journal of Economics and Management Strategy*, 1: 151–174.

Barney, J. B. (1986) 'Organizational culture: Can it be a source of sustained competitive advantage?', *Academy of Management Review*, 11: 656–665.

Belch, G. E. and Belch, M. A. (1987) 'The application of an expectancy value operationalization of function theory to examine attitudes of boycotters and non boycotters of a consumer product', *Advances in Consumer Research*, 14: 232–236.

Boush, D. and Loken, B. (1991) 'A process-tracing study of brand extension evaluation', *Journal of Marketing*, 28, 1: 16–28.

Brealy, R. and Myers, S. (1988) 'Principles of Corporate Finance', New York: McGraw-Hill.

Brown, T. J. and Dacin, P. A. (1997) 'The company and the product: Corporate associations and consumer product responses', *Journal of Marketing*, January, 61: 68–84.

Camerer, C. and Vepsalainen, A. (1988) 'The economic efficiency of corporate culture', *Strategic Management Journal*, 9: 115–126.

Caves, R. E. and Porter, M. E. (1977) 'From entry barriers to mobility barriers', *Quarterly Journal of Economics*, 91: 421–434.

Chakravarthy, B. (1986) 'Measuring strategic performance', *Strategic Management Journal*, 7: 437–458.

Cramer, S. and Ruefli, T. (1994) 'Corporate reputation dynamics: Reputation inertia, reputation risk, and reputation prospect', Paper presented at the National Academy of Management Meetings, Dallas.

Dawar, N. and Parker, P. (1994) 'Marketing universals: consumers' use of brand name, price, physical appearance, and retailer reputation as signals of product quality', *Journal of Marketing*, 58, 2, 81–95.

Deng, Z. and Lev, B. (1997) 'Flash-Then-Flush: The Valuation of Acquired R and D in Process', New York University, Stern School of Business, Accounting Department Working Paper.

DiMaggio, P. J. and Powell, W. W. (1983) 'The iron cage revisited: Institutional isomorphism and collective rationality in organizational field', *American Sociological Review*, 48: 147–160.

Dutton, J. E. and Dukerich, J. M. (1991) 'Keeping an eye on the mirror: Image and identity in organizational adaptation', *Academy of Management Journal*, 34: 517–554.

Dutton, J. E. and Penner, W. (1992) 'The importance of organizational identity for strategic agenda building', in Johnson, G. and Hendry, J. (Eds.), 'Leadership strategic change, and the learning organization'.

Etzioni, A. (1988) 'The Moral Dimension', New York: Free Press.

Fishbein, M. and Ajzen, I. (1975) 'Belief, Attitude, Intention and Behavior', Reading, MA: Addison-Wesley.

Fombrun, C. J. (1996) 'Reputation: Realizing Value from the Corporate Image', Cambridge, MA: Harvard Business School Press.

Fombrun, C. J. and Rindova, V. (1996) 'Who's Tops and Who Decides? The Social Construction of Corporate Reputations', New York University, Stern School of Business, Working Paper.

Fombrun, C. J. and Shanley, M. (1990) 'What's in a name? Reputation-building and corporate strategy', *Academy of Management Journal*, 33: 233–258.

Fombrun, C. J. and Zajac, E. J. (1987) 'Structural and perceptual influences on intraindustry stratification', *Academy of Management Journal*, 30: 33–50.

Freeman, R. E. (1984) 'Strategic Management: A Stakeholder Approach', Boston, MA: Pitman Press.

Granovetter, M. (1985) 'Economic action and social structure: The problem of embeddedness', *American Journal of Sociology*, 91: 481–510.

Grossman, S. and Stiglitz, J. (1980) 'On the impossibility of informationally efficient markets', *American Economic Review*, 70: 393–408.

Kapferer, J. N. (1992) 'Strategic Brand Management', London: Kogan Page.

Keller, K. L. (1993) 'Conceptualizing, measuring, and managing customer-based brand equity', *Journal of Marketing*, January, 57: 1–22.

Klein, B. and Leffler, K. (1981) 'The role of market forces in assuring contractual performance', *Journal of Political Economy*, 89: 615–641.

Kotler, P. (1991) 'Marketing Management: Analyses, Planning and Control', 8th ed. Englewood Cliffs, NJ: Prentice-Hall.

Lev, B. and Sougiannis, T. (1996) 'The capitalization, amortization, and value-relevance of R and D', *Journal of Accounting and Economics*, 21: 107–138.

Lippmann, W. (1922) 'Public Opinion', New York.

Lydenberg, S. D., Marlin, A. T. and Strub, S. O. (1986) 'Rating America's Corporate Conscience', Reading, MA: Addison-Wesley.

Maathuis, O. J. M. and Van Riel, C. B. M. (1996) 'The Added Value of the Corporate Brand', Management Report Series, Rotterdam School of Management, Rotterdam.

McGuire, J. B., Sundgren, A. and Schneeweis, T. (1988) 'Corporate social responsibility and firm financial performance', *Academy of Management Journal*, 31, 4: 854–872.

Meyer, A. (1982) 'Adapting to environmental jolts', *Administrative Science Quarterly*, 27: 515–537.

Miles, R. with Cameron, K. (1982) 'Coffin Nails and Corporate Strategies', Englewood Cliffs, NJ: Prentice-Hall.

Milgrom, P. and Roberts, J. (1986) 'Relying on the information of interested parties', *Rand Journal of Economics*, 17: 18–32.

Myers, S. and Majluf, N. (1984) 'Corporate financing and investment decisions when firms have information investors do not have', *Journal of Financial Economics*, 13: 187–221.

Nayyar, P.R. (1990) 'Information asymmetries: A source of competitive advantage for diversified firms, *Strategic Management Journal*, 11: 513–519.

Olins, W. (1978) 'The Corporate Personality', London: Thames and Hudson.

Park, C. W., Milberg, S. and Lawson, R. (1991) 'Evaluations of brand extensions: The role of product feature similarity and brand concept consistency', *Journal of Consumer Research*, 18, 2: 185–193.

Petty, R. E. & Cacioppo, J. T. (1986) 'Communication and Persuasion: Central and Peripheral Routes to Attitude Change', New York: Springer Verlag.

Poeisz, T. B. C. (1988) 'The Image Concept: Its place in consumer psychology', *Journal of Economic Psychology*, 10: 457–472.

Porac, J. F. and Thomas, H. (1990) 'Taxonomic mental models in competitor definition', *Academy of Management Review*, 15: 224–240.

Rao, A. R. & Ruekert, R. W. (1994) 'Brand alliances as signals of product quality', *Sloan Management Review*, Fall: 87–97.

Rindova, V. and Fombrun, C. J. (1997) 'Constructing competitive advantage', *Strategic Management Journal*, forthcoming.

Ross, S. A. (1977) 'The determination of financial structure: The incentive-signalling approach', *Bell Journal of Economics*, 8: 23–40.

Scheutze, W. (1993) 'What is an asset?', *Accounting Horizons*, 7: 66–90.

Schultz, D. E., Tannenbaum, S. I. and Lauterborn, R. F. (1994) 'Integrated Marketing Communication', Chicago: NTC Books.

Shapiro, C. (1983) 'Premiums for high-quality products as returns to reputations', *Quarterly Journal of Economics*, 98: 659–681.

Shapiro, S. P. (1987) 'The social control of impersonal trust', *American Journal of Sociology*, 93: 623–658.

Shrum, W. and Wuthnow, R. (1988) 'Reputational status of organizations in technical systems', *American Journal of Sociology*, 93: 882–912.

Stigler, G. J. (1962) 'Information in the labor market', *Journal of Political Economy*, 70: 49–73.

Stiglitz, J. E. (1989) 'Imperfect information in the product market', in Schmalensee, R. and Willig, R. (Eds.), 'Handbook of Industrial Organization', Chapter 13, pp. 769–847, Amsterdam, Holland: North-Holland Press.

Wartick, S. L. (1992) 'The relationship between intense media exposure and change in corporate reputation', *Business and Society*, 31: 33–49.

Weigelt, K. and Camerer, C. (1988) 'Reputation and corporate strategy: A review of recent theory and applications', *Strategic Management Journal*, 9: 443–454.

White, H. C. (1981) 'Where do markets come from?', *American Journal of Sociology*, 87: 517–547.

Wilson, R. (1985) 'Reputations in games and markets', in Roth, A. E. (Ed.), 'Game-Theoretic Models of Bargaining', Cambridge: Cambridge University Press.

Chapter 12

Stephen A. Greyser

ADVANCING AND ENHANCING CORPORATE REPUTATION

From *Corporate Communications: An International Journal* 1999, 4 (4): 177–181

EDITORS' COMMENTARY

Stephen A. Greyser is Richard P. Chapman Professor (Marketing/Communications) Emeritus at Harvard Business School. He is a regular commentator and speaker on issues related to corporate communications, identity, and reputation. He is in great demand as a speaker and makes regular appearances at the International Corporate Identity Symposium.

Of note are the sizable number of Harvard Business School case studies written by Greyser on the above areas. One of his most recent Harvard-style case studies, written for the Design Management Institute with Peter Phillips, is to be found in Section Six. His launch of the popular elective "The New Corporate Communications" as part of Harvard's MBA syllabus in the late 1980s provided a stimulus to the study of corporate-level constructs such as corporate identity, communication, and reputation. Harvard was one of the first of an international group of leading business schools to acknowledge the cardinal importance of corporate communications, identity, reputation, and branding to contemporary organizations. Today these areas have become an integral feature of the pedagogical approach adopted by several leading business schools around the globe.

In 1995 Greyser worked with John Balmer and others in establishing the International Corporate Identity Group (ICIG), which had the primary objective of raising the profile of understanding of corporate identity and related issues by both scholars and the business community. It has had decisive, if not defining, influence on this front. The same year, he and Balmer developed the first version of the ICIG ("The

Strathclyde") Statement on corporate identity. This is reproduced in the introduction to Section Two of this anthology.

The main focus for the ICIG's activities today is the annual symposium during which a memorial lecture is delivered on identity-related issues in memory of the group's Honorary President, Lord Goold. The first of these lectures was instituted in 1998 and was delivered on June 18 by Professor Greyser. Entitled "Advancing and Enhancing Corporate Reputation," this paper was read by Professor Greyser at the Fifth International Corporate Identity Symposium, which in 1998 was held at The Queen Elizabeth the Second Conference Centre, Westminster, London. The edited version of that lecture is included here, as it subsequently appeared in *Corporate Communications: An International Journal*.

Since then the Lord Goold Memorial Lecture has, variously, been delivered by others who have distinguished themselves in the broad area of corporate identity and branding, namely Wally Olins,[1] David Bernstein,[2] and Lord Browne of Madingley, Group CEO of the BP Group.

In his article Professor Greyser draws extensively on research undertaken by the Opinion Research Corporation's (ORC) CORPerceptions research. This worldwide study among 10,000 managers in over sixteen countries was undertaken over a three-year period. (Professor Greyser is a nonexecutive director of ORC and was intimately involved in the development of the study and the analysis of the data.)

A number of valuable insights emerged from the study relating to corporate reputation. Among them: corporate reputation can be managed, can give strategic benefits, and can be altered and affected by exogenous factors such as industry and cultural forces. Account also needs to be taken of corporate behavior, which can be a very potent factor affecting reputation.

Explaining the drivers that underpin corporate reputation management, Professor Greyser revealed that the CORPerceptions study highlighted six key factors: competitive effectiveness, market leadership, customer focus, familiarity/favorability, corporate culture, and communications. The research revealed that the international picture was not entirely homogeneous. For example, executives in France and in Germany place greater store on corporate social responsibility than do their US counterparts. High-calibre management has a higher significance in Japan than in the USA. French and British managers give greater significance to companies that are industry leaders than do their North American colleagues. Familiarity also fluctuates among cultures, whereas the Japanese regard this as a prerequisite of business.

A major theme of this study is that *credibility* is the central link between corporate behavior and public confidence. All too often there is a "promise–performance gap" – a chasm that can exist between customer expectations and product or service delivery.

The lecture was delivered with aplomb, as befitting a veteran Harvard academic (drawing on one of Stephen's phrases) and a former radio sports commentator to boot!

NOTES

1   Olins, W., "Global Companies: The Inexorable Rise of the Corporate State?" The Second Lord Goold Memorial Lecture, delivered at Templeton College, Oxford University, November 1999 at the Sixth International Corporate Identity Symposium. Published in a Special Edition on Corporate Identity and Corporate Marketing: *European Journal of Marketing* 2001, 35 (3/4): 485–496.

2   Bernstein, D., "Corporate Branding: Back to Basics." The Third Lord Goold Memorial Lecture delivered at Bradford School of Management, November 2000 at the Seventh International Corporate Identity Symposium. To be published in a Special Edition on Corporate and Services Branding: *European Journal of Marketing* 2003 (forthcoming).

Introduction and key points

MY PURPOSE IN THIS PAPER is to help us all try to advance and enhance corporate reputation. By this I mean both to advance our understanding of the corporate reputation phenomenon, and to advance our advocacy of measuring and enhancing the importance of corporate reputation in our companies.

Let me preview my five key points:

(1)   Executives worldwide believe that companies can affect their reputations.
(2)   Three very different major strategic benefits (and goals) of strong corporate reputation can be identified – and are supported by both attitudinal and empirical company reputation assessment.
(3)   Six key factors emerge from a battery of image attributes as drivers of corporate reputation.
(4)   These drivers vary in importance based on different countries, different industries in the same country, and the above-mentioned three different strategic goals.
(5)   What undercuts corporate reputation, in my view, is company behaviour, especially relative to public expectations.

Time out

Before I dig into these topics, let me take a brief "time out" to offer a preliminary comment – or perhaps minor "truth in labeling" announcement. I serve as a non-executive director on the board of Opinion Research Corporation International; at ORC, I also work with Dr Jim Fink, Jeff Brown and their colleagues on the conceptual development of ORC's corporate reputation practice – but not on

company studies. The data reported here come from the CORPerceptions reputation research, based on a total of over 10,000 interviews with a cross-section
of executives worldwide (or at least in 16–19 countries) over the past three
years. I appreciate their permission to report some of the aggregate data publicly
here. Now back to my main themes.

1 Companies can affect their reputations

First, some context. Question: "Is a company's image a captive of its industry?"
Executives resoundingly say "no". In response to the statement, "there isn't much
a company can do to improve its image beyond that of its industry in general,"
only 2 per cent of UK executives surveyed strongly agree, and only 17 per cent
strongly+somewhat agree. In the US, the numbers are 2 and 14 per cent respect-
ively, just about the same. These 1997 percentages are similar to those in the
previous two years. Remember, the respondents are a cross-section of executives
– not solely advertising and corporate communications executives (who might
be characterized as "the usual suspects").

A separate question – on whether "a company's image is mostly shaped by
outside forces which are beyond the company's control" – yielded similarly
minimal agreement among UK executives: only 2 per cent strongly agree and
11 per cent strongly and somewhat agree.

The net message is that companies can affect their corporate image, their
reputation.

2 Three major strategic benefits

What are the benefits of a positive corporate reputation? People in business used
to speak of the benefits largely in general terms – warm feelings toward the
company, but feelings infrequently identified in a specific way.

Now we can identify at least three major zones in which corporate reputation clearly manifests itself. These are:

(1) Preference in doing business with a company when several companies'
     products or services are similar in quality and price.
(2) Support for a company in times of controversy.
(3) A company's value in the financial marketplace.

As I mentioned, in the past three years ORC has surveyed literally thousands of
executives worldwide to explore and illuminate these propositions in the course
of measuring company reputations. Executive opinion consistently reinforces
each component of the triad. More specifically:

●   *Company preference.* Among executives in the UK, 57 per cent strongly agree
    and 92 per cent strongly and somewhat agree that "when several com-
    panies' products or services are similar in quality and price, the companies'

respective corporate reputations often determine which product or service the customer will buy". (The US data are 63 and 97 per cent.) This 92 per cent UK executive endorsement in 1997 is virtually the same as that shown in the 1996 data (95 per cent) and 1995 data (92 per cent). The consistent strong endorsement is the storyline. Let me note that in virtually all countries surveyed, executives respond in a rather similar fashion. In 1997, executives in all 16 countries showed 90 per cent or more agreement on this question.

A related perceived benefit of a strong reputation in terms of business preference is the ability to charge a premium. The question [was put]: "A company with a strong corporate reputation can normally charge more for its products and services than a company without a strong corporate reputation"; among UK executives responding, 29 per cent strongly agree, 69 per cent strongly and somewhat agree. (Among US executives, the figures are 22 and 72 per cent.) To support the substance of this point: we know that in supermarket channels in the USA, the top brands are often able to exact a higher manufacturer's price without the shelf price being proportionately higher than that of competitors.

- *Support in troubled times.* "A strong corporate reputation can sustain a company in times of controversy." That is the statement. Among UK executives in 1997, 46 per cent agree strongly, 95 per cent agree strongly and somewhat. (Among US executives, the numbers are 52 and 95 per cent.) Only in Japan is the "strongly agree" percentage very low: only 13 per cent, although an additional 65 per cent agree somewhat. My hypothesis is that in the Japanese culture only public shame (corporate self-flagellation, if you will) can cleanse a company fraught with trouble.

  Again, these responses are consistent across the three years of ORC studies – both for the USA, and for Japan.

- *Value in the financial marketplace.* The statement is: "A strong corporate reputation has considerable financial value." In the UK, 51 per cent of executives agree strongly, 95 per cent strongly and somewhat. The US figures were 66 per cent agree strongly and 96 per cent agree strongly and somewhat (in the 1997 study). In every country studied, the "strongly agree" percentage is above 50 per cent (for 1997).

These executive opinions, in summary, provide a meaningful attitudinal foundation for advancing our understanding of where strong corporate reputation can affect a company. But what are the empirical components – the key drivers – of actual company reputations? Further, do these drivers vary in different parts of the world? Do they vary meaningfully across major industries? And – perhaps most important to corporate strategy – do they vary based on which of the three key effects is the company's primary focus, i.e. business preference, support in controversy and the financial marketplace?

The answers, according to extensive analysis of the ORC database of three years and scores of companies, are:

- six key drivers, derived from about 25 image factors;

- yes, there are important country differences;
- yes, there are industry differences, in the same country; and
- yes, some drivers have much more leverage on one of the three key effects than on others.

3 Six key factors

The ORC corporate reputation structure is based on about 25 separate image questions (including awareness and familiarity) asked about a small group of companies in a particular industry. Over time, many companies in many industries (and many countries) have been assessed. Modelling and analytics have clustered the questions into six key factors (or drivers). These combine to generate an overall corporate brand equity score for a company in a country, relative to key competitors.

The six key drivers are:

(1) *Competitive effectiveness* (including attributes such as high-calibre management, invests strategically in R & D, financial strength, etc.).
(2) *Market leadership* (including industry leadership, well-differentiated products, in touch with today's marketplace, etc.).
(3) *Customer focus* (including offering good value for the money, committed to customers, a clearly defined image, etc.).
(4) *Familiarity/favourability*.
(5) *Corporate culture* (including high ethical standards, recognize social responsibilities, high-quality employees, etc.).
(6) *Communications* (effective advertising, sponsorship of major events, etc.).

The overall importance of these factors (or drivers) ranges in the USA from 24 per cent (for competitive effectiveness and for market leadership) down to 8 per cent for corporate culture and 6 per cent for communications, when the issue is preference for doing business with a company.

4 Differences in importance

Let us now look at three kinds of differences. First, to respond to the question of country differences . . . yes, there are differences in the importance of the drivers, and of individual attributes. For example, executives in France and Germany put more emphasis than do US executives on "recognizing corporate social responsibilities", in terms of impact on preference in doing business with a company. In Japan, "high-calibre management" is more highly valued than in the USA. And French and UK executives put more emphasis on industry "leader rather than follower" than US executives do. Conversely, "high standards of ethical business practice" are less emphasized by executives in China, Korea, Taiwan, Japan and Singapore compared to US executives.

The impact of familiarity varies considerably geographically, even among mature countries. For example, 100 per cent of Japanese executives agree that "I need to know a company very well before giving it a major piece of business". The US percentage is 74, and the UK percentage is 60. These are just a few examples.

On another question I raised – about industry differences in the same country – again yes . . . there can be significant differences. In the USA, for example, customer focus is the most important driver among telecommunications companies (27 per cent) and corporate culture seems to play a small role (8 per cent). But among consulting firms, corporate culture is very leveraged (21 per cent) while customer focus is far less so (15 per cent).

A final set of differences seen in the data relates to the three strategic goals. In the USA, as noted, competitive effectiveness and customer focus are most salient in terms of impact on "prefer to do business". When the issue is "willing to support in times of controversy", corporate culture becomes key (29 per cent). (Think about Johnson and Johnson in the Tylenol tragedy.) And when the issue is the financial marketplace ("willing to invest"), market leadership (23 per cent) is almost as important as competitive effectiveness (27 per cent).

Let me offer a comparison of UK and US data that points to some key country differences. The industry context is the technology sector, the strategic goal is "prefer to do business". In the UK, market leadership is most important (27 per cent) and competitive effectiveness is only 12 per cent. In the USA, the situation is almost reversed – market leadership is only 12 per cent and competitive effectiveness is 22 per cent. Obviously, one must not assume that each of the key drivers has the same weight around the world.

5 Corporate reputation and corporate behaviour

Now I want to go beyond data and ask a new question: "What undercuts corporate reputation?" Answer (my opinion): company behaviour. Repeat: company behaviour, particularly relative to public expectations.

I believe that credibility is the central link between company behaviour and public confidence. This pertains whether the issue is the fit between company behaviour and public expectations, whether it is the congruence of product claims and actual product performance, or whether it is the match of good corporate intentions and company actions.

Let me mention some specific company experiences – without the details, since those with even modest familiarity with corporate crises will know them:

- Intel Pentium.
- Perrier's peculiarly "natural" bubbles.
- US Air and safety.
- UK Shell and Brent Spar.
- Exxon Valdez.

What is the lesson learned from all of these experiences?

When a company's behaviour runs counter to public expectations (or at least the expectations of a large part of the public), the company will suffer a major loss of reputation – and often a loss of business . . . and share price as well.

There are a variety of reasons why consumer trust in companies declines. As we have seen, one key reason is a sudden exposure of the company's failure to live up to public expectations. Another is when there is a discernible gap between product performance and marketing claims – what I term "the promise/performance gap". This is the gap between consumer expectations (even after the consumer applies a "discount" to advertising claims) and the perceived "delivery" of the service (or product).

Think of your own experiences regarding your expectations for product and service quality. Consider how for many years company efforts to squeeze out costs actually led to decreases in product quality – or at best, no meaningful improvements. Think of advertising (not all of it) that substitutes "puff" for "stuff". All these fuel the promise/performance gap.

Higher expectations, higher risk – let me point to a particular set of companies for which concern over the promise/performance gap should be even more salient than normal. These are companies which strongly position themselves as firms which behave in a socially responsible way. The Body Shop, and Ben and Jerry's (in the USA), are two corporations with especially high visibility as companies that embrace what has been termed "caring capitalism". However, such positioning carries risks, risks not shared by most other companies. The promise/performance gap constitutes a serious potential trap for these companies.

When critics accused companies of exaggerating their environmental and social responsibility activities, this raised credibility questions. Indeed, I believe that when "100 per cent pure" natural products are less than that, when environmental standards are not met, or when promises of charitable contributions are not maintained – then there is the prospect of real trouble for any firm that has conspicuously promoted its higher standards. In these instances, the public's expectations of corporate behaviour have risen to a higher level – one that generates disappointment (even a sense of public betrayal) when not matched by revealed reality. The public's reaction is: "After all, you're the ones who said you were holier than thou."

Conclusion

Finally, let me return briefly to the theme of "advancing and enhancing corporate reputation". At the outset of my remarks I offered four key points about corporate reputation that in my view are data-supported. These points in combination advance our understanding of the complex phenomenon of corporate reputation. Of particular pertinence are the conditional generalizations (as social scientists would call them) about the variations in what drives corporate reputation in different countries, industries, and strategic situations.

In my fifth key point, above, I alluded to the erosion of corporate reputation. Other than highly visible company crisis-type situations such as those I mentioned, one rarely reads about only modest deterioration of corporate reputations. Rarer still are data-based reports of company reputation in situations of either crisis or modest decline. While we need to learn more about building reputation, we also need to learn about rebuilding it (if company behaviour permits). The Texaco situation since its well-publicized race incident and subsequent company initiatives would be instructive.

In closing, I hope we can all join in advocating for the multi-faceted importance of corporate reputation, in tracking and measuring it (including its components), and – as might be expected from a veteran academic – in reporting interesting data and interpretations (even in somewhat disguised form) to help us all advance and enhance corporate reputation.

The corporate brand: an organization's covenant

Decus et·tutamen
("An ornament and a safeguard")
This Latin inscription appeared on the rim of the 1662/1663 crown coin of
King Charles II of England.
It is now used as one of the inscriptions found on the rim of British pound coins.
To us it epitomizes the worth of another currency: that of corporate branding.

EDITORS' INTRODUCTION

Having the Midas touch

UBIQUITOUS, VENERATED, COVETED, SOUGHT, and bought, brands represent one of the most fascinating perspectives on the business environment in the twenty-first century. Brands are adored in equal measure by customers and organizations alike. For customers they serve as an additional guarantee of product (or service) quality. For organizations they accord a distinctiveness to their products and services, and sometimes to the *corporation as a whole*, that is not easily replicated.

Brands appear to be invested with the Midas touch.

Their importance is irrefutable.

Brands provide a means of reconnoitering the business environment as a prelude to decision-making: relating to purchases, employment, and investment. They are used as a navigational tool by a variety of stakeholders for a miscellany of purposes.

Brands have a blend of properties that make them distinct. They transcend boundaries of both time and space. They represent a new language – a language that is far removed from its origins as a patois spoken predominantly by marketers. Their allure has enthralled scholars, including management theorists such as John Kay.[1]

In essence, brands have become a lingua franca – a language that is international in scope. A language that is of pivotal importance in a world saturated by images. Whether for better or for worse, brands have become integral to our everyday existence. They represent a contemporary societal phenomenon – a phenomenon that one anthropologist[2] has christened "*brandscapes.*"

Brands are here to stay.

"Brandscapes": erstwhile, established, and emergent

Traditionally, two types of branding definitions have been identified.[3] We call these *erstwhile* and *established*.

Erstwhile. In its simplest sense a brand denotes a name, logotype, or trademark and was originally used to signify ownership, as with the branding of livestock. These are, increasingly, seen to be points of entry to the essence of a brand rather than the essence of branding per se.

Established. This refers to the added values that a brand brings to a product. Products may or may not have brand values. Product brand values are superimposed by the organization by its marketing and communications experts and advisers. They are made memorable. In the main, such values are fashioned in the mind; not on the production floor. They are, essentially, synthetic. Whereas products are made in a factory, brand values exist in the mind. Brands can be timeless in a way that products may not be.

However, there is a *new* understanding of branding. We call this aspect of branding *emergent*.

Emergent. While the category most certainly is established, the fundamental differences between this category and the other two are only beginning to be appreciated. This category refers to brands at the *corporate* level. Corporate brand values are not contrived; they need to be bona fide. The role of personnel and of "culture" in establishing and maintaining and understanding corporate brand values is of the essence. As a consequence, personnel and the influence of "culture" become important.

For the above reasons, corporate branding has manifestly distinct characteristics that delineate it from product brands. Corporate brands often appear to be indistinguishable from corporate identities. However, they are more first cousins than doppelgängers.

What are corporate brands?

Corporate brands are found in organizational bodies of every category. While the construct is equally applicable to countries, regions, cities, etc., it is more usually applied to corporations and to their subsidiaries. Corporate brands also boundary-span organizations. The corporate branding philosophy, at its core, represents *an explicit covenant* between an organization and its key stakeholder groups, including customers.

This covenant is set forth by senior management in terms of a clearly articulated corporate branding proposition. It is professed via the multiple channels of communication. It is experienced through corporate and staff behavior, and, importantly, through the organization's products and/or services.

A corporate brand, although it creates awareness and recognition via a name or logo, needs to articulate its accord with key stakeholders by demonstrating, *unceasingly* and *over time*, that it has kept its corporate branding pledge. As such it became a mark of assurance.

What of visual and verbal identifiers? A clever design has little intrinsic value of its own. However, it can achieve significant leverage when the promise explicit in the corporate brand has been kept and has been experienced consistently and over time. *Only then* will such verbal and visual identifiers potentially have enormous intrinsic worth.

Corporate brands: a superior organizational lens?

Corporate branding represents a related, but manifestly distinct, corporate-level construct to that of identity, reputation, and communication. It is another manifestation of corporate meaning; another way of comprehending, and revealing, the organization.

In an era where corporate boundaries have become less distinct, where there is a blurring of the margins, the corporate brand has come into its own. It too is a fashionable concept; a concept of our era. It is also a concept which more than any other helps define the boundary-spanning characteristics of organizations in ways that are surprising if not inspired. It transcends the internal and external dimensions of corporations, as well as those between organizations and industries (including the supply and distribution chains). It is a concept that is redolent of a new dynamic that renders traditional perceptions of brand management, if not marketing, wanting if not redundant.

From our analysis of corporate brands several observations can be made:

1   Corporate brand is a construct distinct from that of identity (in its different manifestations).
2   The demarcation between corporate identity and corporate branding is becoming less distinct.
3   For many organizations the corporate brand is the primary instrument for achieving distinctiveness.
4   It is not a prerequisite, or necessarily desirable, for an organization to have a corporate brand.

How do corporate brands differ from corporate identities?

The identity concept is applicable to *all* entities in a way that the corporate branding concept is not. However, where an organization has, or desires to acquire, a corporate brand, then the organization's identity elements need to be in alignment with the promise(s) that is/are intrinsic to the corporate brand covenant. The corporate brand thus becomes the template by which an organization's identity is evaluated.

There are other differences:

- Corporate brands typically have a longer gestation than identities.
- Corporate brands have mainly an external focus.
- Corporate brands strive to achieve a high profile.
- Corporate brands are typically supported by enhanced corporate communication and by strong visual and verbal identifiers.
- Corporate brands may be portable in a way that identities may not be.
- Corporate brands can be accorded significant financial goodwill.

There are noticeable *similarities* however. The importance of personnel,[4] of subcultural groups,[5] the need for ongoing senior management and CEO support[6] are referred to in the literature. The multidisciplinary roots of both corporate identity and corporate branding are another, similar theme.[7]

To summarize, we think that corporate brands augment the identity of the organization through added uniqueness in terms of values, style, or experiences.

The new alchemy? The new alchemists?

If corporate brands are the new alchemy, then corporate brand managers and consultants, in theory, are the new alchemists. This is because a well-respected brand (corporate or otherwise) has an ability to generate goodwill that can be worth well in excess of the company's value.[8] This aspect is nothing new, as the following quotation from 1923[9] referred to by Newman[10] testifies:

> The good will of certain well-established names and brands is valued in the millions of dollars, and ranks high among the assets of the companies responsible for them. In the great majority of fields . . . practically every one discriminates between brands in making a purchase. In many lines it has come to be regarded as the simplest and surest way to obtain standard quality and service.

However, there is still a reluctance on the part of many businesses to acknowledge the financial worth of brands – particularly corporate brands – for their balance sheets.[11] The consequence of that reluctance is significant if not downright misleading. This is because corporate brands are seen as a cost: while the value of corporate brands is not formally documented, the cost of supporting them is. Such accounting practices, to all intents and purposes, emasculate the worth and strategic importance of corporate brands.

Corporate branding architecture

Classical and tripartite

The importance of corporate brand management has resulted in a corollary concern: the management of brand architecture. Brand architecture refers to the relationship among corporate, company (subsidiary), and product brands. Such relationships embrace products and services, or a mixture of the two across the hierarchy of brands. However, such relationships are no longer confined within the corporation.

Olins's[12] well-known categorization of brands according to a tripartite structure reflects the 1970s business environment. Comparatively speaking, that environment had a transparency and stability. Accordingly, strategy formulation was less complicated and subject to change. Olins characterized brands into three types: monolithic, endorsed, or branded. This classical tripartite classification provides a useful preamble to any consideration of brand architecture.

Contemporary

How times have changed!

Contemporary organizations face new and more complex challenges. Brand management has become not only more important but also more intricate and complex. One of these challenges is that new branding categories have emerged.

Such relationships and structures are, according to Aaker and Joachimthaler,[13] not dissimilar to the challenges confronting architects who need to design interiors, buildings, complexes, and, sometimes, whole cities. Balmer[14] concurs with those authors regarding the increased complexity of the branding architecture. However, his point of departure is different. He reflects on the new branding environment taking an organizational perspective on branding. In relation to corporate (and company) brands he argues that they have a driver role not only for customers but for employees, would-be employees, stockholders, and other stakeholder groups.

His analysis has resulted in the identification of six new corporate/transcorporate categorizations and a greatly extended branding architecture. Five of them appear to have secured a firm existence within the *contemporary* environment. Those five categories are as follows:

- *Familial:* the sharing/adoption of the same corporate brand by two entities within the same industry sector. Example: the two companies that have rights to the Hilton brand name.
- *Shared:* as above, but with the companies operating in distinct, though sometimes related, markets. Example: Rolls-Royce the UK-owned engineering and aero engines group, and Rolls-Royce the German-owned car subsidiary of BMW.
- *Surrogate:* a franchise arrangement whereby one organization's products/services are branded as those of another. Example: British Regional Airways' use of the British Airways brand.
- *Multiplex:* the multiple use and sometimes multiple ownership/rights of a corporate brand among a variety of entities in a variety of industries. Example: Virgin Atlantic Airways, Virgin Trains, Virgin Blue (airline), Virgin Radio, Virgin Activity Clubs, Virgin Car Hire, etc.
- *Federal:* the creation of a new corporate brand by separate companies that pool their resources in a joint venture to, in effect, create a new identity as well as a company and corporate brand. Example: Airbus.

The sixth, and final, category is discussed below.

Avant-garde and postmodern

New, avant-garde quasi-corporate branding categories may also emerge. The following is the sixth example. It would appear to be in its formative stages of growth and development.

- *Supra:* a quasi, "arch" brand used to supra-endorse company brands. The type is particularly common within the airline sectors. The brand is virtual insofar as it does not have a tangible identity in the same way as most organizations do.

The potential for such alliances to metamorphose into strong brands may be seen as avant-garde. Example: Airline alliances such as One World, Star Alliance, and Qualifier Group.

The notion that an organization's primary competence is seeking leverage from a set of brand values may seem extraordinary, if not postmodern. At Richard Branson's Virgin it is already a reality. It could also be at Ford. Ford is progressively stressing its core competences in terms of design, marketing, sales, and branding; less so in production. To some, the long-term prognosis is clear: "*Ford will not make but it will brand*."[15] If that prediction is fulfilled, then Ford's identity will change in important ways: in terms of culture, structure, skills, staffing, and communication. At the same time, Ford's policy of "outsourcing" components and production will mean that Ford's partners are likely to embrace key elements of Ford's branding covenant. In the process, important aspects of *their* identities may possibly be transformed.

The example of Ford reveals how, in this age of corporate branding, identities are undergoing a metamorphosis in ways that were unimaginable fifty years ago. We may see a hitherto yet unknown Ford Corporation – an organization grounded on an idea, on a promise, on a covenant. It will be more of a church than a business.

Linking identity with branding: the AC³ID Test™ [16]

Corporate brands can therefore be regarded as a new type of corporate entity; a new type of corporate organism. It can be called the "*covenanted identity.*" It can, drawing on the AC²ID Test™,[17] detailed in the opening section of this anthology, be viewed as an additional "identity type." Exhibit 1 accommodates the corporate brand as an additional (a sixth) element of what now becomes the AC³ID Test™ (*Actual, Communicated, Conceived, Covenanted, Ideal, and Desired*).

The process of identity management (where organizations have a corporate brand) may necessarily involve _R_evealing the six identity types, _E_xamining the interfaces between them, _D_iagnosing the misalignments, _S_electing the most pressing identities to be aligned, and, finally, developing a _S_trategy.

The "Covenanted Identity" is shown as a five-pointed star outside the original pentagon. This reflects some of the characteristics of corporate brands: that they can be applied to other identities and entities, can be shared with other organizations, and have a life and worth of their own.

One important point to remember about the corporate branding covenant is that it does not exist in a vacuum. As Lord Browne,[18] the CEO of the BP Group, told us while delivering the Fourth Lord Goold Memorial Lecture on Identity: "Without a clear business strategy, there can't be a clear and credible brand." He noted that BP's brand is underpinned by "values which match strategy and which are expressed in performance." Using the AC³ID Test as a template, it becomes clear that an attempt is being made to bring the various identity types into alignment.

Thus corporate brands can be viewed as another "identity type" – something that, while an ornament, also serves as a safeguard to stakeholders as well as to

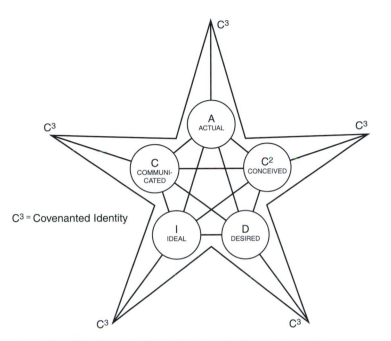

Exhibit 1 The AC³ID TEST™ (trademarked by J. M. T. Balmer, 2001)

organizations. This explains their allure and that pervasiveness as an international currency par excellence; they are an ornament and a safeguard: "*Decus et tutamen.*"

Aperçu

From our analysis of corporate brands, our final summary, or *aperçu*, consists of the following observations on corporate brands:

1   Corporate brands are not the same as corporate identities.
2   The current environment is characterized by a less distinct demarcation between corporate identity and corporate branding.
3   Increasingly the corporate brand is being deployed by corporations as a vehicle for achieving distinctiveness.

We also believe that it is not a prerequisite, or necessarily desirable, for every organization to have a corporate brand.

The articles

Three chapters have been selected for this section on corporate branding. The section opens with what we view as a seminal paper on the subject by the advertising consultant and guru Stephen King of the WPP Group. It provides an early and insightful overview of why organizations need to accord greater attention to their corporate brands. Such was its importance that it was accorded lead-article status in the *Journal of Marketing Management*. The second chapter is by two of the world's leading scholars of branding: Professors Kevin Lane Keller and David A. Aaker. It reports the findings of their empirical research, which showed the important role that corporate marketing activity can have on corporate brand extensions. The final chapter, by Balmer, may be seen to build on the earlier work of King: it articulates the importance of corporate brands, their differences from product brands, their benefits and characteristics. Balmer concludes, by making reference to case histories, that corporate brands are vulnerable to life-threatening illnesses through all stages of their life cycle.

TOPICS FOR DISCUSSION AND REFLECTION

1   "A brand is a promise, and in the end, you have to keep your promises. A product is the artifact of the truth of the promise" (Watts Wacker, futurist). Explore this statement in the context of corporate brands.

   What are the artifacts of the truth of the promise for the following corporate brands:
   (a)   Microsoft;
   (b)   Jaguar;
   (c)   CNN;
   (d)   the Body Shop;
   (e)   Harvard University;
   (f)   your organization/another organization with which you are familiar?

2   Why (or why not) is the corporate brand a superior corporate-level construct vis-à-vis corporate reputation and corporate identity?

   Select a product or service brand and corporate brand of your choice. Explain their differences and similarities.

3   "It takes genius, faith and perseverance to create a brand" (David Ogilvy, 1911–1999, advertising practitioner). Discuss this observation in relation to Disney, Virgin, Jaguar, Sydney (the city), American Express, and Lego.

4   Hilton is a corporate brand that is shared by two corporations: one operating hotels in the U.S.A. and the other in the rest of the world. What communication issues does this raise for the management of the corporate brand?

   What steps would you take to ensure that the branding covenant is delivered across both organizations?

   What functions, if any, should be shared across both organizations?

   What strengths and/or weaknesses result from the above?

5   Consider the strengths and weaknesses of King's New Brand Management model (the pentagon). What changes, if any, would you make?

6   "I am irresistible, I say, as I put on my designer fragrance. I am a merchant banker, I say, as I climb out of my BMW. I am a juvenile lout, I say, as I down

a glass of extra strong lager. I am handsome, I say, as I don my Levi's jeans" (John Kay, British economist and university don). Discuss the notion and significance of "brandscapes"/the branding covenant in the context of the above.

Make a list of the things you do, wear, use, consume, and buy on a typical day off. What brands, if any, are associated with the list?

How many of them are *corporate* as opposed to product brands?

What implications (if any) flow from the above?

7   Critique Keller and Aaker's article "The Impact of Corporate Marketing on a Company's Brand Extensions" (this volume, Chapter 14).

8   Discuss Balmer's (2001) statement that a corporate brand may be a corporation's principal asset.

9   "In the factory, we make cosmetics: in the store, we sell hope" (Charles Revson, cosmetics manufacturer). Provide, in no more than twenty words, similar descriptions for the following types of organization. Start by identifying the core promise/covenant of your corporate brand:

(a)   a bank;

(b)   a car manufacturer;

(c)   a home appliances manufacturer;

(d)   a travel agency;

(e)   a fast-food chain;

(f)   a business school;

(g)   a top baseball and/or football (soccer) team;

(h)   a rest home/funeral director;

(i)   your organization (or another if yours does not have a corporate brand).

10   "Those are my principles, if you don't like them I have others" (Groucho Marx, 1890–1977, comic genius); "Go ahead and be inconsistent. You're not a wind-up toy. If they are consistent in values, which they are, then we have nothing to worry about" (Herb Kelleher, airline executive). Why (or why not) and where (and where not) is it important to have consistency in corporate brand values (the corporate brand covenant)?

Consider the difficulties (if any) that ethically-positioned corporate brands such as Ben and Jerry's, the Body Shop, Tom's of Maine, and the Co-operative Bank (U.K.) have in delivering their covenant to a wide range of stakeholder groups. (Begin by considering customers and stockholders.)

Explore the notion of "profits with principles" vis-à-vis corporate brands.

Discuss to what degree (if any) an organization's operating framework (a mutual, a cooperative, a privately owned company, a publicly listed company, a publicly listed company in two countries) impacts on consistency across stakeholder groups of an ethically-positioned corporate brand.

NOTES

1   Kay, J., *Foundations of Corporate Success*, Oxford: Oxford University Press, 1995.

2   Sherry, J., in Barwise, P., Dunham, A., and Ritson, M., "Ties That Bind: Brands,

Consumers and Businesses," in J. Pavitt (ed.) *Brand New*, London: V and A Publications, 2000, p. 73.

3   Barwise *et al., op. cit.*

4   Balmer, J. M. T., "Corporate Branding and Connoisseurship," *Journal of General Management* 1995, 21 (1): 22–46; Ambler, T. and Barrow, S., "The Employer Brand," *Journal of Brand Management* 1996, 4 (3): 24–46; De Chernatony, L., "Brand Management through Narrowing the Gap between Brand Identity and Brand Reputation," *Journal of Marketing Management* 1999, 15 (1–3): 157–179.

5   Balmer, J. M. T., "Corporate Identity, Corporate Branding and Corporate Marketing: Seeing through the Fog," Special Edition on Corporate Identity and Corporate Marketing: *European Journal of Marketing* 2001, 35 (3/4): 248–291; Harris, F. and De Chernatony, L., "Corporate Branding and Corporate Brand Performance," Special Edition on Corporate Identity and Corporate Marketing: *European Journal of Marketing* 2001, 35 (3/4): 441–456.

6   King, S., "Brand Building in the 1990s," *Journal of Marketing Management* 1991, 7 (20): 3–13; Balmer, "Corporate Branding."

7   King, *op. cit.*; Balmer, J. M. T. and Wilkinson, A., "Building Societies: Change, Strategy and Corporate Identity," *Journal of General Management* 1991, 17 (2): 20–33; Knox, S., Maklan, S., and Thompson, K. E., "Building the Unique Organization Value Proposition," in M. Shultz, M. J. Hatch, and M. H. Larsen (eds) *The Expressive Organization*, Oxford: Oxford University Press, 2000, pp. 138–156; Keller, K. L., "Building and Managing Corporate Brand Equity," in Shultz *et al.* (eds) *op. cit.*, pp. 115–137; Macrae, C., Brand Reality Editorial, *Journal of Marketing Management* 1999, 15 (1–3): pp. 1–24.

8   Newman, K., "The Sorcerer's Apprentice? Alchemy, Seduction and Confusion in Modern Marketing," *International Journal of Advertising* 2001, 20: 409–429.

9   Hotchkiss, G. B. and Franken, R. B., *The Leadership of Advertised Brands*, New York: Doubleday, p. 1923.

10   Newman, *op. cit.*

11   Chajet, C. and Schachtmann, T., *Image by Design*, 2nd edition, New York: McGraw-Hill, 1998; Tollington, T., "UK Brand Asset Recognition beyond Transactions or Events," *Long Range Planning* 2001, 34: 463–487.

12   Olins, W., *The Corporate Personality: An Inquiry into the Nature of Corporate Identity*, London: Design Council, 1978.

13   Aaker, D. and Joachimsthaler, E. A., "The Brand Relationship Spectrum: The Key to the Brand Architecture Challenge," *Californian Management Review* 2000, 42 (4): 8–23.

14   Balmer., J. M. T., "Corporate Brands Ten Years On: What's New?," Paper delivered at the Eighth International Corporate Identity Symposium in 2001, published in *The Working Paper Series, Bradford School of Management*, no. 02/07, March 2002.

15   Olins, W., "How Brands Are Taking Over the Corporation," in Schultz *et al.* (eds) *op. cit.*, p. 51.

16   AC³ID Test™ trademarked by J. M. T. Balmer, 2001.

17   *Ibid.*

18   Lord Browne, Fourth Lord Goold Memorial Lecture, delivered at the Eighth Inter-
      national Corporate Identity Symposium entitled "Corporate Brands: Making a Dif-
      ference?," London: November 2001.

FURTHER READING

Articles

Aaker, D. and Joachimsthaler, E. A. (2000) "The Brand Relationship Spectrum: The Key
      to the Brand Architecture Challenge," *Californian Management Review* 42 (4): 8–
      23.

Ambler, T. and Barwise, P. (1998) "The Trouble with Brand Valuation," *Journal of Brand
      Management* 5 (5): 367–377.

Barwise, P., Dunham, A. and Ritson, M. (2000) "Ties That Bind Brands, Consumers and
      Businesses," in J. Pavitt (ed.) *Brand New*, London: V and A Publications.

Bernstein, D. (2003) The Third (2000) Lord Goold Memorial Lecture: "Corporate
      Branding – Back to Basics," Special Edition on Corporate and Service Brands:
      European Journal of Marketing, forthcoming.

Berry, L. (2000) "Cultivating Service Brand Equity," *Journal of the Academy of Market-
      ing Science* 28 (1): 128–137.

Bickerton, D. (2000) "Corporate Reputation versus Corporate Branding: The Realist
      Debate," *Corporate Communications: An International Journal* 5 (1): 42–48.

Biehal, G. J. and Shenin, D. A. (1998) "Managing the Brand in a Corporate Advertising
      Environment," *Journal of Advertising* 28 (2): 99–110.

Dawar, N. (1998) "Product-Harm Crises and the Signaling Ability of Brands,"
      International Studies of Management and Organization 28 (3): 109–119.

De Chernatony, L (1999) "Brand Management through Narrowing the Gap between
      Brand Identity and Brand Reputation," *Journal of Marketing Management* 15:
      157–159.

Elliot, R. (1994) "Exploring the Symbolic Meaning of Brands," *British Journal of
      Management* 5: 13–19.

Ewing, M., Pitt, L., de Bussy, N., and Berthou, P. (2002) "Employment Branding in the
      Knowledge Economy," *International Journal of Advertising* 21 (1): 3–22.

Farquhar, P. H. (1989) "Managing Brand Equity," *Marketing Research* 1 (3): 24–33.

Handy, C. (1995) "Balancing Corporate Power: A New Federalist Paper," in C. Handy
      (eds) *Beyond Certainty: The Changing Worlds of Organisations*, London: Hutchin-
      son, pp. 35–56.

Harris, F. and De Chernatony, L. (2001) "Corporate Branding and Corporate Brand
      Performance," Special Edition on Corporate Identity and Corporate Marketing:
      European Journal of Marketing 35 (3/4): 441–456.

Ind, N. (1998) "An Integrated Approach to Corporate Branding," *Journal of Brand
      Management* 6 (5): 323–329.

Keller, K. L. (1999) "Brand Mantras: Rationale, Criteria and Examples," *Journal of
      Marketing Management* 15: 43–51.

Keller, K. L. (2000) "Building and Managing Corporate Brand Equity," in M. Schultz, M. J. Hatch, and M. H. Larsen (eds) *The Expressive Organization*, Oxford: Oxford University Press, pp. 115–137.

Knowles, J. (2000) "Protecting Brands from Downside Risk," *Professional Investor*, p. 17.

Knox, S. D. (1999) "Positioning and Branding the Organisation," in M. McDonald, M. Christopher. S. D. Knox, and A. Payne (eds) *The Value-Driven CEO: Building a Company for Customers*, London: Financial Times Management.

Knox, S. D., Maklan, S., and Thompson, K. E. (2000) "Building the Unique Organizational Value Proposition," in M. Schultz, M. J. Hatch, and M. H. Larsen (eds) *The Expressive Organization*, Oxford: Oxford University Press, pp. 138–153.

LaForet, S. and Saunders, J. (1994) "Managing Brand Portfolios: How the Leaders Do It," *Journal of Advertising Research* September–October: 64–76.

Low, G. and Fullerton, R. (1994) "Brands, Brand Management and the Brand Management System: A Critical Historical Evaluation," *Journal of Marketing Research* 31 (May): 173–190.

Maathuis, O. (1999) "Corporate Branding: The Value of the Corporate Brand to Customers and Managers," unpublished PhD thesis, Erasmus University, Rotterdam.

McDonald, M., De Chernatony, L., and Harris, F. (2001) "Corporate Marketing and Service Brands," Special Edition on Corporate Identity and Corporate Marketing: *European Journal of Marketing* 35 (3/4): 335–352.

Macrae, C. (1999) Guest Editorial, Special Edition on Brand Reality: *Journal of Marketing Management* 15: 1–24.

Mitchell, A. (1999) "Out of the Shadows," *Journal of Marketing Management* 15: 25–42.

Newman, K. (2001) "The Sorcerer's Apprentice? Alchemy, Seduction and Confusion in Modern Marketing," *International Journal of Advertising* 20: 409–429.

Olins, W. (2000) "How Brands Are Taking Over the Corporation," in M. Schultz, M. J. Hatch and M. H. Larsen (eds) *The Expressive Organization*, Oxford: Oxford University Press, pp. 51–65.

Olins, W. (2001) The Second Lord Goold Memorial Lecture, "Global Companies: The Inexorable Rise of the Corporate State?" delivered at Templeton College, Oxford University, 1999, Special Edition on Corporate Identity and Corporate Marketing: *European Journal of Marketing* 35 (3/4): 485–496.

Saunders, J. and Guoqun, F. (1997) "Dual Branding: How Corporate Names Add Value," *Journal of Product and Brand Management* 6 (1): 40–48.

Tollington, T. (2001) "UK Brand Asset Recognition beyond Transactions or Events," *Long Range Planning* 34: 463–487.

Urde, M. (1999) "Brand Orientation: A Mindset for Building Brands into Strategic Resources," *Journal of Marketing Management* 15: 117–133.

Books

Christopher, M., Payne, A., and Ballentine, D. (1991) *Relationship Marketing*, Oxford: Butterworth-Heinemann.

Gregory, J. R. (1997) *Leveraging the Corporate Brand*, Lincolnwood, IL: NTC Business Books.

Hotchkiss, G. B. and Franken, R. B. (1923) *The Leadership of Advertised Brands*, New York: Doubleday Page.

Ind, N. (1996) *The Corporate Brand*, London: Macmillan.

Knox, S. D. and Maklan, S. (1998) *Competing on Value: Bridging the Gap between Brand and Customer Value*, London: Financial Times/Pitman Publishing.

Schmitt, B. and Simonson, A. (1997) *Marketing Aesthetics: The Strategic Management of Brands, Identity and Image*, New York: Free Press.

Chapter 13

Stephen King

BRAND-BUILDING IN THE 1990s

From *Journal of Marketing Management* 1991, 7: 3–13

EDITORS' COMMENTARY

Stephen King, a director of the WPP Group, is well known for his commentary on branding, as his publications attest.[1] In the history of ideas relating to the corporate-level constructs examined in this volume, Olins is to corporate identity what Bernstein is to corporate communications and King is to corporate branding.

His article "Brand-Building in the 1990s" is, we believe, a classic. It is significant because it provides one of the earliest commentaries on corporate branding. Being ahead of its time, the article has not been accorded the recognition it warrants.

King's article provides a synopsis of the attributes, significance, and trials involved in the metamorphosis of the branding concept from being a product-focused construct to one that applies to corporations. An indication of this article's significance can be detected in the decision by the editor of the *Journal of Marketing Management* (*JMM*), Professor Michael J. Baker, to accord King's paper the status of lead article. For an academic journal such as the *JMM* this is a rare honor indeed, even for a paper penned by a luminary of the stature of Stephen King.

The article is insightful and challenging in equal measure. It is insightful because King sketches out the differences between product brands and what he calls company brands. He argues that nothing short of a radical reappraisal needs to take place when applying the branding concept to corporations. He contends that corporate brands are more complicated, require board-level support, and are of greater strategic impact than their product brand counterparts. Of additional note is the emphasis he gives to personnel and to the human resources department in the building and maintenance of corporate brands – something that still appears to be overlooked by many human resources departments and scholars. It is clear that there is still a veritable chasm between the conceptualization of brands at the product level as opposed to brands at the corporate level.

The challenges posited by King are radical and revolutionary. Yet comparatively few of his suggestions have been taken up by marketers and those who write on company branding. In essence corporate brand management requires a multidisciplinary approach. The importance of corporate branding to different stakeholder groups means that it needs to be underpinned by multiple channels of communications – in other words, by corporate communications.

King identifies another impediment in relation to corporate branding and its management. This may be seen as a new variant of marketing myopia.[2] In his view there needs to be a radical reappraisal of the marketing mix and philosophy, especially when applied to corporate entities.[3]

This can be detected at the outset of his chapter. It represents a powerful *cri de coeur* that needs to be mused upon by marketers. King says:

> It's always easy to drift on with the old ways of doing things, simply because social and economic movements are gradual and it never seems the right day to make a change. A new decade (and we can still just think about the 1990s as that) can at least prod us to look again at our marketing methods and maybe revise the textbooks. I think we need to.

Quite. But as the distance between the present and 1991 grows ever greater, marketers ignore at their peril not only King's advice but also the classical injunction *periculum in mora*.[4]

NOTES

1   King, S., *What Is a Brand?*, London: J. Walter Thompson, 1970; King, S., *Developing New Brands*, London: J. Walter Thompson, 1984; King, S., "Another Turning Point for Brands?," *ADMAP* 1985, 21 (October): 480–484.

2   "Marketing Myopia" – the famous *HBR* article by Levitt in which he inveighs against organizations that have a production rather than a customer focus. See Levitt, T., "Marketing Myopia," *Harvard Business Review* 1960 (July–August): 24–47.

3   Balmer, J. M. T., "Corporate Identity and the Advent of Corporate Marketing," *Journal of Marketing Management* 1998, 14 (8): 963–996.

4   *Periculum in mora* – a Latin expression counselling against inaction. Literally "danger in delay."

New pressures

IT'S ALWAYS EASY to drift on with the old ways of doing things, simply because social and economic movements are gradual and it never seems the right day to make a change. A new decade (and we can still just about think of the 1990s as that) can at least prod us to look again at our marketing methods and maybe revise the textbooks. I think we need to.

However gradually they've grown, the pressures on companies during the past decade have become formidable, and they seem likely to intensify in the 1990s. Let me pick out six of them: three to do with people and three to do with the companies themselves.

1 More confident consumers

In almost all markets, consumers have become more confident, readier to experiment and trust their own judgement. They're less tolerant of products and services that don't contribute to their own values. By the end of the '90s they'll be more mature (roughly 10% more over-35s and 10% fewer under-35s in Europe). They'll have more disposable income and wealth and be more worldly-wise. They'll have an even greater understanding of marketing, advertising, public relations and direct response. They'll ensure that customers in business-to-business marketing become more demanding too.

Underlying this new confidence is rampant individualism. Despite all the talk about "globalism", there has rarely been a time when people have been more aware of the tribes to which they belong. The individualism is likely to transcend national cultural differences: there will be more differences, say, within Germany than between the "average" German and the "average" Briton.

2 New concepts of "quality"

People will still be looking for high quality and personal added values, variants, style and fashion changes. But their interpretation of "quality" seems to be changing quite fast. It's increasingly based on what they feel are *real values* – not superficial styling. They are searching for the "full life"; one in which they find meaning and culture in everything they do and buy. There are certainly excesses in much that currently surrounds "greenism", but it's an indication of a growing social awareness. People are increasingly willing to pay a little extra for a clear conscience.

3 Shortage of skills

A combination of demographic changes (especially in Germany) and a weakness in educational and training systems (most notably Britain's in the intermediate vocational area) means that there is likely to be a severe shortage of the skills needed to meet these new demands for quality.

4 The competitive screw tightens

Competition is intensifying in almost all fields, typified maybe by Japanese investment in Europe, up by some 350% over 4 years. In 1989 the number of Japanese companies with plants in Europe went up by 23% to over 500. The real pressures from all this investment have yet to come, but it is clear that there will be over-capacity in many markets.

At the same time, there are stirrings in the European retail trade, as the most national of companies start looking outside their traditional boundaries. Some of the international but decentralized companies, such as Auchan or Tengelman, are looking at centralizing their buying. Pan-European buying groups are emerging. Aldi has invaded the UK, sending out some ominous signals about price wars. All the signs are that the balance of power between manufacturers and retailers is still going the retailers' way.

5 Side-effects of new technology

New technology has perhaps been talked about more than it has actually affected brand-building so far. But that will surely change in the 1990s. There will be shorter product and service life-cycles and faster technological leapfrogging, with more discontinuities than we've seen before, via new materials, electronics and biotechnology. Constant innovation will be a necessary part of normal commercial life, but few companies will be able to rely on having any *demonstrable* product or service advantage for more than a few months.

Retailers will get better at using the power of the data on turnover, stocks and profits that scanning has put at their fingertips. So far, this information has been used mainly as just another weapon in the long bouts of arm-wrestling with their suppliers. Now the more innovative retailers, such as Vons in California and Generale Supermercati in Italy, are using the detailed information they have about individual local customers to develop more accurately tailor-made services for them. There is a huge opportunity in new technology for retailers to become the consumer's friend and helper in a way that few manufacturers will be able to match.

6 Restructuring

In just 2 years, take-overs of the really big companies (those worth over 1 billion ECUs) have gone up by two and a half times. There has been a wave of mergers, take-overs, MBOs, LBOs, bundling, unbundling and all sorts of barbarians at the gates. There may now be a temporary pause for breath, but the process will surely start up again. John Harvey-Jones has suggested that at least half the companies in

Europe will disappear by the mid-'90s. Even when company structures are left unchanged, there are often huge corporate alliances – such as Philips/Thomson in high-definition TV, Sumitomo/Yuasa/Lucas in car components, Volkswagen/Ford in the development of a vehicle to challenge the Renault Espace.

Many organizations and people must be wondering who they are, to whom they owe loyalty and what their corporate culture is.

Brand-building

In such times of pressure and rapid change, how are companies to ensure that they stay on the right side of John Harvey-Jones's dividing line? How are they to retain and build their customer base and their margins? If they are constantly being restructured in some way, how are they to succeed in building any enduring link with their consumers?

Most people in marketing would agree that success will depend critically on developing skills in *brand-building*. That is, on using all the company's particular assets to create unique entities that certain consumers really want; entities which have a lasting personality, based on a special combination of physical, functional and psychological values; and which have a competitive advantage in at least one area of marketing (raw materials/sourcing, product/design/patents, production systems, supply/sales/service networks, depth of understanding of consumers, style/fashion, and so on).

Most would say (e.g. Doyle 1989) that brand-building is the only way in these circumstances:

– to build a stable, long-term demand
– to add the values that will entice customers and consumers
– to build and hold decent margins
– to provide a firm base for expansion into product improvements, variants, added services, new countries, etc.
– to protect the company against the growing power of intermediaries
– to transform an organization from a faceless bureaucracy to a company that is attractive to work for or deal with.

All this is hardly new. Does it simply mean that the message for the 1990s is exactly the same as for the 1980s? For some brands, the answer must be "yes". For the "classic" brand leaders in packaged grocery products (such as Coke, Pepsi, Marlboro, Ivory, Lux Toilet Soap, Persil, Oxo, Bovril, Mars, KitKat, Andrex), it will be the mixture as before. There seems no reason why such brands should not prosper more or less indefinitely, given adequate tender loving care. If they can be given consistent branding and marketing expenditure, regular innovation and extension, based on sensible economies of scale and cost control, they will surely be brand leaders in 20 years' time, just as most of them were 20 years ago. The evidence is overwhelming that their sort of market share, based on high product quality and supported by a high proportion of advertising in the marketing mix, is linked to a high return on investment (Abraham 1990; Buzzell and Gale 1987; The Ogilvy Center 1989).

But with the changes that are coming in the 1990s, it seems to me that such brands will become steadily rarer and a smaller part of consumers' expenditure than we have been used to. It's been clear for many years that nowadays successful new single-line brands are a great rarity (Madell 1980; Tauber 1988), and indeed that many of the classic brands would simply never have made it if they had been launched in today's circumstances. We can get a hint of what's been happening by looking at which brands spend most on press and TV advertising. In 1969, of the 25 top-spending brands in the UK, 19 were repeat-purchase packaged goods; in 1989 it was just one.

We are going to have to get out of the habit of using the old classic brands as the models to which we should aspire. I believe that brand-building in the 1990s is entering a new mode. It is not simply a matter of these more demanding pressures, but also that the long-promised "service economy" seems genuinely to be happening in the new Europe. (Or at least that it will burst forth after the next period of recessionary battening down of the hatches.)

People are increasingly valuing non-functional rewards more, even if the style of those rewards may be changing somewhat from one of glitz and designer everything to one of authenticity and greenism. White-collar service is now the employment mode of the majority. More people work in IT and entertainment and communications and financial services, less in satanic mills. The norm in Europe is adding values, not basic production.

We must get better at recognizing the key marketing implication of this sort of economy. It is not simply that more of people's money will be spent on "services" rather than on "products". It is more that virtually everything we buy is a combination of product and service (Foxall 1985) and that, for a brand to be successful, the service element is going to have to become more dominant (Christopher 1985).

This in its turn will imply, in an era of rapid technological leapfrog, that increasingly the *company brand* will become the main discriminator. That is, consumers' choice of what they buy will depend rather less on an evaluation of the functional benefits to them of a product or service, rather more on their assessment of the people in the company behind it, their skills, attitudes, behaviour, design, style, language, greenism, altruism, modes of communication, speed of response, and so on – the whole company culture, in fact.

In essence, brand-building in the 1990s will involve designing and controlling all aspects of a company, leading people and activities well beyond the traditional skills of the marketing department and the agencies that it employs. It will be a lot closer to the marketing of services (such as airlines, hotels, retailers, building societies) than to the brand-building of the classic brands.

But the problem is that the whole idea of branding in services is relatively new. There is no very well-established body of either readable academic findings or practical folklore. Conferences on service marketing tend to treat it as a specialist subject rather than as the new centre of brand-building. And many service companies, especially those in financial services, have rushed into a quick purchase of the brand managers, methods and communication media of the classic repeat-purchase brand companies – sometimes with rather unhappy results.

There's a lesser but still obstructive problem of language. Most managers outside marketing (and indeed some in it) are not used to thinking of companies as "brands" – the word has been linked too firmly in their minds with trivial things in packages in grocery stores. The term "corporate identity" is used by many to mean roughly what I mean by "company brand"; but since it's even more widely used to mean the company logo, it seems to me to be a dangerous (as well as a cumbersome) phrase.

There is still a lot to do in simply establishing what will be new about brand-building in the 1990s.

What's different about a company brand?

In fact there are some fairly obvious differences between the classic brands and the "new" service-based company brands:

The consumers are different

When the classic brands were launched, people looked to authorities for their opinions. Attitudes were inherited and respect was shown. Such people as teachers, doctors, bank managers, lawyers, MPs (maybe even journalists and financiers) were looked up to. A classic brand could become the authority in its own field, and mass marketing was quite feasible. Today, there's not a great deal of respect for any authority, and marketing companies face not an admass but a lot of people who want to be treated as individuals.

Most service-based products can be readily copied

Most of the classic brands had a good run before copies came onto the market and had time to establish themselves. Many of them were based on genuine product inventions, sometimes patents. This is simply not true of today's service-based products: think of the many "products" produced by banks and building societies. However ingenious, they can be quickly and easily copied, and usually are.

The points of contact for a company brand are more diverse

For the classic brand, some of the traditional marketing rules of thumb (like, for instance, the 4Ps) work well enough. If product, packaging, pricing, distribution and advertising are more or less right, it is likely that all will be well. Final consumers and retailers make up the only really important points of contact for the brand.

When the company is the brand, there are clearly far more points of contact. They range from the closest to home (employees) to the furthest distant (the community in general) – with, in between, shareholders, Government departments, institutions (the City, trade unions, etc), journalists, experts, MPs, suppliers, customers, retailers, pressure groups and consumers of the company's products/services. These groups are by no means self-contained: the trade unionist negotiating a wage claim is probably a reader of the advertisement in the *Financial Times* proclaiming the company's 14th consecutive year of record profits.

Because of this diversity of contact, there is a far greater diversity of communication media used. For the classic brand, advertising and packaging are overwhelmingly important. For the company brand, it can range from the most personal (face-to-face) to the most impersonal (general publicity) via the telephone, demonstrations, print material (both personal and broadcast), design in general, packaging, promotions and advertising. Anything up to half a dozen departments, with jealously guarded budgets, can be responsible for important communications on behalf of the brand.

It's clear that co-ordinating all this, so that the company brand is presented coherently and consistently, is a far harder task than anything faced by a classic brand. Many companies have barely started dealing with it.

Discriminators are based on people, not things

The classic brands had tangible products that stood out from their variable competitors. Most gave instant sensual satisfaction and the consumers knew immediately whether they liked them or not. Even when it was copied, the unique personality of a brand was based ultimately on the product. The source of success for these brands was repeat-purchase of a standard article, based on the familiarity and consistent quality of an old friend. They became a habit; they were one more agonizing decision that didn't have to be made.

Consumers repeat-buy the company brand too and they compare it with competitors (Brouillard Communications 1988), but it is no standard article. The discriminator is a changing collection of people, values, styles and behaviour. What binds the people together is very intangible – a complex set of norms, conventions, methods, examples, organizational patterns, rules and personalities.

With such major differences in consumers, products, points of contact, media use and discriminators, we may have to abandon the marketing rules derived from the classic brands and go back to basics in our approach to brand-building. This is no dreary solemn duty: the opportunities opened up are extraordinarily stimulating.

Building the company brand

In fact we may have to take a new look at every aspect of brand-building. But let me here just pick out four that seem to be particularly important:

1 The staff as brand-builders

The idea that the employees of a company will be the key element in brand-building and a major communication medium in the 1990s is a liberating one. To take just a few of the implications:

—   *The role of the Personnel Director.* Maybe he/she should be thought of primarily as a marketing person and should have direct experience in it. At the moment, there tends to be an almost complete barrier between personnel and marketing departments; there are different strands of theoretical background, consultants, research agencies, communication methods – and this is surely wrong. The criteria used for selection and evaluation of employees should certainly take into account individuals' skills in reflecting, contributing to and presenting the corporate brand.

—   *Expressing company strategies.* There clearly should be a full programme of explaining brand (i.e. company) strategies to *all* members of the staff and indeed of using the staff's reactions at times to modify the strategy. For many companies the discipline of explaining could make a useful test of whether the strategy makes sense.

—   *Training, motivation, leadership.* There are some clear lessons from the best companies – for instance, McDonald's with their Hamburger University; Sainsbury, completion of whose retail training course is accepted as one-third of a university degree; British Airways, whose staff training was central to its turnaround. But there are plenty of black spots too. For instance, some research has shown that about half the people who take a test drive in a car end up by buying it; yet other research suggests that only in 10% of cases do salesmen in franchised car dealers offer the enquirers a test drive. Another recent "mystery shopper" survey showed that, when cashiers were asked for information on their bank's (brand's) mortgage services, most handed out leaflets, but only 15% took the enquirer's name and address. Not the staff's fault – just a symptom of thoughtless training and leadership.

—   *Internal communications.* Some companies do it well enough, some not so well. But relatively few programmes of employee communications derive from brand-building and the planning of the company brand values. The editor of the house journal should be an important member of the brand-building team.

2 Organization

It's arguable that in a competitive situation getting the company branding right is the most important job for the management. Equally, it's clear that not many companies have organized their management structures with that in mind. The companies behind the classic brands are not by any means a good model (indeed they may be increasingly wrong for their own purposes). They tend to rely too much on the traditional "family tree" type hierarchy. That means they are too split by function to lead naturally to the innovation and imagination that any brand constantly needs. Decisions tend to be made too tactically, too low down in the organization, with too little guidance from the top.

The right organization for a company brand implies that brand management should reside right at the top. And since inventive organizations tend to be based on small, flexible, interactive, multi-disciplinary working groups, I think that our model (at a symbolic, rather than organization chart, level) should be something like the diagram below.

The skills needed for this management working group would be those of *production* (the organization and efficient running of the company's products/ services); *personnel* (recruitment/training/inspiring of the people who make up the corporate brand); *communications* (all aspects of communications, marketing and consumer/customer research); and possibly as a separate skill that of *brand designer* (a new type of animal, concerned with design in its broadest sense (Lorenz 1986), from R and D to adding services to products and vice versa, with a passion for the totality of the brand). The whole group to be led by the *CEO* – he's the real brand *manager*.

However such a model is translated into reality, it seems to me that many companies need to take a new look at their organization charts, with brand-building in mind. Most authorities (e.g. Pascale and Athos 1981; Doyle, Saunders and Wong 1990) seem to agree that there will have to be a more flexible and less hierarchical approach, with more informal networking, in order to get the rapid response and to attract the rare skills that a successful company brand needs.

It clearly goes a lot further than organization. What the best company brands represent is a common culture – common aims, standards, language, approaches and style. A common personality, rather than a book of rules. This may sound a little abstract and qualitative, but it is what consumers value in company brands (IBM, ICI or Marks and Spencer, for instance). That puts an enormous premium on sheer leadership from the top (Hamel and Prahalad 1989). A company brand cannot succeed if the individuals doing the detailed work are zombies who aren't allowed to take any initiatives. Equally, it will not be a brand at all if there are no common links or if they don't know how they're expected to behave.

3 Common methods for communicating brand values

Charisma will not do the whole job. If the brand is to be established as a coherent and consistent entity, there must be a common approach to the strategies and tactics of communication. This common approach will have to be followed both by those in the company and by the specialist outside agencies. At the same time it has to be established without constricting the imagination which is the basis of all effective communication.

Precisely how that's done will differ by company, but these seem to me to be the areas in which there should be common methodology and common language:

— *Consumers' buying systems*. Ways of analysing the processes and cycles by which people buy and use and re-buy the company's products/services, as a basis for deciding what methods of communication are best for what purpose at each stage.
— *Brand audit*. Auditing where the company brand stands in people's minds, compared with competitors, and why.
— *Brand positioning and brand personality*. Clear and evocative expressions of *what* the brand should be seen to offer and *who* it should be seen to be.
— *Brand strategy*. What at the strategic level is to be done to the products and the brand to bring them nearer to the desired positioning and personality.
— *Briefing*. Methods of briefing that aim to ensure that the brand is always presented consistently and in line with these strategic decisions, while allowing the maximum of inventive freedom at the tactical level.

It's an extremely demanding and time-consuming job to establish such working methods and common languages, and even more so to get them followed. But I think it will be both easier and more effective than trying to break up the empires and budgets of all those in the company who are communicating in some way about the brand. Rigid centralization and a hierarchical line of command are not really options for communications.

4 The brand idea

Many of the best of the classic brands are famous at least partly because they have had a vivid and enduring advertising idea. By contrast, research (Biel 1990; Gordon and Ryan 1983) has shown that people are scornful of the more hackneyed themes and campaign types, especially on television – the musical wallpaper, the side-by-side comparisons, the talking heads, the computer graphics, the miracle-everything-slashed-unique-opportunity sales. They are equally aware of some very entertaining advertising for some brand whose name has temporarily slipped their mind. The value of a good advertising idea linked inexorably to a brand is enormous. It is clear that this would be even more valuable to a company brand, because its products/services are likely to be even less distinguishable from the competitors' and because its contacts with consumers are likely to be even more diverse. It would have to have something broader than an advertising idea, simply because of the wider range of communication vehicles used.

It's easier to recognize a good idea years later than to see it at the time or to describe it. But on the whole a good communication idea for a company brand would be an *original metaphor for the brand's personality*. That is, the brand would be borrowing from the outside something with the same personality characteristics, which could be *uniquely* associated with it; that could be reasonably long-lasting; and that in some way illuminated and enhanced the brand itself.

There are many examples from the advertising of the classic brands:

- *Marlboro:* the cowboy. The individual facing the elements.
- *Esso:* the tiger. Graceful, powerful, aggressive.
- *Andrex:* the puppy. Soft, durable, wholesome.
- *Persil:* mother love. Metaphor for taking care of clothes.
- *Mr Kipling:* the voice. Tone of voice as metaphor for traditional craftsmanship.

Of course it is a very great deal harder to find an adequate metaphor for the personality of a whole service-based company, usable in a much wider range of media than advertising. It's not easy to think of many examples – there is Lloyds Bank's black horse, Legal and General's brolly, the Prudential's Rock of Gibraltar, Merrill Lynch's thundering herd. Some companies have used the personality of the founder for a brand idea (Habitat, Laker, The Body Shop, Next) but of course that can mean a rather dangerous impermanence. There are some good "brand gestures" (some public policy designed to symbolize a company's personality), such as Marks and Spencer's no-quibble exchange of goods or John Lewis's no-quibble return of cash if shown to be undersold. But on the whole there seem to be a lot of missed opportunities for company brand ideas.

Fun for all

The intriguing thing is that if one accepts these basic notions of what brand-building will be like in the 1990s – the move from the model of the classic brand to that of the service-based company brand – there is no shortage of ideas on what to do about it: quite the reverse. New research methods are emerging too (Baird *et al.* 1988). And in this area I think we can be less shy about using ourselves and our experiences as a research source. It is clear that many people in companies and many teachers of marketing will be able to have a very enjoyable time starting again from first principles.

References

Abraham, M. (1990), *Fact-based Design to Improve Advertising and Promotion Productivity*, 2nd ARF Advertising and Promotion Workshop.

Baird, C., Banks, R., Smith, P. and Morgan, R. (1988), *The SMART Approach to Customer Service*, Market Research Society Conference.

Biel, A. L. (1990), "Love the ad. Buy the product?", *Admap*, September.

Brouillard Communications (1988), *The Winning Edge*, New York, Brouillard Communications.

Buzzell, R. D. and Gale, B. M. (1987), *The PIMS Principles*, New York, The Free Press.

Christopher, M. (1985), "The strategy of customer service". In: *Marketing in the Service Industries*, London, Frank Cass.

Doyle, P. (1989). "Building successful brands: the strategic options", *Journal of Marketing Management* (5): 77–95.

Doyle, P., Saunders, J. and Wong, V. (1992), "Competition in global markets: A case study of American and Japanese competition in the British market", *Journal of International Business Studies* 23 (3): 419–442.

Foxall, G. (1985), "Marketing *is* service marketing". In: *Marketing in the Service Industries*, London, Frank Cass.

Gordon, W. and Ryan, C. (1983), *How do Consumers Feel Advertising Works?*, Market Research Society Conference.

Hamel, G. and Prahalad, C. K. (1989), "Strategic intent", *Harvard Business Review* May/June: 63–76.

Lorenz, C. (1986), *The Design Dimension*, Oxford, Blackwell.

Madell, J. (1980), "New products: How to succeed when the odds are against you", *Marketing Week*, February 22.

The Ogilvy Center for Research and Development (1989), *Advertising, Sales Promotion and the Bottom Line*, The Ogilvy Center.

Pascale, R. T. and Athos, A. G. (1981), *The Art of Japanese Management*, New York, Simon & Schuster.

Tauber, E. M. (1988), "Brand leverage: Strategy for growth in a cost-control world", *Journal of Advertising Research*, Aug/Sept: 26–30.

Chapter 14

Kevin Lane Keller and David A. Aaker

THE IMPACT OF CORPORATE MARKETING ON A COMPANY'S BRAND EXTENSIONS

From *Corporate Reputation Review* 1998, 1 (4): 356–378

EDITORS' COMMENTARY

With stellar reputations as branding scholars, Professors Kevin Lane Keller and David A. Aaker have almost become brands in their own right. Professor Keller is the E. B. Osborn Professor of Marketing at Amos Tuck School of Business, Dartmouth College. His book *Strategic Brand Management: Building, Measuring and Managing Brand Equity*[1] enjoys wide currency. Professor Aaker is E. T. Grether Professor of Marketing Strategy at the Haas School of Business, University of California, Berkeley. His books *Building Strong Brands*[2] and *Managing Brand Equity*[3] are two of the most authoritative texts on branding.

Keller and Aaker's article "The Impact of Corporate Marketing on a Company's Brand Extensions," reproduced here, is, we believe, important in three regards: (a) the importance it accords to company brands; (b) its empirical basis; and (c) the utility of corporate marketing programs.

The chapter opens with the authors outlining the two principal modes of brand extensions. The first is product based, where there is little awareness of the corporation behind the brand. The second makes an explicit link with the corporate brand and, as a consequence, with the organization generally.

The authors go on to frame four hypotheses relating to the effect of corporate marketing activities on the evaluation and external perceptions of corporate brand extensions. Their hypotheses were tested in a laboratory-style experiment among 256 undergraduates from a major public university in the west of the USA. The findings revealed that corporate marketing activity directly benefited the acceptance of new products by consumers. However, the research showed that there were significant variations, dependent upon whether or not corporate marketing activities focused on the corporation's stance in relation to one of the following: product innovation, environmental credentials, or community action.

The most effective stance was when corporate marketing activity drew on a corporation's prowess in product innovation. Corporate marketing communication platforms focusing on environmental concern or community action had no effect on consumer buying behavior. However, an approach based on environmental concern did enhance consumer perceptions of the corporation's trustworthiness and amiability.

The central message from Keller and Aaker's study is that there is considerable merit in utilizing the corporate brand in launching a new product, especially where the organization is known for its prowess vis-à-vis product innovation.

NOTES

1   Keller, K. L., *Strategic Brand Management: Building, Measuring and Managing Brand Equity*, Englewood Cliffs, NJ: Prentice Hall, 1998.
2   Aaker, D. A., *Building Strong Brands*, New York: The Free Press, 1996.
3   Aaker, D.A., *Managing Brand Equity*, New York: The Free Press, 1991.

Introduction

BUILDING, MEASURING, AND MANAGING BRAND EQUITY has become a top priority for many companies.[1] One important strategic branding decision is the proper role of the corporate or company brand name. Companies choose among three principal naming options:

–   to apply the corporate name to all products
–   to create brand names that are distinct from the corporate name
–   to pursue a hybrid or sub-branding strategy that combines the corporate name with different brand names.

When an existing brand name is used to introduce a new product, it is called a brand extension. A company makes a product brand extension when it uses an existing brand name distinct from its corporate name to introduce a new product outside its current product offerings. With product brand extensions, consumers are often completely unaware of the company involved. In contrast, a company makes a *corporate brand extension* when it relies on its corporate name to launch a new product. A corporate brand extension clearly identifies an organization with the product, and so evokes different reactions from consumers than a product brand extension. A corporate brand may create associations in consumers' minds that reflect the values, programs, and activities of the firm. For example, many of the strongest brands — such as Sony, Hewlett-Packard, Kodak, 3M, and IBM — are corporate brands that convey organizational associations in addition to product associations. These corporate-level associations may be only tangentially related to the company's products. An important research question involves asking how corporate-level associations impact the product decisions that consumers make, and how they evaluate brand extensions.

Extensive research has examined the process by which consumers evaluate product brand extensions.[2,3,4] Many researchers have also examined the conceptualization, antecedents, and consequences of corporate image.[5,6,7] Despite the prevalence and importance of corporate branding strategies, relatively little research, however, has examined how corporate-level associations affect the success of brand extensions.

Among the few such studies, Aaker[8] showed how the sequential introduction of brand extensions influenced consumer evaluations of a corporate brand extension by affecting perceptions of corporate credibility. Their study examined how the 'stretch' of the corporate brand was influenced by the level of quality of the parent brand as well as the number and nature of intervening brand extensions. The study did not, however, examine different types of corporate associations nor did it distinguish different underlying dimensions of corporate credibility.

This paper reports a laboratory study that we conducted to examine several types of marketing activity that a company can undertake to influence perceptions of its credibility and thereby affect the evaluations that consumers make of extensions introduced under the corporate name. Specifically, we consider the effects on consumers of providing them with information that identifies actions taken by a company as being one of the following:

— innovative
— concerned with the environment
— involved with the community.

We hypothesize that these common types of corporate marketing activity will impact dimensions of corporate credibility in different ways, and so affect consumers' evaluations of the company's brand extension. We also explore whether corporate marketing activity affects brand extension evaluations when the brand extension is also advertised. After developing a set of hypotheses, we report the results of a laboratory experiment that we conducted and discuss theoretical and managerial implications of our findings.

Conceptual background

Corporate marketing activities are publicly visible programs and actions that companies initiate and that are not identified with a single product or brand sold by the company. Different mechanisms can explain how corporate marketing activities affect evaluations of a new product or service. We begin by briefly reviewing research on how consumers evaluate brand extensions in general before turning to the topic of corporate brand extensions. We then consider how different types of corporate marketing can impact consumer evaluations of corporate brand extensions both in the presence and absence of supporting product advertising.

Brand extension research

Research on consumer responses to extensions of product brands[9,10,11] suggests that two key factors influence consumer evaluations:

–   the types of associations that make up the parent brand image
–   the relationship between the parent brand and the extension product.

These factors affect consumer beliefs about whether the new product fits as a member of the brand line.[2,3,12] Prior research has distinguished between functional or product-related associations and user or usage-based, non-product-related associations.[13,14,11,12] Broniarczyk and Alba,[4] however, showed that any unique brand-specific association can constitute 'fit' and lead to favorable evaluations of the extension. In sum, the record therefore suggests that a variety of different associations for the parent brand can be transferred to an extension, assuming a basis of fit exists. However, prior research has not examined closely on the role of corporate-level associations in influencing extension evaluations.

Corporate brand extensions

When a company uses its corporate name on a product extension, it evokes different associations. A corporate brand is more likely to evoke associations for its own managers and employees, for consumers with past or present ties to the company and its employees, and those more familiar with corporate activities that reflect the social responsibility, values, and goals of the company. A corporate brand can also be associated with features of the company's product brands – eg, attributes, benefits, and attitudes – especially if the company's product portfolio consists of highly-related products. In general, however, a corporate brand is more likely to possess intangible attributes or organizational characteristics that span product classes.

A corporate brand can therefore influence extension evaluations in diverse ways. Since a corporate brand represents the maker of the product or service, perceptions of the company have the potential to provide source credibility to any product or service that the company sponsors. Source credibility is known to affect how people respond to persuasive messages.[15,16,17] For instance, Goldberg and Hartwick[18] found that advertiser reputation affected acceptance of advertised claims, especially when claims were more extreme (see also Craig and McCann and MacKenzie and Lutz).[19,20]

More recently, Aaker[8] examined the impact of corporate credibility on consumer evaluations of new products. He defines corporate credibility as the extent to which consumers believe that a company is willing and able to deliver products and services that satisfy customer needs and wants. These findings indicate that successful brand extensions lead to enhanced perceptions of corporate credibility and to improved evaluations of dissimilar brand extensions. Based on past research,[21] Aaker identifies three dimensions of corporate credibility:

(1) *Corporate expertise* is the extent to which a company is thought able to competently make and sell its products and services
(2) *Corporate trustworthiness* is the extent to which a company is thought to be honest, dependable, and sensitive to consumer needs
(3) *Corporate likability* is the extent to which a company is thought likable, prestigious, and interesting.

In the next section, we examine how specific corporate marketing activities impact consumer evaluations of a corporate brand extension. We first consider the baseline case where the consumer knows only about the company introducing the extension and where no information about the new product has been advertised.

Effects of corporate marketing in the absence of advertising

Three major types of corporate marketing impact evaluations of a corporate brand extension:

–   activities that demonstrate product innovation
–   environmental concern
–   community involvement.

We examine here the impact of those activities on five key measures of extension evaluations:

–   the perceived credibility of the company
–   corporate fit
–   product attribute beliefs
–   perceived quality
–   purchase likelihood.

The first three measures are known to be important mediators of extension evaluations; the latter two are typical outcomes of interest in a brand extension.

Corporate marketing that demonstrates product innovation

Corporate marketing activity that demonstrates a company's innovativeness typically involves developing new and unique marketing programs with respect to product or service improvements and new product or service introductions. Being a product innovator induces perceptions of the company as modern and up-to-date, investing in research and development, and employing the most advanced product features and manufacturing capabilities.

Perceived innovativeness is a key competitive weapon and priority for firms in many countries. In Japan, many consumer product companies such as Kao, and more technically oriented companies such as Canon want to be perceived as innovative. In Europe, such companies as Michelin ('Driving Tire Science') and Philips Electronics ('Let's Make Things Better') try to distinguish themselves through their ability to innovate and successfully invent new products. Similarly, such US companies as 3M ('Innovation Working For You') and DuPont ('Better Ideas for Better Living') try hard to foster and communicate their innovation capabilities.

Corporate credibility

Innovative companies draw heavily on technology, engineering, and other specialized skills. A company perceived as innovative should therefore have higher perceived corporate expertise. Consumers may also have more respect, liking, and admiration for a company that is competently doing new things and finding new solutions, thereby enhancing perceptions of corporate trustworthiness and likability.

Fit and beliefs

Perceived corporate innovativeness should induce consumers to believe the company more capable of generating successful new products outside of its area of operation, with two consequences. First, the perceived expertise associated with an innovative company should enhance perceptions of fit. Aaker and Keller[2] showed how fit is based on the perceived applicability of the company's manufacturing skills and assets. A dissimilar extension may seem a better fit for a company with an innovative reputation. Secondly, corporate expertise should increase the likelihood that consumers will infer an extension product to be both well-designed and well-made. Consequently, consumers should form more favorable beliefs about specific attributes of the extension.

Evaluations

Positive perceptions of corporate credibility, extension fit, and extension attribute beliefs should result in higher perceived quality and purchase likelihood ratings for a corporate brand extension.

We therefore propose the following hypothesis:

H1: Corporate marketing activities that demonstrate a company's *innovativeness* will increase consumer perceptions of:
   – corporate expertise, trustworthiness, and likability
   – fit of a corporate brand extension

- attribute beliefs about a corporate brand extension
- quality of a corporate brand extension
- purchase likelihood of a corporate brand extension.

Corporate marketing that demonstrates environmental concern

Companies indicate sensitivity to environmental concerns through marketing programs designed to protect or improve the environment or to make more effective use of scarce natural resources. Environmental concern reflects a growing social trend that is reflected in the attitudes and behavior of both consumers and corporations. Among consumers, 83 per cent of Americans say they prefer buying environmentally safe products.[22] Twenty-three per cent of Americans also report making purchases based on environmental considerations.[23] Companies have developed various 'green marketing' initiatives to capitalize on these trends. For instance, many leading firms (eg, GE, Disney, and Bechtel) have top 'green' executives or departments that chart environmental policy. Other firms have built their corporate identities around environmentally-friendly policies (eg, Body Shop, Ben and Jerry's, and Patagonia).

Corporate credibility

Companies perceived as environmentally concerned signal to consumers that the company is interested not only in financial matters and profits, but also in improving the quality of life of the society in which it operates. A probable implication is that the company will be perceived as more understanding of customer needs. Insofar as consumers believe that environmental concern is a worthwhile and socially responsible corporate endeavor, these activities should result in enhanced perceptions of corporate trustworthiness and likability. Consumers may also feel that many environmental problems require fairly sophisticated technological solutions, suggesting that an environmentally involved firm is also more likely to have specialized expertise.

Fit, beliefs, and evaluations

Perceived environmental concern is unlikely to improve consumer perceptions of fit or increase the favorability of product attribute beliefs not related to the environment. Nevertheless, insofar as consumers want to support the environment, they may be more inclined to evaluate a corporate brand extension favorably if it comes from an environmentally concerned firm. Moreover, if a company is liked and trusted, then consumers are likely to be more comfortable and proud to buy its products. An affect transfer could therefore operate.[24,25]
We therefore suggest the following hypothesis:

H2: Corporate marketing that demonstrates a company's *concern with the environment* will increase consumer perceptions of:
- corporate likability, trustworthiness, and expertise

 — quality of a corporate brand extension
 — purchase likelihood for a corporate brand extension.

Corporate marketing that demonstrates community involvement

Companies often demonstrate community involvement through marketing pro-grams designed to contribute to the welfare of the community in which the firm is associated, as well as to society as a whole. McDonald's, Toyota, Levi-Strauss and many others have active, visible ties to local communities in an effort to improve the quality of life of local citizens. Many companies also participate in national efforts that convey a sense of social responsibility.[26] For example, Master-Card's 'Make A Difference' program ties credit card usage to charitable donations. American Express's 'Charge Against Hunger' campaign donates funds to feed the hungry based on card use. The Body Shop is active in numerous cause-related marketing programs, and Ben and Jerry's donates a percentage of its pre-tax profits to various causes.

Credibility, fit, beliefs, and evaluations

We expect perceived community involvement to have similar effects as per-ceived environmental concern. Insofar as consumers believe that companies should behave in socially responsible ways, they should find those companies more trustworthy and likable. In turn, increased perceptions of trustworthiness and likability should translate into more favorable ratings of extension quality and purchase likelihood.

We therefore suggest the following hypothesis:

H3: Corporate marketing that demonstrates *community involvement* will increase consumer perceptions of:
 — corporate likability and trustworthiness
 — quality of a corporate brand extension
 — purchase likelihood for a corporate brand extension.

The effects of corporate marketing with product advertising

If a company heavily advertises its product, can corporate marketing activity still have an effect on extension evaluations? We argue that the congruity or consist-ency of the advertised product positioning with the corporate marketing activity will influence the added value of corporate marketing. In particular, corporate marketing should prove beneficial if it reinforces and supports the product positioning. Consumer expectations are less likely to be violated and make it easier to establish the product position. Favorable product perceptions and enhanced credibility in the new product context should then induce higher extension evaluations.

Thus, corporate marketing that demonstrates product innovation should help a corporate brand extension that is positioned as innovative; corporate marketing that demonstrates environmental concern should help an extension that is positioned as environmentally sensitive; and corporate marketing that demonstrates community involvement should help an extension that is positioned as beneficial to the community.

We therefore suggest the following hypothesis:

H4: Corporate marketing will be more effective at enhancing evaluations of a corporate brand extension if product advertising is congruent with information conveyed by corporate marketing activities than if it is incongruent.

Method

Procedure

Two hundred and fifty-six upper-class undergraduate students from a major public university in the western US participated in this study as part of a course requirement. Young adults aged 20–25 represent a key target for many marketers because they are just beginning to form buying habits, and develop loyalty and preferences. Participants were placed in groups of 20 in large classrooms.[a] They were told that the purpose of the study was to learn more about a new product testing service that gathered consumer reactions to potential new products that companies were considering introducing. With the service, participants were told, consumers would be given a brief company description which summarized the main products of the company and some noteworthy aspects of their business, followed by an ad describing a new product that they were considering introducing. They were also told that, although they might normally have more information than would be provided when they really made product purchase decisions, companies wanted to learn what consumers thought even when they had little information. After examining the ad, subjects responded to a series of questions measuring their reactions to the company and its new product. The same procedure was followed for four different companies and their new product introductions.

Design and manipulations

The basic design of the study was a four (corporate marketing activities) by four (product positionings) full factorial design. The design was replicated for hypothetical companies marketing products in four categories:

(1) *over-the-counter drugs* (aspirin and aspirin-free pain relievers and cough and cold remedies)
(2) *baked goods* (cakes, biscuits, cookies, breads, cake mixes, biscuit mixes, and cookie mixes)

(3)   *personal care products* (shampoos, conditioners and facial soaps and skin cremes)

(4)   *dairy products* (milk, butter, ice cream, and yogurt).

All products sold by a company used the company's name, including the proposed new product. We used neutral company names that conveyed no specific product information. Product categories were familiar to all participants.

Company descriptions included an opening paragraph describing the products currently offered by the company, followed by two paragraphs describing the corporate marketing activity. Corporate marketing was manipulated to signal either product innovativeness, environmental concern, or community involvement. A control for 'no corporate marketing' was also included. Figure 1 presents the complete text of the manipulations for the company making Baron over-the-counter drugs.

Product positioning was manipulated by the content of the ad for the new product. The new product chosen was a corporate brand extension that was not within the product categories currently served by the company, but not so dissimilar that there was not a basis for 'fit.' Specifically, a pretest sample of 40 respondents from the same subject population as the main study were given the first paragraph description of the products currently sold by the corporation (as described above) and asked to rate the degree of fit for proposed new products on an 11-point scale (0 = Extremely Poor Fit, 10 = Extremely Good Fit). The new products chosen were perceived as basically 'moderate' in fit, with ratings that ranged from 4.65 to 7.38.

New products were positioned by ad copy, headline, and picture in one of four ways – as innovative, environmentally-sensitive, beneficial to the community, or a control. The first two paragraphs were constant across all ad types and provided some brief introductory comments. The following paragraphs, headline, and picture then expanded on the particular image of the product. For example, the ad for innovative positioning showed a picture of a calendar for the year 2000. Its headline stated that the new product was the first of the 21st century, noted that 'technological advances have created new standards,' and that the product contained a breakthrough ingredient or was made by a newly-patented production process. The environmentally-sensitive positioning ad showed a picture of a tree. Its headline stated that the product was 'good for you and good for the environment,' noted that 'all packaging uses material that is either recyclable or biodegradable' and was 'manufactured with a special production process that doesn't harm or pollute the environment.' The community-benefit positioning ad showed a picture of a panda. Its headline appealed to 'help yourself and your local zoo,' and stated that 25 cents would be donated to support the local zoo for every box sold. Finally, the control ad showed a picture of a 'bull's-eye' and provided neutral, descriptive information about the product and noted that it was now available in consumers' favorite supermarkets and drugstores. Figure 2 presents the complete text of the ads for the Baron eye drops extension.

Subjects saw four of the 16 possible combinations of corporate marketing activity and product positioning as a result of crossing the corporate marketing

All companies
Baron Corp. makes a variety of over-the-counter drugs. Their main product sellers are Baron Aspirin and Aspirin-Free Pain Relievers and Baron Cough and Cold Remedies.

Corporate Marketing Demonstrating Product Innovation
Baron Corp. is widely recognized as being the most innovative firm in the markets in which they compete. Their corporate philosophy is to introduce products with technological advances that provide superior product performance.

Baron Corp's strategy to achieve that goal is to exceed competitive expenditures on product research and development. Baron out-spends the industry average on R&D in order that they can: 1) better understand what consumers need and want and 2) design and manufacture innovative products that better satisfy those consumer needs and wants.

Corporate Marketing Demonstrating Environmental Concern
Baron Corp. has distinguished itself selling products that are 'environmentally friendly' and are good for consumers. Their corporate philosophy is to make and sell products that set industry standards for minimizing the possibility of any negative side effects to the environment.

Baron Corp's products are manufactured in plants that have received national recognition for the ways in which they help to protect the environment. All disposable elements used in their business and manufacturing operations are recycled. All packaging, which is minimized to conserve resources, reduce waste and save customer's money, is also made out of recyclable and biodegradable material.

Corporate Marketing Demonstrating Community Involvement
Baron Corp. is known for their strong involvement with the community. Their corporate philosophy is to improve the quality of life in the communities in which their products are made and sold. Baron Corp. believes that they can contribute to consumer satisfaction, well-being, and welfare not only by their customers' consumption of Baron products, but also by their commitment to organizations and activities that improve the cultural and spiritual sides of consumers' lives too.

To achieve these goals, Baron Corp. has been involved in a variety of programs. They are one of the biggest sponsors of local activities of the United Way. They have provided sizable donations to a number of Arts functions related to symphonies, ballets, operas, folk festivals, museums, art exhibits, etc. They have also been financial supporters of a number of youth programs related to sports, career development, and drug rehabilitation.

Control Corporate Marketing Activity
Baron Corp. has manufacturing plants in several Western States and has their headquarters in Phoenix, Arizona. Baron Corp. has been in business for 25 years.

Figure 1 Corporate descriptions (over-the-counter drugs company)

activity and product positioning factors to form a Latin square design. Consequently, subjects saw each type of corporate marketing activity and product positioning exactly once. Subjects were randomly assigned to the four different exposure sequences produced by the Latin square. Additionally, the exposure sequences were counterbalanced by product category and order of presentation so that each combination of corporate marketing activity and product positioning were seen for each product type and each position in the exposure sequence (1st, 2nd, 3rd, or 4th).

Innovative Positioning Ad

Introducing Baron, the First Eye Drops for the 21st century
Introducing revolutionary new Baron Eye Drops, the sensible way to take care of your eyes. It's the perfect way to refresh and protect your eyes! Baron Eye Drops provides unsurpassed comfort to your eyes. Technological advances have produced the most effective eye drops ever available. Baron contains oxhydogener, a new patented ingredient that lubricates more effectively than anything previously available. Whatever your eye care needs, Baron's breakthrough new ingredient will give you fast, soothing relief. No other eye drop can promise the same effective performance. Innovative new Baron Eye Drops has just set the standard for eye drops for the 21st century.

Environmental Positioning Ad

Baron Eye Drops are good for you and good for the environment
Baron Eye Drops are the new eye drops that are both good for you and good for the environment. Baron Eye Drops are the sensible way to take care of your eyes. It's the perfect way to refresh and protect your eyes! Baron Eye Drops are also made with the good of the environment in mind. All of the packaging for Baron Eye Drops comes from either recyclable or biodegradable material. And it is manufactured with a special production process that doesn't harm or pollute the environment. So when you use Baron Eye Drops, you are getting the best possible product both for you and for the environment.

Community Positioning Ad

Help yourself and your local zoo. Try Baron Eye Drops
Do yourself a favor and try new Baron Eye Drops. Baron Eye Drops are the sensible way to take care of your eyes. It's the perfect way to refresh and protect your eyes! And for every box of Baron Eye Drops sold, we will donate 25 cents to support your local zoo. By helping to preserve our natural heritage, we hope to make life a little better for everyone. When you buy Baron Eye Drops, not only do you get effective eye care for yourself, you also help to improve the lives of the animals at your local zoo and increase the enjoyment gained by thousands of visitors. So help yourself and your local zoo. Try Baron Eye Drops.

Control Ad

Introducing Baron Eye Drops
Try new Baron Eye Drops. Baron Eye Drops are the sensible way to take care of your eyes. It's the perfect way to refresh and protect your eyes! Baron Eye Drops are now available in all of your favorite drugstores and supermarkets. So try new effective Baron Eye Drops.

Figure 2 Advertising stimuli (eye drops extension)

To illustrate, subjects in the first exposure sequence, product category, and ad order conditions evaluated:

—   a new sun block positioned as innovative from an innovation-oriented personal care products company (Profile)

- a new rice positioned as environmentally sensitive from a community–
  oriented baked goods company (Medallion)
- a new eye drops positioned as beneficial to the community from an over-
  the-counter pharmaceutical company with no specific corporate image
  (Baron)
- a new salad dressing with no specific product positioning from an environ-
  mentally-oriented dairy products company (Monarch).

Measures

After examining the company description and ad for the corporate brand extension, respondents completed various scales. First, they evaluated the new product on three seven-point scales with respect to *quality*; three seven-point scales
with measuring *fit*; and an eleven-point scale measuring *purchase likelihood*.

Participants were then asked to rate whether the new product matched ten
different descriptions. Four items assessed whether consumers believed the new
product possessed key attributes in the product class,[b] and two items each
assessed whether the product was seen as innovative, environmentally sensitive,
and beneficial to the community.

Finally, participants were asked to provide their reactions to the company
making the product on seven-point scales (higher numbers indicating greater
levels of agreement). Two items each were used to measure company *quality* (has
quality products; has superior products), *innovativeness* (innovative; has advanced
products), *environmental concern* (good for the environment; no negative side
effects to the environment), *community involvement* (good for the local community; helpful to the local community), *expertise* (expert; good at manufacturing),
trustworthiness (trustworthy; concerned about customers), and *likability* (likable;
prestigious). Because all composites exhibited satisfactory reliability (coefficient
alphas exceeding .80), summary scales were formed by averaging the appropriate items.

Finally, three covariate measures of product category involvement were
collected to capture the product category attitudes and behaviors of participants
that could potentially affect their evaluations of the new products. The measures
assessed *usage frequency, knowledge*, and perceived *quality differences* among brands
in each product category. These measures were combined to form a scale of
category involvement with a satisfactory coefficient alpha reliability estimate of .72.

Results

The hypotheses were tested by planned comparisons, with product category
type, product category involvement, presentation order, and data collection
period (see endnote a) as covariates.[c] Tables 1 and 2 contain the means for all
dependent variables for the 16 cells. For ease of exposition, planned contrasts are
referenced by the appropriate cell number.

Table 1 Cell means of product ratings

Cell (N)	Innovative corporate	Quality	Purchase likelihood	Fit	Beliefs	Innovative-ness	Environ-mentally sensitive	Community beneficial
1 (67)	Innovative product	5.38	6.22	5.02	5.26	5.24	4.37	4.43
2 (70)	Environmental product	5.47	6.32	5.31	5.01	5.22	5.96	5.25
3 (53)	Community product	5.33	5.98	5.22	5.15	4.65	5.12	5.15
4 (69)	Control	4.90	5.72	4.94	4.88	4.41	4.36	4.06
	Environmental Corporate							
5 (53)	Innovative product	5.25	5.84	4.58	5.14	5.26	5.46	5.06
6 (69)	Environmental product	4.96	5.59	4.64	4.86	4.74	6.48	5.59
7 (67)	Community product	4.53	5.13	4.35	4.55	3.85	5.70	5.76
8 (69)	Product control	4.26	4.18	3.96	4.44	3.66	5.57	4.97
	Community Corporate							
9 (67)	Innovative product	5.09	5.34	4.43	5.09	4.96	4.49	4.84
10 (53)	Environmental product	4.90	5.96	4.88	4.85	4.67	5.69	5.68
11 (71)	Community product	4.64	5.77	4.78	4.64	3.99	4.98	5.96
12 (67)	Product control	4.12	4.14	4.13	4.31	3.30	4.34	5.06
	Control Corporate							
13 (69)	Innovative product	4.57	4.91	3.96	4.79	4.77	4.25	3.99
14 (66)	Environmental product	4.37	4.71	3.96	4.35	4.12	5.60	5.06
15 (68)	Community product	4.09	4.67	4.25	4.43	3.50	4.61	5.35
16 (53)	Control	3.91	3.86	4.12	4.33	3.34	4.02	3.65

Table 2 Cell means of company ratings

Cell (N)	Innovative corporate	Quality	Innova-tiveness	Environ-mentally concerned	Community involved	Expert	Trust-worthy	Attrac-tive
1 (67)	Innovative product	5.62	5.72	4.45	4.66	5.47	5.50	5.42
2 (70)	Environmental product	5.75	5.84	5.81	5.41	5.61	5.73	5.51
3 (53)	Community product	5.73	5.64	5.04	5.88	5.46	5.79	5.52
4 (69)	Control	5.57	5.51	4.43	4.45	5.46	5.29	5.09
	Environmental Corporate							
5 (53)	Innovative product	5.27	5.54	5.81	5.44	5.40	5.49	5.24
6 (69)	Environmental product	5.14	5.38	6.44	5.72	5.27	5.78	5.36
7 (67)	Community product	4.74	4.63	5.89	5.79	4.94	5.41	5.06
8 (69)	Product control	4.75	4.69	5.77	5.25	5.00	5.21	4.78
	Community Corporate							
9 (67)	Innovative product	5.23	5.23	4.58	5.86	4.95	5.46	5.07
10 (53)	Environmental product	5.06	4.95	5.66	5.99	4.94	5.67	5.02
11 (71)	Community product	4.77	4.63	5.36	6.21	4.65	5.71	5.28
12 (67)	Product control	4.51	4.19	4.82	5.90	4.50	5.40	4.92
	Control Corporate							
13 (69)	Innovative product	4.82	4.90	4.12	4.10	4.82	4.47	4.60
14 (66)	Environmental product	4.66	4.53	5.36	5.06	4.73	5.03	4.77
15 (68)	Community product	4.38	3.95	4.62	5.52	4.42	4.79	4.63
16 (53)	Control	4.29	3.67	3.89	3.81	4.34	4.31	4.24

Manipulation checks

Corporate marketing activity

The success of the corporate marketing manipulation can be tested by comparing the effects of corporate marketing that demonstrate product innovation (PI), environmental concern (EC), and community involvement (CI) on the ratings for the corresponding corporate image dimensions against the same ratings for the base case (BC) where no corporate marketing activity was reported, with no product positioning information advertised in each case (ie, cells 4, 8, and 12 vs. cell 16). This analysis reveals that the company engaged in corporate marketing activity related to product innovation was seen as significantly more innovative (BC = 3.67, PI = 5.51; $p < .01$), the company engaged in corporate marketing activity related to the environment was seen as significantly more environmentally concerned (BC = 3.89; EC = 5.77; $p < .01$), and the company engaged in corporate marketing activity related to the local community was seen as significantly more community involved (BC = 3.81; EC = 5.90; $p < .01$) than the base case control.

Product positioning

The success of the product positioning manipulation is demonstrated by comparing the ratings of the innovative (IP), environmentally-sensitive (ES), and community-beneficial (CB) positions on the corresponding product image dimensions to the same ratings for the base case (BP) where no product information was advertised, with no corporate image information provided in each case (ie, cells 13, 14, and 15 vs. cell 16). This analysis reveals that the product positioned as innovative was seen as significantly more innovative (BP = 3.34, IP = 4.77; $p < .01$), the product positioned as environmentally sensitive was seen as significantly more environmentally sensitive (BP = 4.02, ES = 5.60; $p < .01$), and the product positioned as beneficial for the community was seen as significantly more beneficial for the community (BP = 3.65; CB = 5.35; $p < .01$) than the base case control.

Effects of corporate marketing activity without product advertising

H1, H2, and H3 suggested possible effects of corporate marketing activities on perceptions of a company's credibility and perceptions and evaluations of a corporate brand extension when no product information had been advertised. The hypotheses were tested by contrasting participants' ratings when corporate marketing activity existed to the base case where no information on corporate marketing activity was provided, when no ads were presented. These tests involved comparisons between cells 4, 8, and 12 against cell 16 in Table 1.

Effects of corporate marketing activity on perceived corporate credibility

H1a, H2a, and H3a are all supported as corporate marketing that demonstrates product innovation significantly enhanced perceptions of corporate expertise, trustworthiness, and likability ($p < .05$); corporate marketing that demonstrates environmental concern significantly enhanced perceptions of corporate likability, trustworthiness, and expertise ($p < .05$); and corporate marketing activity that demonstrates community involvement significantly enhanced perceptions of corporate likability and trustworthiness ($p < .05$) (see Table 3). Note, however, that although corporate marketing activity that demonstrates environmental concern led to higher ratings of perceived corporate expertise, these perceptions of expertise were still significantly lower than those obtained from corporate marketing activities that demonstrate product innovation ($p < .05$).

Effects of corporate marketing activity on evaluations of a corporate brand extension

Only corporate marketing activity related to product innovation led to greater perceptions of extension fit and more favorable product attribute beliefs ($p < .01$), supporting H1b and H1c (see Table 4). As expected, corporate marketing activity related to environmental concern and community involvement did not have such product-related effects ($F < 1$).

All three types of corporate marketing activities were hypothesized to affect the perceived quality and purchase likelihood of the extension. Only corporate marketing activity related to product innovation, however, had a substantial impact on perceived quality and purchase likelihood ($p < .01$), consistent with H1d and H1e. Although corporate marketing activity related to environment concern had a significant (albeit modest) impact on perceived quality ($p < .05$), consistent with H2b, it did not significantly affect purchase likelihood ($p > .10$),

Table 3 Corporate marketing activity effects on corporate credibility dimensions[d]

Corporate marketing activity	Corporate expertise	Corporate likability	Corporate trustworthiness
Innovative	1.12	0.85	0.98
Environmental	0.66	0.54	0.90
Community	0.16	0.68	1.09

Table 4 Corporate marketing activity effects[e] on extension evaluations

Corporate marketing activity	Fit	Attribute beliefs	Perceived quality	Likelihood of purchase
Innovative	0.82	0.55	0.99	1.86
Environmental	−0.16	0.11	0.35	0.32
Community	0.01	−0.02	0.21	0.28

failing to support H2c. Finally, corporate marketing activity related to community involvement did not have a significant impact on either measure ($p > .10$), failing to support both H3b and H3c.

Effects of corporate marketing activity in the presence of product advertising

H4 addressed the effects of corporate marketing activity on evaluations of a corporate brand extension when product information was also being advertised for the extension. H4 asserted that corporate marketing activity would provide a greater improvement in evaluations for a corporate brand extension when it was congruent with the advertised product positioning, as compared to when the corporate marketing activity was unrelated to the product positioning information. Thus, H4 can be tested by comparing how much ratings for a corporate brand extension improved when information on corporate marketing activity was provided, as compared to when it was absent, when the product positioning for the extension was congruent (cells 1 vs. 13, 6 vs. 14, and 11 vs. 15) vs. when the product positioning was different from the corporate marketing activity (cells 5 and 9 vs. 13, 2 and 10 vs. 14, 3 and 7 vs. 15).

Table 5 shows the improvements in perceived quality and purchase likelihood for the corporate brand extension when product positioning information was either congruent or unrelated to corporate marketing activities. For example, a product advertised as being innovative received a higher quality rating (+0.81) if it came from a company associated with innovative products rather than one having a neutral reputation. All forms of corporate marketing significantly enhanced extension evaluations when product positioning was both congruent *and* unrelated ($p < .05$), failing to support H4 – with two minor exceptions. First, corporate marketing that demonstrates environmental concern did not significantly improve purchase likelihood ratings when the product had been positioned as beneficial to the community ($p > .10$). Corporate marketing that demonstrates community involvement also did not significantly improve purchase likelihood when the product had been positioned as innovative ($p > .10$). Note that across all product positionings, corporate marketing that

Table 5 Corporate marketing activity effects on extension evaluations: the impact of advertised product positionings[f]

Product positioning	Innovative corporate marketing activity		Environmental corporate marketing activity		Community corporate marketing activity	
	Quality	Likelihood	Quality	Likelihood	Quality	Likelihood
Innovative	0.81	1.31	0.68	0.93	0.52	0.43
Environmental	1.10	1.61	0.60	0.88	0.54	1.25
Community	1.22	1.31	0.44	0.46	0.55	1.10

Table 6 Corporate marketing activity effects on extension evaluations (*cont.*): the impact of advertised product positionings

Product positioning	Innovative corporate marketing activity		Environmental corporate marketing activity		Community corporate marketing activity	
	Fit	Beliefs	Fit	Beliefs	Fit	Beliefs
Innovative	1.06	0.47	0.68	0.51	0.47	0.30
Environmental	1.35	0.66	0.62	0.36	0.94	0.50
Community	0.97	0.72	0.10	0.18	0.53	0.21

demonstrates product innovation significantly improved extension evaluations ($p < .05$) compared to corporate marketing that demonstrated environmental concern or community involvement.

To examine the factors affecting extension attitudes, Table 6 shows the improvements in perceived fit and attribute beliefs for the corporate brand extension when product positioning information was either congruent or unrelated with corporate marketing activity. As with extension attitudes, and again contrary to H4, corporate marketing activity worked as well when the corporate brand extension was positioned on another dimension as it did when the advertised product positioning reinforced the corporate marketing activity. Consistent with the results for extension purchase likelihood, the only exceptions to this pattern were that corporate marketing demonstrating environmental concern did not significantly improve fit or attribute beliefs when the product had been positioned as beneficial to the community ($p > .10$). Similarly corporate marketing demonstrating community involvement did not significantly improve attribute beliefs when the product had been positioned as innovative ($p > .10$). Additionally, corporate marketing that demonstrates community involvement did not significantly improve fit or attribute beliefs when the product was positioned as beneficial to the community ($p > .10$).

Mediating effects on extension attitudes

We developed H1–H4 based partly on assumptions concerning how corporate marketing activity would affect different corporate credibility dimensions, perceived fit, and attribute beliefs for a corporate brand extension and how these factors, in turn, would affect extension attitudes. To provide further insight into these mediating effects on extension attitudes, we performed two additional analyses. First, regression analyses were conducted based on participants' responses from all 16 cells, with mediating factors as independent variables and perceived quality or purchase likelihood as dependent variables. The results of both analyses were consistent and showed that corporate expertise, corporate likability, extension fit, and extension attribute beliefs were all significantly related to extension attitudes ($p < .05$).

Secondly, the mediating factors were added as covariates into the planned comparison model for those cells where corporate marketing activity had a large, significant effect on perceived quality and purchase likelihood, ie, for corporate marketing demonstrating product innovativeness. With the mediating factors present, the planned contrast for the corporate marketing factor became statistically insignificant (p > .20). By far the strongest predictors in these analyses were extension fit and extension attribute beliefs, although corporate credibility, especially corporate expertise, also played an important role in mediating the effects of corporate marketing activity on extension evaluations.

These supplementary analyses lend credence to the conceptual model and theorizing about how corporate marketing activity affects perceptions of corporate credibility, extension fit, and attribute beliefs to influence extension evaluations.

Discussion

The experimental results are summarized in Figure 3. Most importantly, the results suggest that corporate marketing activity can provide a direct marketing benefit by improving perceptions and evaluations of a corporate brand extension. One key advantage of engaging in corporate marketing activity, creating a corporate image, and employing a corporate branding strategy is that it can facilitate the acceptance of new products. The nature and extent of that impact, however, depends on the type of corporate marketing activity (see Figure 4).

Corporate marketing activity was manipulated by providing background information on a firm with the following emphasis:

(1) Product innovation: Reputation as innovative and its philosophy of introducing technologically advanced products.
(2) Environmental concern: Policy to sell 'environmentally friendly' products and manufacture products in an environmentally safe fashion.
(3) Community involvement: Corporate philosophy to improve the quality of life in local communities through various activities and programs.
(4) Control: Location and years in business.

Product positioning strategies for these extensions were manipulated by providing advertising information that emphasized:

(1) Innovative: Technological advances in the ingredients of the product or production process.
(2) Environmentally sensitive: Environmental advantages of the product packaging and production process.
(3) Beneficial to the community: Corporate donations to the local zoo on the basis of product sales.
(4) Control: Neutral, descriptive product information.

Figure 3 Summary of experimental manipulations

Empirical Support[a]	Hypotheses		
	H1:		Corporate marketing activity related to *product innovation* will increase perceptions of:
Y, Y, Y		a)	Corporate expertise, trustworthiness, and likability,
Y		b)	Fit of a corporate brand extension,
Y		c)	Attribute beliefs about a corporate brand extension,
Y		d)	Quality of a corporate brand extension, and
Y		e)	Purchase likelihood for a corporate brand extension.
	H2:		Corporate marketing activity related to *concern with the environment* will increase perceptions of:
Y, Y, Y		a)	Corporate likability, trustworthiness, and expertise,
Y		b)	Quality of a corporate brand extension, and
N		c)	Purchase likelihood for a corporate brand extension.
	H3:		Corporate marketing activity related to *community involvement* will increase perceptions of:
Y, Y		a)	Corporate likability and trustworthiness,
N		b)	Quality of a corporate brand extension, and
N		c)	Purchase likelihood for a corporate brand extension.
N	H4:		Corporate marketing activity will be more effective at enhancing the evaluations of a corporate brand extension if the product positioning information for the extension is congruent with the information conveyed by the corporate marketing activity than if it is unrelated.

[a] Y designates statistically significant support (p <.05); N designates a failure to obtain statistically significant support (p >.10)

Figure 4 Summary of hypothesis tests

Corporate marketing activity that demonstrates *product innovation* provides the most valuable enhancements to a corporate brand extension. Specifically, it led to the most favorable perceptions of corporate expertise and, most importantly, was the only type of corporate marketing activity to enhance the perceived fit of the extension and the evaluation of its attribute beliefs. Given the important mediating role of these factors, it is not surprising that it was the only type of corporate marketing activity to increase ratings substantially of both perceived quality and purchase likelihood.

Corporate marketing activity that demonstrates *environmental concern* also provided a number of benefits. In particular, it enhanced perceptions of corporate trustworthiness and likability. It had no impact, however, on either perceived fit or favorability of attribute beliefs for the extension. Consequently, it had only a fairly modest impact on the perceived quality of the corporate brand extension, substantially lower than that for corporate marketing demonstrating product innovation, and had no significant effect on purchase likelihood.

Corporate marketing activity that demonstrates *community involvement* had more limited effects than the other two types of corporate marketing. As expected, it enhanced perceptions of corporate trustworthiness and likability, but did not affect perceptions of corporate expertise, extension fit, or extension attribute beliefs. Consequently, it did not increase ratings of perceived quality or purchase likelihood for the extension.

Corporate marketing effects with product advertising

The impact of corporate marketing did not appreciably differ depending on the type of product positioning for the extension, and improved extension evaluations in almost all cases. There are two noteworthy aspects to this finding. First, all three types of corporate marketing affected consumer evaluations of a corporate brand extension when the extension had also been advertised. Thus, even though corporate marketing demonstrating environmental concern and community involvement did not improve extension attitudes when no product information had been advertised about the extension, these activities did have an effect when more relevant, product-related information was made available. Product information concerning the innovativeness or environmental sensitivity of the extension appeared to be necessary to provide sufficient expertise or credibility in the new business context. Consistent with this conjecture, in all cases but one, *better extension evaluations were linked to greater perceptions of fit and more favorable attribute beliefs*. The only exception was for corporate marketing activity demonstrating community involvement: it improved extension attitudes when the extension was positioned as beneficial to the community even though extension fit and attribute beliefs were not affected.

The second important aspect to this finding is that corporate marketing significantly improved extension evaluations when congruent, as well as unrelated, product information positioning the extension was advertised. The lack of congruence and reinforcement may have been compensated by the fact that product positioning information suggested credible information about attribute dimensions which were weak or otherwise missing from the corporate image.

Finally, we note how similar were the effects of corporate marketing on extension evaluations whether or not product positioning information had been advertised. In both cases, corporate marketing demonstrating product innovation provided more favorable evaluations of the extension than corporate marketing demonstrating either environmental concern or community involvement. Corporate marketing demonstrating product innovation and the resulting perception of corporate expertise appeared to make a substantial difference in consumer judgments about the ability of the company to introduce the extension.

Implications

We suggest five major implications from the findings of this experimental study. First, by showing that corporate marketing related to product innovation enhances perceptions of corporate credibility and extension fit, and thus more favorable extension evaluations, this study extends the findings of Aaker[8] that showed similar benefits for brands with reputations for high quality products. The study also reinforces the findings of Brown and Dacin[27] who showed how corporate ability and corporate social responsibility associations can influence consumer beliefs and attitudes towards a corporate brand extension.

Secondly, this study extends Aaker's[8] findings by providing a more detailed account of the relative effects of particular dimensions of corporate credibility, namely corporate expertise, trustworthiness, and likability. Corporate expertise appeared to play a more influential role in evaluations of a corporate brand extension than either corporate trustworthiness or likability. The fact that expertise was a key predictor of extension evaluations is also consistent with the finding in Aaker[8] that one important predictor of extension success is the ability of a firm's manufacturing skills and assets to transfer from one product context to another.

Thirdly, the findings suggest the merits of leveraging a strong brand to introduce a new product. One advantage of using a brand extension strategy to name a new product is that a less concerted advertising effort may be necessary.[28] To the extent that brand extensions are able to leverage existing parent brand associations in consumer memory, a company should find it easier to achieve a brand image with an extension branding strategy instead of giving a new product a new brand name. The fact that corporate marketing activity impacted consumer evaluations of a corporate brand extension in the absence of any product-specific advertising is further empirical support for the benefit of adopting a brand extension strategy.

Fourth, the fact that corporate marketing activity significantly influenced extension evaluations even when the extension was advertised on the basis of another image dimension points to another advantage of corporate branding strategies. With a corporate branding strategy, associations created through corporate marketing permit freedom in introductory advertising campaigns to communicate other product information about the extension. That is, because corporate image associations are more likely to transfer to an extension on the basis of the branding strategy, an introductory advertising campaign for a corporate brand extension can concentrate on other dimensions of the extension product and communicate new information about its unique attributes or benefits. As a result, advertising can be more impactful because it can provide complementary rather than redundant information.

Finally, the findings also raise important issues about strategic emphasis. Many companies face tradeoffs in their brand strategies – specifically, whether to reinforce a strong association, strengthen a weak association, or create a new association. In some cases, existing associations may be so strong that they would not be responsive to marketing actions, and companies may be better off emphasizing other information to fortify a weak or supply a missing association. This research also points to the power of innovative corporate image associations. Such associations, by affecting perceptions of corporate credibility and fit, can boost a new product that is offered under the corporate brand name even if that product is beyond the company's current product scope.

Limitations and future research directions

The findings from this experiment were based on consumer responses after reading a description of a well-defined, hypothetical corporation and examining an ad on a forced-exposure basis for a new product it was planning to introduce. In reality, consumers' knowledge of, and impressions about, a company form and evolve as a result of countless exposures to and experiences with the products, communications, and reported actions of a company. Although certain associations with a company may be stronger as a result, others could be weaker, and, in general, the corporate image arising from corporate marketing activity may not be as well-defined as was the case here. Because certain associations making up the corporate images may not be as accessible as in the experimental setting, the effects of corporate marketing activity on corporate brand extension evaluations that were observed may be exaggerated when compared with more realistic stimuli and exposure conditions.

In this light, the lack of efficacy of corporate marketing demonstrating environmental concern and community involvement is noteworthy. It may be that these types of activities have more impact on consumer decisions with respect to existing products and brands than with new products or brand extensions. Certainly much corporate investment in these areas is based on the expectation that there will be a transfer of affect or 'goodwill' inducing consumers to do business with companies they most like and admire. Nevertheless, as numerous commercial studies indicate,[29] positive feelings towards environmentally friendly corporate actions do not necessarily translate into more favorable product decisions.

The circumstances by which perceptions of corporate trustworthiness and likability actually influence consumer decisions must be identified in terms of the types of products, consumers, and situations. For example, are the effects of corporate marketing activity designed to benefit the environment or community more likely to be manifested under decision settings characterized by lower involvement than was present in this study? Certainly the elaboration-likelihood model[30] would predict that likability and other such source perceptions should play a more important role in decision-making as a peripheral cue when consumers lack the motivation or ability to make brand evaluations. These and other possible moderating factors should be investigated in more detail.

In a broader sense, this study suggests that there are important research issues that remain in inter-relating corporate marketing activities, corporate images, and corporate brand extensions. In general, marketing managers need guidelines to help them understand how to define a corporate branding strategy that outlines when and how to use their corporate brand name. Managers also need guidelines for how to build and establish a corporate image and effectively manage corporate brands to improve the success and profitability of their marketing programs. A more thorough examination of the process by which corporate marketing activities exert their influence on consumers could help suggest conditions under which corporate image effects are more or less likely to operate. This study provides preliminary evidence for the mediating role of various corporate credibility dimensions and perceptions of the fit and attribute beliefs of the extension. Nevertheless, the effects of these and other mediating factors should be explored in more detail to better assess the causal mechanisms involved. Moreover, the effects of corporate images on other types of consumer decisions also should be explored.

Finally, to enhance the external validity of the study, it would be useful to replicate the study findings using a set of real corporate brands. Since this study involved only a limited number of product classes and a student sample, it would be useful to systematically explore these issues using a broader set of products classes and market segments.

Endnotes

(a)   Subjects came from two different course offerings, separated in time by about six months. Both data collection efforts involved random assignment to the 16 cells. Although there was no reason to suspect any possible contaminating effects from the intervening time, a check of the equality of the two samples was conducted. Specifically, ANOVA analyses for all dependent variables reported in the paper were conducted with all main and interaction effects of the corporate image and product positioning factors and a dummy variable for data collection period as independent variables. There were no statistically significant main effect or interaction terms for data collection period. Thus, the time lag between the two data collection periods did not appear to contaminate the results in any important way. Nevertheless, a dummy variable for data collection period was added as a covariate to all planned comparison analyses reported below.

(b)   The attribute beliefs were effective, convenient, soothing, and fast acting for Baron eye drops; effective, convenient, gentle, and strong protection for Profile sun block; fresh tasting, convenient, delicious, and easy to prepare for Medallion rice; and good tasting, convenient, delicious, and easy to prepare for Monarch salad dressing, rated on a seven point scale (1 = Not at all, 7 = Very).

(c)   All planned comparisons involved between subject comparisons because they always contrasted two cells with at least common corporate marketing activity or product positioning (and the Latin square design meant that subjects saw *each* type of corporate marketing activity and product positioning only once). Consequently, two-sided tests were employed that used the pooled mean square error from the overall ANOVA analysis (with 1 and 1002 d.f.), consistent with the guidelines by Keppel (pp. 428–432).[31] The only significant covariate in the analyses beside data collection period (see endnote a) was product category involvement which, in general, was positively associated with more favorable perceptions and evaluations.

(d)   To illustrate how Table 2 was calculated, the first entry, 1.12, results from subtracting the corporate expertise mean for the control corporate image and control product positioning (cell 16), 4.34, from the innovative corporate image and control product positioning (cell 4), 5.46.

(e)   To illustrate how Table 3 was calculated, the first entry, 0.82, results from subtracting the perceived extension fit mean for the control corporate image and control product positioning (cell 16), 4.12, from the innovative corporate image and control product positioning (cell 4), 4.94.

(f)   To illustrate how Table 4 was calculated, the first entry, 0.81, results from subtracting the perceived quality mean for the control corporate image and innovative product positioning (cell 13), 4.57, from the innovative corporate image and innovative product positioning (cell 1), 5.38.

References

(1)   Morris, B. (1996) 'The Brand's the Thing', *Fortune* (March 4), pp. 72–98.

(2)   Aaker, D. A. and Keller, K. L. (1990) 'Consumer Evaluations of Brand Extensions', *Journal of Marketing*, 54 (January), pp. 27–41.

(3)   Boush, D. M. and Loken, B. (1991) 'A Process Tracing Study of Brand Extension Evaluations', *Journal of Marketing Research*, 28 (February), pp. 16–28.

(4)   Broniarczyk, S. M. and Alba, J. W. (1994) 'The Importance of the Brand in Brand Extension', *Journal of Marketing Research*, 31 (May), pp. 214–228.

(5)   Barich, H. and Kotler, P. (1991) 'A Framework for Marketing Image Management', *Sloan Management Review*, 32(2), pp. 94–104.

(6)   Dowling, G. R. (1986) 'Managing Your Corporate Images', *Industrial Marketing Management*, 15 (May), pp. 109–115.

(7)   Schumann, D. W., Hathcote, J. M. and West, S. (1991) 'Corporate Advertising in America: A Review of Published Studies on Use, Measurement, and Effectiveness', *Journal of Advertising*, 20 (September), pp. 36–56.

(8)   Aaker, D. A. (1991) 'Managing Brand Equity', Free Press.

(9)   Farquhar, P. H. (1989) 'Managing Brand Equity', *Marketing Research*, 1 (September), pp. 24–33.

(10) Keller, K. L. (1993) 'Conceptualizing, Measuring, and Managing Brand Equity', *Journal of Marketing*, 57 (January), pp. 1–22.

(11) Keller, K. L. and Aaker, D. A. (1992) 'The Effects of Sequential Introduction of Brand Extensions', *Journal of Marketing Research*, 29 (February), pp. 35–50.

(12) Park, C. W., Milberg, S. and Lawson, R. (1991) 'Evaluation of Brand Extensions: The Role of Product Level Similarity and Brand Concept Consistency', *Journal of Consumer Research*, 18 (September), pp. 185–193.

(13) Aaker, D. A. (1996) 'Building Strong Brands', Free Press.

(14) Bridges, S. (1990) 'A Schema Unification Model of Brand Extensions', unpublished doctoral dissertation. Graduate School of Business, Stanford University.

(15) Hovland, C. I., Janis, I. L. and Kelley, H. (1953) 'Communication and Persuasion', Yale University Press, New Haven, CT.

(16) Ohanian, R. (1990), 'Construct and Validation of a Scale to Measure Celebrity Endorser's Perceived Expertise, Trustworthiness, and Attractiveness', *Journal of Advertising*, 19 (3), pp. 39–52.

(17) Sternthal, B., Phillips, L. W. and Dholakia, R. R. (1978) 'The Persuasive

Effect of Source Credibility: A Situational Analysis', *Public Opinion Quarterly*, 42, pp. 285–314.

(18) Goldberg, M. E. and Hartwick, J. (1990) 'The Effects of Advertiser Reputation and Extremity of Advertiser Claims on Advertising Effectiveness', *Journal of Consumer Research*, 17 (September), pp. 172–179.

(19) Craig, C. S. and McCann, J. M. (1978) 'Assessing Communication Effects on Energy Conservation', *Journal of Consumer Research*, 5 (September), pp. 82–88.

(20) MacKenzie, S. B. and Lutz, R. J. (1989), 'An Empirical Examination of the Structural Antecedents of Attitude Toward the Ad in an Advertising Pretest Context', *Journal of Marketing*, 53 (April), pp. 48–65.

(21) Sternthal, B. and Craig, C. S. (1982) 'Consumer Behavior', Prentice-Hall, Englewood Cliffs.

(22) Dagnoli, J. (1991) 'Consciously Green', *Advertising Age* (September 16), p. 14.

(23) Joseph, L. E. (1991) 'The Greening of American Business', *Vis a Vis* (May), p. 32.

(24) Lynch, J. G., Jr., Mamorstein, H. and Weigold, M. (1988) 'Choices from Sets Including Remembered Brands: Use of Recalled Attributes and Prior Overall Evaluations', *Journal of Consumer Research*, 15 (September), pp. 169–184.

(25) Wright, P. L. (1975) 'Consumer Choice Strategies: Simplifying vs. Optimizing', *Journal of Marketing Research*, 11 (February), pp. 60–67.

(26) Drumwright, M. E. (1996) 'Company Advertising with a Social Dimension: The Role of Noneconomic Criteria', *Journal of Marketing*, 60 (October), pp. 71–87.

(27) Brown, T. J. and Dacin, P. A. (1997) 'The Company and the Product: Corporate Associations and Consumer Product Responses', *Journal of Marketing*, 61 (January), pp. 68–84.

(28) Smith, D. C. and Park, C. W. (1992) 'The Effects of Brand Extensions on Market Share and Advertising Efficiency', *Journal of Marketing Research*, 29 (August), pp. 296–313.

(29) Manly, L. (1992), 'It Doesn't Pay to Go Green When Consumers Are Seeing Red', *Adweek* (March 23), pp. 32–33.

(30) Petty, R. E. and Cacioppo, J. T. (1986) 'Communication and Persuasion', Springer-Verlag, New York.

(31) Keppel, G. (1982) 'Design and Analysis: A Researchers Handbook', 2nd ed., Prentice-Hall, Englewood Cliffs, NJ.

Chapter 15

John M. T. Balmer

THE THREE VIRTUES AND SEVEN DEADLY SINS OF CORPORATE BRAND MANAGEMENT

From *Journal of General Management* 2001, 27 (1): 1–17

EDITORS' COMMENTARY

John M. T. Balmer, Professor of Corporate Identity at Bradford School of Management and coeditor of this anthology, is no stranger to the corporate branding concept. His initial inquiry into corporate brands is to be found in his article "Corporate Branding and Connoisseurship."[1] It is one of the earliest expositions on corporate brands and the precursor to the article included here. Both articles appeared in the *Journal of General Management* (*JGM*).

In his earlier article Balmer voiced the imperative of ongoing custodianship of corporate brands by senior managers. Although seemingly innocuous, this observation exemplified the seismic shift that was required in order to meet the demands of managing brands at the corporate level. For example, he noted that a multidisciplinary approach would be *de rigueur* in underpinning corporate brand management.

Of particular significance was the important role he accorded to personnel in corporate brand-building and continuance.

A characteristic of both Balmer's and King's articles is the failure to make a clear distinction between the concepts of corporate identity and the corporate (company) brand. The same tension is sometimes found in current articles on corporate branding where corporate branding is used as a surrogate for identity.

Balmer predicted that by the turn of the millennium, organizations would accord increasing importance to corporate brands. The advance of the concept would be inexorable. This prediction has come to fruition. Indeed, the corporate branding construct has entered the management lexicon with considerable speed and energy. The literature utterly mirrors this trend.[2]

Five years after "Corporate Branding and Connoisseurship" Balmer delivered a keynote address to a Confederation of British Industry (CBI) Seminar on Corporate Branding. Entitled "The Three Virtues and Seven Deadly Sins of Corporate Brand Management," the lecture appeared in print a year later as the lead article of the *JGM*. It is this article that is reproduced here.

Balmer observes what he sees as an indubitable truth: namely that a corporate brand may be a corporation's principal asset. A correlary premise is that an organization's success, perhaps even its survival, may well be dependent on the desirability, durability, dynamism and intrinsic worth of its corporate brand (or, indeed, corporate brands).

The chapter advances the general deliberation on corporate brands in at least four regards. The differences between corporate and product brands are elucidated. This is undertaken by discussing their: *B*enefits, *C*haracteristics, *D*ifferences, and *E*volution.

Benefits

Summed up by the following: C+D+E. As such, a corporate brand should

*C*ommunicate the corporate brand covenant;
*D*ifferentiate the brand from others;
*E*nhance the esteem (and loyalty) in which the brand (and organization) is held by key stakeholders.

This formula could be used to determine the salience of any corporate brand.

Characteristics

The characteristics of corporate brands are enumerated be making references to a quintet of attributes that form the acronym C^2ITE. They have *C*ultural roots, require total organizational *C*ommitment, they are multidimensional and multidisciplinary in scope and thus are *I*ntricate in nature; furthermore, they are experienced through *T*angible as well as *E*thereal dimensions.

Differences

Corporate brands differ from product brands in terms of management, responsibilities, disciplinary roots, focus, values, and supporting communications.

Evolution

The upshot of the above is that nothing short of a root and branch reform is required of branding when applied to corporate entities. Accordingly, the emerging theory relating to corporate branding represents an important stage in the evolutionary development of the branding concept.

Balmer observes that although corporate brands rarely appear on a balance sheet they are real assets all the same. They can be of inestimable value. However, they demand intense parenting and are vulnerable through all stages of their life cycle to serious and life-threatening illnesses as exemplified by his seven deadly sins of corporate brand management. Any failure with regard to the latter can be perilous for the brand, the organization, and senior management.

Two tenets suffuse this article and Balmer's approach to corporate brand management. The first is that corporate brands are invaluable. The second is that effective corporate brand maintenance necessitates total commitment to the corporate covenant. This should be made evident *over space* and *over time*, leading to *consistency in conviction, communication, and experience.*

NOTES

1   Balmer, J. M. T., "Corporate Branding and Connoisseurship," *Journal of General Management* Autumn 1995, 21 (1): 22–46.

2   Gregory, J. R., *Leveraging the Corporate Brand*, Lincolnwood, IL: NTC Business Books, 1997; Ind, N., "An Integrated Approach to Corporate Branding," *Journal of Brand Management* 1998, 6 (5): 323–329; Ind, N., *The Corporate Brand*, London: Macmillan, 1996; Harris, F. and de Chernatony, L., "Corporate Branding and Corporate Brand Performance, Special Edition on Corporate Identity and Corporate Marketing: *European Journal of Marketing* 2001, 35 (3/4): 441–456; Olins, W., "How Brands Are Taking Over the Corporation," in M. Schultz, M. J. Hatch, and H. L. Mogens (eds) *The Expressive Organization*, Oxford: Oxford University Press, 2000, pp. 51–65; Knox, S., Maklan, S., and Thompson, K. E., "Building the Unique Organization Value Proposition," In M. Schultz, M. J. Hatch, and H. L. Mogens (eds) *The Expressive Organization*, Oxford: Oxford University Press, 2000, pp. 138–156; Special Edition on Corporate and Services Brands: *European Journal of Marketing*, 2003, forthcoming.

The well-being, indeed survival, of many organizations rests on the success of their corporate brands.

IN AN ARTICLE ENTITLED 'Corporate Branding and Connoisseurship' [1] appearing in the *JGM* in 1995 it was argued that the new millennium will herald increased management interest in the corporate brand. Five years on, this prediction is coming to fruition. The recent media coverage accorded to the introduction of new, and exotic sounding, corporate brand names including Accenture (*Andersen Consulting*), Corus (*British Steel*), Consignia

(*The Post Office* in the UK), Innogy (*National Power*), Thales (*Thomson CSF*), and Uniq (*Unigate*) is one recent indicator of this trend. However, corporate brand names and systems of visual identification should be regarded as the trappings rather than the substance of corporate brands. What is clear is that the concept of the corporate brand has entered the management lexicon with a vengeance and is the focus of books, academic papers and conferences. A number of contemporary writers accord the area a good deal of attention [2], [3].

The virtues of strong, and favourable, global corporate brands are considerable: they differentiate organizations from their competitors; lead to the fostering of loyalty from a wide range of stakeholder groups and networks and accord leverage to an organization – particularly those operating in traditional or in mature consumer markets – as well as providing an aureole to new technology companies such as Microsoft and Intel.

There is evidence which demonstrates the benefits of a favourable corporate brand. Research undertaken by the British opinion research consultancy MORI among 166 corporate brand/corporate identity managers found that they viewed the benefits of a strong corporate brand in terms of increased (a) public profile, (b) customer attractiveness, (c) product support, (d) visual recognition, (e) investor confidence, (f) encapsulating organizational values, and (g) staff motivation [4].

It should be pointed out that the management, and maintenance, of the tangible and emotional benefits of a corporate brand differs from classic product brand management in several, crucially different, ways. First, everyone in the organization has responsibility for the corporate brand and its maintenance; it requires the constant attention of the chief executive and management board; it is inherently strategic in effect and, thus, should be a factor in the organization's strategic planning. Corporate brands need to meet the expectations of a whole range of internal and external stakeholders, stakeholder groups and networks, all of whom are crucial to an organization's success. Reinforcing, and maintaining, awareness of the functional and emotional values of the corporate brand is complicated. A corporate brand is made known, and experienced, through multiple channels of communication. Thus, senior managers need to focus on total corporate communications rather than on marketing communications. Corporate branding is multidisciplinary in scope and does not neatly fall within the remit of the traditional directorate of marketing. Lastly, and perhaps most importantly, the cornerstone of a corporate brand is the cluster of values held by personnel. These find expression in the organization's sub-cultures (see the second deadly sin, below). Figure 1 makes a comparison between corporate and product brands.

C²ITE: corporate brand characteristics

In enumerating the characteristics of a corporate brand it is possible to *cite* five elements: *C²ITE* stands as an acronym for the five distinctive attributes of corporate brands.

The following section provides a short overview of the five characteristics of corporate brands.

	Product brands	Corporate brands
Management	Middle manager	CEO
Responsibility	Middle manager	All personnel
Cognate discipline(s)	Marketing	Strategy/multidisciplinary
Communications mix	Marketing communications	Total corporate communications
Focus	Mainly customer	Multiple internal and external stakeholder groups and networks
Values	Mainly contrived	Those of founder(s) + mix of corporate + other sub-cultures

Figure 1 A comparison between corporate and product brands

(a)   *Cultural*: a corporate brand is a construct with 'cultural' roots. An organization's distinctiveness finds its source in the mix of sub-cultures found within it. Personnel may be regarded as an organization's key 'stakeholder group'. Personnel communicate an organization's uniqueness through everything they do, say or 'make'. HR departments need to appreciate their rôle in managing, maintaining and enhancing the corporate brand.

(b)   *Intricate*: a corporate brand is inherently intricate in nature, as evinced by the four other dimensions. The dimensions consist of a mix of 'soft' and 'hard' elements comprising a corporate brand. A corporate brand is multi-dimensional and multidisciplinary. It impacts upon many internal and external stakeholder groups and networks, transcending traditional organizational boundaries. Corporate brands are made known by 'controlled', 'uncontrolled', and by tertiary/word-of-mouth communications [5].

(c)   *Tangible*: a corporate brand encompasses tangible elements such as business-scope, geographical coverage, performance-related issues, profit margins, pay scales, recruitment, etc. It also includes elements such as architecture (buildings), and graphic-design-features such as interior design and logos, etc.

(d)   *Ethereal*: a corporate brand encapsulates a host of soft and subjective dimensions which evince an emotional response from stakeholders and stakeholder groups. These include the ethereal elements of the brand as well as the emotional response relating to country-of-origin and industry.

(e)   *Commitment*: there is, however, a crucially important element which, although implicit in what has thus far been mentioned, has not been articulated – commitment. An essential element of corporate branding is the need for *total organizational commitment*. Also, sight must not be lost of the fact that CEO and board-level commitment is a *sine qua non* of effective corporate brand management.

The management of a corporate brand is a far from easy task. Consider the case of Doug Ivester, the former Chairman of Coca-Cola. Under his leadership, this most coveted of corporate brands suffered a string of debacles. In effect, the brand came under attack from a barrage of criticisms and complaints from a variety of key stakeholder groups: there was the accusation of unfair competition in both Belgium and Italy; its planned acquisition of Cadbury-Schweppes was blocked by British, American and Mexican governments; and the French government blocked its acquisition of Orangina. Furthermore, the organization was accused of poisoning 200 children in France and Belgium. For all his undoubted management skills, Ivester was unable to steer Coca-Cola out of these difficulties. More unfortunately, he exacerbated the situation in several instances. For example, he travelled back to the USA from Europe at the start of the poison scare. This was badly received within France and Belgium. His frankness with the Brazilian press did little to endear him to customers in South America. The news that Coca-Cola was examining a technology that would enable its vending machines to raise prices in line with any increase in outside temperature is another case in point [6], [7].

What is apparent is that whilst Ivester was a conscientious corporate brand manager, it appears that he failed to share the burden of managing what may be regarded as the world's greatest corporate brand. Furthermore, he lacked the crucial communication skills which increasingly are *sine qua non* of an effective CEO and corporate brand manager. As such, he was unable to ameliorate the loss of confidence felt by a variety of key stakeholder groups including investors.

The seven deadly sins

This article marks a further advance in operationalizing the emergent theory of corporate brand management, and the related area of corporate identity management, by articulating seven questions, which need to be addressed by strategic planners on a more-or-less frequent basis. The writer envisions this as a corporate brand star. (See Figure 2.) A failure on the part of senior management to address any one of the seven questions may, to draw on catholic theology, result in corporate death. A failure to manage a corporate brand properly is mortal rather than venial in degree. The seven deadly sins of corporate brand management posited are failure to:

- understand the company's business;
- understand the company's cultures;
- understand the company's identity;
- understand the company's structure/architecture;
- understand the importance of total corporate communication;
- understand the corporate brand image and reputation;
- understand the impact of environmental forces.

It is essential, of course, that senior managers should demonstrate adroitness

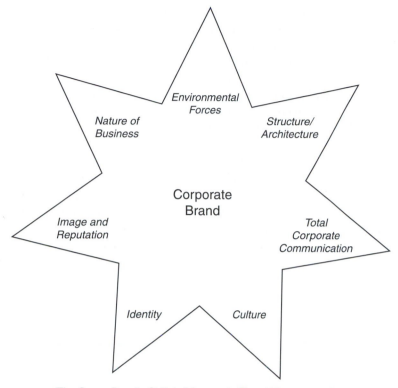

'The Seven Deadly Skills' of Corporate Brand Management

Figure 2 The corporate brand star

in the fiduciary concerns of the organization and should place the wants and needs of customers at the heart of their concerns.

This article argues that a corporate brand demands intense parenting. It has a long gestation. It is demanding of time and resources and is vulnerable, throughout all stages of its life cycle, to serious and life-threatening illnesses.

First deadly sin: 'a failure to understand the company's business'

This deceptively simple, but nonetheless fundamental, issue which Peter Drucker [8] has championed is one that needs to exercise the minds of senior management on a regular basis. Addressing this question should be regarded as one of the most taxing but crucially important tasks confronting strategic planners and would-be connoisseurs of corporate brand management.

A failure to appreciate the nature of any business will, inevitably, sow the seeds of terminal decline. However, a successful resolution of this question provides senior managers with a platform upon which they can address a whole palette of corporate branding concerns such as organizational structure, finance, marketing and human resources. The quintessence of a company's business should draw on the cerebral prowess of the chief executive and management board as well as those managing individual directorates. All of the afore-mentioned should be charged with having responsibility for the corporate brand and this should complement their functional mandate. Addressing the question, 'What is our business', is anything but straightforward.

> Actually, 'what is our business' is almost always a difficult question which can be answered only after hard thinking and studying and the right answer is anything but obvious.
>
> (Peter Drucker [9])

Peter Drucker's celebrated dictum has lost none of its resonance even after the passing of 40 years. Drucker takes no hostages *vis-à-vis* senior management's duty to tackle this issue. He insists that addressing this question is the most pressing task of senior management, and that the ability to tackle it should be a pre-requisite for an individual's appointment to the management board. Indeed, this author would argue that incompetence in this arena is legitimate reason enough to remove an individual from holding high corporate office.

But the last half-century is replete with examples of failure on the part of senior management to answer this question. The US railways and Hollywood are two classic examples of this failure. The former failed to realize it was in the transport business, whilst the latter failed to notice that it was in the entertainment business. There are more recent examples.

Consider Saatchi and Saatchi which, in its heyday, grew to become the world's largest advertising agency. Saatchi's phenomenal growth during the 1970s and 1980s utilized the agency's latent creative prowess, which it deployed in a corporate environment which had acquired an insatiable appetite for global marketing communications campaigns. By the 1990s, the company had unwittingly manoeuvred itself on to a precipice and faced the real prospect of bankruptcy. Saatchi's spectacular decline may be attributed, in part, to a failure to manage its corporate brand, and, in particular, there was a lack of perspicacity on the part of senior management in addressing the nature of the Saatchi and Saatchi business. The company's insatiable thirst for expansion led to the agency acquiring consulting companies. The effect of this approach was that Saatchi and Saatchi cannibalized the equity that was inherent in its corporate brand. It has been observed that this expansion resulted in a lack of synergy across its activities. The reputation for innovation, which was a key feature of Saatchi and Saatchi's core business, was not a salient attribute of its consultancy activities. Furthermore, the imposition of a financial control system, common throughout its newly acquired consultancy businesses, had a deleterious effect on its advertising activities [10].

More recently, two UK based companies have undertaken a radical reappraisal of their business activites. Bass, although having a corporate brand name which, at least among the British general public, is redolent of that organization's roots in the brewing industry, plans to divest its brewing concerns and concentrate on its hotel and leisure activities. For its part, P&O plans to sell off its cruise business and concentrate on its ports, ferries and logistics concerns. What seems certain is that both organizations will keep the question of 'What is the company's business?' at the forefront of their strategic deliberations.

Second deadly sin: 'a failure to understand the company's cultures'

Arguably, the most pressing task of managers is to instil a sense of pride among personnel, and a feeling of commitment in the organization and its brand. However, failure on the part of senior management to accord due diligence in understanding an organization's *mix* of corporate sub-cultures will almost certainly have a deleterious effect on the above and, over time, with the equity associated with a corporate brand. Recent research undertaken with the BBC and a major UK high street bank found that the notion of a single company culture was largely a myth: it was more appropriate to speak of an organization's cultures and identities [11].

Contemporary writers on corporate brand management emphasize the importance of personnel and of an organization's mix of sub-cultures in the underpinning of world-class corporate brands. The implications of this are profound. This is because human resources managers should occupy a position of pivotal importance in supporting the corporate brand. Waterstones, a leading UK retail book shop, had recognized the efficacy of this approach; they regard recruitment as an integral component of corporate brand management [12].

Recent research undertaken by human resource scholars from Oxford and Sheffield Universities found that company culture(s) is a useful guide *vis-à-vis* company performance. The researchers found that company profits can be enhanced by 10 per cent as a direct result of cultural factors [13]. Another study supported the saliency of culture in the underpinning of successful global corporate brands [14].

What is implicit in the above observation is that senior managers who accord a high degree of importance to corporate culture are more likely to attract, and retain, personnel.

The Dutch electronics company Philips is a case of an organization where, in the past, senior managers only paid lip service to their corporate culture and, as a consequence, undermined the leadership rôle of their corporate brand. The ethos at Philips placed great store on technological prowess and on rational technological considerations. However, undue attention was accorded to customers' concerns. As a consequence, other corporate brands with a focus on service quality and performance have eclipsed Philips' primacy.

Third deadly sin: 'a failure to understand the company's identity'

Corporate identity provides the grit around which the pearl of a corporate brand is formed.

The myriad of elements forming the corporate identity mix play a pivotal part in imbuing unique tangible and emotional qualities to a corporate brand. The author's definition *vis-à-vis* the characteristics of an organization's identity is as follows:

> An organization's identity is a summation of those tangible and intangible elements which make any corporate entity distinct. It is shaped not only by the actions of corporate founders and leaders, by tradition and the environment, but also by the mix of employee values and affinities to corporate, professional, national and other identities. It is multidisciplinary in scope and is melding of strategy, structure, communication and culture. It is made manifest through multifarious communication channels and encapsulates product and organizational performance, controlled communication and stakeholder and network discourse.

Clearly, there is a considerable overlap between an organization's identity and its corporate brand. The relationship between the two will be briefly outlined in the final part of this article in the author's definition of a corporate brand.

In exploring the concept a little further, reference can be made to the small, old established English brewery of Shepherd Neame. The brewery has distinct identity attributes which make its corporate brand unique.

It is the sole surviving independent brewery in Kent and is family owned. Five successive generations of the Neame family have managed the company and, significantly, Shepherd Neame brews ale using traditional methods. More crucially, the vast majority of its 360 inns are managed by its tenants rather than by company managers. The latter accords particular distinctiveness to the Shepherd Neame identity and imbues its corporate brand with emotional and tangible attributes which are difficult to emulate.

Another example is the UK's largest friendly society, Liverpool Victoria, which has, over recent years, been beset by a string of *faux pas*. Financial commentators attribute the corporate brand's difficulties to the failure to nurture its core identity. This has led to a chronic loss of direction. The Liverpool Victoria belongs to the dwindling group of institutions which have mutual status, whereby their owners are those who use the institution's services and who are regarded as members rather than shareholders. As such, profits are ploughed back into the organization for the good of its present and future members. Thus, the organization's espoused identity is philanthropic. The reality of Liverpool Victoria, as recent events have shown, is somewhat different. The cause of the society's malaise rests with its acquisition of the Frizell insurance company. This introduced an alien ethos and culture to the society. The sharp practices used by Frizell's commission-seeking salesman sat uncomfortably with the society's benevolent raison d'être. Unsurprisingly, the society received a sharp rebuke and a huge fine from the British regulatory authority covering financial institutions. More wounding, however, was a loosening of the trust between the Liverpool Victoria and its members and its failure to meet the probity and decency demanded of its heritage as a mutual institution. Liverpool Victoria's malaise is a direct result of a failure to appreciate its identity, which draws on strong philanthropic roots.

Fourth deadly sin: 'a failure to understand the company's structure/architecture'

Management psychosis *vis-à-vis* an organization's architecture (structure) can also play a rôle in weakening the corporate brand. The oft quoted dictum that structure follows strategy may be extended by stating that branding follows structure and strategy. In addition, the author argues that reversing the whole cycle may reveal important insights.

An example of a company which undermined its company brand by failing to foresee the inextricable link between strategy, structure and corporate branding was GKN – a UK component manufacturer. Its strategy of dominating competition in its markets through acquisition seemed eminently sensible.

However, the failure on the part of senior management to anticipate the structural implications of this initiative and its effect on the corporate brand became apparent all too soon. The lack of central co-ordination by the parent company meant that the newly acquired companies were, *de facto*, cannibalizing the organization's core business. As such, this led to an undermining rather than an enhancing of the corporate brand.

This case may be contrasted with the huge global food behemoth Nestlé. Nestlé's senior managers are assiduous in the attention they accord to Nestlé's corporate structure, umbrella corporate brand, subsidiary corporate brands and its 140 product brands. Thus, whilst Nestlé marshals the immense power of the umbrella corporate brand in many of its activities, its eight strategic business units have considerable autonomy in terms of managing brands in their local markets and this allows them to respond to changes in the environment in different regions of the world. The multifarious relationship between Nestlé's head office and its business units and product brands accommodates the vagaries of local markets whilst drawing on the equity of the umbrella of a corporate brand. This policy has reaped rich rewards for Nestlé in terms of growth, profits and enhanced corporate brand power.

Lazards, the eminent corporate advisory partnership with a venerable corporate brand name which enables it to punch above its weight, has recently decided, all the same, that a rationalization of its byzantine operating structure was a necessary step to support the enviable reputation associated with its corporate brand name.

For its part, one of the biggest names in California's silicon valley, Hewlett-Packard, has concluded that it not only needs to restructure its business architecture but can, through this means, capitalize on its strength by launching a new corporate brand which will embrace its manufacture and test-marketing of equipment. Other American leviathans have also enhanced corporate brand leverage through restructuring. A case in point is AT&T which split up its business to form three companies – AT&T, Lucent, and NCR.

Fifth deadly sin: 'a failure to understand the importance of total corporate communication'

One trap confronting senior managers in managing their corporate brand is a failure to make a distinction between marketing communications and total corporate communications (TCC). Marketing communication is, for the main, aimed at customers and marshals the marketing communication mix of advertising, sales-promotion, direct-marketing, and packaging. The aim is to deliver a consistent message and create an effective 'positioning' for the brand. The task is inherently more complicated with regard to corporate brands.

This is because (a) the corporate brand can be of interest to a wider palette of stakeholders with their attendant networks, and (b) there are more channels of communication involved. At the corporate level, organizations need to have a dialogue with a wide range of stakeholders: investors, personnel, suppliers, alliance-partners, governments, the media, local communities and the industry. The task is made more complicated by the fact that individuals invariably belong to several of the stakeholder groups mentioned above and will belong to discrete and not-too-discrete networks. Many, of course, will be customers.

As Shell have noted:

> We cannot be accountable solely to shareholders or customers. Our business touches too many lives for us to evade our wider role in society. We must communicate our values and demonstrate that we live up to them in our business practices [15].

Total corporate communications may be broken into three categories: primary; secondary; and tertiary [16].

Primary communication refers to the messages emitted *vis-à-vis* the behaviour of company products, managers and staff, and company policies. Secondary communication pertains to 'controlled' communication, which encompasses marketing communications, corporate advertising and promotion. Tertiary communication relates to word-of-mouth between a company's stakeholder groups and networks.

There is another dimension to total corporate communications, namely the need for congruency – in relation to vertical communications (through multiple channels) and horizontal communications (congruent over time).

Consider Audi, the premium corporate brand of Germany's Volkswagen group: it provides a lesson in terms of the communications effects of primary communication. Five, fatal incidents involving Audi's TT Coupé undermined the corporate brand's reputation, and, more tellingly, adversely affected Volkswagen profits by an estimated $75.1m [17].

Another example is Marks and Spencer, the venerable *grande dame* of the British high street. M & S is licking its wounds after a catastrophic decline in sales and a boardroom *coup d'état*. It has recently announced that it is embarking on a corporate communications campaign. The Marks and Spencer corporate brand traditionally enjoyed immense esteem among the British public, yet, somewhat belatedly, senior management at M & S realized its over-reliance on its reputation and that what they perceived as unswerving customer loyalty might not be enough to weather the current storm engulfing the M & S corporate brand.

Traditionally, M & S has eschewed corporate and marketing communications. This approach is evinced by that fact that M & S's former chairman barred anyone other than himself from speaking to the media. The malaise underpinning the M & S brand has resulted in the marshalling of total corporate communication as a key ingredient in its strategy for (a) revitalizing its flagging corporate brand, and (b) countering inaccurate perceptions. M & S's new head of marketing remarked that in a world in which there is a cacophony of sound, whispering about M & S's activities was no longer deemed to be apposite. He concluded that unless M & S communicated to its key stakeholders it deserved what would happen to it.

Sixth deadly sin: 'a failure to understand corporate brand image and reputation'

The concepts of corporate image and corporate reputation are of importance to the notion of the corporate brand. These are the means by which a company is positioned in the mind of key stakeholders. Indeed, the whole notion of the corporate brand may be regarded as a closely related concept to that of the corporate image and corporate reputation. All three concepts are built on perceptions held of the organization by individuals and stakeholder groups. However, corporate brand image and reputation draws on the ethereal as well as tangible attributes assigned to the organization. By such means, a corporate brand instils a company with distinctiveness and equity. These corporate brand attributes are inferred to an organization by its diverse stakeholder groups, and the corporate brand reputation can act as a powerful standard by which an organization's decisions, activities and behaviour are evaluated. As such, the corporate brand's attributes can be used as a benchmark by which an individual and company's behaviour and activities are evaluated utilizing the so-called D.E.A.R. [18] approach – Decisions, Evaluated, Against, the Reputation of the corporate brand's complex, cultural, ethereal and tangible attributes.

A case in point is the British Broadcasting Corporation (BBC), an organization which regularly undertakes research into the perception of its global brand. One of the most high profile arms of the Corporation is the BBC World Service. The latter may be regarded as a semi-autonomous corporate brand.

Research undertaken by the World Service revealed there to be considerable confusion as to the quintessential nature of the World Service brand. Part of the problem was attributed to the lack of consensus among senior managers as to the core corporate brand values of the radio service and, as such, contradictory and mutually cancelling messages were being emoted by senior managers. Not surprisingly, the BBC has embarked on a clearer corporate positioning and communication strategy for this service.

The importance of perception cannot be overstated. Research undertaken by Robert Worcester at MORI has, over the years, shown a strong correlation between favourability and familiarity [19], [20].

Seventh deadly sin: 'a failure to understand the impact of environmental forces'

The acquisition, and maintenance, of a favourable corporate brand reputation means that it is incumbent on strategic planners to take cognisance of environmental forces. This reflects a point made by the authors of *Built to Last* [21]. Environmental forces are particularly germane to the health of a corporate brand where organizations have accrued a reputation which is closely aligned to a particular technology, product or service category. It is the task of senior management to anticipate the symptoms of terminal decline and, where feasible, to marshal the corporate brand reputation, particularly its emotional equity, as a means of transferring to new areas of activity.

Olivetti is an example of an Italian corporate brand which became too closely aligned to the manufacture of typewriters. Senior managers failed to anticipate the revolution that was to occur in computing technology. The same is true of the shipping company Cunard, which steadfastly positioned itself as a small, exclusive, ocean cruising concern. Senior managers failed to capitalize on the huge upturn in popularity in cruises which has occurred over the last decade. Ocean cruising is no longer the preserve of the well-heeled but has become popular with a much larger public.

In contrast, the Miami-based Knight-Ridder is an example of a corporate brand which has seized the opportunities presented by changes in the environment. The migration of 250,000 Cubans to Florida and the advent of new technologies has resulted in Knight-Ridder launching a daily newspaper in Spanish, an on-line view service and a pay channel. This is quite a departure for an organization which, at the turn of the 20th Century, had as its main focus the publication of *The Miami Herald*.

Environmental forces have also conspired to form a new category of the corporate brand: that of the global alliance. Of particular interest are the alliances emerging in the airline sector: the two major players being the Oneworld Alliance centred on the British Airways/American Airways axis and the Star Alliance whose main partners are United Airlines and Lufthansa. Senior managers in the airline business have concluded that the endorsement of a global alliance brand with ethereal and tangible brand attributes will, over time, have the potential to bolster the strength of individual corporate brands.

CDE: the three virtues and the cornerstone of corporate brands

At this juncture, the defining characteristics of a corporate brand and its relationship to corporate identity may be explained as follows:

> A corporate brand involves, in most instances, the conscious decision by senior management to distil, and make known, the attributes of the organization's identity in the form of a clearly defined branding proposition. This proposition underpins organizational efforts to communicate, differentiate, and enhance the brand *vis-à-vis*

stakeholder groups and networks. The proposition may be viewed as the organization's covenant with its customers, stakeholder groups and networks. As such, a corporate brand proposition requires total corporate commitment from all levels of personnel. It particularly requires CEO and senior management fealty as well as financial support.

Whilst the management of a corporate brand is complex and is fraught with difficulties, there is, on the positive side, the promise of securing a long-term competitive position in an organization's market or markets.

This is the major reason why the acquisition of a corporate brand is such a coveted strategic objective. The author has identified three virtues which can be assigned to successful corporate brands. This framework may be used on a template for evaluating the saliency of a corporate brand. Thus, a corporate brand should:

Communicate; differentiate, and enhance.

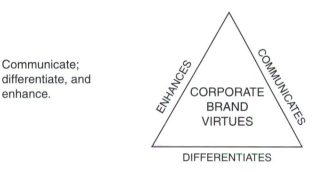

Figure 3 outlines the three virtues of corporate brands in more detail. Referring back to Coca-Cola's Ivester, it becomes clear that if his focus had been on these three elements he might have been able to limit the damage inflicted on the brand. The same would also apply to Ayling, British Airway's former Chief Executive, whose repositioning of that airline's brand failed to win the support of staff and of British business travellers.

The three virtues may be used as a template for evaluating the saliency of whatever hue of the corporate brand is relevant.

C+	*Communicates* clearly and consistently the promise which is intrinsic to the corporate brand.
D+	*Differentiates* the corporate brand from that of its competitors.
E	*Enhances* the esteem and loyalty in which the organization is held by its customers as well as by stakeholder groups and networks.

Figure 3 Corporate brands: the three virtues (C+D+E)

Commitment: the cornerstone of corporate brand management

There is, however, a crucially important element which cannot be over-emphasized: total organizational commitment. In addition, CEO and board level commitment should be seen as a prerequisite for the effective management of a corporate brand. In order to assist senior general managers with this task, the author posits six questions which managers can use in auditing their commitment to their corporate brand or brands (subsidiary brands for example).

The six questions are as follows:

(a)   is it strategically managed?
(b)   is its *raison d'être* made explicit?
(c)   does rhetoric mirror behaviour?
(d)   is there adequate, on-going financial support?
(e)   is pride instilled among personnel?
(f)   is there congruent communication which is both vertical (through multiple channels) and horizontal (congruent over time)?

Conclusions

In an era when it is becoming increasingly difficult to sustain a competitive advantage, strategic planners are realizing that a strong and favourable corporate brand can be a powerful weapon in their armoury. The $84bn valuation placed on the Coca-Cola brand and of another fifty-nine brands with a minimum $1bn price tag is indicative of this trend [22]. Another indicator is the annual survey of the USA's most revered corporate brands dating back to 1990. Conducted by Corporate Branding, a consulting firm based in Stamford, Connecticut, this elicits the opinions of 8,000 executives in relation to 575 corporate brands. Their recent survey reveals basic tenets underpinning corporate brand management with consumers and investors having limited 'brand-width'. In other words, there is a finite number of corporate brands which can be accommodated. Corporate Brand's Managing Director commented that some organizations are neglecting or mishandling communications campaigns [23]. The efficacy of effective corporate identity and corporate brand management is far from *de novo*. The following is, ironically, taken from an annual report by Philips, from the 1970s – an organization which has, in recent years, experienced a decline in its corporate brand power:

> In this age of technology and competition, the buying public is being increasingly faced with a wide choice of similar designs and features within each price range for all kinds of products. It is clear that when there are no obvious differences in price, quality design and features, the purchase decision may increasingly be influenced by a positive reputation of the brand and of the manufacturer. [24]

If anything, the above quotation has a greater saliency and resonance with the passing of over two decades. The author concurs with the doyen of the European corporate branding and identity industry, Wally Olins, in his observation that corporate brands are clearly emerging as the company's unique asset [25]. However, the old, moribund ways of conceptualizing brands require nothing less than root and branch reform. The issue of corporate brand management is indicative of the radical shift that will be required of organizations. In conclusion, the author addresses two questions, namely '*What are the skills required of corporate brand managers?*' and '*Who is the organization's corporate brand manager?*'

With regard to the former question, the author predicts that two types of corporate brand manager will emerge. Both will be versed in the art of corporate brand management. For their part, talented corporate brand managers will reveal their astuteness by circumventing the seven pitfalls outlined in this article. Cognoscenti of the art will, in contrast, demonstrate not only that they possess considerable cerebral prowess, perspicacity, creativity and élan but that they are catholic in their organizational expertise and perspective. Moreover, they will deploy what may be appropriately called the seven deadly skills of corporate brand management to particular, if not to dramatic, effect. Who is an organization's corporate brand manager? It is none other than the organization's chief executive. This was a point made in the *JGM* article 'Corporate Branding and Connoisseurship' in 1995 [26]. This *sine qua non* of corporate branding is ignored by organizations at their peril. As this article has illustrated, the well-being, indeed survival, of many organizations may well rest on the success of their corporate brand.

References

[1] Balmer, J. M. T., 'Corporate Branding and Connoisseurship', *Journal of General Management*, Vol. 21, No. 1, Autumn, 1995, pp. 22–46.

[2] *Ibid*.

[3] de Chernatony, L., 'Brand Management through Narrowing the Gap between Brand Identity and Brand Reputation', *Journal of Marketing Management*, Vol. 15, No. 1–3, 1999, pp. 157–179.

[4] Lewis, S., 'Let's Get This in Perspective', unpublished presentation given at the *Confederation of British Industry Branding and Brand Identity Seminar*, University of Bradford Management Centre, Bradford, England, 24 February, 2000.

[5] Balmer, J. M. T. and Gray, E. R., 'Corporate Identity and Corporate Communications: Creating a Competitive Advantage', *Corporate Communications: An International Journal*, Vol. 4, No. 4, 1999, pp. 695–702.

[6] McKay, B., Deogun, N. and Lublin, J. S., 'How Coke's Ivester Blurred the Image of a Global Icon', *Wall Street Journal (Europe)*, 18–19 December, 1999, p. 1 and p. 9.

[7] Wright, R., 'Ice-Cold Times for Icon', *Independent on Sunday*, 30 January, 2000, p. 27.

[8] Drucker, P., *The Practice of Management*, Oxford: Butterworth, Heinemann, 1955.

[9] *Ibid.*, p. 46.
[10] Collis, D. J. and Montgomery, D. J., 'Creating Corporate Advantage', *Harvard Business Review*, May–June, 1998, pp. 70–83.
[11] Balmer, J. M. T. and Wilson, A., 'Corporate Identity: It is More than Meets the Eye', *International Studies of Management and Organizations*, Vol. 28, No. 3, 1998, pp. 12–31.
[12] Ind, N., *The Corporate Brand*, Basingstoke: Macmillan, 1997.
[13] Coyle, D., 'There's Profit in Empowerment of Your People', *Independent*, 3 March, 1999, p. 4.
[14] Hankinson, P. and Hankinson, G., 'Managing Successful Brands: An Empirical Study which Compares the Corporate Cultures of Companies Managing the World's Top 110 Brands with those Managing Outsider Brands', *Journal of Marketing Management*, Vol. 15, No. 1–3, 1999, pp. 135–155.
[15] Lewis, S., *op. cit.*, 2000.
[16] Balmer, J. M. T. and Gray, E. R., *op. cit.*, 1999.
[17] Harnishfeger, U., 'Audi Suffers Damaged Image', *Financial Times*, 7 February, 2000, p. 27.
[18] Balmer, J. M. T., 'Corporate Identity and the Advent of Corporate Marketing', *Journal of Marketing Management*, Vol. 14, 1998, pp. 963–996.
[19] Worcester, R. M., 'Corporate Image', in Worcester, R. M. and Downham, J. (Eds), *Consumer Market Research Handbook*, London: McGraw-Hill, 1986, pp. 601–666.
[20] Worcester, R. M., 'Managing the Image of your Bank: The Glue that Binds', *International Journal of Bank Marketing: Special Edition on Corporate Identity in Financial Services*, Vol. 15, No. 5, 1997, pp. 146–152.
[21] Collins, J. C. and Porras, J. I., *Built to Last*, London: Century, 1996.
[22] 'The $1bn Brands', *Survey by Interbrand Branding Consultancy*, London, June, 1999.
[23] Alsop, R., 'Big US Companies Lose Brand Power, According to Survey', *Wall Street Journal (Europe)*, 22 March, 2000, p. 28.
[24] Quoted in Kennedy, S. H., 'Nurturing Corporate Images: Total Communications or Ego Trip?', *European Journal of Marketing*, Vol. 11, No. 1, 1977, pp. 120–164.
[25] Olins, W., 'How Brands are Taking Over the Corporation', in Schultz, M., Hatch, M. J. and Larsen, M., *The Expressive Organization*, Oxford: Oxford University Press, 2000, p. 65.
[26] Balmer, J. M. T., *op. cit.*, 1995.

Note

This article is based on unpublished papers delivered by the author at a *Confederation of British Industry Seminar on Corporate Branding* on 24 February, 2000 and at the *7th International Corporate Identity Symposium* held on 9 and 10 November, 2000. Both were held at Bradford School of Management, UK.

Case Study: Bank One – "The Uncommon Partnership"

Ab uno disce omnes
("From one example learn about all")

SECTION SIX

Case Study: Bank One – "The
Uncommon Partnership"

BANK ONE: "THE UNCOMMON PARTNERSHIP"

THIS CASE STUDY ADDRESSES a significant brand identity situation in a major US financial services entity, Bank One. It provides insight into the development of the company's brand identity strategy over several decades, the changes that took place over time, and the implementation issues associated with the strategy. These introductory comments offer an overview of the case and its primary elements, a set of study questions to guide consideration of the case, and a description of some key issues involved.

Note that this case study is not a complete case "history," in that the information included is intended to focus on the principal topic of the case – here, branding and identity.

Overview

This case chronicles the thirty-year evolution of Bank One's business strategy of growth through acquisition, and the resulting branding issues encountered by the need to re-brand the acquired existing entities.

The case begins in 1968, at the start of the newly formed First Banc (with a "c") Group of Ohio, Inc. – a holding company created by the McCoy family in order to acquire other small banks in the state of Ohio. The banks were to be renamed "Bank One" (with a "k"). The case continues through the next thirty years of growth, marketing innovations, and expansion to many states beyond its Ohio base. This period of growth and change produced numerous challenges to the company's identity.

The principal focus of the case is on the major branding obstacles associated with Bank One's merger with First Chicago NBD, a very large commercial bank. First Chicago NBD represented the first major *commercial* bank to become a member of the Bank One family of dominantly *retail* banks. Issues encompass whether the First Chicago NBD name should be changed to Bank One, as had been done for all previous retail bank acquisitions over the years, or its name retained, using only the endorsement "A Bank One Company."

Further complicating the situation is a major Bank One brand development initiative intended to implement the Bank One brand identity in new ways for all Bank One entities. Consequently, readers must address the relationship between Bank One's corporate strategy and its brand identity, as well as understand and critique the process of brand development over the years.

The case provides an opportunity to follow the process used by a company at the time of critical changes in its identity and positioning in the marketplace. Hence, it is important to understand the several changes in Bank One's identity over the years. This understanding encompasses what the company did, why it was done, how it was done, and what occasioned the next changes. It is also essential to confront the differences between First Chicago NBD and prior Bank One "retail banking acquisitions." Readers also have the opportunity to examine the detailed process of institutionalizing a brand identity.

The case includes extracts from Bank One's "Toolkit," which provide substantial insight into the company's brand identity system. This illuminates what a "brand position" can be, both for a financial services firm and – more broadly – for any company.

Study questions

Below are ten suggested study questions intended to guide the consideration of this case. These questions offer a mix of more strategically oriented brand issues as well as those addressed to the process and implementation of a branding system.

1 Over a period of years, Bank One altered its identity several times. For each change in identity:
   ● What did the company do?
   ● Why did it do it?
   ● How did it do it?
   ● Why did it make the next change?

   Both strategic factors and issues of effectiveness should be considered. The "publics" (i.e., "audiences" or stakeholders) for the identity changes should be identified. Also, refer to the "multiple identities" concept in Section One. What misalignments, if any, characterized Bank One's identity evolution?

   Key changes over the years included:
   ● Renaming City National Bank "Bank One."
   ● First Banc Group of Ohio becomes "Banc One."
   ● 1979 – move to consolidate names of all affiliates to "Bank One."
   ● Review Exhibit 2, "List of acquisitions and dates."
   ● Creation of "The Uncommon Partnership" in 1978.
   ● Demise of "The Uncommon Partnership" in 1995; a strategic shift to a "national financial services company."
   ● 1980s – Retail-oriented marketing innovations, product line expansion, electronic banking innovations, and geographic expansion.
   ● 1996 – Standardization and centralization as a "retailer" of financial services.
   ● 1998 – Bank One merger with First Chicago NBD – "commercial vis-à-vis retail positioning."
   ● 1999 – "What we stand for" statement emphasizes a brand position from a consumer perspective.

2 The McCoy family created a holding company to buy established, profitable, well-known local Ohio banks. In 1979 John G. McCoy decided to create a new monolithic identity for all the banks under the master brand "Bank One." The stated purpose was to identify the banks more clearly to investors. What are the pros and cons (risks) of changing a familiar and trusted name?

3 Because of early technicalities in Ohio banking regulations, the holding com-

pany was called Banc One and the banks were called Bank One. Does this seem sensible to you?

4   What was the "Uncommon Partnership" strategy? How well did it work initially? Why? How well did it work in the longer term? Why?

5   How applicable is the "What We Stand For" statement (p. 340) to Bank One after the merger with First Chicago NBD?

6   What was the purpose of the Toolkit? From the description of its contents, how do you think it facilitated/impeded institutionalizing the brand? (*Note*: The "Toolkit" provided primarily technical detail regarding the visual presentation of the brand. Readers should consider the effectiveness of this approach to an audience largely consisting of nondesign employees. How effective is technical detail for this audience?)

7   Brad Iversen makes it very clear he believed that branding and advertising are two different things. Do you agree or disagree? Why?

8   Bank One approached the process of developing a brand as a "marathon," not a "sprint." What are your reactions to Bank One's approach?

9   On the basis of this case (and your own experiences), what factors make identity consolidation easier vs. more difficult?

10   In light of numerous bank mergers in recent years, how relevant is it to spend a great deal of time, energy, and resources on developing a strong bank brand?

Two interesting overview questions are: "How important is a strong bank brand if your bank's business strategy is based upon growth through acquisition?" and "How important is a strong bank brand if your bank's goal is to be acquired?"

Some key issues

A major issue in the case is the challenges of implementation for Bank One's branding approach created by the merger with First Chicago NBD. These challenges represent a major fork in the road for Bank One: different market sectors, retail vis-à-vis commercial banking; different corporate cultures; relative importance of branding to each company; and relationships with customers. A key question for consideration is "What is Bank One just before this merger?"

Separately, it is essential to return to 1968 and address the evolution of the Bank One brand as a core component of the company's basic business strategy.

Chapter 16

Peter L. Phillips and Stephen A. Greyser

BANK ONE

"THE UNCOMMON PARTNERSHIP"

Design Management Institute Case Study, 2001

"**I**F LOU GRANT COULD only see me now!" Mason Adams said as he stepped onto the rooftop of the 24-story Columbus Center, the headquarters of Banc One Corporation. It was October 1979. Adams was there to begin filming a new series of Bank One TV spots. As reported by Johanna M. White, Marketing Administrator of Banc One Corporation, the Friday night filming ran well into early Saturday morning as the 40-degree weather and high winds continued throughout the filming. "The site for the announcement of our name change spot was selected to dramatize the moment of change," explained John A. Russell, at that time Bank One Vice President and Director of Marketing.

Mason Adams, more popularly recognizable as Ed Asner's boss on the *Lou Grant Show*, had been selected as spokesman for City National Bank, renamed Bank One, and all of the corporation's affiliate banks in Ohio. "We'll look back on October 22, 1979, the first day for our use of our unified identification, as a very important event in the history of our holding company and our affiliate banks," Adams said in his special filmed message to all associates of Bank One. Adams had been engaged by Bank One as a spokesperson only for the campaign announcing the new name.

The first edition (Vol. 1 No. 1) of the *BANK ONE Wire*, the corporation's employee newsletter, explained the change in identity.

"October 22, 1979 was the day when a new name took its place on the Columbus skyline and on the main streets in cities and towns across Ohio.

This case was prepared by Peter L. Phillips, at the Design Management Institute, in collaboration with Stephen A. Greyser, Harvard Business School, as a basis for class discussion rather than to illustrate either effective or ineffective handling of an administrative situation.

Although the people, their work, and the buildings from which they serve their customers remain the same, familiar names like City National Bank, Farmers Savings and Trust Company, Security Central, or Coshocton National Bank are no more. In their place a new name will grace the building signs and appear across checks, deposit tickets and literally hundreds of other forms. The similar corporate name will replace First Banc Group in stock market listings. The new name is BANK ONE, the corporate identity BANC ONE." (Logos for Bank One and Banc One Corporation are shown in Exhibit 1.)

Banc One President (since 1958) John G. McCoy explained the decision was made to move to a common identity for all banks affiliated with the Banc One Corporation to keep pace with the new Ohio bank branching law, to make possible more effective marketing, and to better identify in the minds of investors the collective success of all banks in the group.

"The conversion will allow group purchasing of certain supplies and the consolidation of a number of forms. Thus far, we have trimmed the 1,017 different forms we used to use in half."

"Perhaps the single most important element in this name change," McCoy stressed, "is that we remember that each bank will continue to operate locally to meet the unique needs of the community it serves. A common identity does not change the uncommon partnership."

The history of Banc One

The history of Banc One Corporation began in 1868 with the formation of Sessions and Company. The McCoy family purchased the bank shortly after the turn of the century and renamed it The City National Bank and Trust Company. The bank continued to be run by three generations of the McCoy family.

By 1968 the McCoy family had created a bank holding company in order to acquire other small banks in the state of Ohio. Originally known as First Banc Group of Ohio, Inc., the name was changed to Banc One Corporation once acquisitions were targeted outside of the state of Ohio. Because the holding company was non-secured and non-insured, Ohio banking law prohibited it from

Exhibit 1 Representation of two logos, one for Bank One and one for Banc One Corporation

using the term "bank" with a "k" in the corporate name. However, they could use the term "bank" (with a "k") for their acquisitions. Consequently, they renamed The City National Bank and Trust Company as Bank One. Bank One records indicate that John G. McCoy was at first not happy with the name "Bank One" for the banks. A large number of names had been suggested, and tested with consumers, but the name Bank One kept emerging as the clear favorite.

The holding company had, until this time, acquired only Ohio banks. The vision, according to John G. McCoy, was to cross state borders and acquire banks nationwide. In order to unify all of these acquisitions under one name, it was believed the term "city" was no longer appropriate. Thus the company created two nomenclature systems: Bank One for the banks, and Banc One Corporation for the holding company.

Patterns of growth and innovation

Over the 30-year period through 1999, the holding company grew from $31 million in assets to over $250 billion, according to Moody's Investors Services.

Banc One Corporation's strategy was to grow through acquisition as well as innovation. The acquisition process started in the state of Ohio. Deane Richardson, chairman emeritus of Fitch, Inc., a design and branding firm engaged by Banc One Corporation to assist in unifying the acquired banks' identities within the holding company, observed the growth process. He stated: "During those early years, mergers and acquisitions were based upon purely financial gain, not marketing or branding strengths. As banks were acquired one after the other in contiguous counties across the state of Ohio, there was often resistance to any change in identity. These banks were very independent." Richardson went on to explain that John G. McCoy recognized that he would have to find innovative ways to convince these acquired independent banks to accept the change and embrace the marketing innovations Banc One Corporation was aggressively pursuing.

Among those marketing innovations, McCoy and his holding company were the first to initiate and introduce a Bank Americard service outside of California, marking the beginning of present day national credit card programs. Banc One was also the first financial corporation to introduce and install plastic card automated teller machines (1970). It was also the first banking organization to handle a group of broker relationships for VISA cash management accounts including Merrill Lynch, Dean Witter, and others (1981).

In 1984 John B. McCoy succeeded his father as CEO of the company. McCoy asked Fitch to evaluate the changing customer activities occurring in bank lobbies. As a result of this evaluation, Fitch designed "The Bank of the Future" in Kingsdale, a shopping center in Upper Arlington, a suburb of Columbus. The "new generation" Kingsdale Financial Center included an interactive video center and a sales boutique environment that offered such services as insurance, real estate, brokerage services, and travel. According to Fitch, the goal was to design a customer-oriented environment that would be perceived as a one-stop center providing an efficient and valuable resource for financial services of all kinds. The Kingsdale Financial Center was the forerunner to the Sawmill Financial Marketplace, opened by Banc One in Columbus in early 1988. The Marketplace, which was open seven days a week, featured investment, travel and trust services, home financing and realtor service, as well as all traditional bank services.

John B. McCoy hired John Fisher, a radio disk jockey from New Jersey, to be Senior Vice President of Marketing. Richardson described Fisher as being "very extroverted, charming, and very easy to like." One of Fisher's first tasks was to create programs to educate the bank's customers on the benefits of using ATM machines and VISA cards. According to Richardson, at first customers didn't trust the devices, or the cards, and the acquired smaller banks had no interest in installing the systems. However, he said Fisher was highly successful in educating both banks and customers so that Bank One was soon considered the most influential of the emerging "electronic banks." Fisher implemented aggressive advertising campaigns that were highly focused on customer needs and benefits and a departure from the traditional "interest rates and services available" advertising style banks were using at the time.

Due to the wide publicity the bank received under Fisher's leadership, the press began to refer to McCoy and Fisher as "The Uncommon Partnership." Fisher used this term as a marketing positioning theme. He reported his intent was to communicate, in a powerful and compelling way, that Banc One banks were "people's banks." McCoy wanted to be certain that all banks in the group would be perceived as "consumer-focused banks." Fisher often referred to them as "Tiffany Banks." The largest and most prestigious competitor at the time was the Bank of Ohio. Banc One's strategy was to differentiate themselves from the older traditional financial institutions by offering "an uncommon partnership" with the bank customer.

Moving beyond Ohio

Changes to banking laws in 1978 had permitted Ohio-based holding companies to purchase banks and conduct business outside the state of Ohio. John B. McCoy gradually expanded the company's holdings first to other midwestern states, and then further west to Arizona, Texas, Colorado, and Utah. (Exhibit 2 lists the acquired companies and dates of acquisition through 1998.) In an article, "Searching for that old Banc One magic," John W. Milligan described McCoy's strategy:[1]

> The strategy was called the Uncommon Partnership, and it worked this way: McCoy would use Banc One's stock, which for years carried one of the industry's richest premiums, to acquire highly profitable, well-run institutions in attractive markets. Banc One would leave the newly acquired bank's management in place and give it considerable local autonomy, while also providing it with the com-

1 *U.S. Banker*, v 106, n 6, pp 26–32, June 1996.

Banc One Corporation – Interstate growth through acquisition of non-Ohio banks

1987 January, acquired American Fletcher Corporation, Indiana
1988 April, acquired Marine Corporation of Milwaukee, Wisconsin
1989 July, acquired Deposit Insurance Bridge Bank, Texas
1990 February, acquired Bright Banc Savings Association, Texas
1992 January, acquired Marine Corporation of Springfield, Illinois
      March, acquired First Illinois Corporation, Illinois
      November, acquired Affiliated Bankshares of Colorado, Inc., Colorado
      November, acquired Team Bancshares, Inc., Texas
1993 March, acquired Valley National Corporation, Arizona
      May, acquired Key Centurion Bancshares, Inc., West Virginia
      December, acquired Central Banking Group, Inc., Oklahoma
1994 August, acquired Liberty National Bancorp, Inc., Kentucky & Indiana
1996 January, acquired Premier Bancorp, Inc., Louisiana
1998 April, acquired First Chicago NBD, Illinois*

* First Chicago NBD had its headquarters in Chicago, Illinois, but also had a dominant presence in Michigan, Indiana, and Florida, as well as international offices in Argentina, Australia, Canada, China, England, Germany, Japan, Mexico, South Korea, Singapore, and Taiwan.

Exhibit 2 List of acquisitions and dates

pany's extensive product set and marketing expertise that rarely failed to further increase profits. This would propel Banc One's earnings, boosting the stock and allowing McCoy to do even more deals. Who wouldn't want to sell out to Banc One under such happy circumstances? Everyone became a winner.

It had to end some time, just as great sports dynasties inevitably run out of momentum and must be rebuilt or reinvented. Banc One's fall from grace occurred in 1994, when concern surfaced over its reliance on derivatives to boost profitability, but in truth, McCoy was finding it increasingly difficult to run such a large company with its old decentralized framework. The Uncommon Partnership was officially eulogized on February 22, 1995, in a McCoy speech to a gathering of his senior executives in Atlanta when he offered a new vision of a new Banc One – this one a national financial services company that would operate with far greater standardization, and in many instances centralization, than previously had been the case. The bank's binding constitution would now be a "National Partnership" built on an obligation to adopt common goals, objectives, and processes, McCoy told his starting team in Atlanta.

Stronger consumer focus

A key implication of the new vision was a strategic shift to stronger consumer-oriented marketing.

In April 1996, McCoy and the board of Banc One Corporation hired Kenneth T. Stevens as chairman and chief executive of Bank One's retail group.

Stevens' background and expertise were in retail marketing to consumers. He had been the president of PepsiCo's Taco Bell Corporation.

Banking Strategies magazine published an interview with Stevens in late 1998 regarding the specific changes he had been instituting at Bank One.[2]

> One of the things that attracted me to Bank One was its reputation on the retail side. It was known as a retail bank. But chief executive John McCoy realized in the mid-1990's that as good as Bank One was from a retail standpoint, it couldn't go to market in a uniform, consistent manner. It was a loose confederation of some 60 to 70 banks. Each one marketed in its own way.
>
> So one of the opportunities was to move to a line-of-business structure. John decided we were going to look, feel and act like a national company. When I got here, we began creating a retail line of business. We established one officially in May 1996.
>
> We aspire to become the premier national retailer of financial services. When we say "premier," we really want to be recognized as the leader – not a leader, not part of the pack, not pretty good, but the leader. And we have developed some metrics to chart where we are on that journey. The second word, "national," means that we go to market in a uniform, consistent manner, that we have national performance standards, national metrics, national products, just like any other company that operates nationally.
>
> "Retailer" is also a very important word to us. We want to be known as a great retailer, not a banking retailer or even a financial services retailer. And what makes great retailers great is that they know more about their customers than anybody else. They're able to take that customer knowledge and use it productively on the front line. The knowledge itself is great, but the ultimate challenge is using it as a foundation for fruitful programs and approaches.

In the same interview published in *Banking Strategies*, Stevens had this to say about his approach to branding at Bank One.

> Our belief is, the way you create a great brand is by delivering or creating that superior customer service experience, having a ubiquitous distribution system, and then wrapping all that in compelling communications. It's the whole package that creates the brand.
>
> The things we do that might be visible – whether it's putting Bank One on a Wheaties box, as we did, or doing a sports sponsorship – only work if they reinforce an experience that we want people to have. That's why every sponsorship or event that we do has to have an integrated program associated with it. It's not about just giving an entity some money and getting your name slapped up there. It's really about experiential branding.

---

2 Kenneth Cline, senior editor, *Banking Strategies* magazine, November/December, 1998.

Stevens was referring to the bank's sponsorship relationship with the Arizona Diamondbacks baseball team. As part of the agreement, the Diamondbacks named the stadium they built in Phoenix Bank One Ballpark; the announcement that the new stadium would be called Bank One Ballpark was made on April 5, 1995, and the stadium opened on March 31, 1998. Bank One put automated teller machines in the stadium. A side panel on the Wheaties box showed the company logo on that stadium. As part of the affinity-marketing program, Bank One offered consumers special checking accounts with Diamondbacks-imprinted checks. Stevens reported that in the first 14 weeks of the promotion the bank opened more than 23,000 accounts. Bank One also initiated similar affinity programs with the Colorado Rockies baseball team.

In 1997, Banc One Corporation acquired a seven-year-old Dallas-based credit card company, First USA, Inc., a division of First USA Bank. First USA, Inc. was generally regarded as a leader in affinity programs, according to Stevens.

Creating the Bank One brand

When Kenneth Stevens became chairman and chief executive of Bank One's retail group in April 1996, he stated that he was impressed with the quality of the bank's various retail products and offerings, but was concerned that the bank was not ready to go to market in a unified and consistent manner. Each of the 70 banks in the group was undertaking its marketing independently under the Bank One name. McCoy and Stevens agreed that to be perceived as a national company, Bank One would have to look, feel, and act like a national company.

Stevens asked the bank's advertising agency, The Martin Agency, to conduct a search for brand consultants to assist in the process. Martin narrowed the search to three firms and finally recommended Fitch to be the brand consultants for Bank One in September 1997.

Fitch had worked with the McCoys and Banc One Corporation in previous years on a variety of projects including the Kingsdale Financial Center (described above). This experience with the corporation during its evolution persuaded Stevens to engage Fitch as Bank One's brand consultant firm.

Separately, Stevens hired Brad Iversen as Executive Vice President and Director of Marketing in August 1997. Iversen had previous experience in developing branding programs while he was in charge of marketing with Nations Bank during their re-branding.

Brad Iversen described his philosophy of branding this way. "The process of developing a truly strong and enduring brand is a marathon – not a sprint. There is no reason to rush. This process is not about advertising or tag lines, it is about strategy, perception, and behavior." Iversen explained that, from his viewpoint, what was needed was a clear, simple way to embrace the needs of all the bank's lines of business. In order to do this it would be critical to take the time to get input from key stakeholders in each business. To be sure each business was represented accurately, Iversen required Fitch to conduct interviews with not only the presidents of each business but also senior executives at least one level down from the president.

Fitch conducted monthly meetings of these line-of-business groups at their Columbus-based agency headquarters for one year. Discussions were not limited exclusively to Bank One or even the banking industry. Participants were encouraged to discuss why and how various brands outside the banking industry worked or didn't work. Iversen explained that the purpose of discussing these brand situations was to coach participants in understanding that branding and advertising were not one and the same.

Iversen and Fitch established four rules for these discussions:

1   Every subject is open and on the table for discussion.
2   The word "No" cannot be used.
3   The phrase, "It can't be done in a bank," was not allowed.
4   No negative attitudes would be permitted.

During these discussions, no one sat at the "head" of the table. Rather everyone was considered to simply be "at" the table. The Fitch team consisted of everyone, at all levels, who would be involved with the project, not just the account executives. The Martin Agency personnel also attended these discussion meetings.

In Iversen's view, the sessions were highly productive and led to a great deal of trust among all parties for the process.

During this one-year period of "discovery" in 1997–8, Iversen said that senior management "really pushed the team hard." The key question was whether the team really could develop a consistent branding strategy that would meet the needs of all the business units equally. From Iversen's point of view, a critical issue was how to communicate this activity internally. "How do you make 93,000 employees aware of the project and its purpose, and how do you get them involved?"

Bill Faust, CEO of Fitch at the time, stated that an internal communications plan was developed during 1998. It included a series of workshops with those in middle management who would have to deal hands-on with branding issues on a day-to-day basis. Each workshop included from 20 to 25 people and participants were called "Brand Purveyors."

In addition to these monthly meetings and middle management workshops, Fitch conducted a visual audit of all current Bank One business materials as well as those of competitors. Forty executives were selected for personal interviews, including Stevens and John B. McCoy. Existing Bank One customer research was reviewed. During the summer of 1998 a draft senior management presentation was developed.

Fitch developed a timeline for the entire project, shown in Exhibit 3. Fitch also created a list of key deliverables that included a brand architecture, brand positioning, a description of brand characteristics, and a "brand toolkit."

Fitch and Bank One also developed a Brand Vision booklet for prospective distribution to all employees in late 1998. The foreword to this booklet explained its purpose:

This book was designed to help you understand our brand vision. The

Brand Development Timeline

Discovery	July–September 1997
Definition (Architecture/Positioning)	October–December 1997
Management Input	January–February 1998
Preliminary Brand Language	March–April 1998
Demonstration Projects	May–August 1998
Management Inputs	September–October 1998
Basic Toolkit	November 1998–April 1999
Additional Guidelines	Ongoing

Exhibit 3 Fitch timeline

brand vision reflects the needs of our customers within all our lines of business. It integrates ideas, comments, and decisions from many of our executives and employees.

Reading and understanding this book is a key step in the evolutionary process toward building and managing the Bank One brand as one of our most valuable assets in the years ahead.

The booklet also explained the company's vision of a successful brand.

Branding is an integral part of doing business and rising above the competition. A strong brand can sum up and symbolize the many facets of a complex organization, its products and services, its philosophy, and its people.

The most effective brands create broad awareness and build loyalty through every interaction and communication. Time has proved that the investment of money and effort yields significant financial results. Brands are highly valued corporate assets.

On the facing page, the draft booklet showed four corporate logos that the company believed represented strong brands: GE, Coca-Cola, IBM, and amazon.com. (Exhibit 4 reproduces the page with the logos and Fitch's accompanying text regarding what successful brands can achieve.)

Merger with First Chicago NBD

According to Iversen and Faust the Bank One branding project was working according to schedule. The timeline had been strictly followed – until the eighth month (April 1998). It was then that First Chicago NBD (a commercial bank) and Bank One agreed to merge. First Chicago and NBD had previously merged in 1995. The decision to merge with Bank One just three years later, according to Iversen, came as a surprise to many people in the banking industry – primarily because Bank One had always been positioned as a retail bank and First Chicago NBD had a strong position as a commercial bank.

Suddenly Bank One was not just a retail bank. Many facets of the evolving brand identity program would have to be revisited immediately.

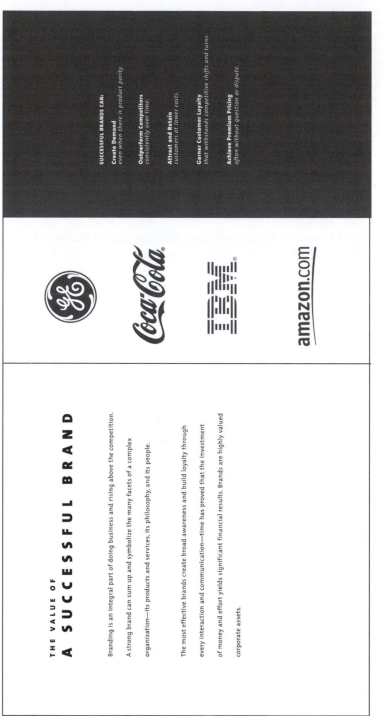

THE VALUE OF
A SUCCESSFUL BRAND

Branding is an integral part of doing business and rising above the competition.

A strong brand can sum up and symbolize the many facets of a complex

organization—its products and services, its philosophy, and its people.

The most effective brands create broad awareness and build loyalty through

every interaction and communication—time has proved that the investment

of money and effort yields significant financial results. Brands are highly valued

corporate assets.

SUCCESSFUL BRANDS CAN:

Create Demand
even when there is product parity.

Outperform Competitors
consistently over time.

Attract and Retain
customers at lower costs.

Garner Customer Loyalty
that withstands competitive shifts and turns.

Achieve Premium Pricing
often without question or dispute.

Exhibit 4 GE, Coca-Cola, IBM, amazon.com logos from vision book

A document produced by Bank One describes First Chicago NBD as follows:

> In 1863, the First National Bank of Chicago began operating under Charter #8, granted by the U.S. Comptroller of the Currency.
>
> Acquisitions of other financial services companies began as early as 1881 and in recent years have included the purchase of many local banks, bank holding companies, and savings and loans. They include American National Corporation, First United Financial Services, Gary-Wheaton Corp., Morgan Shareholders Services Trust Company, and Lake Shore National Bank.
>
> The roots of NBD are in Detroit, where in 1933 it was capitalized equally by General Motors Corporation and the Reconstruction Finance Corporation. Both General Motors and the RFC divested their interests in the bank during the 1940's.
>
> Through a number of acquisitions, NBD went on to become the largest banking company in Indiana and Michigan and gained significant trust presence in Florida.
>
> The 1995 merger of equals between NBD and First Chicago Corporation joined two major and respected Midwest financial services institutions.
>
> In 1998, [the now-named] First Chicago NBD had a dominant presence in Michigan, Indiana, Florida, and Illinois, as well as international offices in Argentina, Australia, Canada, China, England, Germany, Japan, Mexico, South Korea, Singapore, and Taiwan.

Immediately upon learning of the merger, Brad Iversen contacted his counterpart at First Chicago NBD to explain the branding initiative that had been underway for eight months at Bank One, and to discuss ways to get the program adapted to and incorporate the needs of First Chicago NBD. The first reaction from First Chicago NBD, Iversen recalled was, "You are a retail bank, we are a commercial bank, and your identity has nothing to do with us." Those involved at the time remember that executives from both organizations reported that it was evident there would be a culture clash between the banks that would have to be addressed carefully.

A new identity challenge

Up until the point of merger with First Chicago NBD, all of the brand development discussions and strategies had been focused on retail and consumer activities. A key issue that was debated by each participating work group had been which of three brand architectures to adopt: monolithic (single master brand), discrete brand (individual brands for different units), or endorsed (individual brands with each unit identified as part of a corporate parent). John McCoy had favored the monolithic, single master brand, approach because, in his view, it would offer greater efficiencies and economies of scale, provide more leverage in the global marketplace, unify what had become a diverse organization, and allow the corporation to capitalize on existing equity. Faust reported that all the work groups had agreed. This strategy had worked well for Banc One for a number of years, while it acquired other smaller, retail banks. During this acquisition period, most of the local bank brands had been deleted. This practice had slowly developed considerable equity in the Bank One name.

First Chicago NBD executives understood what the Bank One Retail Bank Group was doing, but resisted becoming part of a brand that was being focused so completely on retail activities. Iversen reported that First Chicago NBD favored an endorsed approach, e.g., "A Bank One Company."

John Tomick, Senior Vice President of Advertising at First Chicago NBD, was the first First Chicago NBD employee hired by Bank One in the fall of 1998. He was made Bank One's Senior Vice President of Marketing Services, instantly becoming an integral member of the brand development team. According to Iversen: "Tomick brought strong branding knowledge and experience to the table, but more importantly he was well regarded by, and credible with, First Chicago management. He had great knowledge of the First Chicago NBD history and culture that would be very important to resolving the issue of how to combine both brands effectively."

John Tomick stated that it was his belief that the overall project had to fall between an integrated brand strategy approach (a strategy to effectively combine each bank's marketplace positioning), and a primarily graphics-based solution. He described First Chicago NBD as a "money center" commercial bank, with the bulk of its profits from business-to-business transactions, even though it had characteristics of a retail bank as well. Bank One was clearly more a retail bank. With its 1997 purchase of the credit card division of First USA Bank, and now with The First Chicago NBD merger, the Banc One Corporation was now engaged in three main areas – retail banking, credit card services, and commercial banking.

To bring these three different core businesses under one brand would require, according to Tomick, starting with building a very strong foundation. He used this analogy: "Like a house, you can paint it, spruce it up, and make some cosmetic changes, but you can't really do major remodeling until the foundation has been strengthened and fixed where necessary." Tomick advocated a knowledge-based brand architecture, "where all audiences of all the diverse businesses are studied to develop a very clear vision and mission." He also wanted the cultural and style differences to be addressed between the two organizations. Bank One had been very action-oriented, even aggressive, according to Tomick; First Chicago NBD had been more conservative and "study" oriented. John Tomick maintained that branding at Bank One was a work in progress that would continue for some time.

With the addition of Tomick to the brand development group, work was undertaken to modify the Bank One brand development initiative to embrace the needs of First Chicago NBD.

The ongoing brand development process

Brad Iversen believed that most brand development projects put too much focus on advertising and not enough on "customer experience." For this reason, he changed the title of the position "Brand Manager" to "Director of Customer Experience."

Bill Faust and the team at Fitch developed an approach to help the various work groups focus on a variety of concepts rather than just words. They developed large collages of photographs, found objects, bank artifacts (such as credit cards, forms, etc.), and even clothing. These collages helped to focus group discussion on the differences among each line of business, its customers, and its individual culture and personality. For example, Bank One (the retail bank) had adopted business casual dress for all employees every day. The more conservative commercial bank, First Chicago NBD, required more traditional business dress each workday. Through a mix of concept photos, clothing, bank artifacts, and competitive materials in these mini-exhibits – work groups were given a springboard for meaningful discussion of a variety of concepts relating to the emerging brand architecture. They even explored a variety of concepts for bank and office environments. (Exhibit 5 shows illustrative photographs of materials used in this process.)

The Fitch process asked the work groups to articulate a positioning statement they thought would work for the whole company as well as for various business groups. Following consensus across the work groups on a positioning statement, the next step would be to develop a definitive set of attributes based on the positioning statement. Faust noted that these attributes were largely aspirational, rather than current reality across the organization. Thus, he said that it was necessary to have a plan that would demonstrate how each business unit could make these attributes a reality within its group.

Eventually Fitch would create a series of demonstration modules for each business unit to show employees exactly how they could try to achieve their goals. The previously-mentioned "Brand Vision" booklet for upper middle management had been developed to guide them in embracing all the elements of the emerging brand and to communicate these elements within their respective organizations consistently.

Implementing the Bank One brand identity

By autumn 1998, agreement had been reached on the brand architecture for the merged companies. All business unit presidents, Stevens, McCoy, and Verne G. Istock, Chairman of the Board, had approved the new brand identity. It was to be a monolithic architecture with all business units operating under the Bank One name.

To support the new identity, Fitch developed a "Brand Toolkit." It contained all of the precise standards, guidelines, templates, and rationale for implementing the brand company-wide. The toolkit took the form of a small, spiral-bound booklet. The stated purpose of the toolkit was to document the elements of the Bank One brand identity system and provide guidelines for their use. Both Istock

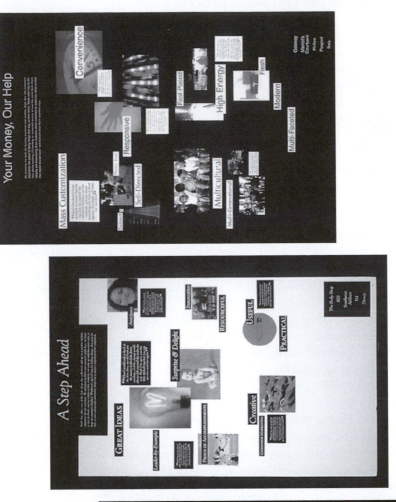
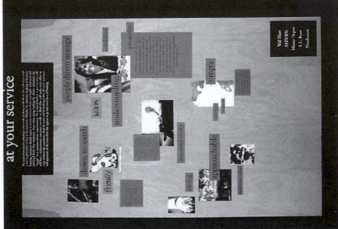

Exhibit 5 Various photos of collages

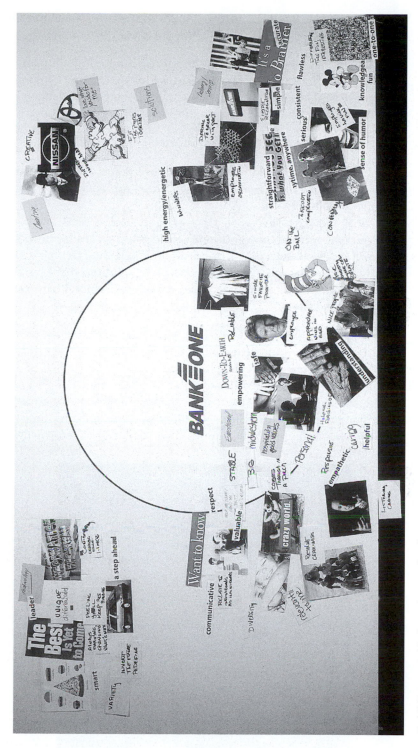

Exhibit 5 cont. Various photos of collages

and McCoy signed the foreword to the toolkit booklet. Addressed to all Bank One employees, it stated in part:

> Bank One's goal is to be among the top three competitors in each of our lines of business and in each market we serve. It's more important than ever that Bank One demonstrate a consistent reflection of our brand to the public and to all commercial and retail customers.

Text from the introduction to the toolkit informed employees that:

> The brand position should reflect how we are perceived by our customers; therefore the statements [that follow] are written from the customers' point of view.
> Our Brand Position:
> Bank One is more than a bank. It's my trusted source for financial services because it does things that are in my best interest. It's committed to delivering the best ideas and the best solutions that I can act on with confidence. It strives to make every experience I have easy and understandable.

The contents of the toolkit were divided into six sections: Statement of the Bank One Brand Position; Core Elements which included the logotype, field of blue, and tone of voice; Secondary Elements including typography, color, and photography; Differentiating elements such as graphic use of the digit "1," graphics in the field of blue, and use of the element of surprise; Marketing Communications application guidelines; and Corporate Communications utilizing both printed stationery and electronic publishing tools. The toolkit also contained support

Exhibit 6 Toolkit cover

materials including reproduction art for the logotype, color chips, and electronic files on CD. (Exhibits 6 and 7 depict the cover and sample pages from the toolkit.)

This toolkit was distributed in November 1998, about six months after the merger had been finalized. The toolkit was delivered to all marketing and communications personnel in each line of business as well as to all external suppliers of goods and services for each division. Fitch set up an 800 number and special e-mail address as hot lines for anyone with a question about the contents of the toolkit. Key groups were given a live presentation by Fitch staff. Other groups were simply sent copies with instructions to speak first with their managers in the event of questions.

The new names and logos (Exhibit 1) were unveiled in November 1998. According to John Tomick, during the initial transition process the corporation used an endorsed approach – "A Bank One Company" – after the name First Chicago NBD. This was emotionally more acceptable to First Chicago employees, customers, and investors, according to Tomick. "All audiences were important and all audiences were looked at. First Chicago NBD had a very clear vision and mission. Bank One did too. But [as noted above] Bank One was more action-oriented and aggressive than First Chicago NBD, which was more conservative and study-oriented. These differences have caused tensions."

Reflections

In mid-1999, about eight months after the initial rollout of the new name and brand strategy, a task force of Fitch staff and Bank One staff began a process to evaluate whether the toolkit and brand precepts were working as planned. Based upon both visual audits and hot line question tracking and analysis, Faust believed there was nothing basically wrong with the system but there were areas which needed greater clarification and needed to be covered in more depth.

The Bank One senior management group and the consultants involved with the branding program, still in its infancy at the time, admitted that it would require ongoing senior management attention. Although many groups in the company had embraced the program intellectually, some parts of the company initially resisted total involvement. Stronger, more compelling communications, according to Iversen, remained a key element in the continuing process.

To address this situation, Tomick and his staff engaged an external communications consulting firm to develop training modules for employees to help them understand branding. As part of this project, a clear and well-articulated corporate vision and mission statement would be developed. The training module would address not only design elements of the brand identity, but also behavior, management style, and marketing philosophy for the company. The stated goal: To effectively integrate and institutionalize the monolithic Bank One brand and its related philosophy into all company cultures as quickly as possible.

OUR BRAND POSITION:

BANK ONE IS **MORE THAN A BANK.**

IT'S MY **TRUSTED SOURCE** FOR FINANCIAL SERVICES

BECAUSE IT DOES THINGS THAT ARE IN MY BEST INTEREST.

IT'S COMMITTED TO DELIVERING **THE BEST IDEAS**

AND **THE BEST SOLUTIONS** THAT I CAN ACT ON

WITH **CONFIDENCE.** IT STRIVES TO MAKE EVERY

EXPERIENCE I HAVE **EASY AND UNDERSTANDABLE.**

WHAT WE
STAND FOR

The foundation of the brand identity system is Bank One's brand vision. This statement, as well as our brand personality, should be conveyed in our words and our actions. They help us express the Bank One brand more consistently.

These aren't the words we say to customers—they are the values behind everything we say and do. They are the guiding principles that help us make the right decisions for our customers and handle all business details appropriately.

The brand position should reflect how we are perceived by our customers; therefore, the statements at right are written from the customer's point of view.

Exhibit 7 Toolkit inside spreads

HOW WE
LOOK, SPEAK, AND ACT

As with all personalities, ours is a composite of many characteristics. These characteristics are the foundation of our personality. They reflect how the Bank One brand should look, feel, and sound. They help us talk to customers in a consistent way.

It is our job to make the sum total of these characteristics much more visible to our customers and to the world. We can also use them as a filter to evaluate what we say and do. Use them to measure and refine the effectiveness of your work and your words.

be One

HONEST
RELIABLE • TRUSTED • CREDIBLE • CANDID
Our customers can depend on us as a reliable resource with an intimate understanding of their needs. We should repay that trust with candor and honesty.

APPROACHABLE
FAMILIAR • INVITING • OPEN • PERSONAL
Our actions and words should be welcoming. We should eliminate the barriers that have historically been placed between banks and their customers.

STRAIGHTFORWARD
DIRECT • RELEVANT • CLEAR • ORGANIZED
Regardless of how complex the subject matter, we should bring order and clarity to every customer interaction.

ORIGINAL
UP-TO-DATE • FRESH • NEW • PROGRESSIVE
Our perspective should be unique. We won't accept the obvious. We will bring fresh ideas and innovative thinking to our customers.

HIGH ENERGY
DRIVEN • VIGOROUS • DYNAMIC • VIBRANT
We should reflect the energy of today's financial marketplace—trading floors, boardrooms, banking centers, and the Internet.

Together, these characteristics establish the spirit of our brand—that dynamic, meaningful presence that customers come to know. When we express them in our actions, interactions, and communications, we strengthen our customer relationships.

Exhibit 7 cont. Toolkit inside spreads

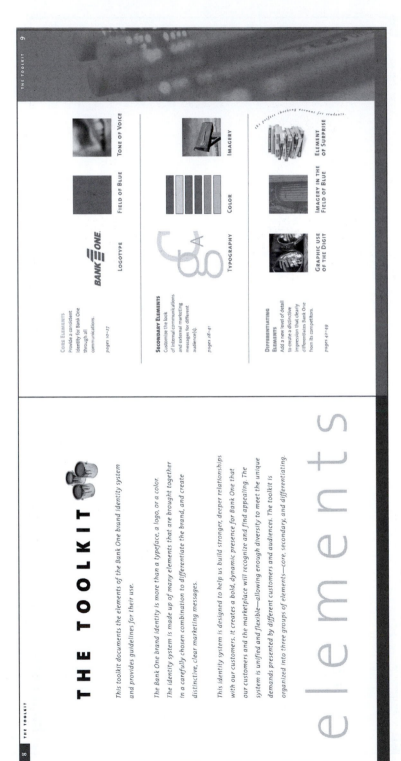

THE TOOLKIT

This toolkit documents the elements of the Bank One brand identity system and provides guidelines for their use.

The Bank One brand identity is more than a typeface, a logo, or a color. The identity system is made up of many elements that are brought together in a carefully chosen combination to differentiate the brand, and create distinctive, clear marketing messages.

This identity system is designed to help us build stronger, deeper relationships with our customers. It creates a bold, dynamic presence for Bank One that our customers and the marketplace will recognize and find appealing. The system is unified and flexible—allowing enough diversity to meet the unique demands presented by different customers and audiences. The toolkit is organized into three groups of elements—core, secondary, and differentiating.

elements

CORE ELEMENTS
Provide a consistent identity for Bank One through all communications.

pages 10–27

LOGOTYPE

FIELD OF BLUE

TONE OF VOICE

SECONDARY ELEMENTS
Customize the look of internal communications and external marketing messages for different audience(s).

pages 28–41

TYPOGRAPHY

COLOR

IMAGERY

DIFFERENTIATING ELEMENTS
Add a new level of detail to create a distinctive impression that clearly differentiates Bank One from its competitors.

pages 42–49

GRAPHIC USE OF THE DIGIT

IMAGERY IN THE FIELD OF BLUE

ELEMENT OF SURPRISE

Exhibit 7 cont. Toolkit inside spreads

Exhibit 7 cont. Toolkit inside spreads

EPILOGUE
Beyond the age of innocence

■ John M. T. Balmer and Stephen A. Greyser

> Now this is not the end.
> It is not even the beginning of the end.
> But it is, perhaps, the end of the beginning.
> (Sir Winston Churchill, 1942)

Retrospective

TO DATE, THE VARIOUS ATTEMPTS to discover the corporate-level equivalent of the Holy Grail – in other words, to "reveal the corporation" – have largely floundered. This failure is, we believe, in part attributable to a failure by scholars and practitioners to comprehend the multidisciplinary and multifaceted characteristics of the domain.

The chapters selected for this anthology chronicle the emergence, ascendancy, and eventual hegemony of various corporate-level concepts that, at various times since the 1950s, have energized the imagination of practitioners and scholars. However, each concept provides *some*, but not *all*, of the insights that explain corporate entities.

Let us remind the reader of some of these milestones (and associated articles, all included in this volume) that we believe are of seminal importance.

Martineau's *Harvard Business Review* (*HBR*) article reflects the fascination with corporate image that characterized the 1950s and 1960s.

The following decade witnessed another *HBR* article – one that de facto marked the epiphany of the corporate identity concept. Written by Walter Margulies, this article set in motion widespread practitioner and, to a more limited degree, scholarly interest in corporate identity. Olins's lecture to The Royal Society of Arts further captures the transatlantic excitement and fascination with the corporate identity concept. Olins's article foreshadowed the broader conceptualization of the identity concept. This became manifest in 1995 with the Strathclyde Statement on Corporate Identity Management (original version), which was penned by Balmer and Greyser after collaborative discussions with scholars and practitioners.

Bernstein's article makes evident the ascendancy of, and widespread interest in, corporate communications that characterized the start of the 1980s. The article by Van Riel records the progression of corporate communications as an academic subject.

Albert and Whetten's seminal article on organizational identification fashioned a new and distinct approach to identity studies, one that marshaled for the first time the organizational behavior literature. This approach has remained in the ascendant in academic circles ever since.

More recently, the articles by Fombrun and by Greyser replicated the wide allure of corporate reputation in the 1990s.

Finally, the work of King heralded a new era which, at the time of our writing, has witnessed a burgeoning of interest in a recent "umbrella" corporate-level construct: corporate branding.

In perspective

To the world of practice the historiography of these corporate-level concepts may be seen to reflect the Zeitgeist of a particular epoch. It certainly reflects the vagaries of fashion, and in some respects a concern on the part of too many consultancies with the self-differentiating trappings rather than with the substance of individual concepts.

Our perspective is markedly different. To us, each of these concepts has a penetrating luminosity. They reveal corporations in ways we believe are original, profound, and sometimes startling.

This raises the question of what *the sum* of the concepts represents. To us the current stage of development with regard to the corporate-level constructs detailed here is not so dissimilar from the painters of the late Middle Ages. They were artists of consummate skill, but artists who had not yet discovered perspective, and thus had failed to grasp and effect multidimensional representations of reality.

Our anthology marks an interim stage between a period of fragmentation to one of consolidation. A move away from simplicity to complexity. A move from adolescence to adulthood. A move beyond the age of innocence.

Marshaling a galaxy of ideas

The opening article of this volume, our "Managing the Multiple Identities of the Corporation," does, we believe, demonstrate the efficacy of marshaling the galaxy of ideas and concepts that have characterized the domain since the 1950s. It has revealed the benefits and richness that accrue from adopting a broad vista and through the assemblage of *multiple* perspectives: of *multiple identities*.

We *do* hold that the identity concept captures the quintessence of the corporation, but here there is an important caveat. Our view is that only when identity is placed in the context of other corporate-level concepts and concerns – image, reputation, communication, and branding, strategy, and leadership – can we fully comprehend the various dimensions of corporate meaning and the inner and outer manifestations of any entity. We believe the AC^{2}ID Test™(and its most recent variant, the AC^{3}ID Test™) largely accomplishes this. It amasses the rich disciplinary inheritance that underpins the identity, corporate communications, image, reputation, and branding constructs into a coherent and memorable whole. It also acknowledges another important dimension: that of time. Different identity types may inhabit different time frames. This is often overlooked. Yet the dimension of time can provide a new lens through which to perceive organizational misalignments.

From an academic perspective it would appear the identity concept provides the most appropriate platform by which the corporation may be revealed. Without doubt, the recent upsurge in academic interest in identity studies from leading U.S. scholars has given a lift to identity scholarship and its standing.

However, account should be taken of the world of practice, where there is increasing avoidance of the term and where, according to some, identity as a concept has reached its nadir.[1] This may be not as discouraging as it sounds. It may even be cathartic. This is because identity is seen by both the *vox populi* and many from practice to be allied with graphic design. That being the case, the demise of identity studies and of practice being viewed in terms simply of graphic design is to be welcomed. (Of course, graphic design remains a component of the identity mosaic.)

If that demise occurs, this could well lead to a renaissance of the identity concept among business practitioners and scholars. It would position the concept as one that at its essence is concerned with the substance of organizations rather than with logotypes alone – in short, an area that at its core is concerned with revealing the corporation.

Every idea has its day, and we firmly believe that this is the case with the identity construct.

A new gestalt of the corporation?

In addressing the question as to what the orchestration of the concepts of identity (organizational and corporate identities), corporate communication, corporate image, corporate reputation, and corporate branding represent, we see them as providing the building-blocks of a new gestalt: a new philosophy of management. This new gestalt is one that should acknowledge, indeed celebrate, the area's rich disciplinary inheritance.

While identity studies offer a new way of envisioning, analyzing, and managing corporations, we feel it incumbent upon us to offer an alternative viewpoint, one that accommodates the myriad perspectives on the area but avoids the linkage of identity to graphic design alone. We believe that the time may be right for what possibly may be viewed as a further evolutionary stage of development, one that more closely aligns this gestalt as a branch of one of the existing areas of management. Such a progression would be efficacious for purely practical reasons. (We reiterate that identity studies is the most frequently used umbrella title for this gestalt.)

Problem children?

We begin by explaining why existing corporate-level concepts may be deemed to be unsuitable.

It has to be acknowledged that *any* umbrella title is likely to be troublesome. Existing concepts, although they all have an immense richness, are either inappropriate, inadequate, or carry much gratuitous baggage.

Some of the concepts examined in this compilation may be viewed as second-order concepts in that on their own they operate in a vacuum. This may be seen in relation to corporate identification, which raises the following dilemma: *identification with what?* The area of corporate communication raises a similar quandary: *communication of what* and *to whom?*

Corporate image is, for many, a problematic, if not imprecise, concept. Corporate reputation, and its management, while immeasurably more compelling and agreeable than the corporate image concept, still has the disadvantage that a corporate reputation per se is no guarantee of business success or even survival – witness Arthur Andersen.

Corporate branding has considerable utility. Its Achilles' heel is that it is manifestly *not* applicable to every entity. Certain companies either have failed to develop a corporate brand or have concluded that the exigencies of their sector mean that such a move would be inappropriate or ineffectual. Thus while subsidiaries may have corporate brands, the holding company might not. For these reasons the corporate brand is ruled out.

The identity concept (more precisely, the corporate identity construct rather than the organizational identification variant) has been typecast from over-emphasis by the graphic design industry. Business often sees corporate identity in terms of logos and systems of visual identification. As such the identity concept is also problematic.

What should be the umbrella title of this new area of management? We believe it should be known as *corporate-level marketing*. We argue that this should be undertaken for historical, practical, and operational reasons.

Corporate-level marketing: What is it? What of it?

"Corporate-level" connotes that the area of concern is with corporate entities in their totality, *including corporate-level networks and partnerships*. As such the designation aims to reflect our view that the area should not be constrained by rigid disciplinary boundaries or past attitudes that "marketing" may be limiting.

First, "corporate-level" denotes that the area of concern is *strategic* in effect.

Its importance is such that the CEO and board of directors should be apprised of the area on a regular basis and should be familiar with its scope and significance.

This brings us to the contentious issue of why this area should have a distinctive "marketing" handle. We contend that there are four advantages that marketing can offer this nascent area, namely its *inheritance, prescience, expedience*, and *assemblance*.

Inheritance

Of all the disciplines that have made a contribution to this collection, the role of marketing has been the most conspicuous. To illustrate our point, consider communication, image, reputation, and branding. These are *key* concepts within the marketing domain, while others, such as identity, are also frequently marshaled by marketing scholars and practitioners.

To date, the above concepts have tended to be narrowly conceived by marketers in terms of products or services rather than corporations. To our mind these concepts can be orchestrated at the organizational level in order to underpin the new gestalt of corporate-level marketing.

Prescience

The notion that marketing should involve itself with corporate-level concerns is far from new. Such a perspective has long been advocated. As far back as 1969, Kotler and Levy[2] had the prescience to articulate that the marketing concept should be broadened so as to encompass *any entity*.

More recently, Webster[3] foreshadowed what has in effect started to occur in the field of identity studies. He advanced the view that it was *de rigueur* for marketing to effect a paradigm shift away from products and firms to people and organizations. Accordingly, there was a requirement for greater scrutiny to be accorded to phenomena that traditionally have been the preserve of psychologists, organizational behaviorists, political economists, and sociologists.

Marketing's entrée into the corporate domain has already become a reality. For example, we have seen the rise of "new" areas of marketing interest such as relationship marketing, the marketing of services, internal marketing, marketing for nonprofits, marketing of the arts, green marketing, and – in the area of communications – integrated marketing communications.

Expedience

Marketing has been particularly effective in demonstrating its utility to managers. Baker[4] observed that marketing (along with architecture, engineering, and medicine) is a synthetic discipline in that it distills insights gained from other fields into a body of knowledge with an immediate and practical relevance. In other words, marketing is adept in operationalizing theories.

Assemblance

Marketing is, and always has been, a repository of insights and theories gathered from other disciplines. Traditional marketing draws heavily from a number of management and nonmanagement disciplines such as psychology, economics, and strategy. The assemblance of diverse perspectives to form a unified whole has been a basic tenet of marketing. Indeed, Borden,[5] who first devised the "marketing mix," was profoundly influenced by the work of Culliton,[6] who in 1948 envisioned the marketer to be first and foremost a mixer of ingredients – in other words, an *orchestrator*.

Quo vadis marketing/corporate-level marketing?

What of the basic marketing concept?

We envision that the notion of profitable exchange relationships will remain an enduring feature of corporate-level marketing, as it does with traditional marketing. What is different is that the emphasis will be on *multiple* exchange relationships. There will also be a greater acceptance that the traditional internal/external boundary lines have all but vanished. Corporations are less concerned with the management or ownership of all aspects of the supply chain or distribution channels: they see themselves as part of a network.[7]

The above perspectives are reflected in the literature. Badaracco[8] challenged the view that there is an identifiable corporation–environment boundary. Moreover, the boundary, such as it is, has virtually disappeared, and thus to us is superfluous. Hence, internal and external groups are not so much stakeholders or publics but *partners*.[9]

This perspective is not without its difficulties. It comes with a realization that individuals do not belong to a solitary stakeholder group but rather to multiple groups, and as such may be engaged in diverse corporate-level partnerships.

We also hold that there is a significant time dimension as well. Corporations will need to be sensitive to past, future, as well as to current stakeholder groups.

Exhibit 1 compares the major components of marketing identified by McGee and Spiro[10] with that of corporate-level marketing identified by Balmer.[11]

Corporate-level marketing mixes

Two of marketing's enduring characteristics, namely expedience and assemblance, are at their most translucent in terms of the marketing mix originally devised by Borden[12] and revised and reduced by McCarthy[13] in a manner that was simple to recall: the "4Ps." Thus, the articulation of a corporate-level marketing mix may

	MAJOR COMPONENTS OF MARKETING (McGEE AND SPIRO)[a]	MAJOR COMPONENTS OF CORPORATE MARKETING (BALMER)[b]
Orientation	*Customer* Understanding customer wants, needs, and behaviors	*Stakeholders* Understanding present and future stakeholders' wants, needs, and behaviors
Organizational support	*Coordinated organizational activities* Undertaken to support customer orientation elicited above	*Coordinated organizational activities* Undertaken to support stakeholder orientation elicited above
End-focus	*Profit orientation* Focus on profit rather than on sales (needs to be adapted for not-for-profit organizations)	*Value creation* Profit maximization is a primary but is not the only focus: it also includes business survival as well as tempering the above, where appropriate, in meeting. . .
Societal obligations	*Community welfare* An obligation to meet customers' and society's long-term interests	*Future stakeholder and societal needs* Balancing current stakeholder and society needs with those of the future. Showing sensitivity to the organization's inheritance where applicable (cooperatives, partnerships, etc.)

Notes:

a   L. W. McGee and R. K. Spiro, "The Marketing Concept in Perspective," *Business Horizons* 1990, 31 (3): 40–45

b   J. M. T. Balmer, "Corporate Identity, Corporate Branding and Corporate Marketing: Seeing through the Fog," *European Journal of Marketing* 2001, 35 (3/4): 248–291

Exhibit 1 The major components of marketing and corporate marketing

Source: J. M. T. Balmer, "Corporate Identity, Corporate Branding and Corporate Marketing: Seeing through the Fog," *European Journal of Marketing* 2001, 35 (3/4): 248–291

serve a similar purpose at the corporate level, with one *crucial* difference. We envisage the corporate-level marketing mix to underpin the philosophy of corporate-level marketing: a corporate-wide orientation based on mutually satisfying stakeholder partnerships. As Drucker,[14] an early advocate of the marketing concept, noted back in 1954, "Concern and responsibility for marketing must permeate all areas of the enterprise."

As does Webster,[15] we view the marketing approach as primarily one about a philosophy rather than one with a concern with processes and the proliferations of departments. The latter has resulted in non-marketers being exonerated from any marketing responsibility.[16] Thus to us, corporate-level marketing is more of a *philosophy* than a *function*. It needs to reside within the mindsets of everyone within the organization. Greyser has traced marketing's evolution towards this perspective.[17]

What are the substantive differences between the marketing mix and the corporate-level marketing mix? There are three: The first is that the elements are broader than the traditional "4Ps" of the marketing mix. The second is that the elements of the traditional mix require a radical reconfiguration. The third is that the

PHILOSOPHY AND ETHOS	What the organization stands for, and the way it undertakes its work
PERSONALITY	The mix of subcultures present within the organization: these contribute to the organization's distinctiveness
PEOPLE	Their importance to the organization's identity (membership of subcultural groups); their interface with external stakeholders; their role in product and service quality
PRODUCT	What an organization makes or does: its core business or businesses
PRICE	What it charges for its products and services, including the goodwill element in the valuation of its corporate and product brands; the price of stock; staff salaries
PLACE	Distribution channels, company's relationship with distributors, franchising arrangements, etc.
PROMOTION	A concern with Total Corporate Communications: the effects of the earlier-mentioned primary, secondary, and tertiary communication; includes visual identification and branding policy
PERFORMANCE	How the organization's performance is rated by its key stakeholders vis-à-vis the organization's espoused philosophy and ethos, and how it is rated against competitors
PERCEPTION	Questions relating to corporate image and corporate reputation. Perception of the industry/country of origin may also be significant
POSITIONING	In relation to important stakeholders, competitors, and the external environment

Exhibit 2 The original corporate-level marketing mix

Source: J. M. T. Balmer, "Corporate Identity, Corporate Branding and Corporate Marketing: Seeing through the Fog," *European Journal of Marketing* 2001, 35 (3/4): 248–291

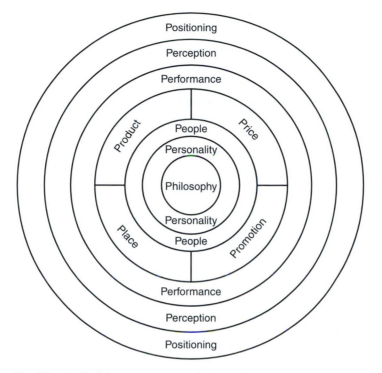

Exhibit 3 The "Ten Ps" of the corporate marketing mix

Source: J. M. T. Balmer, "Corporate Identity and the Advent of Corporate Branding Marketing," *Journal of Marketing Management* 1998, 14 (8): 963–996

mix elements have distinct *disciplinary* traditions. They also transcend the traditional organizational boundaries.

In his initial attempt at articulating the "new" marketing mix in 1998, Balmer[18] extended the marketing mix to ten elements, as described in Exhibit 2 and illustrated in Exhibit 3. However, the number of elements contained in the mix makes it difficult to operationalize, and to recall, especially when compared to McCarthy's[19] 4 Ps. (The problem is not so dissimilar to the early marketing mix of Borden.[20])

The new corporate-level marketing mix

As a means of circumventing the problem above and with the didactic needs of faculty in mind, Balmer developed a new mix.[21] This forms the acromymn HEADS[2]: this stands for what an organization *HAS, EXPRESSES, its AFFINITIES, what it DOES, how it is SEEN,* and lastly *its STAKEHOLDERS.* (The mix of course needs to take account of the environment, and hence for pedagogical purposes a *seventh* element might be added, namely *ENVIRONMENT,* which would result in the mnemonic HE[2]ADS[2].)

We hope that the loss of richness that occurred with McCarthy's simplification of Borden's mix is not replicated here. Indeed, we hope that the later formulation *adds* richness. Compared with the marketing mix, these mix elements have a far greater *dynamism*.

The basic, six-element form of the corporate-level marketing mix is explained as follows, and is shown in diagrammatic form in Exhibit 4:

1   What the organization *HAS.* Includes the organization's structure, history and legacy, property and equipment, reputation, investment interests in other organizations.

2   What the organization *EXPRESSES.* Integrates primary communication (products and services performance), secondary (formal communication policies), and tertiary communications (word of mouth, media communication, competititor communication, and spin).

3   The *AFFINITIES* of employees. Includes the degree of positive or negative associations with employees to various subcultural groups including corporate ones (old, new, ascendant, subsidiary, departmental).

4   What the organization *DOES.* Includes all the elements of McCarthy's 4Ps mix with the exception of promotion (see *EXPRESSES* above).

5   How the organization is *SEEN.* Includes data regarding current perceptions of the organization's image and reputation, and organizational awareness and profile; data on past performance, knowledge, beliefs, and expectations; salience of the corporate branding covenant.

6   The organization's key *STAKEHOLDER* groups and networks. Noting and prioritizing the organization's key groups, networks, and individuals in the context of the organization's strategy, and in the context of different markets and situations.

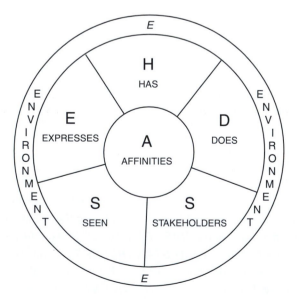

Exhibit 4 The new corporate-level marketing mix

Source: J. M. T. Balmer, "Corporate Identity, Corporate Branding and Corporate Marketing: Seeing through the Fog," *European Journal of Marketing* 2001, 35 (3/4): 248–291

Historical parallels?

There is also a historic parallel between the development of the marketing function in the organization and what we are witnessing now with corporate-level marketing. Exhibit 5 compares the two. The above-mentioned piece by Greyser (p. 352) describes the development of traditional marketing in considerable detail.

TRADITIONAL MARKETING	CORPORATE-LEVEL MARKETING
PRODUCT ORIENTATION	ORGANIZATIONAL ORIENTATION
Nineteenth century (variable)	
A focus on the product itself. Selling what we make. Making what we are good at.	A focus on the organization simply in terms of a machine. Efficiency. Providing a profitable return for stockholders.
SELLING ORIENTATION	IMAGE ORIENTATION
Early twentieth century (variable)	
Emphasis on pushing products into markets with limited analysis of whether there is a need or want or a market for them.	Emphasis on transmitting an image of the corporation that meets desired corporate goals but may not be based on reality. Considerable use of the the most readily controllable and highest-profile forms of communication such as advertising and graphic design and logos.
MARKETING ORIENTATION	CORPORATE-LEVEL MARKETING ORIENTATION
Current	
(Mid-twentieth century onwards) Meeting the wants and needs of customers profitably. Based on company's capabilities and environmental forces. Involves blending the marketing mix (product, price, place, promotion) and sometimes people.	(Late twentieth century onwards) Meeting the wants and needs of stakeholders profitably. Based on company's capabilities and environmental forces. Involves blending the corporate-level marketing mix, which integrates identity, image, reputation, communication, and corporate brand management.
(Late twentieth century) Philosophy should imbue entire organization	Philosophy should imbue entire organization.

Exhibit 5 Historical parallels

The desert generation

In bringing this anthology to a close we are mindful that nigh on forty years has elapsed since Margulies coined the phrase "corporate identity." In a very real sense the journey we have retraced in this compilation is akin to that of the *dor ha-midbar*: the desert generation who have wandered for forty years in the desert. The irony here is that it is *we,* the children of *dor ha-midbar*, who for the most part are still in the shadows. For the desert generation is to be found not within the covers of this anthology but among those in business, consultancy and academe who still perceive the dimensions of corporate meaning examined in this collection to be obtuse, ethereal, immaterial, or simply hogwash!

Thankfully, the literature relating to the corporate-level constructs examined in *Revealing the Corporation* is developing apace, with integrative approaches and frameworks under development. However, such perspectives still remain the exception rather than the rule. We often think of a swimming pool as an appropriate metaphor in this regard. Invariably, most of the noise and activity take place in the *shallow end* of the pool. It is there that most of the children are to be found!

New beginnings

In closing this Epilogue, let us remind readers that this anthology includes only a small selection of the literature focusing on insights into the various dimensions of corporate meaning. A good deal more exists, as detailed in our suggested readings, and more will surely follow. What is clear to us is that there are multiple approaches in contemplating the dynamic organism that is the corporation.

Victor Hugo[22] made the prescient observation that nothing can stop an idea whose time has come. In the sphere of management there is nothing more vital, commanding, and insightful than revealing the corporation through an identity lens. Its renaissance is long overdue.

NOTES

1   Aldersey-Williams, H., "Ten Reasons why Corporate Identity Is Dead," *RSA Journal* 2000, 148, 4 (4): 4–5.

2   Kotler, P. and Levy, S. J., "Broadening the Concept of Marketing," *Journal of Marketing* 1969, 3 (January): 10–15.

3   Webster, F. E., "The Changing Role of Marketing in the Corporation," *Journal of Marketing* 1992, 56 (October): 1–17.

4   Baker, M. J., "Marketing – Philosophy or Function?," in M. J. Baker (ed.) *The IEBM Encyclopedia of Marketing,* London: International Thomson Business Press, 1999, pp. 3–17.

5   Borden, N., "The Concept of the Marketing Mix," *Journal of Advertising Research* 1964 (June): 2–7.

6   Culliton, J. W., *The Management of Marketing Costs*, Cambridge, MA: Harvard University Press, 1948.

7   Ford, D., *Understanding Business Markets: Interactions, Relationships, Networks*, London: Academic Press, 1990.

8   Badaracco, J. L., *The Knowledge Link: How Firms Compete through Strategic Alliances*, Cambridge, MA: Harvard Business School Press, 1991.

9   O'Malley, L. and Patterson, M., "Vanishing Point: The Mix Management Paradigm Re-visited," *Journal of Marketing Management* 1998, 14 (8): 829–851.

10   McGee, L. W. and Spiro, R. K., "The Marketing Concept in Perspective," *Business Horizons* 1990, 31 (3): 40–45.

11   Balmer, J. M. T., "Corporate Identity, Corporate Branding and Corporate Marketing: Seeing through the Fog," Special Edition on Corporate Identity and Corporate Marketing: *European Journal of Marketing* 2001, 35 (3/4): 248–291.

12   Borden, *op. cit.*

13   McCarthy, E. J., *Basic Marketing: A Managerial Approach*, Homewood, IL: Irwin, 1960.

14   Drucker, P., *The Practice of Management*, New York: Harper, 1954.

15   Webster, F. E., "The Changing Role of Marketing in the Corporation," *Journal of Marketing* 1992, 56 (October): 1–17.

16   Gummesson, E., "Marketing-Orientation Revisited: The Crucial Role of the Part-Time Marketer," *European Journal of Marketing* 1991, 25 (2): 60–75.

17   Greyser, S., "Janus and Marketing: The Past, Present, and Prospective Future of Marketing," in D. Lehmann and K. Jocz (eds) *Reflections on the Futures of Marketing*, Cambridge, MA: Marketing Science Institute, 1997, pp. 3–14.

18   Balmer, J. M. T., "Corporate Identity and the Advent of Corporate Marketing," *Journal of Marketing Management* 1998, 14 (8): 963–996.

19   McCarthy, *op. cit.*

20   Borden, *op. cit.*

21   Balmer, "Corporate Identity, Corporate Branding;" see note 11, above.

22   Hugo, V., as referred to in A. Ries and J. Trout, *Positioning: The Battle for Your Mind*, New York: McGraw-Hill, 1986, p. 189.

Index